Grand Opportunity

Irish Studies

James MacKillop, *Series Editor*

Grand Opportunity

The Gaelic Revival and Irish Society, 1893–1910

Timothy G. McMahon

SYRACUSE UNIVERSITY PRESS

Copyright © 2008 by Syracuse University Press

Syracuse, New York 13244-5290

All Rights Reserved

First Edition 2008

08   09   10   11   12   13   6   5   4   3   2

∞ The paper used in this publication meets the minimum requirements
of the American National Standard for Information Sciences—Permanence of Paper
for Printed Library Materials, ANSI Z39.48-1992.

For a listing of books published and distributed by Syracuse University Press,
visit https://press.syr.edu.

ISBN-13: 978-0-8156-3158-3 (cloth)   ISBN-10: 0-8156-3158-8 (cloth)

ISBN-13: 978-0-8156-3184-2 (paperback)   ISBN-10: 0-8156-3184-7 (paperback)

Library of Congress Cataloging-in-Publication Data

McMahon, Timothy G.

Grand opportunity : the Gaelic revival and Irish society, 1893–1910 / Timothy G. McMahon. — 1st ed.

p. cm. — (Irish studies)

Includes bibliographical references and index.

ISBN: 978-0-8156-3158-3 (cloth : alk. paper)

ISBN: 978-0-8156-3184-2 (pbk. : alk. paper)

1. Ireland—Intellectual life—20th century. 2. Ireland—Intellectual life—19th century. 3. Gaelic League
(Ireland) 4. Irish language—Revival. 5. Language and culture—Ireland. 6. Popular culture—Ireland.
7. National characteristics, Irish—History. 8. Celtic philology. I. Title.

DA959.1M287 2008

941.5082'1—dc22

2007049510

Manufactured in the United States of America

Contents

Tables

TIMOTHY G. MCMAHON was educated at Washington and Lee University and at the University of Wisconsin-Madison. He is currently assistant professor of history at Marquette University, where his research focuses on the study of identity and its expression through popular culture.

Acknowledgments

I have accumulated numerous obligations since this book was first conceived, and I would like to acknowledge them at this time. I have received financial assistance without which I would not have had access to the training and archival resources necessary for completing the work. I would, therefore, like to thank the Department of History at Washington and Lee University, the Department of History at the University of Wisconsin-Madison, the Graduate School at the University of Wisconsin-Madison, and the Henry Vilas Trust for their generous support. I would also like to thank the Helen Way Klingler College of Arts and Sciences at Marquette University for its support in the later stages of the book's preparation.

Several individuals with personal connections to the Gaelic revival shaped this work through their advice, questions, and encouragement. In Ireland these included Nioclás Mac Craith of Ring, Co. Waterford; Finian Ó Fathaigh of Galway city; and Sister Íte Ó Fathaigh, also of Galway city. Their local and familial knowledge were particularly helpful at various stages in the development of this project. Also, Seán Mac Mathúna of Conradh na Gaeilge (the Gaelic League) offered his valuable insights into the workings of the organization as well as access to materials in the headquarters of the League on Harcourt Street in Dublin during the early development of the book.

The staffs of several libraries and archives in the United States and the Republic of Ireland have shared their collections and expertise with me over the years as well. Among them, I wish to thank the staffs of the National Library of Ireland; the National Archives of Ireland; the National University of Ireland—especially the Archives Department and the Irish Folklore Department of University College, Dublin; the Cork City and County Archives (formerly the Cork Archives Institute); Mount Melleray Abbey; Trinity College, Dublin; the Raynor-Memorial Library at Marquette University; and the Memorial Library at the University of Wisconsin-Madison. I would be remiss if I did not mention the tireless assistance of Ed Duesterhoeft, Judy Tuohy, and Dineen Grow at the Memorial Library in Madison. Dineen must also receive special mention for having been my first teacher of Irish. Without her, this project could not have proceeded.

Further, I would like to acknowledge the many archives and institutions that have granted me permission to cite materials from their collections in the present work. Specifically, I would thank the Cork City and County Archives, for use of the C. T. O'Leary and Liam Ó Buachalla papers; the Director of the National Folklore Collection, University College, Dublin, for access to the 1918 memoir of Douglas Hyde; the National Archives of Ireland and the Director of the National Archives, for permission to cite the Chief Secretary's Office Registered Papers, the minutes of the St. Grellan's branch of the Gaelic League, and various Constabulary reports; the Mount Melleray Abbey Trust, for use of the papers of Abbott Maurus Ó Faoláin; the Archives Department of University College, Dublin, for access to the Eoin MacNeill and W. P. Ryan papers; and Conradh na Gaeilge for permission to cite their early reports, minute books, and correspondence. Further correspondence with Eoin MacNeill, as well as the papers of Fionán MacColuim, John Glynn, Joseph McGarrity, and various committees of Conradh na Gaeilge are cited with the permission of the Board of the National Library of Ireland. Last, chapter three of the present work is a slightly updated version of an article published in 2002 in the journal *Éire-Ireland,* and I would like to thank the Irish American Cultural Institute and the editors of *Éire-Ireland* for granting permission to republish that material here.

I owe my greatest intellectual debts to the Washington and Lee University and the University of Wisconsin-Madison. In Lexington, Robert J. de Maria, I. Taylor Sanders II, J. D. Futch III, M. Kirkland Follo, and the late B. S. Stephenson provided exemplary tuition. In Madison, Johann Sommerville, Jonathan Zeitlin, Rudy Koshar, Suzanne Desan, Robert Koehl,

Mary Magray, Philip Herring, and Richard Begam taught and inspired, and Sandy Heitzkey, Jane Williams, Judy Vezzetti, James Schlender, and the late Judy Cochran provided much needed assistance. My fellow students—including Matthew O'Brien, Sean Farrell, Michael de Nie, Kurt Gingrich, David Holmes, Peter Thorsheim, Robert H. Landrum, Patrick Tally, Thea Lindquist, Thomas Lekan, and Joel Ryan—provided (and provide) friendship and questions that remain invaluable to me. No individual has shaped this project more than my doctoral advisor, James S. Donnelly Jr. His exemplary scholarship, teaching, and commitment to our profession have motivated me, as much as his questions and advice have guided me.

I am, moreover, grateful to the wider Irish studies community in Great Britain, Ireland, and the United States for comments offered in formal and informal settings, usually associated with meetings of the American Conference for Irish Studies. In particular, I wish to thank Emmet Larkin, David W. Miller, A. C. Hepburn, Philip O'Leary, Lucy McDiarmid, James Rogers, and Nancy J. Curtin. I wish further to acknowledge the late Lawrence McBride, whose early death left a hole in our ranks. My own generation of historians has been equally open and critical, and I would be remiss if I did not thank Breandán Mac Suibhne, James Patterson, Fergus Campbell, Enda Delaney, Stephen Ball, Paul Townend, Jason Knirck, Tim O'Neil, and Benjamin Novick. Three others deserve special mention: Úna Ní Bhroiméil, whose familiarity with the Gaelic revival and its Irish-American supporters is truly remarkable; Frank Biletz, whose insights into the connections between various elements of the Irish-Ireland movement merit wide recognition; and the prolific and generous Patrick Maume, who sets the table for many of the rest of us.

At Marquette, colleagues such as James Marten, Julius Ruff, Carla Hay, and John Krugler have offered encouragement and support, while former colleagues Andrew Donson, Alan Singer, Mary Conley, Sara Sewell, Barbara Fox, Allyson Delnore, Sean Field, Gregory Milton, Andrew Larsen, and Lance Grahn offered assistance at critical points in the revising process. And at Syracuse University Press, I wish to thank James MacKillop, Glenn Wright, their outside readers, and staff for their assistance in preparing the present book. A special thank-you goes to Julie DuSablon, whose keen eye has saved me from making numerous errors in the present text. It goes without saying that any remaining errors are my own.

My greatest debts, however, I owe to my family. Maureen and the late Patrick McMahon were always there for me, and I cannot thank them enough for everything. I am glad to know that dad at least saw the completed dissertation from which this work emerged. At various points, Sidney and Mary Coulling have provided unparalleled help to Anne and me, and I sincerely thank them. Liam and Mary Catherine have grown up with this book. I hope that its appearance will remind them that all things are in fact possible. Most important, I thank Anne, the one person without whom this book would never have seen the light of day. Her patience and faith have been as constant as her love. I dedicate this work to her.

Grand Opportunity

Introduction

> I wonder if the promoters of these gatherings think of the grand op-
> portunity they afford of driving home a few simple truths regarding the
> fight for Irish nationhood to the minds of the people who come together
> to enjoy the dancing, the singing, and the music, and all the other attrac-
> tions of the open air gatherings.[1]

S tudying the complex phenomena of group identities—for example,
of classes, nations, or political allegiances—is a daunting task: one
must read minds as well as texts. Historians undertaking such studies
must clear the further hurdle of translating their reading through time,
for the meanings attached to concepts in one era do not necessarily reflect their meanings in another. Yet we persist in this probing because
societies, like individuals, undergo repeated periods of intense reflection about who they are, where they have come from, and what will be
their destiny.

Such questions never really leave the public sphere, especially in societies as given to self-analysis as is the Irish. From the popular media, in
columns such as "The Irishman's Diary" in the daily *Irish Times,* to academic circles, where the so-called revisionist debate spawned a virtual
cottage industry among historians and political scientists in the 1990s,
national identity remains a central concern in Ireland, north and south.[2]

As investigations moved from the superficial treatments necessitated
by general or biographical works to more specific case studies, the level
of analysis about Irish nationalism and national identity has increased
dramatically. For example, whereas F. S. L. Lyons devoted a chapter of his
Ireland since the Famine to the "Battle of Two Civilizations" waged between

Gaelic and Anglo-Irish revivalists at the turn of the twentieth century, Tom Garvin and John Hutchinson, among others, have written extensive and illuminating accounts that apply sophisticated analytical frames to the same era.[3] In particular, Hutchinson has championed this shift away from what he refers to as "the claustrophobic intensity with which the Irish are wont to examine themselves" as a means to "internationalize" Irish history through comparative perspectives.[4]

One cannot turn to any standard account of the revival era without encountering some discussion of the quintessential Irish-Ireland organization, the Gaelic League, and its guiding lights, Douglas Hyde and Eoin MacNeill. When they established the League in July 1893, Hyde and Mac-Neill did so ostensibly "for the sole purpose of keeping the Irish language spoken in Ireland."[5] By turning to the language, they hoped to appeal to people of all political and religious persuasions through a sense of Ireland's unique cultural heritage, distinct from that of England or Britain, and in so doing, to release the creative energies of the Irish people. Throughout much of the next quarter-century the League formed the nucleus of a popular movement that sponsored Irish language classes and cultural events, encouraged Irish industries, pressed for bilingual education for native-speaking children in the National School system, and campaigned for a compulsory Irish-language requirement for matriculation in the National University of Ireland.[6] In short, the Gaelic League was in the van of Irish cultural nationalism at the turn of the twentieth century in that it sought to maintain and develop native culture—however one defined native—without explicitly calling for Home Rule or Irish independence.

Historians have tended to portray the League in one of two related ways. First, those exploring the development of Irish nationalism generally and the republican movement specifically have suggested that the League acted as a "quasi-political association" in the years following the death of the parliamentary leader Charles Stewart Parnell. Because the official policy of the League until 1915 was to remain "non-political," the thrust of this line of research has explored the validity of the policy and the means by which the League was transformed into "a sort of school for rebellion."[7] The other and overlapping theme in the research has been the attempt to elucidate the contribution of the League to cultural diversity in Ireland and to show how this diversity sidetracked efforts to create a "fused" or consensus culture in anticipation of Irish Home Rule and, later, in the wake of partition.[8] In these accounts adherents of the Irish-Ireland movement generally appear as if they were of one mind in their approach to the Ireland of their day; hence, when scholars do highlight internal debates within the movement, they present them as reflecting the readily apparent divisions in Irish society, that is, the political and religious.

To be sure, although neither Garvin nor Hutchinson used Irish-language sources for their investigations of the revival, they have nevertheless both presented sophisticated and compelling arguments linking it to revolutionary politics and Catholic antimodernism. For example, Garvin's assessment moved significantly beyond earlier studies by linking the development of revolutionary politics to the socioeconomic transformation of Ireland in the wake of the Great Famine. Drawing on the writings of Moore, Tilly, and Hroch, he posited the theory that Irish revolutionary nationalism developed in "compact, unindustrialized, and developmentally intermediate zones," in which "capitalism had developed enough to generate problems, but not enough to offer solutions."[9] In particular, he highlighted the southern province of Munster, which produced a disproportionate number of leaders in the revolutionary era, as the key intermediate zone in the postfamine Irish context, although aside from citing its disproportionate number of revolutionaries, he provided no other clear reason for his southern focus. According to Garvin, these undefined problems of development were felt most acutely by men of the lower middle class, which, he declared, was composed of "the following social categories: the artisanate, shopkeepers, and smaller capitalists; professionals, in the broad sense, including teachers, lower civil servants, lower and middle management, and clerks, and excluding only the higher professions, such as senior positions in law, medicine, and accountancy; the highly skilled working class, or significant portions of its upper level; small and middle-sized farmers and peasantry; army NCOs; intellectuals, again in the very broad sense, to include writers, artists, journalists, and entertainers. Another important category in the Irish case is the lower clergy, which should also be included."[10] Garvin continued that these middlemen only took control of revolutionary movements once they had already been started, presumably by the landed elites, the upper-echelon professionals, or the laboring poor, as these are about the only categories missing from his rather loosely defined "lower middle class."

Hutchinson, meanwhile, offered another provocative study of the revival, using it as a test case for Anthony Smith's thesis that nationalism arises out of a crisis of "dual legitimation."[11] Essentially, Smith argued that intellectuals turn to nationalism as a dynamic solution to the identity struggle they face when the ethos of a "scientific state" interposes itself on a traditional culture.[12] The crisis manifested itself in Ireland, according to Hutchinson, when the expanding civil service and the relatively stagnant number of professional positions failed to provide enough opportunities for the aspiring youths of the increasingly well-educated Catholic middle and lower-middle classes. Exasperated with the nationalist political leadership of the Irish parliamentary party, which these intellectuals saw as too committed to the British connection, they turned to Gaelic revivalism as a way to draw together modernizing urban-oriented journalists such as Arthur Griffith and W. P. Ryan, reforming priests and their allies such as D. P. Moran, and "neo-traditionalist" clerics such as Father Patrick Dinneen and Canon Peadar Ua Laoghaire.[13]

This approach had many virtues, not the least of which is that it recognized that revivalists themselves debated what direction their efforts should take, but it also suffered from several deficiencies. First, the trigger mechanism Hutchinson has identified for the dual-legitimation crisis does not stand up to scrutiny. As will be seen in chapter 3, professionals in Ireland largely held aloof from the Gaelic League, much to the chagrin of some of its leading proponents.[14] Further, Peter Murray pointed out in 1993 that the League did not "exert a peculiarly strong gravitational pull on those experiencing blocked mobility frustrations or moral subversion fears. Grievance over inequality of opportunity was focused elsewhere— principally on banks, insurance companies, and railway companies—and was articulated by other movements."[15] Indeed, Hutchinson did not even attempt a systematic study of League membership to see whether revivalists fit the criteria of Smith's model.[16] Second, Hutchinson assumed too great a connection between the ideals of the Gaelic revival and the political challenge to the Irish parliamentary party posed by Arthur Griffith's

Sinn Féin party. To be sure, the Gaelic revival arose during the years when the Parnell split had fractured nationalist parliamentary unity, and Griffith and his followers, as leading proponents of the language cause, could claim to incorporate its ethos in their political program. But this did not mean that cultural politics emerged in the 1890s to fill a political vacuum, nor does it imply that all or even most Gaelic Leaguers were nascent Sinn Féin supporters.

Certainly elements of these accounts are incontrovertible: many of the men and women who helped to found the Irish Free State (and later the Irish Republic) had been revivalists in their youth; advanced nationalists wrested control of the League from its moderate founders in 1915; and conservative clerics, such as Ua Laoghaire, actively denounced English culture as "evil" in revivalist newspapers such as Moran's *Leader*. But such provocative statements and actions must be placed in proper context in order to recognize—along with P. J. Mathews and Philip O'Leary—the countless, significant examples of cooperation between revivalists and other elements in contemporary Irish society.[17] Perhaps the vehemence and finality of the language in controversies about the Irish stage or among political rivals have blinded us to the quieter moments when ideological disputants joined hands on one project or another? That Irish men and women battled rhetorically and yet banded together should, however, not surprise us, as contemporary observers were well aware that violent disagreements—both physical and rhetorical—were part of the sport of Irish debate. What is surprising is that it has not been recognized as such in hindsight.[18]

Moreover, drawing general conclusions about the revival from select controversies still assumes too great a unity of thought among revivalists over time. In reality, disputes about the movement's means and aims were endemic among Irish-Ireland's leading spokespersons, as a careful reading of the contemporary press would show. For example, throughout the first decade of the century Moran deprecated the Sinn Féin political program, caricaturing Griffith and his followers as a "Green Hungarian Band." Griffith returned the favor by hammering away at Moran's desire to "capture the King," after Moran advocated that Irish nationalists take their demands directly to King Edward VII in order to preempt unionist claims to be the only Irishmen loyal to the Crown.[19] Similarly, the opinions of ideologues themselves developed and changed over the course of their careers. For example, the future revolutionary Patrick Pearse, as an eighteen year old in 1899, denounced the Irish Literary Theatre as a threat to the Gaelic League led by an English poet of the "third or fourth rank" (W. B. Yeats). That same Patrick Pearse, as the editor of the Gaelic League's newspaper *An Claidheamh Soluis* from 1903 until 1909, portrayed the Irish National Theatre Company as an asset to Irish-Ireland and Yeats as a man with a sincere interest in Irish nationhood.[20]

The most significant drawback of the focus on ideology, however, has been that it has necessarily limited our understanding of how the Gaelic revival changed the Irish people's perceptions of themselves. To borrow from the Czech scholar Miroslav Hroch's typology, controversies in the press are situated in Phase B of the development of a nationalist movement, that is, the articulation of the philosophy or ideology of the movement.[21] To be fair to those scholars who have adopted this approach, they have followed a time-tested methodology for studying nationalism through those who articulate a program to be followed.[22] What is missing in such work is attention to Hroch's Phase C—the popular phase of a nationalist movement—or what I call nationalism in practice. And it is to this final phase that one must look in order to understand the impact of the revival on the Irish people generally.

It is the contention of this study that the issues of participation and identity formation were inextricably linked through an assimilative process in which people's responses to ideologies were notional, that is, partial, constructed, and shaped by the social environments in which they were propagated and through the cultural forms used by the people who adopted them.[23] A critical component of the assimilative process is multivalence: those who declared allegiance to a specific ideology need not have understood that ideology in precisely the same way; indeed, it was unlikely that they would.[24] Rather, just as specific historically identifiable circumstances shaped each community and each individual, communities or individuals more similarly shaped would interpret and graft on the aspects of an ideology that spoke most directly to them. Thus, even if an ideologue articulated a program consistently and coherently over a significant period of time—itself an unusual occurrence—the reception of all or part of that message would necessarily be contingent upon a number of factors: How did a person learn of the ideology? How did a person perceive it in relation to her/his existing circumstances? Did a person see a place for that ideology in her/his life?

Using Irish- and English-language sources, the present study will attempt to trace the ways that Gaelic Leaguers propagated their ideas in their local milieux in order to understand better how Irish men and women reconfigured notions of Irishness in the decades prior to partition. Chapters 1 and 2 begin by placing the Gaelic revival in the context of Ireland at the turn of the twentieth century, in particular discussing its relationship to the most important sociocultural institution on the island—the Roman Catholic Church. Chapter 3 examines internal League records, newspaper and police reports, census data, and local directories to establish a comprehensive profile of League membership in order to test whether, in fact, the revival appealed to people of "all creeds and all classes" as Hyde and others proclaimed. Chapter 4 turns to the activities of Gaelic League branches and points out that the most underappreciated aspect of the League program was its effort to inculcate the Victorian concept of independence, that is, the ability to stand on one's own. Crucially, the interest of revivalists in sobriety and economic advancement served as bridge builders between people of different social and economic backgrounds, but they also diverted attention from what was ostensibly the primary goal of the revival—preserving the Irish language.

If such multiple understandings were possible within Gaelic League branches, how much more diffuse did the meaning of the revival become as its proponents spread their messages through annual festivals and processions? Irish historians, like their counterparts elsewhere, have lately paid great attention to the construction of mass spectacles and to the implications that these events had for Irish politics in the nineteenth and twentieth centuries, and chapters 5 and 6 engage this growing corpus of literature.[25] Drawing particularly upon the insights of Clifford Geertz, Victor Turner, and Frank Manning, this examination of League festivals (feiseanna) and processions contextualizes and assesses the interplay between Gaelic Leaguers and their neighbors in these shared communal celebrations.[26] Of special importance is Turner's observation that celebrants and audiences associated the objects that were constructed for use as celebratory texts (for example, tableaux and songs) with the emotions and impressions experienced during the celebrations themselves. Hence, when events were repeated over a period of time—as were League functions—people invested these objects with special meanings "even when they are products of a culture hitherto unknown to the observer."[27] By examining celebratory texts and the milieux that influenced their construction and reception, therefore, it is possible to interpret how people invested specific objects, such as the Irish language, with particular meanings.

What we will find is quite striking: the Gaelic revival succeeded and failed simultaneously. It succeeded in creating an atmosphere conducive to the study and appreciation of the Irish language, but it failed to arrest the decline of vernacular Irish in the Gaeltacht—the very areas in which the founders of the revival hoped to have the most impact. The purpose of this study, then, is twofold. First, I will address the questions of who participated in the revival and why? Second, I will show that although revivalists did not preserve the so-called traditional culture of Ireland, they created a form of Irish culture, which had varied meanings for the island's people.

1

The Strange Case of O'Growney's Bones

Young and old, men and women, priests and laymen, rich and poor, were all represented in the ranks. The sight was, certainly, one fully calculated to arouse an interest commensurate with the solemn and pathetic function of the day.[1]

Throughout the morning of 26 September 1903, excited crowds gathered on the streets outside of the Catholic Pro-Cathedral in Dublin. Most of the growing throng wore black crepe armbands emblazoned with the likeness of Fr. Eoghan (Eugene) O'Growney—the man whose memory they were assembling to honor. O'Growney, the author of the Gaelic League's popular series of *Simple Lessons in Irish* and the former professor of Irish at St. Patrick's College, Maynooth, had died nearly four years earlier in the United States, a victim of tuberculosis brought on by overwork. After much fitful effort, Irish Americans had financed the transfer of his remains from Los Angeles to Ireland in a progress that featured requiem masses in seven cities presided over by nine bishops and concelebrated by dozens of priests.[2] At Maynooth, the final destination on this journey, the entire staff and student body gathered around the coffin, at which point the white-robed seminarians performed a *caoin* specially written for the occasion.[3] But the main event of the progress had taken place that afternoon, a procession that snaked its way through downtown Dublin to the Broadstone Station. As marshals mustered the gathering crowd into their appointed staging areas on the side streets and quays outside of the Pro-Cathedral, O'Growney's family and close friends attended a midday mass inside. Then, shortly after one o'clock, they fell into line marching shoulder-to-shoulder, four across, behind hurlers whose *camans* were also draped in black. Their ranks—estimated by the Dublin Metropolitan Police at about 6,000 people—stretched continuously for almost a mile and a quarter.[4] Along their route, they passed tens of thousands of onlookers, many of whom were simply out for a Sunday stroll, but many others had concentrated at particular vantage points to watch the proceedings.

According to the *Freeman's Journal*, the O'Growney funeral recalled similar events through the Irish capital—for example, the return of Terence Bellew MacManus's corpse from the United States in 1861 and the funeral for Charles Stewart Parnell in 1891. Whereas "the Parnell funeral was one intense sob for a great leader gone in his prime, and the MacManus funeral was a political demonstration meant to give the warning note of the Fenians," the O'Growney funeral "took the character of both. It was a requiem and a tocsin combined."[5] "What Father O'Growney had done for his people needed not to be said at his graveside," the article concluded hyperbolically. "It was there in the long line of children and young men and women, which stretched for miles behind his coffin across the city."[6]

But what precisely had O'Growney done for his people? The short answer would be that he had helped to found the Gaelic League, the organization most associated with the spread of what Mathews has called the "self-help" ethos of the Irish-Ireland movement.[7] Certainly the priest's name, if not his biography, was well known because his five-volume *Simple Lessons* series—known popularly as "O'Growney's"—was the doorway through which most League members and hangers-on came into contact with the Irish language. By 1903, the League had published more than 320,000 copies of the first volume of the series alone.[8] At the time of the priest's death, the traveling organizer Tomás Bán Concannon reported that "O'Growney's name is spoken with affection" wherever he visited.[9] And Arthur Clery, a Gaelic activist and frequent contributor to the *Leader*, recalled years later that as Gaelic classes "became the rage" at University College, "Sophocles and O'Growney, Higher Plane Curves and O'Growney, Hegel and O'Growney, became the recognized diet of the various classes of students."[10]

This posthumous fame would undoubtedly have surprised the shy and sickly priest. Within a year of the League's foundation, his health had failed him, and the college trustees had authorized a six-month leave of absence and a generous pension to facilitate his recuperation in the United States. But he never regained enough strength to contemplate seriously returning to Ireland, and on 18 October 1899 he died at a hospital in Los Angeles. As we will see in chapter 2, however, he had already played a central part in transforming the attitude of Ireland's Catholic clergy toward the Irish language.

Beyond testifying to O'Growney's personal renown, his funeral procession highlights the strengths and weaknesses of themes prevalent in the existing scholarship about the Gaelic revival. The marchers, for example, came primarily from Ireland's Catholic and nationalist communities. The ratio of priests to lay marchers in the procession (a staggering 1 in 60) dwarfed the ratio in society as a whole (roughly 1 in 1,200), a fact that almost certainly played a role in contemporary accounts emphasizing the large number of priests in attendance.[11] If one also considers that large contingents from the Christian Brothers's schools in the city, as well as sodalities and temperance societies, marched, the overwhelming number of participants in the procession would have been overtly Catholic in sentiment. Such a sight undoubtedly confirmed the opinion of those, such as the controversialist Michael J. F. McCarthy, who had denounced the League the previous year as a "priestly institution,"[12] and it lends credence to the perception that the Catholic character of the League widened the gulf between those seeking to create a cosmopolitan Irish culture and those seeking to insulate the country through the Irish-Ireland movement.[13]

It is similarly noteworthy that Irish-American Fenians paid for the disinterment and transportation of O'Growney's body, and that members of the Old Guard Union, the Cumann na nGaedheal, and the Celtic Literary Society—all groups carefully watched by the Constabulary's Crime Special Branch because of their ties to republicanism—made up the so-called "general section" of the funeral procession. More respectable, constitutional nationalists also attended, including five members of parliament, the lord mayor and lord high sheriff of Dublin, and nineteen members of the city corporation, who marched in the "representative section."[14] The presence of both advanced and moderate elements of the nationalist spectrum suggests that the potential already existed for the internecine struggle for the League's machinery that Garvin outlined two decades ago.[15]

But the funeral also highlights an underappreciated aspect of the revival: its connection to the hoped-for economic regeneration of Ireland. The most boisterous segment of the procession was its industrial section, which included numerous trade society bands. Contrary to the received opinion that the Gaelic League was the preserve of middle-class dilettantes, marchers included contingents from the silk trade, the slaters union, the bakers and confectioners trade society, the Amalgamated Society of Carpenters and Joiners, the Dublin pork butchers, and the Kingstown (Dun Laoghaire) Laborers' Society.[16]

Their presence—alongside clerics, politicians, members of the Gaelic Athletic Association (GAA), and student groups—brings into firm relief an enormously important fact about the Gaelic revival: it was the product of a specific conjuncture of the social and political transformations that shaped modern Ireland and not merely an epiphenomenal expression of the island's political and religious divisions. To be sure, an extraordinary cadre of leaders spearheaded the movement, including such familiar names as O'Growney, Douglas Hyde, Eoin MacNeill, and Patrick Pearse, but also including lesser known figures, such as Padraig Ó Dalaigh, the indefatigable secretary of the League from County Waterford; Patrick Ingoldsby, who organized massive processions through Dublin in the years after the O'Growney funeral; and Agnes O'Farrelly, who founded a Gaelic summer college in County Donegal and served continuously for more than a decade on the executive committee of the organization. However, were it not for economic modernization, the expansion of political participation, and the devotional revolution of the nineteenth century, these men and women would have had a very different movement to lead. The following tells the story of how language revivalists tapped into the hopes and fears of the Irish people at a time when these transformations were recasting their expectations. It also argues that the Irish people were not passive recipients of that revivalist message; rather, they adapted it to suit their everyday lives.

THE WORLD THAT THEY KNEW

Because several Gaelic Leaguers had storied if not always successful careers in other walks of life, it is easy to overlook the haphazard nature of their organization. The League was (and remains) volunteer based, and in the 1890s, it was extremely informal. Between 1893 and 1898, interested individuals affiliated with the Dublin founders regardless of their proximity to the city, though as early as 1894, provincial activists in Cork, Galway, and Belfast determined to form their own branches. These *craobhacha* maintained a loose, confederal association with their Dublin counterparts, who offered them advice and coordinated information. Branches in the 1890s recognized Dublin's first-among-equals status through a series of constitutions ratified at an annual congress, or Ard-Fheis, which was more like a gathering of friends than a strict caucus. The most important of these meetings took place in 1899 when delegates formally established a national executive committee (the Coiste Gnótha) to manage the League on a day-to-day basis. Branches were now answerable to the congress through the executive. In practice, this meant that Dubliners retained a disproportionate influence on League administration for two reasons: first, provincial representatives were less likely to attend executive-committee meetings than were city representatives; and second, until 1902 administrative work continued to be performed by volunteers who necessarily lived in the city.[17]

After the congress recognized the need to professionalize the executive staff in 1902, League records became more systematized, but the improvement was far from complete.[18] Paid staff still dealt with volunteer local officers who often failed to submit fees and reports, creating tensions between national officials and local leaders: copies of countless pro forma reminders litter the executive's correspondence books, serving as polite testimony to what must have been a frustrating aspect of this work.[19] William Bulfin, an émigré to Argentina who chronicled one of his extended trips home in a newspaper series later published as *Rambles in Eireann*, has left a particularly colorful description of the hectic workday at headquarters. Under his watchful eye, Ó Dalaigh "repeatedly performed the following things simultaneously: written letters; spoken in Irish and English; checked branch reports; read press notices—and smiled. When anyone with a grievance comes in and threatens to wreck the movement, he is folded in the magic of the secretary's smile, and his anger is put to sleep."[20]

Despite this breezy image, the pressure of business weighed heavily on central staff. In 1899 MacNeill, who kept his full-time job as a clerk while serving as volunteer secretary of the League and editor of its newspaper *An Claidheamh Soluis,* suffered a physical breakdown. For the rest of his life he endured recurring headaches and bouts of "lassitude."[21] Nine years later, treasurer Stiofán Bairéad developed insomnia because of his constant concern that branches failed to remit their dues promptly enough to cover the day-to-day expenses of the organization.[22]

When the League was at its largest between 1906 and 1908, it included branches in every county in Ireland. There were more than 50,000 dues-paying members in nearly 700 domestic branches at that time, as well as thousands more in branches throughout the Irish diaspora. Critically, these figures underreport the overall number of members during the period under review because people joined, participated actively for a time, left, and were replaced by new blood. That circulation of members had the impact of broadening the reach of the revival and lessening the depth of understanding that individual members—and their contemporaries—had for what Moran called *The Philosophy of Irish Ireland.*[23]

Instead, their understanding of the revival was conditioned by the world that they knew, a world that had been profoundly reshaped over the preceding century. For example, the population had declined steeply since the island's prefamine total of more than 8 million people (6.5 million of whom were Catholics), to approximately 4.5 million (3.3 million Catholics) in 1901.[24] Of direct concern to language revivalists, the proportion of the population speaking Irish had fallen even more precipitously: whereas roughly half the population could speak Irish prior to 1845, only about 14 percent could in 1901. Worse still, only one-half of 1 percent of the population claimed to be monolingual Irish-speakers.[25]

In fact, the famine had catalyzed migration patterns that were developing prior to 1840, benefiting larger population centers within Ireland and leading many Irish men and women to seek their futures abroad. The overall share of the population living in towns with at least 1,500 inhabitants had increased from only 15 percent in 1841 to 32 percent in 1901, but this aggregate change reflected the enormous growth of Belfast (to nearly 350,000 people) and the continuing relative importance of Dublin to the island's population.[26] Many smaller towns and villages—the very places where we will see in chapter 3 that the League established beachheads outside of Dublin—actually declined in size during the same period.[27]

A major cause of this latter phenomenon was emigration spurred by the lack of employment in the country, which, Gaelic Leaguers would argue, forced young people to look for work abroad. Since the 1840s, the social structure of the rural population had indeed been altered at the expense of redundant laborers and household servants and to the benefit of strong farmers who emphasized pasturage on large and medium-sized farmsteads.[28] After 1870, redundancy also hit towns and villages more intensely than it had previously because the ongoing shift away from tillage farming adversely affected inland mill towns: less access to local grain supplies made inland milling operations economically vulnerable.[29] In towns such as Nenagh, Ballymahon, and Clonmel, mills closed rapidly after 1880, and as Cullen has shown, "employment in milling was halved between 1881 and 1901."[30] Moreover, cheap factory-made goods—many imported from Britain and carried throughout Ireland by the railways, which had expanded rapidly since 1850—undercut local craftsmen.[31] For instance, with the growth of the factory-made shoe industry, the number of bootmakers in Ireland fell by over a third between 1871 and 1891, and it declined at the same rate again between 1891 and 1911. More dramatically, factory-produced nails made nailers almost obsolete. According to Cullen, the number of nailers in Ireland was "almost halved in the 1870s, halved again in the 1880s, and halved yet again by 1901."[32]

From a macroeconomic perspective, such changes are understandable as an Irish manifestation of the impact that growing international economies of scale had on traditional production techniques. But these changes were wrenching for those who lived through and adapted to them. Along the Atlantic seaboard, the Irish-speaking districts were among the poorest parts of the island, and parents—motivated by an instinct for survival—bred insurance for export. Adults became so adamant that their children learn English that they refused to speak to them in their native language: these youthful policies needed to be outfitted with the key to success, so that they could emigrate or become migrant harvesters reaping the means for the family's survival on its meager homestead.[33] Emigration statistics reflect the impact of these actions on the Irish-speaking districts. In the last three decades of the nineteenth century Connacht and Munster contributed disproportionately to the exodus. In 1901, their combined populations represented 42 percent of the Irish total, yet almost 70 percent of emigrants came from these two provinces.[34]

The communities they left behind were largely devoid of social outlets. Elizabeth Malcolm has shown that traditional entertainments, such as Gaelic games, patterns, and festivals, had already declined in the first half of the century. Political campaigns and temperance crusades provided intermittent communal excitement, but most contemporary commentators agreed that provincial villages and rural districts were "tiresome and monotonous."[35] As the lexicographer Fr. Patrick Dinneen told the Central branch of the Gaelic League in 1901, an Irish village was "a place without prosperity, happiness, or brightness."[36]

Market forces filled this social vacuum with a popular culture that was largely derivative of English popular culture. Cheryl Herr has shown in the case of music halls and Christmas pantomimes that Dublin and Belfast theater owners imported shows and performers from England rather than maintaining troupes of local performers.[37] Although traveling companies adapted the content of shows to include local references, they also followed strict conventions of style and subject matter. Entertainments originating in Britain and traveling to towns in Ireland often contained references that were more topical in London or in areas fully attuned to metropolitan sentiments.[38] For example, Herr points out that a production of *Sleeping Beauty* in 1902 contained a song that suggested an "utter lack of any popular desire for Home Rule" and contained a refrain extolling Australia, India, and Canada for having "proved themselves in Africa/A patriotic pattern to the world."[39] As we will see in chapters 4 through 6, such entertainments inspired revivalist attempts to create a culture that would no longer turn "the mind of Ireland to England."[40]

"WE WERE REALLY BUILDING UP A NATION"

This specific complaint was also at the heart of revivalist ideologues' disdain for the island's fractious political culture, which was dominated in the 1890s and early 1900s by the question of whether parliament would grant Home Rule to Ireland.[41] Of course, the old salt spilled by W. B. Yeats that political stagnation after the Parnell split had opened the way for a cultural awakening has long since been swept away.[42] In fact, these were years rich in political activity. After enduring the acrimony of the split, for instance, Home Rulers of various stripes reenergized and reunited under the aegis of the agrarian agitation carried on by the United Irish League (UIL). Eventually they gained the necessary leverage over their Liberal allies to put Home Rule firmly on the United Kingdom docket in 1912.[43] More advanced nationalists, meanwhile, limped into the twentieth century, poorly funded and more poorly organized, though Griffith's fledgling Sinn Féiners vividly articulated their concerns. As for the revolutionary underground, the Irish Republican Brotherhood (IRB) was so disorganized that it could not even muster a decent showing at the funeral for John O'Leary in 1907; it was only around 1910 that Bulmer Hobson, Sean MacDermott, and Patrick MacCartan reinvigorated their ranks.[44] Concurrently, opposition to Home Rule brought together several disparate strands of thought—ranging from liberal unionist to aristocratic/conservative and plebeian/Orange influences—in an uneasy fusion of interests known as "unionism."[45] Some scholars have detected differences between southern unionism, as represented by Sir Horace Plunkett's pursuit of constructive reformism, and its more sectarian northern counterpart, though as Alvin Jackson has pointed out, reformism and sectarianism could be found among unionists throughout the island.[46]

For the purposes of the present study, two points are important to keep in mind about these developments. First, the language revival drew its membership from across this political spectrum, thanks in no small part to the commitment of Gaelic Leaguers to remain "nonpolitical" and "nonsectarian." "I was always able to boast," Hyde wrote in 1918, "that though our movement did not contain the whole of any body of thought or of religion in the country, still there was no body or religion that it did not draw some of its adherents from, and as it took every sort to make a nation, we were really building up a nation very effectively."[47] Hyde's claim, as we will see in chapter 3, was plausible because "Gaelic zealotry happened, and mattered, at a different level from that of politics."[48] To be sure, League members came overwhelmingly from nationalist back-grounds, and they included numerous politicians in their ranks.[49] Further, some of the organization's employees became members of the IRB and used their positions to push radical opinions, and the League did become a political tool after the IRB used proxy delegates to seize control of the or-ganization at the Ard-Fheis in August 1915.[50] But until that point in time, the efforts of politically motivated actors to "work" the revival were con-fined to a few branches and were generally snuffed out by leaders and or-dinary members.[51] As late as April 1915, the Inspector General of the Royal Irish Constabulary (RIC) concluded that attempts to introduce political questions had been thwarted by "members interested in the League for its own sake from an educational point of view, [who] have from time to time drawn attention to the necessity for preserving its nonpolitical character." The League, he determined, was "not a political society."[52]

The emerging unionist community, meanwhile, responded in a vari-ety of ways to the implications of the revivalist idea—that Ireland had a distinct nationality. Some, such as the leader writer of the *Dublin Evening Mail*, rejected such claims categorically, believing that "the Irish language campaign is only another side of the eternal political agitation with which Ireland is cursed."[53] And there can be little doubt that similar fears in-formed the occasional attacks made by Orange or loyalist gangs on men and women returning from League gatherings.[54] Still, others expressed sympathy with the revival on patriotic grounds. For example, the Rev-erend R. R. Kane, who had organized one of the largest anti–Home Rule rallies in Belfast in 1892, was among the earliest adherents of the fledgling League branch in the city in 1895. Kane, who stated publicly that he con-sidered himself Irish first and a citizen of the United Kingdom second, was often quoted by Hyde as having said that he could never forget that his "real name" was Ó Catháin.[55] There is nothing to indicate that Kane's was more than a nostalgic or antiquarian interest in Irish, but similar sen-timents informed the members and patrons of bodies such as the Gaelic Society at Queen's College, founded in 1906. Among its important patrons was the Reverend Thomas Hamilton, a prominent Belfast unionist who remained a patron until at least 1915.[56] Others, meanwhile, viewed the lan-guage as a curiosity, worthy of study but not as a subject that should be imposed upon the public generally. Intriguingly, Ulster unionist members of parliament, including James Craig and Ronald McNeill, expressed these sentiments during the Home Rule debates in October 1912. (McNeill, later one of the most influential early historians of unionism, even acknowledged that he had made efforts to learn Irish himself.)[57] More important, one can point to several unionists who were active revivalists, such as the surgeon and president of the Belfast Gaelic League, Dr. John St. Clair Boyd; the liberal unionist aristocrat, Lord Castletown, who resided at Doneraile, Co. Cork; and Robert Lindsay Crawford, editor of the *Irish Protestant* and from 1903 to 1908 the Imperial Grand Master of the Independent Orange Order. Crawford was even a candidate for the Coiste Gnótha in 1906 and appeared in Strabane in January 1909 to advocate for the adoption of compulsory Irish in the National University of Ireland.[58] Thus, while many unionists viewed the language revival generally, and the League specifically, with skepticism, Ó Cobhthaigh's contemporary and measured assessment appears an accurate gauge of unionist response to the revival: "The average member of that party, even if he did not sympathize with the objects of the League, regarded it with benevolent indifference."[59]

Second, politicians of all stripes found it difficult to dictate to their (sometimes unruly) constituents because new political synergies were emerging out of the combination of Ireland's century-long tradition of mass mobilization and the increasing literacy of the expanded electorate. Scholars are only beginning to decode this phenomenon, but one need merely consider two examples to see that elite politicians and their supporters did not always see eye to eye. First, in 1907 the leader of the parliamentary nationalists, John Redmond, had to come out publicly against the Liberal Party's devolutionary Irish Councils Bill after UIL branches overwhelmingly rebuffed it at a party conference. Redmond had had private reservations about the scheme, but he had been silent enough about them prior to the convention that his erstwhile colleague William O'Brien was "amazed" at its rejection. At the same time, UIL leaders faced a second, running challenge from small farmers and landless laborers who engaged in the so-called Ranch War. Their cattle drives and calls for the redistribution of ranch lands attacked the very element whose financial support was crucial to the party leadership. And though the conflict cooled after

1910, its lack of resolution fueled lingering resentments against the parliamentary party that redounded to the benefit of Sinn Féin in the years after 1916.[60]

THE "MASSIVE MIDDLE GROUND"

Similar dynamics conditioned the relationship between the island's religious elites and their flocks, especially among the Catholic majority. Since the middle of the nineteenth century, Irish Catholics had undergone what Emmet Larkin has called a "devotional revolution," which expressed itself through more active lay participation in the sacramental devotions of the church and which received direction from an increasingly well-organized and growing clerical workforce. Accordingly, Catholicism provided the majority of the population with a "substitute symbolic language and offered them a new cultural heritage" that compensated for the social and cultural dislocations described earlier.[61] To cite just one manifestation of this increased devotionalism, church attendance increased dramatically after the famine. Prior to the 1840s, fewer than 40 percent of lay Catholics (outside of southeastern Ireland) attended mass regularly; by 1890 the figure was more than 90 percent.[62] Some of this upsurge must be attributed to similarly dramatic expansions in church facilities and personnel. Thus, if one looks only at the church's human resources, one sees that the number of priests increased from approximately 2,500 to 3,200 between 1850 and 1870, and the number of nuns grew from 1,500 to more than 3,700. By 1901 approximately 3,700 priests and 8,000 nuns, as well as about 1,100 teaching brothers, made up the total Catholic institutional workforce.[63]

These personnel figures represented the continuation of longer term institutional developments, but the push for Irish Catholicism to conform more fully to Roman norms gained coherence after the arrival of Paul Cullen as archbishop of Armagh in 1849.[64] The epicenter of this change was the national seminary, St. Patrick's College (Maynooth), which the bishops had founded in 1795 with the consent of and a grant from parliament.[65] On the eve of the famine, Maynooth already had trained the majority of Ireland's bishops, seventeen of whom served as the trustees of the college.[66] But Cullen's appointment gave the voice of the Irish hierarchy greater unity because his views came to dominate the church in Ireland.[67] He saw to it, for instance, that only those men who agreed with him received promotion to bishoprics on the island, and the door to the episcopacy opened increasingly through the seminary. Eleven of the twelve professors of theology who taught at Maynooth between 1867 and 1895 were elevated to Irish sees, the lone exception being Fr. Walter McDonald, whose challenges to orthodoxy made him suspect in the eyes of his superiors both in Ireland and at Rome.[68] The bishops met as a unit twice each year, and a standing committee of the four archbishops and five or six of the suffragans ensured continuity by handling any ecclesiastical business that arose between meetings.[69]

The educational philosophy at Maynooth did not encourage intellectual curiosity among its students. According to the bicentennial history of the college, the typical late nineteenth-century seminarian "learned to preach from his dogma lectures; to administer the sacraments he learned from the deans' instructions and, most specifically, from his course in moral theology, which taught him to be a good confessor."[70] Although a small percentage of students did indeed go beyond rote learning, the grim picture painted of the student experience by Gerald O'Donovan is probably not far removed from reality. In his largely autobiographical first novel, *Father Ralph*, a prizewinning seminarian acknowledged to the eponymous protagonist that he memorized the Latin notes from their dogmatic-theology course without understanding the language: "'Oh, I never bother about the meaning in English,' he said, 'as long as I have the Latin words. Sure, no one can deny the meaning is in them, right enough.'"[71] Such performers could succeed because, as O'Shea has noted, the seminary faculty aimed to create "a body of professional men capable of carrying out the spiritual and administrative duties of parish life."[72] The goal at Maynooth, in fact, was merely to produce "good average men."[73] Equally important, since diocesan seminaries and Irish colleges on the continent modeled their curricula on that of the national seminary, the limited course of study in St. Patrick's College had ramifications for the entirety of the Irish Catholic establishment.[74] Nevertheless, Maynooth and these diocesan seminaries graduated more than enough priests during the latter half of the nineteenth century to serve ably in parishes throughout Ireland, with the surplus staffing what came to be known as the "Irish mission" overseas.[75]

In addition to mass attendance, of course, Irish Catholics engaged in a variety of practices, both inside and outside their homes, which placed religion at the center of their lives.[76] Parish missions, temperance crusades, communal rosary sessions, confraternities and sodalities, and stations were among the more important activities sanctioned by the institutional church. Significantly, however, pilgrimages and other practices remained from the pre-Cullen era, particularly in areas of the south and west, and their continuance occasionally led to friction with representatives of the new institutional order.[77]

Seamus Fenton, a school inspector in the west of Ireland at the turn of the twentieth century, recalled a singular example of this clash of religious cultures that took place on (North) Iniskea Island off the Mayo coast. There the local population continued to pray before a wooden statue of their patron, St. Columcille, which they swathed in cloth and kept in a niche of their ruined church. When the English press drew attention to this worship of an "idol," supposedly known as the "Neu Woge" [*sic*], clerical concern grew on the mainland. A curate from Binghamstown visited the island, tore the covering off the statue, broke the wood apart, and tossed the pieces into the sea. Fenton explained the cultural content of the islanders' devotion:

> The islanders, if questioned in their own speech, could have told the journalist, the young priest, and Sir Henry Robinson that the statue from the niche of the ruined island church, that of their guardian saint famous from Iona to Vienna, was also fitted on the very prows of their larger boats, boats named *naomhoga* (naov-oga, new woge! [*sic*]) from that Irish word for statue. The islanders, whose education was mainly from oral tradition, could have told of miracles performed by the island guardian saint in saving seamen from drowning, similar to those attributed to him as related in Adhamhnan's *Life of Colmcille* (Book II).[78]

Women religious and women generally also played crucial roles in the gradual shift from one cultural regime to another. Not only did the increased number of women religious far outdistance that of priests and brothers by 1900, but from about 1850 onward the leaders of female religious communities tended to fall more pliantly under episcopal control than had their predecessors. Most significantly, they directed their substantial and growing resources toward achieving the aims of the devotional revolution.[79] This drive had specific implications in the realm of education, where women religious oversaw the schooling of Catholic girls. The education they offered emphasized moral orthodoxy, quiet submissiveness, and social respectability.[80] As Catholic girls grew up, married, and had their own families, it was often they who encouraged strict adherence to church teachings and taught "proper" devotional practices to their children. Whether through enforcing the nightly saying of the rosary—with its attendant "trimmings," or additional prayers, for special concerns—or by tenderly passing along admonitions against shocking one's guardian angel by performing "unseemly" acts in bed, Irish mothers brought the church into the lives of their children. Indeed, many of the young men who entered the priesthood in the nineteenth century cited their mother's encouragement, prayers, and devotion to the church as having played a seminal role in their vocation.[81]

Within the Catholic milieu, pride of place among the religious went to the priests, whose special position was based on both their sacred and their secular functions in Irish society. First and foremost, they were ministers, ordained to perform the ancient rites of the church, and this set them apart from their parishioners. Buonaiuti, for instance, noted of the Gaelic-speaking "peasant" in County Donegal that although "he addresses everyone else in the second person singular, [he] addresses the priest in the second person plural, because the priest is not alone; God is in him." Similarly, the Longford priest-novelist Canon Joseph Guinan maintained that the priest "dwelt 'behind the veil' where they [his parishioners] durst not enter . . . they would treat me with a reverence almost amounting to fear."[82] On religious matters and moral questions, according to the Frenchman Paul-Dubois, the priest's "authority is indisputable and undisputed."[83]

Behind this reverence lay vestiges of traditional beliefs in a holy man's divinely endowed supernatural abilities. For instance, one of Guinan's characters, Fr. Bernard Melvill, attained a reputation as "the greatest cow docthor [sic] priest that ever came into this part of the country" when the dying cow of one of his parishioners recovered after eating salt blessed by him.[84] One might justifiably question the value of such a fictional account, but other evidence points to the persistence of magical beliefs among the laity. During the heated days of the Parnell split, for example, a priest from the diocese of Meath threatened to turn a parishioner into a goat if he voted for the Parnellite candidate![85] Moreover, people in Gweedore, Co. Donegal, attributed *cumhachtaí* [powers] to their pastor, Canon James MacFadden, who gained national notoriety as their leader during the Land War. Some parishioners believed that MacFadden's powers enabled him to enter and leave meetings without fear of arrest, *and* that he possessed the ability to make an *eisiomláir* of his enemies, that is, that he could deform them so that they would be recognizable as evil-doers.[86]

Augmenting their sacred position, priests carried out countless secular functions for their flocks as well. Limited though their Maynooth training may have been, priests *had* received an education, and they possessed experience of the world beyond the parish boundaries. Particularly in country districts, this wider experience elevated the priest in the estimation of his parishioners. There was also a significant class dimension to the priests' leadership role: since the earliest days of Maynooth, young men seeking vocations came overwhelmingly from the strong-tenant farming class. More than three-fourths of late nineteenth-century clerics came from such backgrounds. They understood the particular concerns of the nascent leaders of rural Ireland, while appreciating, perhaps less fully, the plight of their poorer parishioners, and they sought to encourage parishioners to adopt the respectable behaviors and norms of their class.[87] In recording his impressions of the typical western parish priest, Paul-Dubois observed that "he seems to be a king in his kingdom, affable, courteous, tolerant with non-Catholics, familiar with his flock, above all 'popular.' He is in truth the father of his people, and no doubt an authoritative enough father."[88]

Over the course of the nineteenth century, in fact, clerics fulfilled many of the roles traditionally associated with local notables or gentry elsewhere in the United Kingdom, especially in the realm of education.[89] As early as the 1820s, Daniel O'Connell had deployed the priesthood to lead laypeople in secular affairs when he called on priests to aid in the campaign for Catholic Emancipation.[90] And although parliament had established the Irish national school system in 1831 as nondenominational, Protestant and Catholic leaders pressed the National Board to change the system to grant more control to churchmen. The most public effort by Catholics occurred in 1859 when Cullen condemned the school program as "very dangerous" after the bishops' semiannual meeting, because "its aim is to introduce a mingling of Protestants and Catholics."[91] In late December of that year, the government agreed to restructure the National Board to include ten Catholic and ten Protestant representatives, and by 1870 the government had placed management of the schools in the hands of local clergy, "allowing each denomination to create its own, *de facto* segregated, system within the National system."[92] Governmental recognition of the clerical control of education was even more obvious when one looked at Ireland's secondary schools: the legislation creating the intermediate system in 1878 never even sought to challenge denominational segregation.[93]

Innumerable contemporary commentators focused on the apparent submissiveness of Irish Catholics to their priests in secular affairs. Observers such as the truculent McCarthy denounced the Catholic Irish as "priest-ridden," and the rogue nationalist politician Frank Hugh O'Donnell criticized the general involvement of priests in Irish society as inimical to developing lay independence.[94] Coupled with their relative advantages in terms of education and their freedom from material concerns, O'Donnell saw the "political" priesthood as the "natural aristocracy" in Ireland. And he concluded acidly that priests deliberately chose to "accept the temporal fruit of such a superiority" because "there is human nature even in ministers of religion."[95]

The most famous comments about the priests' potentially stultifying role in Irish society came from Sir Horace Plunkett, the pioneer of agricultural cooperation in Ireland. In 1904, Plunkett published a far-ranging book, *Ireland in the New Century,* touching on the factors in Irish life that he believed would shape the future of the island.[96] Generally sympathetic to the historical plight of Irish Catholics, Plunkett nonetheless created a firestorm by discussing—even briefly—the role of the clergy in perpetuating "deficiencies" in the character of Irish Catholics.[97] Most significantly, he asserted that the clergy bore a "direct and personal responsibility" for the "morale" of the people, which he found wanting.[98] In Plunkett's analysis such deficiencies manifested themselves in the relatively weak economic position of Ireland vis-à-vis Britain, a position exacerbated by what he called the "undue" influence of the clergy. Of particular concern to him was the "over-abundance" of church building in nineteenth-century Ireland, which may have attenuated more general economic advance by diverting capital investment from more productive enterprises.[99] Although more recent analysis has shown that such an interpretation cannot be sustained, at the time of writing Plunkett's opinion—coming from someone who had worked to improve the rural economy and to instill self-reliance among the small-farming population—lent credence to those who feared or decried clerical activity in secular affairs.[100]

Those who interpreted clerical actions more positively responded aggressively to such criticisms. Famously, Monsignor Michael O'Riordan, then a curate in St. Michael's parish in Limerick city and afterward the rector of the Irish College at Rome, wrote a multipart rebuttal (one could hardly call it a review) of Plunkett's analysis in the pages of the *Leader* under the pseudonym, "M Ó'R." The collected rebuttal appeared subsequently as *Catholicity and Progress in Ireland*.[101] O'Riordan denied that character could be equated with economic spirit, but at the same time he traced examples of the latter among Catholics in Ireland and elsewhere.[102] On the central issue of clerical involvement in temporal affairs, O'Riordan maintained that priests participated "not as a duty of justice but of charity." He also pointed out that priests found themselves in a no-win situation. On one hand, they were often asked by their parishioners or by the government to engage in secular affairs; on the other hand, they became subject to criticism whether they participated or not.[103]

Others who were appreciative of clerical participation in secular affairs argued that priests did not abuse their special position in society. Paul-Dubois, for example, detected little basis for charges that priests had aggrandized themselves through their temporal—or indeed their sacerdotal—role, though he recognized that individual exceptions might be found.[104] Buonaiuti noted the potential for abuse because of the great confidence placed in priests by lay Catholics; nonetheless, he felt that the individual priest "respond[s] conscientiously to the people's trust, and ever prompt to their call for the legitimate assertion of their rights, never turn[s] to his own profit the veneration of which he is the object."[105] To commentators such as these, Irish priests were the "good average men" they were trained to be: relatively well educated, relatively capable and respected in secular affairs, absolutely indispensable in spiritual matters.

Three points must be made, however, before leaving this basic discussion about developments in Catholic society in the nineteenth century. First, contemporary generalizations about pastoral relationships often ignored the significant ambiguities created by local circumstances. Over time and in changed conditions, the same cleric might appear in an entirely different light. MacFadden, for example, with his "powers" and his personal charisma, came across as the stereotypical "soggarth aroon" (or beloved priest) while leading his parishioners through the Land War in socially monolithic Gweedore. His secular work on their behalf augmented his attempts to advance the cultural program of the devotional revolution, with its more regularized rituals and its emphasis on middle-class social values. When transferred to the more socially stratified parish of Inishkeel, where he continued to stress social improvement, his readiest allies came from the shopkeeping element in the town. MacFadden's actions, however, exacerbated their already contentious lending relationships with the "mountainy men" from country districts, who were also less willing to acquiesce in the imposition of the cultural and social program espoused by the priest. Thus, the MacFadden of Inishkeel emerged as a "gombeen-priest" (or friend of the usurious shopkeepers) who alienated a significant portion of his parishioners.[106] As Mac Suibhne has argued, both images of the canon had validity; indeed, at Inishkeel, where one's relationship with the priest varied depending on social class and cultural background, these conflicting images *coexisted*.

Second, contemporary and subsequent commentators have failed to tease out the precise nature of the pastoral relationship because they generally have not appreciated the subtleties inherent in the uneven power relationship between priests and people. This failing is particularly evident when they have focused on the deference of lay Catholics to priests in secular affairs. Although it is certainly accurate to note signs of public respect—ranging from the tipping of one's cap, to the cautious use of language when addressing the priest, to the continual requests for clerics to serve as presidents of local organizations—such signs did not necessarily reflect the unwavering subjection of people to their priests. As James C. Scott has noted about observers of peasant societies generally, by concentrating on the extreme behaviors of abject deference or violence, they have neglected the "massive middle ground [of behaviors], in which conformity is often a self-conscious strategy and resistance is a carefully hedged affair that avoids all or nothing confrontations." Scott posits a continuum of actions in which subordinate classes or individuals withhold a part of their opinion "in favor of a performance that is in keeping with the expectations of the powerholder."[107] In such conditions the line between "deferential behavior" and "resistance" becomes blurred to both the powerholder and outside observers as public conformity masks private and semiprivate resistance.[108]

Third, it is contextually significant that discussions about the secular activities of priests were occurring in Ireland at the turn of the century. The coincidence of such discussions with the more heated debates about clericalism in France raised concerns for some priests and key members of the hierarchy.[109] The basis of their concerns, however, was not simply that they feared an anticlerical Ireland per se, but rather that they already knew that they walked a finer line in secular affairs than most commentators acknowledged. In day-to-day life, priests acted as guides and spokespersons, but they recognized that the confidence of at least some of their parishioners was not boundless. It had to be earned *and* retained, and it could be lost, if only temporarily.[110] This is not to deny that bishops and priests behaved as if they were above criticism, particularly when they acted to restrain violence or to take potentially controversial political stances.[111] But flashpoint moments, such as the bitter disputes arising from Parnell's fall, were reminders even to these churchmen that their authority, however extensive, had limits.

"YOU DID MORE TO MAKE HIM KNOWN HERE THAN ANYONE ELSE"

Given the confessional character of Irish politics and society, *and* the overtly Catholic sentiment of leading revivalists such as Moran, it is critical to conclude this discussion of context by noting that revivalists were far less exclusionary than some of their more strident statements might suggest. Moran the practicing journalist, for instance, was more open-minded than Moran the polemicist appears in retrospect. Although he believed that the Irish nation was in essence Catholic, he did not believe that this position necessarily precluded Protestants from participating in the nation. In 1903 he addressed this question explicitly in answer to a correspondent who accused him and his contributors of fostering religious exclusivism.[112] Readers, he cautioned, should not assume that the views expressed by contributors to his paper reflected his own opinions.[113] Moran then took the correspondent to task for equating his attacks against Protestants (for looking, in the main, to England as their social and cultural model) with an intention to exclude Protestants from Ireland. Rather, he offered what he called a more "logical parallel":

> For an Irish-Ireland, as things stand, the Irish language is necessary, and also the recognition of Ireland as a Catholic country in the sense that England is a Protestant country. English-Englishmen can be and are Catholics, though they recognize that the proper place for a great national thanksgiving is St. Paul's Cathedral; Irish-Irishmen can be Protestants or anything else, and recognize that Ireland is a Catholic country so long as, as a matter of fact, it remains a Catholic country.[114]

Moran emphasized that his conception of Ireland as a Catholic country was conditional: "If the million or so non-Catholics became Irish-Irelanders, there would be about 25 percent Irish non-Catholics, and the right of Ireland to be called a Catholic country might be problematical. If in the course of time a large proportion of Irish-Ireland 'Idolators' became Irish-Ireland 'Saved,' and that only 25 percent remained Catholics then, most certainly, Ireland would have ceased to be a Catholic country."[115] He wrote about Irish Catholics, he said, because Irish Protestants had their eyes turned to England, but he and the *Leader* "would be the first to welcome a strong Irish-Ireland movement among Irish Protestants."[116] And in practice, the *Leader* did include contributions from such Protestant Irish-Irelanders as the novelist Lily MacManus and the poet and journalist Alice

Milligan, as well as from a few unionists, such as the Reverend Dudley Fletcher, Anglican rector of Portarlington.[117]

The other major foundation on which discussions of Gaelic exclusivism have been built is the alienation of the Anglo-Irish litterateurs from the Irish-Ireland movement caused by revivalist claims that Irish literature could be written only in Gaelic and by Griffith's overt calls for art to be subordinate to politics.[118] In the seminal statement of Gaelic exclusivism, Moran denounced the Young Ireland literary tradition, and his declaration that "the Gael must be the element that absorbs" seemed a clarion call for Irish-Ireland to turn its back upon Anglo-Irish culture.[119] That Yeats would later defend his theatrical company against revivalist objections to J. M. Synge's works, especially *The Playboy of the Western World*, confirmed the impression of growing intolerance in the debates about the meaning of culture and identity in Ireland.[120]

Without question Moran took aim at some of the most important writers of the day, including Yeats, Synge, and G. W. Russell (Æ), in *The Philosophy of Irish Ireland* and in the *Leader*, but he was hardly the monocular cultural champion that James Joyce and others have painted him to be.[121] Indeed, when he was attempting to popularize the distinction between "Irish" (meaning "Gaelic") and "Anglo-Irish" writing in 1899 and 1900, Moran explicitly endorsed the Gaelic League's bilingual stance that Irish should be used as the primary educational medium in Irish-speaking districts, but that it should remain an elective option in areas with English-speaking majorities. "No one ever suggested," he wrote, "that those who have acquired a cunning mastery over the English language as a medium for expressing what is in them should lay down their pens or hold their tongues until they can use Irish. [Irish literature in English] is a permanent institution and one to be cultivated, for, after all, the extreme aim of the League is to make the Irish a bi-lingual people."[122] Moran was convinced that the Irish language had to be preserved as a spoken language, but he also recognized that the cultural, economic, and social center of Ireland was now in its English-speaking regions, which was why he directed his biting wit at the English-speaking people of Ireland: "Their point of view at present is utterly wrong, and that point of view has got to be turned."[123]

Dissecting such discussions is, however, only a marginally productive way of determining the impact of the language revival on Irish identity because many of the principal participants believed that the language revival and the Anglo-Irish literary movement were parts of the same process *in spite of their occasional clashes*. Fr. Jeremiah O'Donovan, for example, emphasized the numerous connections between the literary and language movements in a submission to the *Irish Ecclesiastical Record* in 1899.[124] And his practical endeavors drew together several apparently disparate revivalist strands. An active Gaelic Leaguer and a noted advocate of agricultural cooperation, he oversaw the renovation of St. Brendan's Cathedral in Loughrea and drew upon the talents of Jack Yeats and the Yeats sisters' Dun Emer industries to decorate its interior. In 1903 he hosted the Irish National Theatre Society when it performed a four-play program—including a one-act play in Irish—at the town hall in Loughrea.[125]

Perhaps no relationship better exemplifies these complex interconnections than the ties between the two most illustrious figures of the revival era—Hyde and Yeats. Having met in Dublin in 1885, they struck up a prickly friendship that would have profound consequences for Irish cultural affairs. Five years the elder, Hyde was gregarious and popular and had already published more than a hundred poems prior to their meeting. Yeats found him to be prone to "diplomatizing" in order to court popularity,[126] but Yeats took advantage of this very quality when he asked Hyde to become president of the National Literary Society in 1892 because he was "a good neutral figurehead." For his part, Hyde occasionally grew exasperated with Yeats's "blather."[127] Still, they moved in many of the same circles and collaborated on collections of fairytales and folklore and encouraged each other in the writing of plays.

When their respective movements gathered momentum in the latter half of the 1890s, Hyde and Yeats diverged somewhat, but their efforts continually reinforced each other's. Even if one noted only those activities that are recorded in Foster's biography of Yeats, their record of mutual aid is impressive: Yeats speaking at Gaelic League functions in 1897, 1899, 1900, 1902, and 1910; Hyde joining in the luncheon that celebrated the launch of the Irish Literary Theatre in 1899; Hyde intervening on Yeats's behalf with Irish-Ireland newspaper editors in 1899 and 1901; Yeats, Hyde, and Lady

Gregory collaborating on the controversial play *Where There Is Nothing* in 1902; Yeats including review comments about Irish-language drama in issues of *Samhain* from 1902 to 1904; and Yeats speaking on behalf of the language revival while touring the United States in 1903 and 1904. When one also notes those activities that Foster omits, the list becomes staggering: Hyde having been one of the original guarantors of the Irish Literary Theatre and serving as vice president of the Irish National Theatre Society; Hyde visiting Coole Park over several successive summers, during which times he, Yeats, and Lady Gregory wrote several important one-act plays, including *Casadh an tSugáin, An Niamh ar Iarraidh, An Teacht na mBocht,* and *An Posadh;* Yeats having donated the proceeds from the sales of *Samhain* in 1902 to endow a prize at the Gaelic League Oireachtas; Yeats having addressed a County Galway Gaelic League function about the place of the Irish language in the theatre in September 1908; and Yeats having encouraged Hyde to make his own trip to the United States.[128]

If one examines their respective American tours, moreover, one can understand why contemporaries in Ireland and the Irish diaspora believed that the language and literary movements were mutually reinforcing. For both, the primary organizer was the Irish-American attorney and cultural patron John Quinn. His deft handling of the many factions in Irish-American circles and his contacts among the emerging elites of Irish America proved invaluable to the success of both trips. Yeats addressed civic and university audiences from New York to San Francisco from the late autumn of 1903 until the spring of 1904. He adapted four standard talks to suit the tastes of his listeners, but throughout, he lauded the work of various friends and causes at home—Lady Gregory and the theatre, Æ and the cooperative movement, Hyde and the language revival. Interestingly, Foster discounts Yeats's most outspoken Irish-Ireland stances at the Catholic University in Washington and at a lecture on Robert Emmet in New York, suggesting that by that point in his travels he was tired and spoke carelessly. But on the eve of the Emmet talk Yeats wrote Lady Gregory a letter that suggests that he spoke deliberately. He would devote three-fourths of that lecture to "general doctrine," he declared, because "it will be hard to speak so long on a more or less political theme, but I shall try and serve the good causes—Hyde in chief."[129] At times, his words about the language revival even led to tangible returns. In one instance, in June 1904, Yeats informed Quinn that a Donegal-born emigrant living in San Francisco had left his modest estate to "Dr. Douglas Hyde and myself, to be expended upon Gaelic propaganda."[130]

In fact, by the winter of 1903, Hyde had been writing to Irish Americans in search of funds.[131] Quinn responded in the summer of 1904 with a donation and the suggestion that Hyde make his own tour of the States to raise money. "Yeats has no doubt told you of his trip here and how badly you are needed to organize the country on behalf of the League," he argued.[132] And indeed, from as early as September 1904, Yeats pressed Hyde to proceed to America.[133] When Hyde finally consented to cross the Atlantic in November 1905, Quinn undertook all the arrangements and set up an ambitious program featuring both university and civic talks. The trip covered more than 50,000 miles and netted in excess of $60,000 for the League. Quinn, modest as to his own part in this achievement, wrote to Yeats and gave him full credit for Hyde's success: "You did more to make him known here than anyone else, and I finished the job that you began. You did it generously and Hyde should never forget it. I imagine he won't. I reminded him and Mrs. Hyde often enough about it."[134]

In providing critically needed money, Hyde's American tour allowed the League to remain solvent for the next five years, years that we will see were critical to the progress of the revival. But the tour also afforded him the chance to spend time with two men who had already performed a signal service for language enthusiasts. These were Fr. Peter Yorke and Laurence Brannick, two of the central figures behind the return of O'Growney's remains to Ireland in 1903. Now two and a half years later, they helped the president of the Gaelic League to collect substantial sums in San Francisco and Los Angeles, respectively.[135] This particular personal connection brings us back to the question posed earlier: what had the late priest done for his people? As the following chapters will argue, in helping to touch off the revival, O'Growney provided them with a grand opportunity to redefine themselves.

2

Priests and People in the Gaelic Revival

In its recent statement of policy the executive of the League deliberately adopted the words, "Those that are not actively with us are against us," and those words have tenfold force in the case of any person, and a hundredfold force in the case of a priest, in the midst of an Irish-speaking population.[1]

Although Protestants of various denominations remained an active minority in the ranks of the Irish-Ireland movement, there is considerable evidence to support the perception that the Catholic church dominated the language movement: members of the Catholic hierarchy spoke frequently and favorably at Gaelic League functions; revivalists paid very close attention to the minutest signs of clerical support for their cause; and many Catholic priests and nuns were prominent in the League, particularly at the branch level.[2] But a close scrutiny of the language revival from 1893 to 1910 suggests that the situation was far more complex. Not only were some of the leading priest-revivalists among the more outspoken advocates of cross-community activity, but lay revivalists did not readily defer to Catholic clergymen on matters they deemed central to language preservation. Indeed, the relationship that developed between priests and people in the Gaelic revival mirrored the general situation described in chapter 1, where clerical engagement with the revival was subjected to critical review, especially when priests acted as social gatekeepers, preventing or denouncing League activities.

CLERICAL ATTITUDES TOWARD IRISH
IN THE NINETEENTH CENTURY

Because priests set the tone for acceptable behavior among Ireland's Catholics and because they controlled what was taught to them, the attitude of the clergy toward the Irish language was a paramount concern to revivalists. Significantly, the vast majority of the nineteenth-century Catholic clergy had taken a utilitarian approach to the language, reinforcing the ethos of the landed and middle-class Catholic strata from which most of them came: if retaining Gaelic would not lead to economic and social advance, then it should be dropped in favor of English.

Perhaps nowhere was this attitude reinforced more effectively than at Maynooth. Just seven years after the foundation of the seminary, the trustees established a chair of Irish. The first two men to hold the chair—Frs. Paul O'Brien and Martin Loftus—were men of ability, but their influence on the college atmosphere was minimal.[3] For two years after Loftus left to take up duty as a parish priest, the chair remained vacant. In 1828, it was finally filled by Fr. James Tully, who did not even meet the trustees' advertised standards, but who was the only candidate to step forward. His tenure lasted nearly five decades! Fr. Walter McDonald took courses from Tully in the 1870s and recalled that college tradition "represented him as having always been uninterested in Irish, and not over-anxious to save it from decay." According to McDonald, Tully's classes consisted almost entirely of the professor calling upon students to read and translate Irish passages aloud; only once in McDonald's hearing did the professor intervene to correct a student or instruct the class.[4] Tully's final few years at Maynooth came shortly after the Irish Church Disestablishment Act took effect, necessitating belt-tightening measures at the college; thus, when he became too feeble to teach, the trustees opted to save money by hiring a senior student rather than a more expensive, experienced person to oversee Irish instruction.[5]

The years after Tully's death in 1876 were, if possible, even bleaker for Irish tuition at Maynooth. At first the trustees assigned the Irish classes without pay to a highly regarded young dean named Michael Logue, who was elevated to the see of Raphoe three years later. After his departure, college officials had postgraduate students on the Dunboyne Establishment teach the Irish lectures, and they allowed students to opt out of the course unless their bishop required them to attend.[6] In practice students were eligible to take Irish only in their fourth year (their second divinity year), and students had the option to attend either a beginners' lecture or an advanced class. One indicator of how poorly regarded the language was by Maynooth men at the time was that only three students—Eugene O'Growney, Laurence (or Lorcan) O'Kieran, and Michael O'Hogan—volunteered for the course in 1886.[7]

Two other factors had strengthened the utilitarian bias against Irish among the priesthood during the nineteenth century, and both were related to missionary activity. On one hand, the heaviest volume of Irish printed material had originated with Protestant evangelizing bodies, such as the Society for Irish Church Missions to the Roman Catholics and the Society for Promoting the Education of the Native Irish through the Medium of Their Own Language.[8] The distribution of Irish-language texts by these and other missionary societies reinforced disdain for the language among Catholic priests, who openly discouraged parishioners from reading printed Irish because it might be dangerous to their faith.[9]

On the other hand, the expansion of the British empire and the waves of emigrants leaving Ireland created vast opportunities for Catholic missionary activity. Many of the surpliced surplus emerging from Irish seminaries after 1850 found themselves sent on the "Irish mission" to parishes in the United States, Britain, and elsewhere in the empire.[10] Kenny points out in her study of the Catholic press that a topic of particular concern in the late 1800s "was the training of Irish priests to be Catholic chaplains on board ships and within the British forces." As she notes, "there was no shortage of pious ladies ready to work tirelessly on committees to supply priests throughout the empire."[11] Needless to say, one prerequisite for evangelizing the empire was to preach in English, thereby relegating Gaelic even further down the list of educational priorities for the clergy.

Of course not all priests shared in the general antipathy toward the language.[12] For example, the Carmelite priest Fr. John Nolan was a founder of the Society for the Preservation of the Irish Language (SPIL) in 1876; the

Cistercian prior of Mount Melleray Abbey, Maurus Ó Faoláin, encouraged students at the Abbey schools to study Irish and maintained an extensive correspondence with numerous language activists with Munster connections; and Fr. Edmund Hogan, S.J., the historian at University College, Dublin, mentored the young clerk Eoin MacNeill in the years immediately preceding the latter's founding of the Gaelic League.[13] Such efforts were primarily scholarly in nature, and their impact on the everyday use of Irish was indirect: Nolan's through the SPIL's successful effort to have "Celtic" introduced as an optional subject in the intermediate schools; Ó Faoláin's through facilitating contacts among his many correspondents; and Hogan's through MacNeill's pioneering work with the League.[14]

But the two most important Catholic clerics who fostered Irish in this period were the long-time archbishop of Tuam, John MacHale, and his secretary and near relation, Canon Ulick J. Bourke. MacHale—who published Gaelic translations of Moore's *Melodies,* the Pentateuch, and the *Iliad*—reputedly refused to ordain any priest who could not speak Irish. Bourke, meanwhile, wrote a series entitled "Self-Instruction in Gaelic" for the nationalist newspaper the *Nation* in the 1850s and early 1860s. In the 1860s, as principal of St. Jarlath's College, the diocesan college in Tuam, he retained the services of John Glynn as a teacher of mathematics and Irish. The canon thought so highly of Glynn's language skills that he secured a second position for him, as editor of the Irish-language column in the weekly *Tuam News,* a newspaper that Bourke's nephew John MacPhilpin managed. Throughout the 1880s and early 1890s, the *Tuam News* was the only weekly newspaper in Ireland to run a regular column of Gaelic news and notes.[15]

It was in the pages of the *Tuam News* that language enthusiasts first read the work of the young O'Growney. Although reared in an English-speaking home, he engaged in intensive language study with the aid of native-speaking classmates after entering Maynooth in 1882. Years later several of his former classmates remembered that fellow students generally viewed him as "a man of no account" because his concentration on Gaelic precluded him from securing any academic prizes while at Maynooth. Those who were aware of his linguistic interests, however, recognized his determination and intellect.[16]

During his seminary years O'Growney also developed a network of contacts who shared his passion for Irish. For example, he joined the Gaelic Union, a small body of activists based in Dublin, which had broken away from the SPIL in 1880. Their guiding light was the retired schoolteacher John Fleming (Seán Pléimeann), a former teacher of Abbot Ó Faoláin's, who was employed by the Trinity professor Robert Atkinson to help edit Old Irish manuscripts.[17] Some idea of O'Growney's progress with the language may be gleaned from a comment made by Fleming in a letter to Ó Faoláin in 1886. Referring to a recent Gaelic Union meeting, he wrote that "we had an excellent student in the chair on Saturday. He is a native of Meath and did not speak a word of Irish a few years ago—he speaks it very well now. During his holidays he goes to the West to speak Irish."[18] O'Growney's regular correspondents eventually included such key figures as Ó Faoláin and Glynn, as well as Hyde and MacNeill.[19] By the time of his ordination in 1889, O'Growney had published numerous items in Glynn's column of the *Tuam News*. And in September 1891 he succeeded Fleming as editor of the Union's journal *Irisleabhar na Gaedhilge* (the *Gaelic Journal*), Ireland's most important periodical dedicated to the Irish language.

The previous November, O'Growney had opened a campaign to change the clergy's attitude toward the language with an article in the journal most widely read by Irish priests, the *Irish Ecclesiastical Record*.[20] Given subsequent events, the appearance of this ten-page piece should be seen as a seminal event in the history of the clerical relationship with Gaelic. O'Growney noted that foreign linguists who visited Ireland were surprised to find that so little Irish was taught in the primary and secondary schools controlled by priests and that politicians and priests seemed unwilling to address Irish-speaking audiences in Gaelic.[21] He lamented the lack of interest in the language among educated Catholics, and specifically priests, because of the damage it did to the country.[22] By refusing to teach through Irish in western and southern districts, for example, "many a mind which might make a stir in Ireland" was left "dark and uneducated." "And," he added in words surely calculated to stir his readers, "not a few people are left without religious instruction through want of one who will teach them in the language they understand."[23]

His most clever appeal to the clergy went to the issue of apostolic descent in Ireland. Catholics, he claimed, were at a fundamental disadvantage in their effort to combat Protestant claims to be the true descendants of the Patrician tradition of Christianity because all of the best scholars of ancient- and medieval-Irish texts at that time were foreigners and Protestants. Men such as the eminent Professor Atkinson, he remarked, "might not see, or might be tempted to slur over, a point in favor of our position."[24] O'Growney was certainly aware that the aged (and devoutly Catholic) Fleming assisted Atkinson in his work. He may not, however, have known that Atkinson was scrupulous not to gloss over points of Catholic doctrine in the manuscripts he published. Whether he knew this or not, however, was irrelevant: his readers would not have known, and O'Growney's intention was to prompt action among the Catholic clergy.[25]

He next contacted MacPhilpin to enlist his support for a public discussion as well. MacPhilpin was an astute choice, and not simply because the priest had been contributing to his paper for several years. MacPhilpin had impeccable credentials in Catholic circles: he was a nephew of both Archbishop MacHale and Canon Bourke, and he had been "the earliest public herald" of the Marian apparitions at Knock.[26] O'Growney sent him a copy of the November *Record,* informing him that he had already received "a lot of letters" in response to it.[27] He then asked MacPhilpin to reprint the piece, and he even included a sample introduction extolling the virtues of this "remarkably rigorous paper." And on 14 November 1890, "The National Language" duly appeared in the *Tuam News* with O'Growney's introductory comments verbatim.[28]

By the time that the priest met MacNeill seven months later, the bishops were considering reestablishing the Irish chair at Maynooth. O'Growney believed Monsignor Robert Browne, the president of the college and future Bishop of Cloyne, had encouraged their thinking.[29] O'Growney confided to MacNeill that he would "have no hesitation in becoming a candidate" if the chair were opened for competition. He had also considered writing a "rousing supplementary article" in the *Record,* but he asked MacNeill to submit one instead, declaring that he "would rather cut off my hand than have people imagine I was doing so to bring myself forward for this Irish chair." In the event, MacNeill's article, "Why and How the Irish Language

Is to Be Preserved," appeared two months after the trustees had offered the reinstituted chair to O'Growney as a junior professorship.[30]

With his new professorship and his editorial post at the *Irisleabhar na Gaedhilge,* O'Growney assumed an enormous and expanding workload. Under his direction, the *Irisleabhar* grew from an occasional publication with fewer than 200 subscribers to a monthly journal with a subscription list of nearly 1,000 names.[31] The new Irish program for Maynooth was also significantly more extensive than had ever existed in the college. All rhetoric and first-year philosophy students now had to attend lectures twice each week, and second-year philosophy students attended weekly lectures. An optional weekly lecture was also available to the three senior theology classes, and O'Growney delivered six public lectures annually about Irish literature and antiquities.[32] Because most of the seminarians had had no prior work in the language, O'Growney additionally had to prepare reading primers and a basic grammar for his introductory courses.[33]

Several factors precluded this industriousness from effecting an immediate change of attitude toward Gaelic within the college. The new professor battled both the clergy's long-standing apathy toward Irish and his own reputation for modest achievement as a Maynooth student.[34] The foremost obstacles in O'Growney's way, however, were his own limitations as a lecturer. Although he certainly cared more deeply about the future of Irish than had the listless Tully, his self-effacing manner did not energize a room full of students sitting through a required course. As one of his former charges recalled, "It is no disparagement of his scholarship to say that his pupils learned but little from him."[35] Those who were interested in Irish often turned for advice to native-speaking senior students, such as Richard Henebry of the diocese of Waterford and Lismore, just as O'Growney himself had turned to class-fellows a few years earlier.[36]

To his credit, the Irish professor recognized and encouraged such extracurricular contacts among his students and focused on laying the groundwork for successful long-term attitudinal change rather than on making a big splash in the classroom. Such an approach was entirely consistent with what his close friend, the fiery Irish-American priest Fr. Peter Yorke, referred to as his "eminently practical" nature:

In non-essentials he was ever ready to yield to expediency. By some this policy was falsely construed as weakness. It was true strength. It is a great mistake to suppose that Father O'Growney was a diffident and timid man. He had a shy appearance, but that was all the shyness was about him.[37]

O'Growney compensated for his lack of lecture-hall charisma through small-group conversations and individual conferences that, according to one former student, "laid bare all the great devotion of his for the old language."[38] He offered his students the same message that he had delivered in the *Record*—that saving the language was a work of patriotic and pastoral urgency. It was the latter point that apparently began to resonate with the faculty and students at Maynooth, where "the study became truly a labor of love and a work of piety, not a mere fleeting fashion of the hour or pedantic trifling."[39]

"FR. O'GROWNEY AND 'IRISH' ARE PRETTY NEARLY SYNONYMOUS"

Outside of the college, O'Growney's initial attempts to alter clerical attitudes also had only a limited impact, as reflected in the early makeup of the Gaelic League. In 1894 only 26 of the League's published membership of 325 (or about 8 percent) were Catholic priests. Further, according to the extant manuscript subscription list, 4 of the 26 never actually subscribed to the League: although "elected" by the Dublin committee, they did not submit the modest dues (2s. 6d.) needed to secure membership. Thus, as there were more than 3,500 clergymen in Ireland in 1894, fewer than three-quarters of 1 percent of them chose to join the League in its first year of operation, a clear indication that the indifference or hostility of the clergy toward Gaelic remained.[40] Through 1897—the last year for which a central list of individual members was kept—only 13 of the original 22 priest members had paid dues to the League for more than a single year.[41]

As sobering as such numbers were, there were promising acquisitions among these few clerical adherents. Three were members of the hierarchy, the bishops of Galway, Raphoe, and Cork; four were members of the Maynooth faculty, including O'Growney himself; and two others were faculty members at Catholic colleges, Fr. Henry Boyle of St. Malachy's College in Belfast, and Fr. Patrick O'Doherty from the seminary at Letterkenny.[42]

Over the next decade, several factors combined to determine the parameters of clerical engagement with the revival: the manner in which League leaders appealed to clerics; the variable nature of episcopal support; and O'Growney's example to Ireland's younger priests. In style and substance leading revivalists avoided confrontations with the Catholic clergy, seeking to connect with priests by appealing to their egos, their intellects, and their practical concerns.[43] Hyde and MacNeill in particular maintained a publicly deferential attitude toward priests that mirrored O'Growney's. MacNeill developed especially cordial relationships with several bishops, and as Miller has observed, their correspondence with him displayed an intimacy and trust far greater than they showed to nationalist politicians such as John Redmond.[44] Hyde's studied caution in public life was, meanwhile, seen as a sign of weakness by some of the more aggressive members of the League and outside observers. But Sean O'Casey—who, like Hyde, was a Protestant revivalist—recognized the latter's resourceful avoidance of controversial stances, "taking ill" to miss a heated meeting or leaving a room for a cigar so as not to stand a toast to the King. True, one of O'Casey's characters, Donal Mac Rory O'Murachadha, also hissed that Hyde "has a bend in his back, looking at episcopal rings."[45] But diplomacy was ultimately an asset for Hyde, and his approach to the clergy included references to the pseudo-historical links between the language and Irish piety. Similarly MacNeill asserted that in learning to speak Irish, "we soon find that it is what we may call essential Irish to acknowledge God, his presence, and his help, even in our most trivial conversation."[46]

Obtaining the goodwill of the hierarchy and clergy had practical benefits as the League expanded. For instance, if the language had suffered from its lack of social cache in the past, revivalists believed that it would be placed in an entirely new position if they received the imprimatur of the hierarchy. The willingness of the bishops to reinstitute the chair of Irish in 1891 and their maintenance of it after O'Growney's departure had been auspicious signs, and throughout the 1890s a growing number of archbishops and bishops openly endorsed aspects of the League's program. In 1893 Archbishop William Walsh of Dublin had encouraged O'Growney to write the newspaper series that became *Simple Lessons in Irish,* and Walsh also pushed the National Board of Education to adopt the revivalist program of bilingual education for schools in the Gaeltacht in 1900.[47] Meanwhile, Bishop Patrick O'Donnell of Raphoe and Bishop Henry Henry of Down and Connor agreed to be patrons for the first League branch in Belfast in 1895.[48] Four years later Bishop Richard Sheehan of Waterford and Lismore instructed the priests in the Irish-speaking districts of his diocese to have the Acts of the Apostles, the rosary, and the sermons "given frequently" in Irish; then, in 1901 he advocated the training of bilingual teachers because "no true education" could "take place in much of the country unless it was through [the medium of] Irish."[49]

Undoubtedly, the most outspoken member of the hierarchy in the Gaelic cause was the archbishop of Armagh himself, Cardinal Michael Logue. In June 1899 he presided at the Oireachtas and told the crowd about his attempts to teach Irish at Maynooth in the 1870s, when "there was a great deal of coldness and a great deal of indifference."[50] Subsequently, he appeared at numerous feiseanna and revival meetings, describing himself as holding "a standing brief for the Gaelic League" at a Limerick event in June 1900.[51] Just prior to the cardinal's Limerick appearance, the hierarchy had spoken collectively, endorsing the League's call for bilingual instruction at its June 1900 meeting at Maynooth. The news of the bishops' resolution was greeted rapturously in the pages of *An Claidheamh Soluis,* which proclaimed that "the toil and effort and propaganda of the last seven years have culminated in a complete and triumphant justification of the aims and claims of the enthusiasts. The movement now stands in a position that defies criticism and fears no opposition."[52]

Such pronouncements spread confidence through revivalist ranks, but there were more mundane reasons for seeking clerical support. In most small towns and villages the only facility large enough to hold classes or social events was the church or school hall, both of which were usually controlled by the parish priest. Therefore, from the time that Concannon became the organization's first paid traveling organizer, he worked to obtain the sanction of the parish priest in any locality before attempting to establish a new branch. When the traveling staff expanded in 1902, the organization subcommittee of the League executive issued a set of instructions that recommended this same practice.[53] Generally, parish priests served as president or patron of provincial branches in exchange for their consent.

O'Growney's example hitherto has not received the recognition it deserves for its impact on clerical views about the language. Even though his illness forced him to leave St. Patrick's College in 1894, he had already made a lasting imprint on Maynooth and its governing body. In 1896, Fr. Michael O'Hickey, of the diocese of Waterford and Lismore, enlisted the aid of his ailing colleague in his campaign to succeed to the Irish chair. O'Hickey wrote to Ó Faoláin that "in their lordships' minds, Fr. O'Growney and 'Irish' are pretty nearly synonymous."[54] He echoed this sentiment five weeks later. Having received a glowing endorsement from the invalid, O'Hickey warned Ó Faoláin that the only danger to his candidacy lay "in the fact that so few of the bishops are competent judges of Irish scholarship." Still, "Fr. O'Growney's letter should decide all waverers," he wrote, because "circumstances give to Fr. O'Growney's testimony in this matter a weight far greater than could attach to anybody else's words."[55] Far more demonstrative, argumentative, and self-promoting than his predecessor, O'Hickey pushed to expand the Gaelic presence within the college. He taught nearly 400 students annually, almost double the number of O'Growney's largest classes, and he attributed the increased student interest to two things—the impact of his required lectures and the fact that one of his students, William Byrne, had secured a £10 prize at the first Oireachtas. "No subject is better studied, and no examinations are better than mine," he trumpeted in February 1898. "They [the students] now understand their duty to the language."[56]

Maynooth students were in fact taking a greater interest in Irish. Corish records that students of the Junior House recited the nightly rosary in Gaelic throughout the latter 1890s, and by February 1898, some 200 students subscribed to the League newspaper *Fáinne an Lae*, even though they were not allowed to receive the paper during school sessions. They petitioned to have this rule changed, and in October 1898 the bishops granted their request. At the same meeting the bishops also sanctioned a new student association—the *Cuallacht Chuilm Cille*, or League of St. Columba— which fostered an appreciation for Irish language, literature, and history in the hope that as future priests, its members "may be more zealous and qualified to labor in promoting, extending, and controlling movements connected with these objects."[57]

The morally upright tone of so much of the League's rhetoric, particularly when reinforced by episcopal endorsement, resonated with Ireland's fin-de-siècle clergy, many of whom feared the impact that English "gutter literature" was having on their flocks.[58] Boyce, Garvin, and MacDonagh have correctly highlighted the way in which the *Leader* spoke to these Catholic clerical fears.[59] Its circulation was the highest of the Irish-Ireland weeklies, and priests made up a significant portion of its readership.[60] In its pages, Moran vented against music-hall entertainments, the popular press, and Protestant "Sourfaces," and prominent League clerics, such as the prolific Fr. Peadar Ua Laoghaire of Castlelyons, Co. Cork, publicly discussed the revival as divinely guided. In 1902 Ua Laoghaire asserted that God had inspired the language movement, and that its ultimate mission was to preserve the morality and spirituality of the Irish [Catholic] people. And in 1908 he deprecated popular English "navvils," concluding that English as a language was "poisonous."[61]

Two points should not be lost in this discussion, however. First, Moran and his contributors could also be highly critical of priests and nuns who did not embrace the Gaelic movement. Second, some of the most visible Catholic spokesmen in the movement expressed a countervailing appreciation for the work that Protestants did and could do for the Gaelic cause—though their comments did not generally appear in the *Leader*. The most important examples in this context were O'Growney and O'Hickey because they served in succession as vice president of the League and because, between them, they oversaw the language instruction of young priests for nearly two decades. Both men certainly emphasized a pastoral duty to promote Irish. We have noted this already in O'Growney's activities, and we can discern a similar motivation behind O'Hickey's undertaking his professorial work. In this context, he made a telling comment to Ó Faoláin about the German Celticist Kuno Meyer while pursuing the Irish chair:

> If the Irish language was to be revived, it should be by the creation of a religious literature. It was so, he [Meyer] said, the Welsh was revived.

> This has been haunting me ever since Father Henebry mentioned it in
> one of our conversations. I think our German friend was right. It is only
> by such a literature we can get at the Irish-speaking classes, if we can get
> at them at all. It is only in this way, too, we can get the Irish-speaking
> clergy back to Irish preaching—if at all.[62]

His desire to cultivate such a literature was again evident at the Maynooth
Union in 1899 when he warmly endorsed the creation of the Catholic Truth
Society, suggesting that "their works should be written from a strong Irish
standpoint," adding that "he hoped the society would see its way in its
program of publications to introduce a number of Gaelic works."[63]

Nevertheless, O'Growney and O'Hickey shared a commitment to the
ideal of cross-community nationalism associated with Wolfe Tone and
Thomas Davis. One of O'Growney's childhood friends, Michael McKenna,
recorded in the *United Irishman* that the priest had lamented the "great
ground lost by not trying more efforts to detach the Irish Protestants from
the side of England."[64] Another close friend, Fr. Lorcan O'Kieran of the
diocese of Clogher, reported that he had introduced O'Growney to "the
'Ninety-Eight literature and everything in book form of the Young Ireland
literature during their student days."[65] By 1889, O'Growney was himself
introducing Young Ireland literature ("real rousers," he called them) to
the two book societies that met in his parish at Ballynacargy,[66] and he
stressed the nonpolitical and nonsectarian appeal of the Gaelic League
up to the end of his life.[67] O'Hickey, meanwhile, came from a family with
a long association with republican and Young Ireland nationalism. His
grandfather had been a United Irishman, and his father and aunt—who
raised him after his mother's death—had known John Mitchel and later
joined the Fenians.[68] A devotee of Thomas Davis's writings, O'Hickey incorporated references to Davis in many of his speeches, and he even made
Davis the subject of one of his required lectures to the student body at
Maynooth. His peroration is particularly instructive:

> To prepare and deliver such a lecture as this has been a dream of mine
> for years. I suppose it is fully ten years ago since it first occurred to me to
> do so. One thing or another has hitherto prevented the realization of my

dream. But after all it is just as well perhaps that its delivery should have been postponed to this time, and reserved for this place. To whom should it be more fittingly delivered than an audience of young Irish ecclesiastics who will soon wield so much influence over an extensive area?[69]

Thus, alongside the exclusivist Catholic rhetoric of certain revivalist priests, there was a more open-minded philosophy expressed by others, a philosophy that did not see an appreciation for Catholic literature in Gaelic as being antithetical to interfaith support for language revival.

"DIFFERENT FROM THOSE OF THAT OLDER GENERATION"

By the late 1890s the changing attitude of some clergymen to the language was becoming evident. For instance, as the hierarchy was considering its aforementioned endorsement of the League's call for bilingualism in the schools, some 183 Catholic school managers from the Irish-speaking districts signed a memorial calling on the National Board to introduce bilingual education in their schools.[70] Moreover, the number of priests joining the League grew dramatically after 1898 and is measurable by the number of priests serving as branch presidents. When branch formation was still in its infancy, only half of the fifty *craobhacha* in Ireland had priest presidents (though the percentage increases to 71 percent if we exclude those branches for which no president was identified).[71] As branches became the normal mode of League operation, the overall percentage increases to 76 percent, if we consider only those branches with known presidents. The manuscript list of branches and officers from 1897 through 1905, summarized in Table 1, confirms this preponderance of clerical presidents in newly formed *craobhacha*.

An indication that traveling organizers directed their appeals successfully to senior clergymen is the fact that more than 68 percent of the 537 priest presidents identified were parish priests, canons, or administrators.[72] And among the clerics who joined the League at this time were several who had and would achieve some eminence in the church, including Bishop Thomas MacRedmond of Killaloe and the future bishop of Limerick, Monsignor Denis Hallinan.[73]

Table 1
Gaelic League Branch Presidents, 1898–1905

Year	No. of Branches	No. of Presidents	No. of Priests	Percentage Overall	Percentage Identified
1900	178	159	124	69.7	74.1
1901	153	143	106	69.3	74.1
1902	151	140	98	64.9	70.0
1903	124	123	98	79.0	79.7
1904	111	108	89	80.2	82.4
1905	40	35	22	55.0	62.9
Totals	757	708	537	70.9	75.8

Source: NLI MS 11,538, Conradh na Gaeilge, *Leabhar-liosta na gCraobh i na n-Oifigeach a Bhíonnta I na Sintiúsí Cinnbliadhna, 1897–1898 go dtí 1905–1906 (i lámh-scríbhneoireacht an Chisdeora i Stiophán Bairéad)*/First List of Branches with Officers and Annual Subscriptions, 1897–1898 to 1905–1906.

A significant number of junior priests also assumed leadership roles in League branches. Some 31 percent of the branch presidents appear in the manuscript list as curates or simply as "reverend," but other evidence shows clearly that curates often served as vice presidents, treasurers, or secretaries under their parish priests.[74] Many of these younger men had personal connections to O'Growney or O'Hickey, either as former classmates or students, and according to Paul-Dubois, the spirit animating them was directly attributable to the "new ideas very different from those of that older generation" at Maynooth.[75]

Further, the reports of the Crime Special Branch of the Royal Irish Constabulary also demonstrate extensive clerical involvement in League branches. The police repeatedly referred to priests "controlling" branches by keeping the "advanced men" from turning the League to political ends.[76] The constabulary highlighted this dichotomy in 1902 in its annual estimate of the "numerical strength of secret societies and other nationalist associations." The Special Branch divided the 258 branches of the League into those "under Fenian control" and those "under clerical control." Significantly, they considered the vast majority—almost two-thirds of the membership—to be under clerical control.[77]

The extent of clerical involvement varied widely, however. In some instances senior priests played a very active role in branch activity. Thus, Fr. Matthew Ryan (1844–1937), parish priest of Knockavilla and Donaskeigh, Co. Tipperary, learned the language in the 1890s after playing a leading part in the land agitation known as the Plan of Campaign. A local history of the language revival even referred to him as "one of the far-seeing patriots who believed that the land and language movements should work together."[78] Ryan hired only Irish-speaking teachers for the six schools he managed, and he oversaw the introduction of Irish instruction by riding his bicycle to each school every week. He served as the national vice president of the Gaelic League from 1909 to 1915—significantly withdrawing when the IRB took over the executive.[79] Often, though, it was curates, such as Fr. Cathaoir Ó Braonáin (1875–1937), who were the more visible clerical participants in League affairs. Ó Braonáin, who studied under O'Hickey, started the first branch in Killarney; he edited a short-lived Irish journal *Loch Léin* from 1903 to 1905; and he published articles and poems in several Irish-Ireland publications, including *An Claidheamh Soluis*, the *Leader*, and the *Irisleabhar na Gaedhilge*.[80]

Such examples of devotion to the movement could be multiplied, but they should be placed beside those of priests who did little to enhance, or who actually retarded, the work of the revival. Clerical inactivity was often rooted in inattention and lingering indifference toward the language. For instance, the secretary of the League in Cahirciveen, Co. Kerry, noted that the president and one of the vice presidents of the branch (i.e., the parish priest and his curate) had not attended a single one of the committee's ten meetings between February and June 1903. The secretary, Thomas MacDonagh O'Mahony, J.P., acknowledged that the president had allowed the branch to make a churchyard collection on behalf of the language fund, an effort aided by "the zeal of the nuns in the matter." Nonetheless, O'Mahony called on the officers "to take an *active interest* in the working of the branch. I also earnestly appeal to the clergy to come to the classes as often as possible. To a great extent the life of the branch depends on this."[81]

Elsewhere clerical inaction was rooted in lingering uncertainty about the intentions of the language campaign. Thus, the *timire* Peadar

Ó hAnnracháin reported to Fionán MacColuim from South Galway that the priests and teachers he met seemed "agreeable," but that "the people have never been interested yet. There is fine Irish [spoken] on all sides but poor spirit." More than eighty priests ministered in this region, which included parishes from the diocese of Clonfert and the united dioceses of Galway and Kilmacduagh, but Ó hAnnracháin named only four priests who had offered him real assistance.[82] Moreover, he found that priests in the region generally misunderstood the League a decade after its foundation and his comment is telling: "They have very hazy ideas of my mission, and in one case they refused to take some pamphlets lest they were dangerous and edited by a proselytizing co[mpany]."[83]

An even more explicit instance of clerical foot dragging caused by fears of Protestant proselytism occurred in 1903 in the Glens of Antrim, where memories remained fresh about a very public dispute involving Presbyterian-backed Irish-language schools in the 1840s.[84] The League was making a concerted effort to organize the Glens in the spring of 1903 when Concannon shifted the focus of his work to Ulster. *An Claidheamh Soluis* described the parish priests in the Glens, including Frs. Edmund Hassett at Glenarm, Murtagh Hamill of Carnlough, and T. Convery of Cushendall, as "convinced of the necessity of the movement" and "flinging themselves into the fray."[85] In July the League published the extensive work program undertaken by the traveling teacher hired for the district, calling it "heartsome and business-like."[86] But by November, Mrs. Annie McGavock of Glenarm reported privately to her brother Eoin MacNeill that Fr. Hassett was "apathetic," and "he is not so bad as the other two gentlemen, Frs Hamill and Convery, who are not passive but active resistors." According to McGavock, their inaction made it difficult for the district committee to collect the funds needed to pay the teacher. The passive Fr. Hassett refused to make collections on behalf of the League, resisting even a personal request from Bishop Henry Henry made in McGavock's drawing room. But she exhibited a special contempt for the actions of the other two priests, who had refused monetary support from interested Protestants in spite of the financial distress of the local League. "It is nothing short of a scandal the way those two Rev. gentlemen, Frs. Hamill and Convery, treated the movement," McGavock wrote.[87]

These actions did not deter McGavock or her Protestant fellow-workers, and Ada McNeill of Cushendun even recruited other Protestants to the movement. Although her efforts allowed the League in the Glens to continue its classes, they did nothing to calm the local priests. Two months later, McGavock observed that the priests feared "the old shadow of Souperism." "I think," she concluded, it "is neither creditable nor courageous to bring this old bogey back to life."[88] In March 1904, she reported further that Henry—at the request of the Belfast Gaelic Leaguer (and Protestant) Francis J. Bigger—had again intervened to calm the situation, declaring his action "providential." The League in Glenarm, she acknowledged, was "narrowing down into such a fine point that we should soon have been imperceptible. This, I hope, will broaden the movement in these parts."[89]

The Glens incident is instructive on four counts. The most obvious point is that the local League persevered in its work in spite of the foot dragging of several priests. Second, Henry's unsuccessful attempt to cajole Hassett into making a collection exemplifies what Miller has termed "the practical constraints on episcopal dictation."[90] Although Henry could have ordered Hassett to make a collection, he did not, partly because the collection was for a strictly non-church-related cause in Hassett's parish. The bishop would have been within his rights to force the issue, but such a transgression against a priest's prerogatives within his own parish could have led to the kind of morale problems that most bishops sought to avoid.

Third, Henry was not likely to force the issue because his own support for the revival was based on a combination of personal and political considerations, rather than on a thoroughgoing adherence to Irish-Ireland ideals. It is significant that his original request to Hassett was made in McGavock's home, as the bishop was a friend of the MacNeill family, having taught Eoin MacNeill at St. Malachy's College in the 1880s. The bishop's continuing contact with his former pupil had played a role in his early adherence to the language movement.

Further, Henry sought to be a political power broker of sorts, founding the Belfast Catholic Association (BCA) in 1896 and aligning himself with Timothy Healy's clericalist parliamentary faction. After the parliamentary nationalists had reunited behind the UIL in 1900, Henry utilized his association as an alternative power base to the UIL in Belfast.[91] Pearse, who dined with the bishop in Belfast in 1904, told a local League officer that he thought that Henry was sincere but did "not understand it [i.e., the League] very well." Rather, his support for the movement sprang "in a sort of subconscious way . . . from his dislike of the UIL. He wants to show that he is as good an Irishman as any in the UIL."[92] Intriguingly, Pearse viewed the bishop's motivations as presenting the Gaelic movement with an opportunity. While he cautioned his Belfast contact against allowing the League to become a "mere appendage" of the BCA, he also thought it worthwhile to "use the latter [i.e., Henry] for all he is worth, especially as regards the schools, etc."[93]

Fourth, McGavock's insights into the situation in the Glens are evident only in private correspondence, but they mirrored much more public complaints made by Gaelic enthusiasts about clerical apathy. An ongoing source of discontent for Irish-Irelanders was the failure of priests and bishops to offer *practical* support to the movement after paying lip service to it. For example, in December 1901, Moran upbraided two curates who served as the president and vice president of a new League branch in Cahir, Co. Tipperary. When accepting their positions, he claimed, the priests had pledged that "they would do their utmost to forward the much-desired movement." Then they reportedly organized a concert that featured "a number of comic songs and mandolin and banjo solos" but included no Irish songs on the program. "When we think of the Cahir concert in connection with the president and vice president of the local branch of the Gaelic League," Moran declared caustically, "we think of the verb 'to say' and the verb 'to do.'"[94]

In no area was clerical activity so routinely scrutinized as in education because, as was seen in chapter 1, the clergy and religious had de facto control over the primary and secondary schools of most of Ireland's Catholics. Thus, at the end of September 1900, when the League received word that the National Board would allow school managers to introduce Irish as an ordinary subject, *An Claidheamh Soluis* characterized it as an opportunity because "the whole initiative of the country in primary education has become atrophied and ossified." It was the duty of the League, the editors insisted, to ensure that school managers understood their new prerogatives, and the analogy they used was startling in its implications: "The bird that has lived half its life in a cage loses the power of flight, and even the instinct to use its freedom. It cannot get itself away from the scene of its captivity. To restore it to its natural life, you must actually train it in the ways of its kind."[95] In short, the Gaelic League was to teach Ireland's priests and nuns their patriotic duty.

For the preceding month, *An Claidheamh Soluis* had anticipated this call in its leading articles. On 1 September 1900, for example, the paper had declared that "the different managers who have signed the bilingual memorial should be approached and requested to back up their signatures by some practical action."[96] In the following week the leading article scrutinized the Christian Brothers, known for having introduced Irish instruction into many of their secondary schools:

> The Christian Brothers deserve every praise for their unfailing support of the national language in the Intermediate, but they would deserve the everlasting gratitude of their race if they would only introduce Irish into their primary schools. As things are, only about one-sixth or one-seventh of the pupils of these schools enter for the Intermediate Examinations. The result is that the other five-sixths or six-sevenths never get a chance of knowing anything of Irish. These should be taught Irish from third book up to the time of leaving school. The Christian Brothers are perfectly free to do this. Why do they not do so? True, they are laboring under great difficulties and are doing work of the utmost public utility, and yet get no remuneration from public funds. But it is to be feared that even they are forced by circumstances to follow the phantom of "a sound English education" and to think it, and it only, can serve their pupils.[97]

Similarly, the female orders, which ran the secondary schools for Catholic girls, received criticism for worrying too much about "respectability" and offering only an English-style education.[98]

Not surprisingly the pace of educational change also became a significant cause for concern among language activists. Although revivalists had welcomed the bishops' endorsement of the bilingual program in June 1900, a correspondent in the *Leader* expressed frustration that their follow-up pastoral made no further reference to the language revival just four months later.[99] Similarly, in October 1902, *An Claidheamh Soluis* specifically highlighted the slow pace with which the bishops were moving to introduce Irish into the diocesan seminaries: "The bishops of Ireland have long since demanded bilingual teaching in Irish-speaking districts and liberty to teach Irish elsewhere; what are the diocesan Schools, UNDER THEIR LORDSHIPS' SOLE CONTROL, going to do for the cause the bishops have so much at heart?"[100]

Such commentary was common in the Irish-Ireland press, as Gaelic activists staked a claim to protect the language—and by extension Irish nationality—from any perceived neglect. With their eyes focused primarily on the Irish-speaking districts, but their gaze scanning the island as a whole, revivalists declared themselves free to criticize anyone who shaped the island's social mores and controlled its key institutions.

THE ARAN CONTROVERSY

Two extended confrontations highlight these tensions. The first occurred in two distinct phases in 1901 and 1902, and it centered on one of the Gaeltacht heartlands, the Aran Islands. Linguists and revivalists had been visiting Aran for decades, and it was in the cottages of Inismeadhon that O'Growney and MacNeill had honed their speaking knowledge of the language. MacNeill also developed a lasting friendship with a native-speaking priest, Fr. Murtagh Farragher, who served as curate in Aran from 1887 to 1891 and returned as parish priest to the islands in 1897. Farragher was a substantial figure in a host of local affairs: in 1898 he helped the League establish its first branch in Aran, and he introduced its bilingual program into the schools he managed; he became active in the UIL's campaign to encourage the Land Commission to purchase and break up the Digby estate (covering most of the islands); and he founded a fisheries cooperative that, with the help of the Congested Districts Board, brought much-needed income to the fisherfolk of the islands.[101] Like many of his brother priests, Farragher was also a man unaccustomed to being challenged in the affairs of his parish. Thus, when "the Aran controversy" erupted in 1901, he took it as a personal attack on his authority.

The central figure in the early stages of the controversy was Farragher's curate, Fr. Charles White, who had arrived in Aran in 1900 after serving a brief curacy in another Gaelic-speaking heartland, the island of Achill. White's offense, in the eyes of some Gaelic activists, was that he knew no Irish and insisted on preaching and administering the sacraments in English. *An Claidheamh Soluis,* which announced that the League executive would be taking a harder line toward prominent individuals who neglected the language, cited his case as an instance of how "the Catholic religion [was] used as a powerful Anglicizing agency." "In Inismeadhon, one of our most Irish-speaking districts," the story went, "an Irish speaker addressed the priest (Fr. White), who had been in the parish some twelve-months, in Irish: 'if you want me, my man,' answered the reverend father, 'you must speak to me in English.'"[102] Interestingly, the League paper primarily blamed White's training for his attitude, though it did hold him accountable for failing to pick up the language over the course of his year among the islanders.[103]

White learned of Irish-Ireland's reaction by reading the original notice in the *Leader,*[104] and he became incensed that anyone would question his actions. By the late autumn, rumors floated through the islands that one of the many League visitors in the preceding summer had suggested to parishioners that they should leave the chapel if White again preached in English. From the pulpit White responded that, had he been aware of this at the time, he "would have banded the men of the island together and we would have got him into a boat and packed him off from the island."[105] *An Claidheamh Soluis* reported in November that he told his flock that "people are complaining that I don't preach in Irish. Everyone understands every word I say in English, and I hope I will never preach but in English."[106] An unknown League enthusiast, a native of Aran and the source of this story, claimed that not one in seven of those present understood this defiant declaration. Moreover, the League paper argued, "if the congregation were able to gather some meaning from the English sermon, Father White's position would still be at fault, for he would be forcing his English sermons on an Irish-speaking congregation."[107] Because his actions were bound to Anglicize this Gaelic heartland, the paper claimed, White had earned the stinging title of "a Trinity College priest."[108]

During October and November, numerous letters and comments appeared in the press about the Aran controversy. Farragher defended his beleaguered curate, demanding that his name be removed from the list of subscribers to the National Language Fund and denouncing the executive's hard-line stance against "passive" support.[109] "A north Connacht parish priest" responded by sending in a guinea to the language fund and asking a series of pointed rhetorical questions:

> Was not the League quite within its rights in criticizing Fr. White in an adverse spirit? By what right has Fr. White to insist that the people learn English—the language of the hated foreigner—for his sake? Was it not Fr. White's duty to sit down and learn the language of the people so that he might be able to instruct them? Are the people of Arann and Inishmaan, &c. [sic], to learn a foreign language before they can be taught the Christian doctrine? Is that not the logical conclusion we must come to?[110]

In the pages of the *United Irishman,* Arthur Griffith declared that the Catholic church was out of line to assign any priest to an Irish-speaking district who was as ill-equipped as White apparently was.[111]

Like Farragher, members of the Monastery branch of the Gaelic League at Achill, Co. Mayo, defended their former curate. In its "Trinity College priest" column of 16 November, *An Claidheamh Soluis* had stated that White had been indifferent to the language while serving in Achill. But according to a branch report from early December, several speakers declared that he had been "one of the most ardent supporters of this branch of the Gaelic League" and had aided their efforts financially and from the public platform.[112] In the following week, a letter appeared from White himself that acknowledged the support from these former parishioners in the face of an "indecent and untruthful article," and in which he advocated their continued study of the Irish language and Irish history, as well as their support of Irish manufactures as championed by the *Leader.* White concluded his expression of thanks by adding, "you will be glad to know that I am, considering the time at my disposal, progressing with the study of our mother tongue."[113] Although he printed White's statement, the editor of *An Claidheamh Soluis,* Eoghan Ó Neachtáin, accepted it rather disingenuously: "We expect to see the proof of that sincerity manifested not on paper alone but in word and deed."[114]

Magnanimity of this sort led White to respond with an extreme clericalist defense of his actions.[115] He claimed, inaccurately, that the League had offered to "pardon" him if he "apologized and said I could not learn Irish." "Pray," he continued,

> to whom would I apologize—to the executive committee of the Gaelic League, to a body of men who would feign arrogate to themselves the right of dictating to a priest what he is to say and do for his people. Now, sir, be my plain answer this—I will never be dictated to by your League or any other League in my relations with the people. I am the mediator between them and God. Furthermore, I am thoroughly conscious of my position, and remember that I shall have to answer for myself before the great tribunal of God, but I never will give an account of myself to the Gaelic League committee.[116]

White concluded that he felt sharp words had been necessary because visitors to the islands had advised his parishioners to leave mass if he preached in English, and, for the first time, he charged that one of these visitors had gone even further: "Another could see no cause for the wrongs of Ireland except the existence of the bishops, priests, and nuns of Ireland. Doctrines such as these, however diabolical and untrue they are known to be, might possibly do untold harm if spread broadcast amongst an innocent-minded peasantry."[117] The condescension toward his parishioners expressed in White's last comment is telling, especially coming from a man unable to converse with many of the adult members of his congregation about even the simplest daily matters. What is critical to our analysis, however, is that the Gaelic League had challenged him about that very inability, and White replied by wrapping himself in the cloak of his office.

Nothing more was heard of the Aran controversy for several months. Then, during the Ard-Fheis in May 1902, some delegates apparently questioned the veracity of the initial claims made about White, indicating that not all branches of the League had been comfortable with the aggressive stance taken by their executive and its organ. When the author of the original piece offered to produce witnesses to substantiate the story, the matter was dropped.[118] Moreover, according to the League paper and two visitors to the islands, White ultimately admitted "the truth of the charges made by the *Claidheamh Soluis*," offering the explanation "that in slighting the Irish language, he only wished to annoy Gaelic Leaguers who were present."[119]

Farragher, however, did not allow the matter to drop. Trouble boiled over in mid-August, when Agnes O'Farrelly and Edith Drury—two Dublin visitors to the islands—organized an open-air concert. The women had secured the priest's sanction for the event, though he later denied that he had assented to their request. One of the conditions that he had placed on them was that "there must not be too many strangers" present, but the arrival of a particular "stranger" on the day before the concert—the vacationing O'Hickey—apparently convinced Farragher that the entire event had been concocted to embarrass him. Concert organizers insisted that O'Hickey only learned of the event while en route to Aran, and he merely attended the concert. When O'Hickey arrived in the islands, he applied to Farragher for permission to say mass, but the parish priest uncharacteristically refused him—an insult that surprised O'Hickey and outraged the League's lay leadership in Dublin.[120] Then, when the regional Connacht feis took place in Galway city at the end of the month, Farragher ordered the teachers who worked in his schools not to attend the festivities, even though the teachers were on vacation.

In retrospect, one can discern that a large number of people—including Aran residents and visitors, Galway language activists, and members of the League executive—knew of these events, but the Aran controversy did not take on its final public form until after two speeches brought national attention to Farragher's actions. The first occurred on 12 September, when the resident commissioner of education, Dr. William Starkie, addressed the British Association in Belfast. Starkie, a Trinity-educated Catholic, gave his audience a brief history of the national-education system, recognizing that its early leaders had tried to "wean it [Ireland] from its language and its religion," and he expressed mild sympathy with some of the revivalist program. In the course of his remarks, however, Starkie touched on the lack of local funds spent on education and on the indifference with which many clerical school managers undertook their responsibilities.[121] Seeing the two points—calls for local (i.e., lay) activity in education and criticism of priest managers—as a frightening recipe for reform, deanery conferences throughout Ireland made spirited defenses of the clerical management system.[122] But Starkie's comments also resonated with those language enthusiasts who were becoming impatient with those bishops and priests who had failed to introduce Irish into their schools.[123] In the course of one such letter, which focused on the "hypocrisy" of Catholic secondary-school managers who passed resolutions that they then flouted, the pseudonymous correspondent "Ua" made a passing reference to "the Aran priest" who had circumscribed his teachers' movements during their off hours.[124] The second address came at the end of September, when Fr. Jeremiah O'Donovan, administrator at Loughrea, Co. Galway, spoke in Dublin to honor O'Growney's memory. He aimed stinging comments at those of his fellow priests who failed to see the language movement as a cause worth supporting. In particular, he focused attention on priests like Farragher who had come out so openly against the League in Aran the preceding summer.[125]

Farragher dispatched a telegram to the *Freeman's Journal* in early October accusing the League of distorting his public actions.[126] MacNeill responded on behalf of the executive, moderately restating the organization's position with regard to White and denying that any untruths had been spoken or written. He acknowledged that Farragher's treatment of O'Hickey had "a double aspect," the ecclesiastical side of which O'Hickey could pursue independently through an appeal to episcopal authorities. But MacNeill (and *An Claidheamh Soluis* in its 1 November edition) drew the logical conclusion that Farragher's snub had resulted only from O'Hickey's association with the League. To be fair, much of the League's information emanated from O'Hickey and other visitors, whose gossip and speculation during the summer shaped League opinion about Farragher's motives. Farragher in turn directed his ripostes against the use of gossip as authentic source material and expressed his continuing anger that the League organ had referred to his curate as a "Trinity College priest," though he readily admitted having banned his teachers from the Connacht festival. "I make no apologies for my actions," he declared.[127]

This embittered (and occasionally petty) debate continued in the columns of the League newspaper throughout October and November, even as the executive and the Aran priest inched toward compromise behind the scenes. Bishop Thomas MacCormack of Galway declined to act as an arbiter in the case, but the hard feelings gradually seem to have dissipated, perhaps because of the friendship between Farragher and MacNeill. In any case, the Aran controversy disappeared from the pages of the newspapers in mid-November and from the minutes of the League executive in January 1903.[128]

Three important points emerged from the Aran controversy. First, were it not for numerous long-term changes in Irish society (such as improved transportation, increased literacy and communication, and the consequent incursions of the "national" into the "local" setting), the dispute might never have developed. Recall that it was visitors to the island who publicized White's use of English; it was visitors who introduced the heterodox notion that parishioners leave the church if he continued to preach in English; it was Farragher's mistrust of "strangers" that led him to react so negatively when O'Hickey arrived in 1902; and it was visitors' stories and rumors that fueled the emerging debates in the Dublin-based press. Visitors had, of course, been coming to Aran for decades, but their numbers had grown as formerly remote vacation spots became more accessible to middle- and lower-middle-class revivalists.[129] All of this is not to say that the islanders had not themselves chaffed at White's use of English: some clearly found it uncomfortable, and they shared their feelings with the outsiders who could criticize their priest more freely than they could themselves.

A second, related point is that the Gaelic League asserted its right to criticize anyone, even a priest. As Ó Neachtáin wrote in the latter stages of the controversy, "It is absurd to say that it is unfair criticism to characterize an Irish priest as West British or as 'a Trinity College priest' if his actions are such as to justify the title. Why should an Irish priest, in so far as his actions affect Irish nationality, be exempt from criticism?"[130] Third, certain members of the executive committee remained uneasy about the manner in which the League had made its point as late as December 1902. In particular, Dinneen, the lexicographer and one of the leading proponents of clerical dictation within the League, introduced a motion at the December executive committee meeting authorizing the executive to pursue arbitration. Critically, his motion included the proviso that "whilst giving this permission, they [the executive] regret that any words used in the controversy have given pain to the reverend gentleman." MacNeill's brother Charles responded with an amendment, omitting any note of contrition and stating simply that "all matters in controversy between Fr. Farragher and the Coiste Gnótha be referred to the arbitration of his lordship the Bishop of Galway." Charles MacNeill's amendment won the day. Later in the meeting, Dinneen and George Moonan, an attorney and a stalwart member of the Central branch in Dublin, attempted unsuccessfully to pass an additional motion specifically referring to potential arbitration between *An Claidheamh Soluis* and Farragher.[131]

THE BATTLE OF PORTARLINGTON

If the League had asserted its right to criticize priests in the Aran controversy, its resolve was tested three years later in the second and heretofore better-known conflict between Gaelic Leaguers and a priest, the so-called Battle of Portarlington.[132] The basic facts of the case have been aired before.[133] In early August 1905, P. T. MacGinley, a Donegal-born inland-revenue officer, had gathered together a number of local men and women to found Portarlington's first *craobh*, the Rory O'More branch. Following the usual pattern of League expansion, MacGinley and his committee received the approval of the parish priest, Fr. E. O'Leary, who agreed to serve as the branch president. Within weeks, O'Leary—who had already introduced Irish-language instruction into the day schools he managed—objected to the holding of coeducational classes in the evenings, believing that such a practice created a morally dangerous situation. When branch members refused to split the class, O'Leary damned the Gaelic League from the pulpit, at one point saying that young women would not even consider going to the mixed classes if the streets of the town were lit.[134] Branch leaders expelled the priest, who established classes for young women at the local convent on Sunday afternoons. Then, on 10 September, Fr. M. Brophy, the parish curate, denounced the lay officers at two masses. MacGinley's wife and children happened to attend the early mass and reported to him what had been said, so when he attended the second service, he interrupted what he later called the priest's "harangue." Brophy called in the police and had MacGinley and Stephen B. Roche, another revenue officer and Gaelic enthusiast, escorted forcibly from the church.

Seeking to establish that the priests had overstepped themselves by introducing secular grievances and violent language into their homilies, the laymen appealed to Bishop Patrick Foley of Kildare and Leighlin. He merely dismissed the priest's language as a "casual observation," though he told the League executive that "so far as lies in his power, the interests of the language will not suffer as the result of the recent painful incidents" and that none of the principal actors would be penalized.[135]

On the ground in Portarlington, however, the bishop's assurance rang hollow. The *United Irishman* claimed at the end of September that O'Leary now denied the branch access to the school, and he threatened to expel anyone remaining in the O'More branch from religious sodalities and the Catholic Young Men's Society.[136] He likewise encouraged the local UIL branch to pass a resolution denouncing the O'Mores, *and* the UIL dismissed its local secretary, a rural district councilor who was subsequently elected president of the O'Mores. Local teachers received warnings not to attend the language class taught by the League, and private businesses pressured employees to sign an apology to O'Leary authored by the priest himself. When the secretary of the O'Mores, Francis MacManus, refused to sign the apology in November 1905, he lost his job as a shop clerk; after several months of unemployment he emigrated to New York with the aid of a "MacManus testimonial" fund organized by Pearse through *An Claidheamh Soluis*. Perhaps most significantly, the *United Irishman* alleged—without contradiction—that Foley himself had made an unsuccessful attempt "to procure a pronouncement against the Gaelic League" at the October 1905 meeting of the Irish bishops.[137]

Throughout the autumn, the Irish-Ireland press contained stories indicating that priests in the diocese of Kildare and Leighlin were indifferent, if not openly hostile, to the language movement. In the middle of October, the *United Irishman* reported that though "a few sturdy priests still stand resolutely by the Gaelic League, others who privately sympathize with it are afraid to take part in the Irish-Ireland movement."[138] In November MacGinley asserted that O'Leary's antipathy was typical of the parish priests in the area. He claimed that he and a companion had visited four priests the previous summer, and that only O'Leary had been sympathetic.[139] MacGinley published this information both to show that clerical standoffishness had predated the scenes in Portarlington church and to inspire "other small branches consisting of stalwarts who will not fear to hold their ground under any system of terrorism adopted."[140]

It should be noted that MacGinley's partner in those summer meetings, Pádraig Lynch of Monasterevan, denied that the priests had expressed any outright opposition to the League the preceding summer.[141] But his understated defense should also be placed in context. It was spurred by an unnamed local cleric who angrily called his attention to MacGinley's article, and it came at a time when other Gaelic enthusiasts in Monasterevan felt themselves subject to intimidation. In quick succession the curate who had worked with them had received a transfer out of the parish, and the parish priest denied them the use of the school for future classes.[142] Lynch, meanwhile, showed himself over the ensuing year to sympathize with O'Leary.

As in the Aran controversy, a central point was the involvement of outsiders. Initially, this meant MacGinley and Roche, whom Brophy singled out because they were "not Portarlington people."[143] In turn, they attracted allies, including prominent revivalists like Pearse, who came as lecturers to the O'More branch.[144] In the spring of 1906, when O'Leary attempted to set up a rival branch in the neighboring townland of Bishopswood, the League executive refused to affiliate it. At almost the same time the executive's publications subcommittee published a lengthy pamphlet authored by the O'Mores, describing the confrontation with the priests and their failed case before the bishop. Then in June, when Hyde returned from his American fund-raising tour, his train paused in Portarlington, and the president of the League "complimented the [O'More] branch on its notable efforts that won the approval of the Gaelic Leaguers far and wide."[145]

These actions convinced O'Leary that the League was rotten at its core, and he launched a two-pronged campaign against the organization that summer. In July, his Bishopswood branch held a feis. Entertaining the occasion may have been, but it lacked the language and musical competitions that were the hallmarks of League festivals. Instead, the main event of the day was O'Leary's welcoming address. According to the *Freeman's Journal,* eighteen priests and the Monasterevan Gaelic Leaguer Pádraig Lynch joined O'Leary on the platform. The priest told his audience that he was "glad to see that the words on your banner have the right ring, 'Rome and Ireland, Faith and Fatherland,' and our fatherland includes our mother tongue. But our faith comes first. For this our fathers bled and died. This is the one great glory of Ireland—our holy religion. It comes first, before fatherland, before the Irish language, before the Gaelic League."[146] In a singularly explosive passage, O'Leary unleashed an attack on Hyde and his organization:

> Douglas Hyde is a Protestant, but he bears the reputation of being a decent, honorable man. He has done great work for the Irish language and has just returned from America with a large sum of money to further this good work. But all the same, Dr. Hyde, the Protestant, compliments the Catholic Rorys on the scandalous outrage they committed in our church during holy mass. Dr. Hyde, the Protestant, highly compliments the Catholic Rorys in refusing to apologize for their outrageous conduct in the church. Dr. Hyde complimented the Catholic Rorys for publishing their scurrilous libels on their clergy, which no Catholic and only one Protestant in the town would sell for them. There is Douglas Hyde for you! But how could he reprove them when it was the Gaelic League that printed the libels for the Rorys? And there is the Gaelic League for you. We are here to tesify [*sic*] solemnly to-day that we won't allow our religion to be insulted by any mongrel League in Dublin, or any Douglas Hyde. We are here to testify that we will work successfully and well for the dear old Irish tongue, but we'll take no domination from outside.[147]

Thus, for O'Leary, the events of the preceding year had revealed the hidden dangers represented by the League: "domination from [the] outside" by a "mongrel League" headed by a Protestant who encouraged "outrage" and "libel" among Catholics.

A few weeks earlier, the Portarlington priest had launched a second and potentially more far-reaching campaign. In mid-June he had sent a circular letter to select priests throughout the country, offering his account of the quarrel with the O'Mores and describing his growing unease with the Coiste Gnótha:

> The bishops and priests of the country have made the Gaelic League the great power it is now universally acknowledged to be in the land. The present executive has shown by its toleration of, and sympathy with, the Rory O'More branch, and its refusal to affiliate the other branch formed in this parish, that it has decided anti-clerical proclivities. I am aware that it counts priests among its members, but they are in a small minority and appear to have little influence on the actions or decisions of the executive. The remedy for this is to have the objectionable elements removed from the executive or rendered harmless; and a number of good Catholic laymen, with a fair representation of the priests, placed on the executive committee. The priests have it quite in their power to effect this.[148]

He then outlined the procedures by which the priests could ensure that "proper and reliable delegates" attend the League's upcoming national congress. "I am sure," he concluded, "you sympathize with my desire to see the government of the Gaelic League—an organization to which so many of our people look with such abounding hope—in the hands of those whose respect for faith and morality cannot be called into question."[149]

A number of priests, apparently unsympathetic to O'Leary, forwarded the letter to the *United Irishman* and the *Irish Peasant,* which published it in early July.[150] Both papers pointed out that the existing executive committee included twelve priests among its forty-five members, and that they were among the most important members of the executive. In hindsight, the editor of the *Irish Peasant,* W. P. Ryan, turned O'Leary's argument on itself. "Why," he mused, "if the ecclesiastics had done everything [for the movement], they had not secured more than a small and uninfluential minority on the executive, his reverence did not explain."[151] He also pointed out that priests already had "more than a fair share of representation amongst the delegates who annually elected the executive" because in many country branches "only the cleric or clerics could find it convenient to spend some days in Dublin." His conclusion was that the congress had chosen its executive "for Irish, not anti-clerical or clerical reasons."[152]

The issue came to a head at the congress in August. According to Ryan, priests did not seem "disproportionately stronger than at earlier Ard-Fheiseanna that I had seen; women delegates were, I thought, more numerous."[153] Some delegates, including the ubiquitous Pádraig Lynch of Monasterevan, had nominated O'Leary for the executive committee and had entered resolutions about the Bishopswood branch and the Portarlington controversy on the agenda. Early in the meeting delegates gave a signal as to the eventual result of these resolutions when MacGinley, who had been a member of the executive for years, rose to speak about an unrelated subject:

> From all parts of the hall he received a spontaneous ovation, extraordinary in its warmth and its fervor, sturdy young priests chiming in with the best, and the ladies excelling themselves. After a few minutes the Ard-Fheis settled down again to business in happy humor with itself. The branches near and far had plainly sent a big majority of men and women whose views were clear and decided.[154]

When the chairman announced the election results for the new executive two days later, MacGinley had received the largest vote total of any candidate, and O'Leary was not among the top forty-five. The congress defeated the resolution about the Bishopswood branch, and the sponsors withdrew the other about Portarlington before a vote took place. Last, the Ard-Fheis drew up stringent requirements about registering feiseanna with the executive and reaffirmed the nonsectarian constitution of the League.[155]

"The battle of Portarlington" highlighted the ambiguities in the developing relationship between Irish-Irelanders and the clergy. To begin with, the issue did not divide its disputants neatly into priests versus laity. The Monasterevan figure Pádraig Lynch can be seen as representative of those laymen who believed that MacGinley and the League executive had acted inappropriately toward O'Leary, while the presence of priests cheering for MacGinley at the Ard-Fheis indicates that not all clergymen objected to his stance. At the same time the congress so upset Monsignor John O'Hara of the diocese of Killala—described by Ryan as "a leading

Connacht individuality who had done worthy work for Irish culture and Irish industry"—that he resigned immediately after being elected to the executive.[156] Second, as in the Aran controversy, the focus was on the place of the Irish language and the Irish laity in society. In both cases, the central priest figure had a history of supporting language tuition but on terms that he controlled. What the League asserted in the former instance was the broad concern of its right to criticize anyone. In the latter case, it raised more specific questions about the priest's presumed right to oversee activities, such as education, in which laypersons increasingly claimed a stake.

Finally, O'Leary's charge of anticlericalism against the League merits exploration. Portarlington was not the first occasion when a priest (or a Catholic layperson) branded the League anticlerical, and it would not be the last.[157] Some of these incidents emerged out of simple misunderstandings, as English speakers found it difficult to differentiate between Conradh na Gaeilge and other organizations with Irish names, such as the progenitor to the Sinn Féin party, Cumann na nGaedheal.[158] Still, the ongoing criticisms in the Irish-Ireland press of lip-service patrons and sluggish school managers were occasionally expressed with what Moran called "an anti-cleric note."[159] And during the battle of Portarlington, O'Leary's control of the schools gave a fillip to such criticism. Hence, M. J. Woulfe of Inchicore wrote to the *United Irishman* in December 1905 and asked whether one man ought to wield so much authority over local education. Declaring that the question would be the same whether the school manager was a priest or a layman, Woulfe asserted that it was illogical to place so much power in one person's hands since schools were built and supported by public money:

> Such an arrangement is contrary to common sense and should give food for reflection to every member of that organization which was "damned" by the parish priest of Portarlington. Considering this question, one naturally asks: Why should not the Irish people follow out the policy of self-help and take over the management of the schools themselves? If we are capable of managing our own affairs, as we say we are, why not manage our own schools?[160]

Anyone sensitive to the maintenance of clerical authority in local affairs would have understood this argument as a call for limiting the priest's role in education. Griffith apparently anticipated such concerns and attempted to distance his paper somewhat from Woulfe's comments: "we do not believe it would be wise to supersede the clerical managership of Irish primary schools, but we think that facts such as Portarlington present show the desirability of the association of a lay element in the managership."[161]

CLERICAL MANAGERS AND "ANTI-CLERICALISM"

In fact, the "clerical manager question" received considerable attention in 1906 and 1907, and Irish-Irelanders expressed a variety of views on it. Not surprisingly, the Rory O'More branch of Portarlington presented the most extreme stance against the existing system in the introduction to its *Autobiography:* "The use made of the schools in this controversy converted some of us to the view that the unlimited control of the schools, and, we may add, of the teachers, now exercised by the clergy constitutes a menace to public liberty in Ireland."[162] Two months earlier, a pamphlet entitled *Irish Education as It Is and Should Be* had proposed the nationalization and democratization of school management.[163] Its appearance spurred considerable commentary, including a cautious early endorsement from Ryan (who thought it was "interesting and suggestive") and a belated, pseudonymous refutation in the *Leader.*[164]

That the subject was even broached disturbed members of the Catholic hierarchy, who had affirmed their support of clerical management at the Synod of Maynooth in 1900.[165] At the Maynooth Union meeting in June 1906, Logue expressed concern about "a difficult and stormy future, of a great struggle in Ireland for the preservation of the faith."[166] Privately he informed Walsh about his trepidation. "It is very ominous," Logue observed,

> to find some of our politicians going through the country advocating thorough local control. I find that even some of the priests who have attached themselves to that party are going in for local control. Why, they

ask, can we not trust our own people? Are they not Cath[olic]s? God help Irish Catholic education in this country if it is put under local control.[167]

Logue remained anxious enough about the endurance of this discussion to contact the proprietors of the *Irish Peasant* in November 1906, threatening to denounce the paper as "anti-Catholic" because Ryan left its pages open to persons on both sides of the question. The cardinal later told Ryan that he did not recall having used the phrase "anti-Catholic," but his explanation to the beleaguered editor was hardly more satisfying: "A newspaper, without denying or impeaching an article of Catholic faith, may do very serious mischief in prejudice of Catholic interests." Two days later, after Ryan pressed him further, Logue concluded that "anti-clerical would have better expressed what was in my mind."[168]

Not every call for lay involvement in education was anticlerical,[169] though some Irish-Irelanders, such as P. S. O'Hegarty, readily accepted the label. In 1909, for example, he wrote in the *Irish Nation* that

> when we are called anticlerical, it really means that we are insisting for the nation as a whole and for every individual in it that the church should confine itself to such matters as come within its province, and that secular matters remain secular. And we are anticlerical, all of us, in that sense, and rightly so.[170]

Such acknowledgments were few, and the Frenchman Paul-Dubois concluded that Irish anticlericalism was "confined to a small group of 'intellectuals,' or self-styled 'intellectuals,' who naively admire the worst anti-clericals of France."[171] Generally, complaints about priestly foot-dragging vis-à-vis the Irish language were not intended as blanket condemnations of the clergy's role in society.

Still, the international context made these demands worrisome for a sizable, if unquantifiable, portion of the Irish priesthood. Irish Catholics were certainly aware of a variety of threats that their coreligionists abroad had faced since the 1840s, whether from Italian troops storming the Vatican or from a German chancellor's Kulturkampf. At the turn of the century, French Radical anticlericalism received special attention in the

Irish Catholic press.[172] And in 1906 and 1907, Ireland's clerical-manager question took on more than a theoretical tone because the Liberal government of Henry Campbell-Bannerman was considering two pieces of legislation of particular interest.[173] The first would have reformed the English educational system, placing all schools maintained by taxation under the control of representative local authorities and raising a frightening parallel for clerical control in Ireland.[174] The second was the ill-fated Irish Councils Bill of 1907, which would have created a new education department, with local control devolved to laypersons. In the event, neither bill reached the statute book. Nevertheless, one can detect in Cardinal Logue's tribulations about "local control" a less-than-secure reflection on France's Separation Act of 1905, which established committees of lay Catholics to administer church affairs in each parish and which inspired the papal encyclicals *Vehementer* and *Gravissimo*.[175] By 1908 the parish priest of Oldcastle, Co. Meath, Fr. Robert Barry, had wearied of the repeated calls for lay input in education, and he denounced the "secularist nobodies" who espoused them. "They are few, as I have found out," he declared, "but they must be met on their own terms if we are not satisfied to have Ireland a second France. Those characters have no support, only their own audacity, and the people are only waiting for the priests to speak out."[176] It would be easy to dismiss such rhetoric as wildly overblown, but for an Irish clergyman trained in the manner described in chapter 1, the presence of forceful lay advocates and the hovering specter of state-imposed lay control of education reinforced the French parallel.

"MAYNOOTH BELONGS TO THE IRISH PUBLIC"

The clerical-manager question lingered throughout the preindependence era, but it was in the realm of third-level education that Irish-Irelanders had their most memorable showdown with Catholic leaders: the debate about making Irish a compulsory matriculation subject in the new National University of Ireland. The bridge from the managerial question to the university debate was a dispute that focused on the epicenter of Irish Catholicism, the seminary at Maynooth. Since 1900, college officials had repeatedly considered returning to the pre-O'Growney regime in which only students required by their bishops would study Irish, thus allowing the growing number of seminarians who took bachelor's degrees through the Royal University of Ireland to focus their study on examination subjects. The trustees officially shifted their attitude toward the Irish courses in October 1904. They instructed the college to teach Irish only "as far as possible" as a university subject; they rescinded the Irish requirement for students beyond the elementary level; and they allowed individual bishops to dispense students from all Irish study. In his review of the trustees' decision, even Moran criticized it as "a retrograde step."[177] O'Hickey feared that these actions would undermine the elementary courses that he taught, and he appealed to Walsh to intervene. Working behind the scenes, the archbishop secured the restoration of the general requirement among the junior classes, though bishops retained the power to dispense students in individual cases.[178] Then, at their October 1907 meeting, the trustees agreed to a program recommended to them by the president of the college, Monsignor Daniel Mannix, which allowed *him* to dispense any student from the Irish obligation who applied on the grounds that his language studies hampered his general university course.[179]

These moves exacerbated existing tensions between the college administration and the students. Since assuming the presidency in 1903, Mannix had reimposed rules that had not been rigorously upheld by his predecessor, Monsignor Denis Gargan. According to Corish, Mannix's "enlightened authoritarianism" created a "general restiveness among students."[180] Additionally, Mannix had angered an ardently nationalist core of students known as "the Sheiks" before even assuming the presidency because he had received King Edward VII and Queen Alexandra when they visited Maynooth on a tour of the country in the summer of 1903. Three years later, most of the students attended a lecture on Irish archeology rather than attending a reception given by Mannix to honor the visiting lord lieutenant, Lord Aberdeen.[181] Many "Sheiks," including the young Laurence Murray of the Armagh diocese, were also active members of the League of St. Columba. To be sure, only a few students prepared in Irish for the Royal University examination, but interest in the language remained high for a large number of the students. A survey published by the Columban League in 1908 indicated that 212 of the 368 students (about

58 percent) in the senior house were either students or speakers of Irish.[182] Thus, it is suggestive that Murray and his friends publicly booed Mannix during the prize-giving ceremony at the bishops' meeting in October 1907, the very meeting at which Mannix recommended watering down the Irish requirement.[183] For much of the rest of the year students refused to organize a number of traditional events (such as the annual concert in the Aula Maxima and the Easter sports festival), and at the end of March 1908 the administrative council dismissed Murray, whom Mannix identified as the leader of these moves.[184]

The Irish-Ireland press reacted with consternation in stories and editorials about the new regime, as some fifty students were exempted from the Irish course within weeks of the bishops' decision.[185] The two stories that were most stunning in their details appeared in *An Claidheamh Soluis* on 16 November and in *Sinn Féin* on 23 November. The former recorded that the administration had dispensed students from fourteen dioceses, including those over which the four archbishops presided, and that only the bishops of Waterford, Kerry, and Galway had "declined to permit any of their students to drop Irish."[186] In the following week *Sinn Féin* went one step farther, listing the names of the dispensed students by diocese and carrying a letter from a student identified only as a "non-Columban Leaguer" in which the correspondent responded defiantly to the new situation. "Irish is rapidly becoming the vernacular of the college," he alleged, "and no human power can raise English or lower Irish to the respective estates both held in Maynooth a decade ago."[187] Students and staff at the college subsequently received warnings from the administrative council that they were not to communicate "the domestic secrets of the bishops and of the college" to the press.[188]

Hearkening back to the Aran controversy, the Gaelic League focused on the implications that these moves might have for the language in the Irish-speaking districts. Through its secretary, Ó Dalaigh, the executive committee sought clarification about the new regulations, but two inconclusive and haughty replies from Mannix failed to inform him about the grounds on which a student could be dispensed from studying Irish at the college or about the types of examinations that incoming students might be required to take in order to be exempted from the elementary course.[189]

Mannix's attitude prompted League leaders to take issue with his apparent dismissal of the public's right to inquire into secular studies at Maynooth. In a leading article entitled "Dr. Mannix and the Coiste Gnótha," Pearse bravely invoked the same types of claims toward Maynooth that some Irish-Irelanders had made about school management:

> Maynooth belongs to the Irish public. It is endowed by the money of the Irish public. The church for whose ministry it is educating its students is voluntarily supported by the Irish public. *Everyone in Ireland—non-Catholic as well as Catholic—has an interest in Maynooth, for Maynooth touches Irish life at every point, and affects, directly or indirectly, the destiny of every man and woman born in Ireland.* The Irish public is no impertinent outsider in this matter, as the president would seem to suggest. It wants to know how its money is being spent, how its sons are being educated, how its vital interests are bing [*sic*] consulted or otherwise. The young men at Maynooth are our own—our brothers, our cousins, our sons. It is we who send them to Maynooth; it is we who pay Maynooth for educating them; it is amongst us they will work when they emerge from Maynooth. Their spiritual education we are content, and shall always be content, to entrust to the hands of those whose special function it is to direct such things; but their secular education is a matter in which we claim to have a voice—a claim which we intend to make good against all who impeach it.[190]

At a special Ard-Fheis in June 1908, League delegates passed a resolution demanding "fair play" for Irish at Maynooth, but aside from raising the issue periodically, Irish-Irelanders were in no position to effect any change within the college.[191] Still, because of the hard feelings generated within the college and without, the Maynooth episode is critical to understanding the debate about compulsory Irish in the National University that erupted between 1908 and 1910.

"THE PEOPLE WILL REMEMBER"

British governments led by both parties had failed during the preceding decades to create a university settlement that balanced the desires of Ireland's Catholic authorities for denominationally sound institutions with Protestant and Nonconformist concerns. Famously, the nondenominational Queen's Colleges established at Cork, Belfast, and Galway by the Peel administration in 1845 were seen as "godless" by the Catholic hierarchy. The Gladstone government's abolition of Anglican religious tests from Trinity College in 1873 also failed to appease the bishops in their calls for a Catholic university. And the Salisbury administration's inability to craft an acceptable proposal led Bishop Edward O'Dwyer of Limerick to denounce parliament in 1895 as so dominated by "British bigotry" that it was unfit to legislate on any matter for the Irish.[192]

The two most important members of the hierarchy to address the university question at the end of the nineteenth century were Logue and Walsh. Beginning in the 1890s, they sought ways to overcome the prolonged impasse. Walsh, for example, seemed willing to consider an enlarged Dublin University consisting of Trinity College and a newly created Catholic College, but such a suggestion was inimical to men like O'Dwyer, and it fell to Logue as cardinal primate to negotiate a unified position.[193] Ultimately, two royal commissions investigated the various options available for a settlement of the university question in 1900 and in 1906. Using information from these investigations, two successive chief secretaries, James Bryce and Augustine Birrell, consulted with Walsh and Logue as they drafted the bill that established the National University of Ireland and elevated Queen's College, Belfast, to university status in 1908.[194]

This settlement masked a denominational university system in nondenominational language, satisfying the bishops and English Nonconformist opinion at the same time.[195] Its provisions created crown-appointed senates to determine policies for both of the new universities, and it also called for Ireland's local governing bodies (the county councils) to vote taxes for scholarships for local students. These final two provisions are crucial to understanding the compulsory Irish debate because they created a situation that was markedly different from that at Maynooth: although the senates determined the curricula, the public, through the power of the purse, was in position to play a decisive part in those deliberations.

Revivalists watched the parliamentary process closely, and Pearse, as one of their experts on education and as editor of *An Claidheamh Soluis*, voiced the concern as early as February 1908 that Birrell was not receiving adequate advice from Logue and Walsh.[196] Pearse distinguished between the Irish people and those he called "benevolent fogies," especially "clerics who for thirty years have not come into vital contact with the practical problems of Irish life at any one point—who pose, and whom we too often implicitly recognize, as the 'leaders of educated opinion' in Ireland."[197] The previous week he had also differentiated between a "national university" and a "Catholic university," noting that in the former "Catholics and other nationalists shall be able to enter without doing violence to any one of their religious or national convictions."[198]

Throughout the spring and summer, he laid out a model program for such a university that included bilingual instruction for Irish-speaking students and professorships and endowments to encourage Irish-language studies.[199] Pearse further suggested a requirement that Irish be a compulsory subject for matriculation, a proposal that had been mooted as early as the 1902 Ard-Fheis. "Let no one start at the word 'compulsory,'" he declared. "If knowledge of any subject is to be a *sine qua non* for admission as a member of the university of Ireland, surely it is knowledge of the language of Ireland?"[200] The national congress met in August shortly after the university bill had received the royal assent, and the congress—acknowledging the role that the university senate would play in determining the program—called for a popular agitation to ensure that compulsory (or as League spinmeisters dubbed it, "essential") Irish be adopted:

> We feel that a clear and definite demand from the people of Ireland that their native tongue must have its rightful place in the university curriculum, and especially in the matriculation examination, would materially strengthen the hands of our friends against any opposition that might be offered.[201]

There was, in fact, very little in the way of agitation in the weeks after this meeting. Perhaps activists were initially complacent because they hoped that their "friends" on the senate, including Hyde and Mac-Neill, would secure a place for Gaelic in the university program. In late

November, however, any such illusions were shattered when the president of University College, Dublin, Fr. William Delany, S.J., told a student gathering that he opposed "compulsion" because it would limit the access of foreign students to the new university.[202] Pearse took this as a bad sign both because Delany also served on the senate and because "his position represents that of many others whose minds seem obsessed by the time-worn fallacy that the mission of our race is to keep English-speaking peoples straight in their morals."[203] At the time Dublin was abuzz with rumors that the Vatican intended to use the Jesuits and the bishops to establish the new university as an educational mecca for British Catholics.[204] Whether true or not, these rumors caused genuine concern among proponents of compulsory Irish because four other ecclesiastics received appointments to the senate in addition to Delany: Archbishop Walsh chaired the senate, and Archbishop Healy of Tuam, Fr. Andrew Murphy (representing school managers), and Monsignor Mannix, the president of Maynooth College, also held appointments.[205] Delany's relatively innocuous comment lit a firestorm.

The following week, at a huge public meeting in Dublin's Rotunda Hall, the League launched its campaign for compulsory Irish. The main speakers included Hyde, MacNeill, Fr. Matthew Ryan from Knockavilla, and O'Growney's classmate from County Monaghan, Fr. Lorcan O'Kieran. The high point of the evening came when Hyde read a scathing letter sent by O'Hickey, in which the Maynooth professor denounced Delany.[206] Referring to a university settlement without essential Irish, O'Hickey declared flatly, "If we tolerate this thing, we are still a race of helots, deserving the contempt and scorn of mankind."[207] In early January, O'Hickey sent similarly pointed letters that were read at the meetings in Athlone, Limerick, and Sligo. And throughout the remainder of 1909, the League sponsored heated meetings throughout Ireland, including a rally attended by nearly 10,000 people outside of Healy's residence in Tuam in early February.[208] From platform after platform Gaelic Leaguers pressed local-government bodies not to vote taxes for scholarships unless the senate approved of essential Irish. In February, against the expressed wishes of John Dillon, a convention of the UIL endorsed the compulsory Irish demand by a three-to-one majority. By early June 1909, 19 of 32 county councils and 130 of 170 urban- and rural-district councils had voted in favor of the League demands.[209]

What leant these meetings their special charge was that the Catholic hierarchy had come out against compulsory Irish. In January 1909 the episcopal standing committee issued a statement declaring the question of compulsion worthy of "fair argument" but announcing that the bishops opposed the League demand.[210] Their major concern was apparently that a strict Irish requirement would frighten Catholic students into attending Trinity College, rather than their long-sought-after prize. They called instead for the creation of "bright centers of Irish study" in the constituent colleges of the National University that would attract students voluntarily.[211] Publicly the League met this suggestion "with regret, but without dismay."[212] Pearse asserted that the declaration meant simply "that their lordships have not yet appreciated the vastness of the change that has come over Ireland since they were young men."[213] The implication here was clear: since the bishops no longer understood the Irish nation, they could not speak for it.

Precisely what "fair argument" meant became contested in the months after the bishops' announcement. Priests in the dioceses of Raphoe and Limerick and in the archdiocese of Tuam received what *An Claidheamh Soluis* described euphemistically as "requests or suggestions from superior authority" not to participate in the compulsory-Irish debate.[214] Among the priests whose cases received attention were Frs. Thomas Wall of Limerick and Patrick Forde of Athlone, both of whom had been students of O'Hickey's and both of whom had read letters from him at rallies in their cities before they were silenced. Another was Fr. Malachy Brennan, curate at Caltra, Co. Galway, a popular and outspoken member of the Gaelic League executive, who had invoked the bishops' endorsement of "fair argument" when he seconded the resolution in favor of compulsory Irish at the aforementioned UIL convention. In May he resigned suddenly from the executive and from the honorary secretaryship of a local festival that he had founded the preceding year. The League newspaper lamented his withdrawal and pointed to Brennan's February speech as "his most signal service in the cause of the Irish language." Pearse also claimed that Brennan was not the first priest in the diocese of Elphin "who has suddenly found it necessary to retire from the League within the past year," and he concluded by raising the more general issue of free expression: "It would be disastrous not only to our organization but also to the country if young clergymen of commonsense and patriotism were to be deprived of the elementary right of freedom of speech and action."[215]

The most explicit denial of "fair argument" came early in March when Healy refused to discuss compulsory Irish at a meeting of the committee that oversaw the League's Connacht summer college.[216] Clearly annoyed at the rally that had recently taken place in Tuam, the archbishop would not even acknowledge that the matter was open to further debate: "The bishops of Ireland have spoken on the point, and their decision binds."[217] When challenged by Colonel Maurice Moore that the "people of Ireland have spoken with no uncertain voice in favor of Irish, and their opinions should be respected," Healy responded:

> The people of Ireland indeed! What do they know about it? Do you mean to tell me that the fellows that kicked football here a few days ago, and held a meeting here, knew or understood what they were talking about? I would not give a pinch of snuff for their opinion.[218]

The archbishop's derisive language brought forth responses that ranged from the deferential defiance described in the previous chapter to confrontational language in the Irish-Ireland press. For example, shortly after his statements became public knowledge, the archbishop was to celebrate his silver jubilee, but leading townspeople in Tuam reacted coldly when approached to serve on a celebration committee. According to Ryan, "people pointed to the fact that on his own showing Dr. Healy did not care a pinch of snuff for their opinion, so why should they go to the trouble of affecting an appreciation which would not be appreciated?"[219] Meanwhile, the priests of the archdiocese—on the suggestion of one of Healy's close allies—subscribed to a fund in the archbishop's honor, but an informant told Ryan that had the question been put to a vote, "it is certain that the result would not be so satisfactory."[220] Meanwhile, a pseudonymous correspondent in the *Irish Nation* suggested that Healy's actions were "calculated to arouse *real* anti-clericalism."[221] Similarly, Pearse declared Healy's "pinch of snuff" to be "strange language for a prelate, in whose pronouncements, however bizarre, one would expect to find at least a little apostolic charity and humility."[222] To the archbishop's question, "What do they know about it?" the editor of *An Claidheamh Soluis* offered a blistering reply:

> We can assure his grace that the people of Ireland, and especially the people of his own archdiocese of Tuam, know a vast deal about this question and have a paramount right to express themselves on it. They know, for instance, of priests sent to minister to them at the altar, in the confessional, and at the bedsides of their dying who do not know a word of their language; they know of doctors who do patients to death because they cannot follow their descriptions of their symptoms; they know of school teachers who do not understand a single syllable uttered by their pupils during the day, while the pupils do not understand a single syllable uttered by them. And when this long-outraged, long-silent people see at last an opportunity of remedying these terrible wrongs and determine to avail of it, their archbishop, instead of proclaiming himself their leader, plants himself across their path, declares that he will thwart them if he can, and meets their demands for redress with flouts and scoffs and jeers.
>
> The people will remember.[223]

One should note that some priests continued to speak out on behalf of compulsory Irish, usually in respectful, measured language.[224] But occasionally, a priest used defiant words to emphasize his points. One such priest was O'Kieran, who told the Monaghan County feis in June 1909 that the bishops

> would not pay for the university, but the people would, and every one of them had as much right to say what language his children should learn as the bishops have. This matters [*sic*] was not in the hands of the priests or bishops of Ireland to decide, but in the hands of the Irish people; and if the bishops were a little less blind, they would see that not merely was the thing [denying compulsory Irish] not in the interests of religion, but that it was directly against the interests of religion.[225]

As potentially foolhardy as such words may have been in any circumstance, they were particularly bold coming at the end of June 1909, for it was in June and July that dramatic confrontations about "fair argument" erupted at Maynooth. First, the bishops punished the leaders of the League of St. Columba for having sent a letter of sympathy to lay students who had demonstrated on behalf of compulsory Irish in February. Five of the signatories were refused promotion to deaconships and a sixth was denied ordination. The students of the Dunboyne Establishment were similarly punished when the bishops closed Dunboyne for a full year and sent its residents on missions outside of Ireland.[226] Last, in an even more startling move, the trustees pressured O'Hickey to resign his post.

The trustees objected to the release of his pamphlet, *An Irish University or Else—*, which contained the strongly worded letters that he had written to the early public meetings in support of compulsory Irish. In them he had made disparaging references to the priests in the university senate, one of whom was Monsignor Mannix.[227] Since O'Hickey held a life appointment, securing his resignation was their only legitimate course, but he was unwilling to oblige them. Throughout July, *An Claidheamh Soluis* and the *Irish Nation* argued repeatedly that O'Hickey had written these letters prior to the pronouncement of the standing committee in January, while *Sinn Féin* persistently invoked the bishops' allusions to "fair argument."[228] There was disingenuousness in the former defense because the pamphlet did not appear until well after the pronouncement, and it included some introductory comments signed and dated by O'Hickey one day after the standing committee issued its statement.[229] When O'Hickey refused to resign, the bishops dismissed him. Obviously aware that this situation was already a cause célèbre, they then issued a formal statement denying that his dismissal had anything to do with the compulsory-Irish question. "The steps in question," they insisted, "were taken solely in discharge of the episcopal duty of maintaining ecclesiastical discipline in the college."[230]

Then, in words that recalled Logue's concerns over the clerical-manager question, they observed solemnly:

Considering the course which, especially of late, is being pursued in this and similar matters by certain newspapers—including one which is generally reputed to be the official organ of the Gaelic League—the bishops feel it to be a sacred duty to warn the people committed to their charge against allowing themselves to be misled by writings the clear tendency of which is antagonistic to the exercise of episcopal authority and which in some instances are calculated to bring into contempt all ecclesiastical authority, not even exempting that of the Holy See itself.[231]

Pearse printed the entire statement in order to defend his paper against it: "No word antagonistic to the exercise of episcopal authority has ever appeared in its columns."[232] What the Gaelic League had defended, he asserted, was the right "to criticize any action of the bishops, as of any other body of Irishmen, which affects the welfare of the Irish language."[233] And as we will see in chapter 6, the League would continue to comment on the O'Hickey case during the Dublin Language procession in September 1909.

Another year passed before the university senate voted on matriculation requirements. In May 1910, senators convened to address the recommendations of the university board of studies. These placed Irish in two of the five examination categories required for admission, but only as an optional testing subject.[234] After a heated discussion, Hyde moved that this proposal be accepted only if those students who did not pass a test displaying their command of Irish at matriculation would be required to attend language and history courses in their first two years at the university. As chairman, Walsh cast the deciding vote in favor of this proposal. He had remained publicly silent throughout the agitation in the preceding year, but had maintained correspondence with MacNeill and other League officers in the hope of working out a compromise solution between the opposition of some of his ecclesiastical brethren and the hard-line position of the League.[235] Even so, the senate decision did not satisfy the League or the county councils, and since the councils controlled the scholarships to the university, the senate had to reconvene. On 23 June 1910, by a vote of 21 to 12, the senate approved Hyde's new motion that Irish be required for matriculation beginning in 1913.[236]

CONCLUSION

The compulsory Irish debate raises two fundamental questions about relations between priests and people during the revival era: How was it that the leaders of the Catholic church in Ireland had so underestimated public opinion on the university question? And how does one explain the enduring belief that the church seized upon a docile language movement as yet another means to control its flock? The answer to the first question lies in the very nature of the pastoral relationship outlined in chapter 1. The clergy had come to expect a high level of deference from the Catholic laity, but what they and numerous observers had failed to appreciate was that public deference often masked forms of private resistance. Thus in 1901, prior to the intervention of League "outsiders," Fr. White in the Aran Islands preached and administered the sacraments in English apparently without causing a stir. But at least some of his parishioners did object to his use of English, and their objections came to light after visitors to the islands publicized them. In the course of the school-management debate in 1906, one of the principals in the "battle of Portarlington," Stephen B. Roche, hinted that the quiescence of the general public should not be mistaken for an endorsement of the system: "The clerical character of the manager and the peculiar position of the priests in Irish life prevents [sic] the great majority of Irish laymen from saying out publicly what *they are saying in private* of the management or rather mismanagement of our schools."[237] In some instances the very act of joining a Gaelic League branch or of attending a League-sponsored function may itself have been an act of covert defiance.[238] As a character told O'Donovan's Father Ralph that "sorra much good the clergy are outside their own business and many of 'em aren't much good at that itself, and to have 'em agin a movement at times isn't the worst thing either."[239] What was consistent throughout the period under review was that the League as an organization provided a platform for people whose behavior toward priests was genuinely respectful, as well as for others who chose to be critical, whether quietly or in a more public fashion.

The answer to the second question is somewhat more complex. First, one must credit the long-term impact of the changes wrought by O'Growney and O'Hickey at Maynooth for drawing a number of priests into the Gaelic movement. All of the evidence examined has indicated that younger priests at the turn of the century were more likely than their seniors both to involve themselves in the revival and to become committed

Irish-Irelanders. This is not to say that all older priests opposed the revival or that all younger priests agreed with it. Rather, a significantly higher proportion of the priests trained at Maynooth from 1890 to 1910 viewed the Irish language in a sympathetic light than ever before, and it would be this generation of priests who would lead the Irish Catholic church in the postindependence era as parish priests and bishops.

At the same time, one also must recognize that those priests who participated in the revival did so for a variety of reasons. Some, including no less a figure than Cardinal Logue, believed that the movement was a means to combat the impact of modernization and urbanization in Irish society.[240] But this view was far from the only one among priests associated with the language movement. Even Guinan, the conservative novelist who despised the dangers of city life, saw the revival as a means to mediate between Ireland's traditional society and modernity.[241] Still others appear to have acted from the belief, usually associated with lay republican revivalists, that the language movement complemented other forms of nationalist activism. In this context it is significant that some senior priest revivalists, such as Fr. Matthew Ryan, had ties to earlier political and land agitations, and some of the younger priests involved in the compulsory-Irish campaign held separatist views for which they later came under suspicion by the government.[242]

Finally, church officials paid close attention to what concerned their flock. When those concerns did not violate Catholic precepts, churchmen often voiced at least some sympathy with them. As one of O'Donovan's laymen crudely put it, "If this move[ment] comes to anything, you'll have plenty of clergy going round spouting in its favor. It's a way they have of backing the winning horse when it's well up to the post."[243] Even when revivalist criticisms angered priests, clergymen still had to pay attention to those criticisms. In this light the compulsory-Irish debate, coming as it did after a series of encounters in which Gaelic revivalists had shown themselves willing to confront clerical dictation, was a critical moment when literally hundreds of thousands of people let it be known in the streets and squares of Ireland that they disagreed with the expressed views of the hierarchy. Ironically, given the efforts of the Gaelic League to distinguish between "national" and "Catholic" claims, the decision of the university senate created the first institutional linkage of Gaelicism and Catholicism in the National University. A more important moment came after 1922, when the government of the Irish Free State instituted compulsory language education in all Irish primary schools. Partition ensured that more than 90 percent of the Free State population was Catholic, and with the continuation of clerical management of schools (and the desire of the church to perpetuate it), it made good political sense for even those doubting priests to become nominal language enthusiasts. In both instances, however, the clergy did not lead. They followed.

3

"All Creeds and All Classes"?

Just Who Made Up the Gaelic League?

There is among the people a latent enthusiasm for the Gaelic language.
But their attitude to the language is effectively one of indifference. This
indifference is the chief danger to the language. The effective indifference has a false basis; the ineffective enthusiasm has a true basis. It
should be our object to remove the indifference and to make the enthusiasm effective.[1]

For all that has been written about Gaelic exclusivism, few have attempted to sketch out who participated in the revival. Garvin has
contended that the League was dominated initially by a coterie of "middle-class scholars and dilettantes," only to be overtaken by a lower-middle-class cabal whose narrow political aims distinguished them from the
more broad-minded founders of the movement.[2] Hutchinson, meanwhile,
has argued that the revival in its mass phase became "a movement of the
relatively educated young against both the established and relatively uneducated strata—farmers, publicans, and shopkeepers."[3] Men and women
of the younger generation, according to Hutchinson, turned to Gaelicism
(and ultimately to Sinn Féin) because they were frustrated by limited career opportunities and faced the choice of being incorporated into a modern "scientific state" or remaining loyal to their traditional culture.

Such conclusions would situate the revival in the mainstream of European romantic or reactionary nationalist movements, particularly those of
central and eastern Europe, where researchers have long identified members of the middle and lower-middle classes as key ideologues, organizers, and participants. Essential to these portrayals is a sense that men and

85

women joined nationalist movements precisely because they were caught "in the middle": although relatively well off in terms of their educations or their earnings, they recognized that their potential for significant social and political advancement was limited by the circumstances of their respective multinational states. Ultimately, when a movement developed under such conditions, widespread recognition of "blocked mobility" created the potential for revolutionary—and paradoxically conservative—events such as the Anglo-Irish war of 1919–21.[4]

But three objections can be raised to this line of argument. First, Hutchinson and Garvin base their conclusions on virtually no empirical study of League membership and therefore on the untested assumption that the social composition of the League changed after an unspecified period of time, so that frustrated lower-middle-class members preponderated. Second, even if such a change occurred, it is—as Crossick, Haupt, and Koshar have shown—short-sighted to assume that persons of the lower-middle classes responded to the uncertainty of their situations in an explosive manner.[5] Third, such claims run contrary to the contemporary claim made repeatedly by revivalists that they appealed to "all creeds and all classes" in Ireland.

All of this suggests several questions central to understanding the impact of the Gaelic revival: Who joined the Gaelic League? Did the character of its membership change over time? And did the League have an impact in Irish-speaking districts, or did it remain solely an urban phenomenon confined primarily to the eastern half of Ireland? As will become clear, the answers to these questions are interrelated. After beginning with an estimate of the size of the organization at its height, I will investigate the social class, gender, and religious backgrounds of several hundred Gaelic Leaguers. What these data indicate is both that the revival was very much like its European counterparts in terms of the social composition of its leadership *and* that it was more representative of turn-of-the-century urban Ireland than has hitherto been appreciated. Moreover, as will be seen, this very representativeness was the result, at least in part, of calculated appeals by the leadership of the League rather than simply of some predilection of various elements of society to join the movement. Finally and ironically, these calculations had the unintended effect of mitigating the impact of the revival in the very areas that it was supposed to influence most—the Irish-speaking districts.

"CONSTANTLY REPLACED BY NEW BEGINNERS"

Answering the question of who joined the League is surprisingly difficult because specific information about membership is scattered and often problematic. For example, the original rosters of League branches are housed in separate locations and display numerous weaknesses as source material.[6] These logs do contain valuable data, such as the names of branch officers and the dates on which a branch affiliated with the central executive committee, but the information was not entered systematically. Thus, when an officer was replaced through resignation or election, his or her name was simply crossed out and the name of the successor written in, without any recorded date. Branches were also listed sequentially, based on their date of affiliation. If, as often happened, a branch folded and later reaffiliated with a new name or new officers, the "new" *craobh* appeared as a separate entry. Further, branches outside Ireland, including those in Britain, the empire, or the Americas, are listed along with those in Ireland. The resulting number of *craobhacha* included in the final account runs to more than 1,500, while the actual number of domestic branches at any given time was considerably smaller than this total.[7] Even after the Ard-Fheis professionalized its headquarters staff, the best-informed contemporaries, such as Ó Dalaigh and Bairéad, inconsistently reported the number of affiliated branches.[8]

Indeed, it may never be possible to agree on the precise number of branches in any given year, since those doing the counting have compared apples to oranges. Certain contemporary writers (and historians relying on them) apparently assumed that the final entry number at the time of viewing the log represented the strength of the organization.[9] More recently, Ó Fearáil and O'Neill have considered only those branches affiliated in a given year, but they used different criteria for their counts: Ó Fearáil included nondomestic foundations in his 1906 total of 964, while O'Neill focused only on Irish foundations for his 1910 tally of 548.[10] The best contemporary estimates available—that is, the official statistics of the League itself—indicate that the largest single-year total of domestic branches came in 1908, when there were 671, two years after the overall peak of 964.[11] If, however, one notes the growing stream of complaints from headquarters about the lack of financial support from these branches, the League was *effectively* weaker in 1908 than it had been in 1906.[12]

What can be established beyond doubt is the general trend of growth and decline in the number of branches. After expanding modestly between 1893 and 1899 (when there were only 80 total branches at the time of the Oireachtas), the League quintupled in size by 1902 and continued to grow, albeit at a slower pace, between 1903 and 1908. Thereafter its organization contracted until it experienced a new period of growth during the Irish war of independence.[13] At its height the League had at least one branch in every Irish county. It was thinnest on the ground in the midlands, where counties Leitrim, Longford, and Queen's had only one branch each in 1903, while the highest concentrations of branches were in counties with large Gaeltacht regions (such as Cork, Kerry, Donegal, Clare, Galway, and Mayo) and large metropolitan areas (such as counties Antrim and Dublin).[14]

If one accepts the figure of 671 branches as representing the highest domestic total, what does that mean in terms of individual membership? Mac Aodha believed that the League had about 50,000 members in 1904, and that it may have grown to as many as 75,000 at its height.[15] He does not cite a source for this information, though he may have drawn his 1904 figure from a lead article in *An Claidheamh Soluis*, in which Pearse asserted that there were 750 branches in the United Kingdom, with an average membership of 70, which he rendered as totaling "upwards of 50,000" individuals.[16]

Pearse's pronouncement is clearly overstated, as the number of branches did not approach the figure he claimed for several years. His methodology is suggestive, however, and the average membership he posits may be near the mark. Constitutionally, local activists needed to enroll at least 15 members before they could affiliate with the central body, but it was not unknown to have branches with as many as 500 people.[17] Not surprisingly, larger branches were concentrated in big urban areas. A tabulation of League strength put together by the Crime Special Branch of the RIC in December 1901 estimated membership at slightly more than 15,000 individuals in some 258 branches, rendering an average of 58 members per branch. If one looks at individual administrative areas, excluding those in which there was only one branch, one finds that those areas with the highest average branch memberships included larger urban centers: County Louth (174), where branches were concentrated around Drogheda; the West Riding of County Galway, including Galway city (143); the city of Belfast (100); the East Riding of County Cork, which included Cork city (95); and County Waterford (91), where branches were concentrated at Waterford city and at Dungarvan.[18]

The impression created by these data is substantiated when one considers branches in the city of Dublin, which were not included in the RIC tabulation but had a higher average membership than the constabulary sample. The largest was the Central branch (or Ard Chraobh), which had more than 440 members as early as November 1899, and which increased that total by 153 over the next seven months.[19] A more general gauge of the Dublin branches is the size of contingents marching in city's annual Language Week procession. For 1904, when press reports first contained relevant data, the average branch contingent was 82—roughly 40 percent higher than the constabulary figure.[20]

Still, O'Neill has argued persuasively that nearly 70 percent of League branches around the country were located in communities with populations of fewer than 2,000 people, and it is likely that the larger urban branches brought the overall average up to the 58 in the constabulary sample.[21] Hence, Pearse's proposed figure is probably toward the high end of the likely spectrum of involvement. More conservatively, one can postulate a range of average membership of from 50 to 70 members. And given 671 branches in 1908, this would place the single-year high-member total at between 33,550 and 47,000 people.

As useful as such calculations may be in gauging League size at a single point in time, there are several reasons why one should be cautious when extrapolating conclusions from them about the overall size and social composition of the membership. Most significantly, membership changed from one year to another. I have already noted that it was not unusual for branches to fail and then reaffiliate at a later date, often with only a modest overlapping of membership. The early experiences of the League in Galway city are illustrative. Founded in February 1894, the Galway branch had ceased to function in the middle of 1896. Local enthusiasts revived it at end of that year, and by March 1897 it included 50 active members, who held classes three nights per week and a general meeting on Sundays.[22] In 1904, Ua Laoghaire despaired of this pattern in the pages of the *Leader*.[23] "I have seen a great many branches of the Gaelic League started in different parts of the country during the past ten years," he commented. "I have seen in connection with them one curious fact: It is the number of them that have been, from time to time, 'revived,' 're-established,' 're-opened,' etc., etc. I have been watching those words as they have made their appearance in the reports of the progress of the movement. They are ugly words, and they tell an ugly story."[24]

Several factors militated against stability. Occasionally, sectarian concerns discouraged both Protestants and Catholics from attending branches. In south Galway and the Glens of Antrim, we have seen that priests feared that the League was secretly a Protestant proselytizing body akin to those which had printed Irish-language pamphlets earlier in the nineteenth century. In County Down, meanwhile, Orangemen employed a variety of intimidatory tactics to keep people away from meetings—surrounding branch sites, beating drums, yelling blasphemies, and shooting off revolvers.[25] Class tensions also dissuaded some people from joining the League or from remaining associated with it for more than a short period of time. Gaelic enthusiasts repeatedly expressed the concern that members of the legal and medical professions in particular showed little active interest in the revival. Moran blamed their aloofness on snobbery and suggested that the League adjust its branch structure along class lines. "Birds of a social feather," he argued, "ought to have Irish gatherings and branches of their own, for they insist on flocking together."[26]

In fact, a pattern of class-specific or occupation-specific branch formation did take place in larger towns and cities, about which more will be said shortly, but in smaller towns and villages the demographics and the status assumptions of the era did not allow for such adjustments. Several months after offering his "birds-of-a-social-feather" formula, Moran complained splenetically about the impossibility of providing different branches for the "forty different grades of society" in the average country town.[27] To an outsider these gradations may have seemed nonexistent because, as one acute observer of town life put it, "one class shades off into another, and there is no rational excuse for social divisions."[28] Nonetheless, in spite of having similar incomes, tastes, and cultural outlets, townspeople and villagers practiced a rigid, status-based exclusivity: they "firmly and decisively refuse to associate with each other on no grounds whatsoever, except that a clerk in a bank and his wife 'do not know' a clerk in a land agent's office; while the clerk in a land agent's office 'does not know' a shop assistant, even though the latter asserts his quality by calling himself 'a young gentleman in a business house.'"[29]

If sectarianism and class pretensions contributed to turnover, the major factor was simply the indifference of average members. When branch activities shifted from propagandist lectures or dances to classroom work, numbers dwindled because most people were drawn into the League for the *craic* (or fun) associated with it. Both activists and outside observers noted, for example, that branches often became dissipated after starting with a flourish. In practice, the number of paying members in a branch typically dwarfed the number of language students. In June 1900, although the Dublin Central branch reported a membership of about 600, its nine classes enrolled just 190 students.[30] The following year in Skerries, more than 500 people attended the meeting that inaugurated a local *craobh*, but only 68 attended the twice-weekly language classes.[31] In 1911, according to the president of the 150-member-strong branch in Killarney, the average attendance at classes ranged from 70 to 100, but only 30 students "showed a real desire to learn the language." "The social side of the branch," he concluded, "seemed to hold a greater interest for the members in general than the more studious side of its activities."[32] Of course, a relatively small percentage of enthusiastic students learned a fair amount of book Irish and attended meetings regularly, but their very zeal drove away the mere curiosity-seekers. In 1907, Moran warned that the "fanatic Gael cannot draw the English-speaking districts; on the other hand, he may repel them."[33]

Recognition of this fluid membership situation leads to two very important conclusions about the extent and impact of the revival in early twentieth-century Ireland. On one hand, it meant that many more people joined the League than even the previously calculated single-year-high total suggested, for the people paying dues in one year were not necessarily the same people who paid in the next. A report from the very active Nenagh branch outlines this process succinctly: we "can boast but few proficient Irish speakers, but this result is easily explained by the fact that most students attending Irish classes do so only for one session or two at the most in succession and are constantly being replaced by new beginners."[34] In fact, the market for the most rudimentary instructional materials was brisk, but that for more advanced texts was much slower. If we compare the circulations of the various volumes of O'Growney's *Simple Lessons in Irish* series, we find that the total for volume 1 dwarfed that for volume 5. By 1903, when the forty-second printing of volume 1 appeared, some 320,000 copies were in circulation; in 1901–2 alone, the League sold 135,000 copies of it! By contrast, in 1902 the executive issued just the fourth printing of volume 5, bringing its total circulation to a mere 23,000, or 17 percent of the *sales* for volume 1 in the preceding year.[35] Obviously, not all who purchased the *Simple Lessons* paid dues to the League, but significantly more Irish men and women than the estimated 47,000 for 1908 had been willing to pay for their "O'Growney" and presumably would also have joined a branch for a period of time. Also, because the propaganda of the revival included very public events, such as the aforementioned Language Week processions, the Oireachtas, and local festivals and concerts, participation at one level or another in Irish-Ireland activities was even broader still.

On the other hand, turnover meant that most individuals experienced the revival in an unsystematic, limited, and ephemeral way. Officers of the League and the editors of *An Claidheamh Soluis* repeatedly complained that members did not understand the aims of the organization, most especially its first object, which was to use Irish as a spoken language. "This point is sometimes forgotten, and sometimes slurred over," observed Eoghan Ó Neachtáin in 1902.[36] "We think it [i.e., speaking Irish] is of sufficient importance to be printed and hung up in the rooms of every *craobh*. It would often prove a healthy reminder to those who are addicted overmuch to talking in English and to magnifying minor points into great questions."[37] Two years later, Pearse acknowledged that even some of the most earnest revivalists "have nevertheless no adequate, accurate, coherent idea of the philosophy of the movement. They have faith, but they are either unable to attempt a justification of their faith or else seek to justify it by arguments which are untenable."[38] Outside the ranks of those earnest few, where turnover was rapid, such apparently spurious arguments were inevitable and led to what journalist Frederick Ryan called the "curious" phenomenon that people who adhered to diametrically opposed political or cultural programs simultaneously supported the League as a boon to their own interests.[39]

In practice, therefore, the impact of the revival cannot be understood by assuming that the ideas espoused by Hyde or Moran permeated Irish society through the coherent conditioning of a generation. The terms "Irish-Irelander" and "Gaelic Leaguer" must account for those whose interest in the language was piqued enough to learn what the Irish refer to as the *cupla focail* (few words), but who came to see the "minor points" of the revival as of nearly equal importance to language preservation.

THE COISTE GNÓTHA

And who were these men and women? Waters and O'Neill have made attempts to answer this question. Waters derived his data from a series of biographical profiles of thirty-one Irish-Ireland leaders that appeared in W. P. Ryan's newspaper, the *Irish Peasant*. These people were a solidly middle-class, highly educated, and energetic group; about half of them came from peasant backgrounds; and three of the thirty-one were Protestants.[40] Waters also cautioned that "the people in this group were not especially typical of the population of Ireland, nor even of the whole Gaelic League membership."[41] Meanwhile, O'Neill compared the membership of the Ballinasloe branch to census returns, identifying 62 of the 125 people who joined the branch in 1902 and 1903. Among others, they included 24 engaged in commercial trade and shopkeeping, 11 professionals, and 12 skilled tradesmen. O'Neill made no attempt, however, to pay attention to gradations of status and power within these broad categories. For example, half of the people in his commercial-trade and shopkeeping category were shop assistants, and their situations would have been markedly different from those of the dozen shopkeepers in his sample. Intriguingly, the presence of both shopkeepers and shop assistants in the same branch contradicts Hutchinson's contention that the young lower intelligentsia, as represented by the assistants, joined the League as a reaction against the established elements, including the shopkeepers. Perhaps most surprisingly, O'Neill found only two clerks and one civil servant, and he noted the presence of two domestic servants and a single agricultural laborer. Thus the picture presented by the Ballinasloe sample appears a bit more diverse than Waters's leadership cadre, though in the main it was still a fairly solid middle-class constituency.[42]

But how typical are these results of the League as a whole? To answer this question one needs to develop a more extensive and geographically diverse sample of members. Given what has been established about turnover, any sample must be viewed as a mere snapshot of the membership of the League; therefore, some attempt must also be made to compare membership over time. In order to make a more extensive examination of League officers and members, I have utilized a variety of sources not employed by either O'Neill or Waters. In addition to consulting the 1901 census returns, I have turned to local directories, which were published annually and which therefore contained information about individuals who had either changed addresses or died between the time they were recorded as joining the Gaelic League and the time of census enumeration. Further, I have benefited enormously from the work of specialist writers who have published numerous works in Irish in honor of the centenary of the organization. The five-volume collection of biographical dictionaries edited by Diarmuid Breathnach and Máire Ní Mhurchú was particularly valuable as it contains entries for dozens of League officers and paid employees.[43]

I have divided membership information into two main categories—officers and general members. Included in the first category are some of the more prominent names associated with the revival, such as Hyde, MacNeill, Ua Laoghaire, Dinneen, and O'Farrelly. For the purpose of analyzing this officer category, I have chosen to examine two sets of national leaders: the executive committees for 1903–4 and for 1913–14, which were elected during two distinct periods of the early history of the League.[44] In 1903 the organization was still expanding, albeit at a slower pace than during the previous three years, and political factionalism was not yet a great concern among the leadership.[45] The Ard-Fheis in 1913, on the other hand, took place after the organization had been declining in size for several years; its treasury needed constant infusions of cash from American supporters; and its councils were divided between more moderate League leaders, who wished the organization to remain nonpolitical, and those who, like Thomas Ashe, wanted it to take overtly nationalist positions on political questions. Ashe's biographer has suggested that the militants carried the day in 1913, but Ashe himself remained frustrated by the continued moderation of the executive and by its refusal to address political questions throughout 1914.[46] By comparing the social characteristics of committees elected under such different circumstances, I hope to begin testing the assumptions of Garvin and Hutchinson.

In almost every measurable way these two samples were quite similar. For example, both committees included only a small number of Protestant members—two in the first set and three in the second.[47] The range of ages for members was also comparable on the two committees (from 27 to 67 years old in 1903, and from 28 to 70 years old in 1913).[48] The 1903 committee did, however, tend to be slightly younger on average, with a mean age of 41.8 years as compared to 44.1 years in 1913. (The median age was 41 in 1903 and 43 in 1913.) One factor contributing to the higher mean and median ages of the second group is the significant overlap of members who served on both committees: seven men and one woman appear in both samples, and obviously, they were each a decade older the second time around.

Furthermore, both committees were overwhelmingly male: in 1903–4, 34 of the 38 who served (almost 90 percent) were men; ten years later, there was virtually no change, as the corresponding figures were 30 of 34 (88 percent).[49] From year to year the number of women serving on the executive varied, but the number never grew to more than seven members of the committee.[50] At the same time women members of the executive attended meetings with greater regularity than many of their better-known male counterparts. For example, between 1903 and 1913, O'Farrelly attended more than 81 percent of the executive committee meetings. By comparison, Hyde attended only 43 percent of the meetings during the same period.[51] Women members of the executive also became prominent leaders of several phases of the revival. Thus, O'Farrelly and Nelly O'Brien were instrumental in founding and serving as headmistresses of two of the summer colleges founded by the League—O'Farrelly at Cloghaneely, Co. Donegal, and O'Brien at Carrigaholt, Co. Clare.

If one looks at the occupations and family backgrounds of the committee persons, one finds significant similarities but also some notable differences between the two committees. In general, committee members pursued similar occupations. In Table 2 I have divided their occupations into five categories corresponding to those of Mary E. Daly and Armstrong and based on the classification of occupations used by the 1851 English census commissioners.[52] On the surface there is little difference between these data sets: neither committee had any members in categories IV or V (the semiskilled and unskilled sectors); the later committee had only a slightly smaller representation of category I (professionals and clergymen) members and slightly higher representations of category II (employers and managers) and category III (skilled artisans and black-coated workers) members. Because the sample sizes are so small, however, such differentials are not very significant, and the breakdown does not seem to indicate any marked increase in the relative importance of lower-middle-class people (who correspond roughly to category III) on the committees.

Table 2
Gaelic League Executives by Occupational Category (Percentages)

Category	1903–4	1913–14
I	47.2	41.4
II	8.3	10.3
III	44.4	48.3
IV	—	—
V	—	—
Total	100	100

Note: Sample sizes: 1903–4, n=36; 1913–14, n=29.

Still, there are signs that the later committee consisted of individuals who were both relatively more urbanized and relatively more provincial than the earlier committee. For example, while one-third of the members of both committees had been raised as native-speakers of Irish—a marker of a rural upbringing in Ireland in the later nineteenth century,[53] fewer members of the second committee (7) actually came from farming backgrounds than had in 1903 (10). Moreover, almost 79 percent of the members in 1903 evinced signs of upward mobility from their parents or had had substantial living or working experiences outside of Ireland. By contrast, only about 65 percent of the members for 1913 had had similar experiences, and nearly a third of these upwardly mobile members were holdovers from the prior committee.[54] While this final contrast may suggest that the 1913 executive was comparatively less cosmopolitan than its predecessor, such a hypothesis would certainly require further investigation before being proffered for acceptance. To judge from these specific data, it would also be wrong to conclude that the later committee was necessarily more prone to political controversy, particularly given what has already been said about the continuing commitment of the League leadership to political neutrality.

"IT WAS PART PLAY"

With regard to the general membership, I have focused on Belfast, Cork, and Dublin because the sources consulted contain better information for members in these large urban areas, and particularly for Dublin.[55] Individuals from throughout Ireland initially joined the movement through the Dublin headquarters, and the League published their names and addresses in its first annual report in 1894.[56] Out of a recorded membership of 330, the list included 143 Dubliners and 81 people from Cork city and county. Moreover, the Belfast Gaelic League recorded information about 177 new members between 1895 and 1897 in its branch minute book, which was published in 1995.[57] Last, between March and November 1899, *An Claidheamh Soluis* carried numerous reports from the Dublin Central branch in which the names and addresses of 168 more new members appeared.[58] Information gleaned about these 570 individuals will serve as the statistical corpus of the following discussion.

To begin with, members tended to be young, but the statistical breakdown suggests that the League also attracted more mature men and women than previous accounts have assumed.[59] While nearly 37 percent of those sampled were 24 years of age or younger, more than 26 percent were aged 40 or older. The mean age was 32.6 years, and the median was 30, and members ranged in age from 6 to 76 years.[60] This broad age range is substantiated by anecdotal information from throughout the country. In south Galway, League classes included young schoolchildren who studied alongside septuagenarians, and on Achill Island old men frequented the children's classes, reading newspapers aloud and helping to teach pronunciation and grammar.[61] Ó Cobhthaigh noted a similar generational mix in Dublin, but he claimed that the intraclass instruction worked both ways: "It is often amusing, when it is not pathetic, to see grey-haired men and women stumbling through the first rudiments of the language while children solemnly correct their mistakes."[62] In short, when the "young men of twenty" went to language school, they did so alongside people who were of their parents' generation.

Those recorded as joining the League in its early years were overwhelmingly men—fully 85 percent of the sample. To some degree, however, the impression created by this aggregate figure is misleading. If one breaks down the numbers to account for the period in which persons joined, one finds that the number of women increased as the organization found its legs. Of the 85 women in this sample, only 9 had joined the Dublin and Cork branches in 1893–94. By contrast, 27 (or about 15 percent) of the Belfast cohort and 49 (nearly 30 percent) of the later Dublin set were women. And in the case of Cork, which had just 1 woman among its first 85 members, a specific factor accounts in part for women's apparent lack of involvement: many of the earliest adherents in Cork were members of the Catholic Young Men's Society, an organization that did not include women among its members. By the time that the central body sent representatives to Cork in April 1895, "a large number of ladies" attended the public meeting.[63]

More important, reports from throughout the country indicate that women made up significant pluralities—if not outright majorities—of those regularly attending the branches over time. As early as September

1899, the Limerick branch reported that the "ladies easily outnumber the men two to one." In Lisdoonvarna later that fall the majority of those who enrolled in the branch were women, and in June 1900 an account from County Monaghan stated that the women students in Castleblayney were "much more serious, earnest, and persevering in the cultivation of Irish than the young men of the town." Almost three years later, when 100 members reestablished the branch at Cahirciveen, Co. Kerry, the classes consisted "mostly of young ladies, boys and girls, the young men being conspicuous by their absence."[64]

Although the evidence is somewhat sketchy, there were a variety of reasons for women's involvement in the Gaelic revival. Recreation was clearly an important draw for women members, as it was for their male counterparts. The Sligo-born author Mary Colum, who joined a Dublin branch while attending University College, remarked of her experience that "like every activity in life that is a success, it was part play. A good time was had by all."[65] Women also found League committees and classes to be more democratic than Irish society as a whole.[66] Earlier, I noted that women were among the most prominent leaders of the Gaelic movement, even though they were in a minority on the executive of the League. In a country where women first received the right to vote in 1898 (and even then only in local elections), and where the largest parliamentary party would not back calls for women's suffrage out of fear that such action might derail the Home Rule cause, the Gaelic League encouraged women's participation. Local notables, such as Lady Augusta Gregory in County Galway, Lady Esmonde in County Wexford, and the Honorable Mary Spring Rice in County Limerick, founded and led branches in their communities.[67] Women who were on the cutting edge of professional education, as well as those whose careers focused on advanced nationalist politics, were also drawn to the League as an outlet for their talents. Thus Mary Hayden, a member of the faculty and the senate of the National University of Ireland, "rejoiced in the freedom" that she found in the nonsectarian, nonpolitical, and mixed-sex activities of the League.[68] Meanwhile, Jennie Wyse Power, whose political engagement began in the Ladies' Land League of the early 1880s and continued through the foundation of the Irish Free State, was elected to the committee of the Dublin Central branch in 1900. Beginning in 1902 she served on the industrial subcommittee of the Coiste Gnótha and as an ex-officio member of the Oireachtas (planning) committee.[69]

Of course, single professional women and married women working outside the home were not the norm in early twentieth-century Ireland, and for all their openness, most Gaelic Leaguers accepted and reinforced traditional gender roles. It was not unusual to find branches forming separate classes for women students, even when general meetings and social events remained mixed. Similarly, women's participation in the planning of major League events was occasionally limited to an auxiliary role. For instance, in 1902 the committee of the Leinster feis—which included men and women—established a separate "ladies'" subcommittee specifically "to deal with decorations, [the] making of badges, &c."[70]

More fundamentally, League members openly called for women to "Irishize" Ireland through their positions in the home rather than by challenging established gender roles in the public sphere. The most prominent such advocate was the novelist Mary E. L. Butler, a child of privilege, who balked at the politics of her conservative Catholic family after reading a copy of John Mitchel's *Jail Journal* and became affiliated with the nascent Sinn Féin movement.[71] In 1900 she published a pamphlet entitled *Irishwomen and the Home Language* in which she declared that "a language movement is, of all movements, one in which woman is fitted to take part."[72] This was so, according to Butler, because she believed that most Irish women shared her distaste for the "'women's rights' class of work":

> Let it be thoroughly understood that when Irishwomen are invited to take part in the language movement, they are not required to plunge into the vortex of public life. No, the work which they best can do is work to be done at home. Their mission is to make the homes of Ireland Irish. If the homes are Irish, the whole country will be Irish. The spark struck on the hearthstone will fire the soul of the nation.[73]

Butler consistently invoked "angel of the house" imagery in her writings, berating educators who failed to instill patriotism in the future mothers of Ireland and extolling women who made sacrifices on behalf of their families and the nation.[74] But as Frank Biletz has pointed out, her arguments were not as conservative as they initially appear. Like Moran and Hyde, Butler did not view nationality as limited to political activity; instead she believed that by championing women in the private sphere, she would expand their role in shaping the "spiritual, intellectual, and economic aspects" of the nation's future.[75] With her focus on the home, therefore, Butler presented Irish women with a picture of themselves that was both personally empowering and acceptable to the wider society.[76]

One woman who dramatically exemplified this early twentieth-century Irish via media was the schoolteacher Jennie Flanagan. Flanagan was 21 years old when she joined the Central branch of the League as part of the 1899 cohort. The daughter of a carpenter, she became one of the most prominent language teachers in Dublin and at Gaelic summer colleges throughout the country.[77] Years later, Sean O'Casey recalled that Flanagan had lectured to his working-class branch in Drumcondra on the role of women in society. When challenged by a member of the audience that "the woman's place was the kitchen," she responded that "the woman's place was an equal place in every movement, national, social, and political, with the men."[78] O'Casey also lamented that Flanagan "ceased to be heard in any movement" after marrying one of her former pupils, Eamon de Valera, in 1910.[79] But this reading of the situation is incorrect and most likely reflects the passage of time and O'Casey's personal enmity toward "the Long Fellow." Sinéad Bean de Valera—as she came to be known—continued to teach in Gaelic colleges and to act as a judge in festival competitions even after the birth of her first two children in 1911 and 1912. In spite of her public activities, she was, according to one of her husband's biographers, a "classic Irish housewife and mother of the period"—gentle and self-effacing outside the home but a power within the family.[80] A contemporary biographer, meanwhile, recalled that Sinéad and Eamon "were to be met constantly in the places where the enthusiasts of the 'Irish-Ireland' movement congregated, talking Irish to each other as far as a limited vocabulary would allow, buying nothing that was not of Irish manufacture, and taking an active part in all the social and educational gatherings organized by the Gaelic League."[81] When her husband's military and political activities took him away from home and family, she did withdraw from much of her language activities. Nevertheless, in addition to raising her six children and steadfastly supporting her husband's political endeavors, she found time in the 1930s to begin publishing dozens of short stories and plays for children in Irish.[82] Thus, as Flanagan/de Valera's career suggests, acceptance of a more traditional career path in the home did not preclude women from contributing to the cultural life of the country.

There is another way in which her story is typical of Gaelic Leaguers generally: she was an upwardly mobile child of the lower middle classes. In Table 3, I have collected occupational data gathered about 191 members of the League, and because more than two-thirds of them came from the two Dublin cohorts, I have included Mary E. Daly's occupational breakdown of the city as a point of reference.

Two points are striking about these figures. First, categories IV and V—the semiskilled and unskilled sectors—are overwhelmingly underrepresented: With the exception of a single domestic servant in the Dublin cohort from 1899, they simply had not joined the League. Second, categories I, II, and III are dramatically overrepresented.

Given that category I includes professionals and clergy and that category II is made up of employers and managers, it is perhaps not surprising to find them joining a movement that has been portrayed as the

Table 3
Gaelic League Members, 1894–99, by Occupational Category

Category	Percentage	Daly (percentage)
I	25.1	5.5
II	19.4	8.9
III	55.0	34.2
IV	0.5	13.5
V	—	25.4
Total	100.2	92.5

Source: Daly (1984, 64–66). Daly's percentages, when added, total only to 92.5 percent, as she also includes an "X" category made up of students not living at home, pensioners, and workhouse inmates. All occupational categories were assigned after locating the individual member in the manuscript census returns for 1901 or in a local directory. See *Belfast and Province of Ulster Directory for 1895; Guy's County and City of Cork Directory for 1894; Thom's* (1894). For *Thom's*, I also consulted subsequent years up through 1905.

preserve of "middle-class scholars and dilettantes" in its early years. But the presence of so many category III persons in the sample is truly noteworthy. This category corresponds roughly to the lower middle classes, as it includes skilled artisans and black-coated workers (i.e., clerks, minor civil servants, teachers, and shop assistants). Their very presence in such numbers—making up 55 percent of the sample—refutes the claim that the lower-middle classes became a significant presence only after the League had developed into a mass-based organization. It also raises serious questions about the assertion that the move to revolutionary politics within the League followed the influx of lower-middle-class members. They were clearly present during the liberal early years of the revival.

If one breaks down the sample to account for the location and the date at which members joined, one can also draw conclusions about the manner in which membership drives and local conditions affected the make-up of provincial branches. In Table 4, I have split out the individual cohorts to reflect the percentage of members in each occupational category by location and, in the case of Dublin, by time frame.

It is noteworthy that the percentage of professionals and clergy is higher in the later Dublin cohort and in both the Belfast and the Cork cohorts than in the earliest Dublin membership group. Moreover, there is a large drop-off in the percentage of employers and managers in the later Dublin cohort, which distinguishes this portion of the sample from the other three. And last, one finds that category III persons continue to make up the largest

Table 4
Occupational Categories of Gaelic League Members, 1894–99, by Location (Percentages)

Category	Daly	Dublin I	Dublin II	Belfast	Cork
I	5.5	19.7	24.1	34.1	28.6
II	8.9	22.5	10.3	22.0	28.6
III	34.2	57.7	63.8	43.9	42.9
IV	13.5	—	1.7	—	—
V	25.4	—	—	—	—
Total	92.5	99.9	99.9	100	100.1

single occupational grouping in each locality, though they are relatively more plentiful in the later Dublin sample and significantly less so in both the Belfast and Cork cohorts than in either of the Dublin groups.

What accounts for these distinctions? Three explanations appear likely. First, one should recognize that the Belfast and Cork samples were smaller than both of the Dublin samples, and this size differential may account in part for the apparently higher concentrations of professionals in those localities. Because "substantial" personalities are more easily identified in sources like directories, the relative percentage of persons in categories I and II is necessarily higher in Cork and Belfast than in Dublin. It is likely that if we were able to identify more individuals in Belfast and Cork, category III may have accounted for a higher percentage of local membership than is apparent in the present data set.[83]

Second, there was also a built-in reason for professionals and clergymen to be even more prominent in the League outside of Dublin. As the organization expanded, it drew disproportionately on local notables to be the cornerstones of provincial branches, and this was by design. In 1893, in the article that *preceded* his call to found the League, MacNeill outlined a plan whereby Gaelic enthusiasts would appeal through local "representative men" to those whom he termed "the common people."[84] Late in 1894 and early in 1895, the Dublin leadership put this idea into practice when MacNeill sent circular letters to potential leaders in counties throughout Ireland.[85] An examination of some of the lists of recipients, which are extant in MacNeill's papers, shows that they included only those persons who had shown a prior interest in the language, through subscribing to the *Irisleabhar na Gaedhilge* or through joining the fledgling League as individuals.[86] Overwhelmingly, those who can be identified were clergymen and professionals (category I) or schoolteachers (category III). In the specific case of Cork five of the six individuals making up the category I sample in Table 4 were on the list of "representative men" for the county.[87] The impression created by the Belfast and Cork data is further substantiated by an examination of the officers from branches in Londonderry city and county, where twelve of the twenty-two individuals identified were clergymen or professionals (i.e., almost 55 percent were from category I), and seven others were schoolteachers (i.e., 32 percent from category III).[88]

Thus, provincial leaders came largely from the same occupational categories as the executive committees examined earlier—they were mainly professionals, clergymen, or teachers. Such a conclusion places the Irish revival in the mainstream of other European nationalist movements. Miroslav Hroch has noted similar profiles for the leaders of parallel movements in Poland, Catalonia, and Finland.[89] But as is clear from the MacNeill papers, this reliance on provincial notables in the Irish case was the result of calculated appeals. It did not emerge simply as the result of some predilection of these strata to challenge existing cultural norms. Furthermore, as seen in chapter 2, the offer of nominal support for the revival *did not* translate into mounting such a challenge for many of the Catholic clergy. Rather, it indicated their willingness to accept yet another honorific chairmanship from parishioners that required little active engagement from them.[90]

A final component of the explanation for the prominence of professionals in the Belfast sample rests in the way that early League branches often originated within existing local organizations. Thus in Belfast the organization took root in the nonsectarian Belfast Naturalists' Field Club, which catered to a middle- and upper-middle-class membership interested in intellectual improvement through outdoor excursions as well as lectures on local history, botany, and archeology.[91] Since 1892 the Field Club had sponsored a weekly "Celtic" language class, and in August 1895 members of the class resolved to affiliate themselves with the Dublin organization as the Belfast Gaelic League.[92]

This connection with the Field Club was auspicious for another reason: it opened the door to cross-creed interest in the language movement in Belfast at a time when the city was experiencing explosive growth and increased denominational segregation. Both Protestants and Catholics had moved into Belfast in great numbers throughout the nineteenth century, though the Protestant portion of this migration outstripped the Catholic share, with the result that Catholics made up somewhat less than a quarter of the nearly 350,000 people in the city in 1901. Competition for jobs and living space, religious tensions, and—from the 1880s—the high-stakes political question of Home Rule for Ireland, all combined to make relations between Protestants and Catholics tense, especially in poorer neighborhoods, which became increasingly monoethnic.[93]

At an elite level, however, there remained a residue of the nonde-nominational cooperation that had marked relations between some Protestants, especially Dissenters, and Catholics in the eighteenth and early nineteenth centuries.[94] The president of the Belfast League, and a member of the original Field Club class, was Dr. John St. Clair Boyd. Belfast Leaguers considered Boyd, who was an Anglican and a union-ist, to be an invaluable asset because he reassured Protestants that they could join the new organization without fear.[95] Together, he and his com-mittee worked to achieve religious balance among their local patrons, who included the Anglican bishop of Down, Connor, and Dromore, Dr. Thomas Welland; the moderator of the Presbyterian General Assem-bly, the Rev. George Buick; the future Anglican bishop of Ossory and archbishop of Armagh, Canon John Baptist Crozier; and the Presbyte-rian minister who had organized the massive anti-Home-Rule congress in Belfast in 1892, Dr. R. R. Kane.[96] These efforts appear to have borne some fruit. At least five of the fourteen professionals in the Belfast mem-bership sample were Presbyterians or Anglicans.[97] It may be that Boyd also helped to recruit other medical practitioners, for half of the category I entrants from Belfast (seven) were medical doctors, the highest such concentration in any of the geographical cohorts. (One of the two lay of-ficers in the Londonderry cohort was also a doctor and a member of the Church of Ireland.)[98]

The smallest proportion of each cohort can be found at the level of em-ployers and managers (category II), representing slightly more than one-fifth of members. The only exception to this generalization comes from the Dublin 1899 cohort, where the percentage dropped to just slightly more than one-tenth of the membership. Rather than indicating a falling-off of support among category II persons, however, I would contend that this apparent decline in Dublin is more indicative of the type of expansion that the organization was starting to experience in that city. It should be recalled that the 1899 sample comes only from the Central branch, and as we will see shortly, this was the very time when language enthusiasts were establishing new branches throughout metropolitan Dublin. Not only would other branches continue to attract category II members; some appear to have consisted almost exclusively of them.

More important, although the people in category II included a few fairly substantial business owners, such as the Cork alderman and flour merchant Thomas Creedon and the Dublin "grocer and wine merchant" J. J. Boland, most owned smaller businesses.[99] Several were individuals whose training might better have qualified them as skilled artisans under category III, but who had apparently amassed enough capital to own their own businesses. Thus in Dublin there was the printer Patrick O'Brien, who worked as a compositor with the *Irish Times* and who ran a small publishing operation catering to Irish-language publications. One of the founders of the League, O'Brien raised cabbages, potatoes, and carrots outside the front door of his tenement home on Cuffe Street—in a building with the paltry rateable valuation of £19.[100] Similarly, among Belfast members one finds the Presbyterian housepainter John Moore, who listed himself in the 1901 census as an "employer/decorator."[101]

Although the largest segment of the membership, category III, included other skilled workers, the vast majority in this segment—about 90 percent—came from the expanding ranks of the black-coated workers. Among representatives of these "new" lower-middle classes in the League, one finds a variety of occupations, the most numerous of which can be classed as civil servants (28 percent of the category III sample); national and intermediate schoolteachers (24 percent); clerks (14 percent); and shop assistants (11 percent). Black-coated workers made up almost all of the category III members in the Dublin cohort for 1894 (98 percent), and they were only slightly less prevalent in 1899 (87 percent); in Belfast and Cork they were still less so (72 percent and 50 percent respectively).[102] Since several of the Dublin-area civil servants worked in the same offices (such as the Land Valuation Office, the Accountant General's Office, and the Inland Revenue Office), it is likely that recruitment into the League was based as much on personal associations as on anything else.

There are two other points worth noting about the black-coated members of the Dublin League, which are elucidated by a closer look at these early cohorts. First, one finds that some, like Jennie Flanagan, emerged from the artisanal milieu. I have traced the parental background of twenty-five members of the 1899 cohort. Of these, eleven were from category III and one was from category IV. Among those parents in category III, one finds an ironmonger, two joiners, an upholsterer, a compositor, and an engine driver at a flour mill; the category IV parent was a carrier. Although these numbers are small (and therefore subject to qualification), they point toward persons striving to move into a different status category.

Second, a significant percentage of these people were not natives of Dublin city or county. Fourteen of twenty members (70 percent) traced in the 1894 cohort and twenty-seven of fifty (54 percent) in the 1899 set were born elsewhere. By contrast, two-thirds of the general city population in 1901 were born in the city or county of Dublin.[103] This overrepresentation of migrants is understandable, however, given the prevalence of civil servants, teachers, and shop assistants in the sample. As the home of the government administration, the central model schools, and various teacher-training colleges, Dublin was a magnet for young people engaged in what Benedict Anderson has termed administrative pilgrimages.[104] Similarly, in the retail and distributive sector both large and small establishments drew their employees disproportionately from outside the city. According to one active Gaelic Leaguer from this period, members who worked in small businesses, such as grocers' shops and public houses, came almost exclusively from country districts.[105] Large department stores, meanwhile, recruited their assistants primarily from country families who paid "employers between £40 and £50 to indenture their child for seven years" and train them for a job that was seen as socially superior to a craft or to general employment.[106] Indeed, nine of the eleven shop assistants in the 1899 cohort (82 percent) were migrants into the city. It is not possible to determine from this evidence how many of these migrants were native speakers of Irish; nevertheless, it is noteworthy that nearly a third of those identified as migrants came from counties with significant Irish-speaking populations, which could indicate that they had at least a passing familiarity with the language before joining the League.[107]

"SIDE BY SIDE WITH THE COMMONEST AND LOWLIEST"

All of these data indicate that in large urban areas the Gaelic League was an organization made up almost exclusively of middle-class men and women, many of whom were striving (with some apparent success) to be

upwardly mobile. But this blanket characterization should itself be qualified. As we have seen, contemporaries throughout Ireland were acutely
aware of status gradations, and what researchers might see as holistic occupational categories represented several distinct "classes" to many people
at the time. Such distinctions were not based entirely on perceptions, as
more objective criteria, such as incomes and working hours, distinguished
certain category III members from others. For example, a first-class clerk
in the Accountant General's Office with an income of £300 per annum
performed routine work, had a great deal of leisure time, and could afford
the usual hallmarks of respectability, including a home, tailored clothes,
more expensive schools, and possibly a servant.[108] By contrast, shop assistants earned anywhere from £15 to £50 per annum, toiled between 80 and
100 hours per week, and lived in cramped and often unsanitary quarters
where their employers supervised and disciplined them almost twenty-
four hours a day.[109]

Moreover, League members at least rubbed shoulders with people of
lower status because they lived in the same milieux. No doubt, some of
those in categories I and II (and at the upper reaches of category III) fit
O'Casey's biting description of "respectable, white-collared, trim-suited"
suburban Gaelic Leaguers "living rosily in Whitehall, Drumcondra, Rathgar, Donnybrook, and all the other nicer habitations of the city."[110] But an
examination of 94 members of the second Dublin cohort reveals that more
lived in central-city neighborhoods in apparently modest circumstances
than lived in those "nicer habitations." To be sure, 27 resided in suburban
areas such as Donnybrook, Pembroke, Rathmines, and Rathgar, but 39
lived in the generally squalid or declining neighborhoods bounded by
the Royal Canal to the north and the Grand Canal to the south and outside of the city's more affluent southeastern quadrant.[111] Furthermore, if
one looks at the rateable valuations of the habitations in which these 39
members lived and compares them to the average property valuations
in their respective wards, one finds that more than half of these Gaelic
Leaguers lived in buildings rated below the average valuation for their
neighborhoods.[112]

At this juncture it is worthwhile to refer to an inspired Marxist cri-
tique of the revival, which lashed out at the "blindness of the Gaelic

League militants when faced with the social problems" of the Dublin slums and the deprivation in most of the Gaeltacht regions.[113] Certainly, as Maurice Goldring argues, League leaders came predominantly from the upper-middle classes, and prior to 1900 their halting efforts to approach working people in Dublin and other cities betrayed breathtaking paternalist arrogance. In November 1899, for example, *An Claidheamh Soluis* published some brief comments about approaching the Irish-speaking working men in every city in Ireland to ensure that they continued to use the language:

> The League means persevering headwork, and it is not every working-man after his day's toil that can be expected to join in such labor. The workingman, so far as thinking goes, usually just vegetates amid the surroundings created for him from outside. Is it possible to create Irish surroundings in which at least a good proportion of Irish-speaking workingmen, for at least an hour or two daily, could simply vegetate as Irishmen? If such a thing can be done, it will be a kindly and charitable act and at the same time a good stroke for Old Ireland.[114]

Within a year, however, the committee of the Ard Chraobh apparently found more diplomatic terms with which to address a similar suggestion to the Dublin Trades Council. At a meeting of the council late in October 1900, the secretary read a letter from the Central branch encouraging trade societies to start up Irish classes, which the council passed along to societies to allow them to decide for themselves.[115]

Perhaps it was this shift in emphasis—encouraging workers to set up classes for themselves—which made the difference, for as the organization expanded after 1900, its membership diversified. In metropolitan Dublin the Central branch had been the only branch until 1899. In that year suburbanites in Blackrock and shop assistants in the city center established the first two branches of what would become an extensive network of fifty-four *craobhacha* in 1902–3.[116] If the addresses of their secretaries provide an accurate guide, twenty-six of these fifty-four branches were in the same central-city areas in which many of the earliest individual members resided.[117] Hence, just as branches appeared in the more affluent townships of Rathmines and Foxrock, so too branches sprouted up in the heart of the Liberties (the home of the city's declining silk industry), near Blackhall Place (the seat of metalworking), and in Inchicore (with three branches), where the Great Southern and Western Railway plant employed more than 1,200 people by the 1870s.[118] In all likelihood most members in every one of these branches would have come from the working classes.

The secretaries' addresses further indicate that organizations with class-specific or occupation-specific characteristics founded League branches. For instance, there were *craobhacha* in associations with category II memberships, such as the Catholic Commercial Club and the Antiquarian Cyclist Society of Ireland.[119] There were also a number of branches consisting of various types of shop assistants: a Purveyors' Assistants' Association branch; a Grocers' and Vintners' Assistants' Association branch; and a Clery's branch, composed of assistants residing in Clery's department store. At least two trade associations of skilled workers founded branches at this time as well. The Metropolitan Housepainters' Union established the St. Patrick's branch in 1900, and a printers' branch (the Clodhóirí) began meeting in the following year at the Dublin Press Club. *Craobhacha* also emerged in clubs that catered to consciously respectable and self-improving skilled tradesmen, such as the Wellington Quay Workingmen's Club, the Inchicore Workingmen's Club, the Dublin Total Abstinence League and Workingmen's Club, and the Father Mathew Loan Fund Society. These four clubs were exclusively Catholic in composition, but their members socialized occasionally with the (Protestant) Conservative Workingmen's Club (which was just a few doors away from the last two named bodies on York Street).[120] Such intraclass social activity is particularly noteworthy because the members of the Conservative Workingmen's Club maintained an active Orange lodge within their club premises, and members of the Inchicore Workingmen's Club and the Father Mathew Loan Society were sympathetic to republican and socialist politics.[121]

Eventually, the League garnered interest among general laborers in the capital as well. In November 1904, for example, Pearse, Ó Dalaigh, and Edward Martyn presided at the foundation of a branch in Ringsend, the old industrial and fishing village in which laborers lived in such squalid conditions that the *Irish Times* claimed that "not even on the west coast of Africa are the natives worse housed than are the humble residents of Irishtown, Ringsend, and Ballsbridge."[122] *An Claidheamh Soluis* reported that members of the branch were "sanguine" that their body would "do much to ameliorate the social and industrial conditions of the district."[123] Moreover, in 1910 and 1911 members of the Irish Transport and General Workers' Union marched in the annual Language Week procession. The fiery leader of the transport workers, Jim Larkin, even addressed the public meeting after the 1911 processions, telling the assembly explicitly that "this question of the Irish language was an economic question."[124]

The growing class diversity of the membership of the Gaelic League was not limited to Dublin. Not surprisingly, local conditions elsewhere determined the specific composition of individual branches, but when viewed as a whole, the pre-1910 League had a varied membership profile. In other urban areas a healthy representation of working-class members became manifest. In Limerick city the branch paid special tribute to railway workers and the Pork Butchers' Society for supporting the language cause.[125] The constabulary, meanwhile, reported in 1902 that the four Derry city branches included "young men and girls" of "the shop assistant and factory hand class," and that membership was "almost exclusively confined to the working-class element."[126] In the following year, while visiting branches in County Down, League organizer Tomás Bán Concannon found that the Gilford branch consisted of 150 people, "nearly all millworkers—and their energy in regard to Irish is in great contrast to the spirit in several of the larger towns adjoining."[127] And in Belfast, where (as previously noted) the leadership tended to be more elite than in Dublin, a correspondent wrote to *An Claidheamh Soluis* that "it is mostly the popular classes, seemingly the more intellectual, that have grasped the significance of the movement and welcomed it."[128]

Information from two communities in the west and the north is also suggestive of the ways in which language activists garnered interest across the social spectrum. Fr. John M. O'Reilly, who founded the branch on Achill Island, told a Maynooth audience in 1900 that "crowds" of pupils "from every side and from every distance" flocked to his classes to study Irish: "The shop assistants, the artisans, the schoolteachers, and the police sat down side by side with the commonest and lowliest of the people."[129] The "main element" among his pupils, he observed, were "the very poor." As a result, the numbers in his classes ebbed when the young adults of the island made their annual migration to Britain as harvesters, leaving the very old and the very young to attend.[130] In December 1900, *An Claidheamh Soluis* carried a further report from Achill stating that many of the harvesters that summer had taken copies of Fr. O'Growney's primers and Archbishop John MacHale's Gaelic translation of Moore's *Melodies* to study while abroad. According to the story, they had "not only retained but improved that knowledge of Irish acquired while attending the classes" in the preceding year.[131]

Similarly, six years later, Fr. Matthew Maguire became parish priest in Kilskeery, Co. Tyrone, and created a model branch in this rural northern district. The largest village in the parish, Trillick, had a population of only 269 people, but it was the commercial center of this rural area,[132] and according to D. P. Moran, it became the base from which Maguire "Irishized" his community. Maguire arrived in Kilskeery a convinced Gaelic enthusiast, having led a branch during his previous posting as a curate in the neighboring parish of Dromore. Within four months of his arrival, 230 boys and 180 girls were attending Irish classes in the national schools under his management. Local shops began stocking Irish-Ireland literature, and ceilidhs and Irish concerts provided regular evening entertainment. Maguire also oversaw four night schools in which children and adults took Irish-language and history classes. Within a year, more than 900 people of this farming community were studying Irish, and at the first feis held under his supervision, some 3,000 people entered its various competitions.[133]

More important than his attracting large numbers of raw recruits to the cause, Maguire used the Gaelic platform to reach out to his Protestant neighbors—a move that contrasts sharply with the received notion of priests dictating Catholic exclusivism through the League. For instance, he encouraged the Anglican minister of another of the local schools to institute Irish classes in Kilskeery, just as he had worked with a minister in Dromore to introduce Irish instruction for the children in the two schools under Presbyterian management in 1905.[134] Protestants also attended Maguire's night schools alongside their Catholic neighbors, where they received instruction in Irish singing and dancing from three Oireachtas prizewinners.[135]

"DIFFERENT CREEDS MEET IN FRIENDLINESS"

To be sure, lingering suspicions about the language cause made it difficult for Maguire and other enthusiasts to encourage Irish Protestants to take an interest in the revival. In 1906 the outspoken clerical conservative Dinneen claimed that most Protestants remained aloof from the movement because they had no traditional associations with Gaelic and because many of them feared that the League was "in reality a political society of a virulent and dangerous kind."[136] Moreover, various spokespersons—from Anglican bishops to Protestant school managers and teachers—argued that the inclusion of Irish as an extra subject in the school curriculum after 1901 was a "foolish" and impractical imposition on Protestant youths in an English-speaking country.[137] Such positions seemed irrefutable to many, but the contorted logic of some spokesmen occasionally damaged their arguments. Thus, in 1902, when school managers in Portadown stated that they preferred teaching Latin to Irish because Irish was no longer a spoken language, *An Claidheamh Soluis* observed with some amusement that, "needless to say, the tenor of the discussion was rather anti-Irish than pro-Latin."[138] Six years later, a League-sponsored survey of the Dublin schools found that the most cited reason for not placing Irish in the curricula of fifty-seven schools under Protestant management was the hostility of the parents to the language.[139] In 1911, *An Claidheamh Soluis* carried word that "a big number" of Presbyterian clergymen had forbidden children in their congregations to study the language.[140]

Nevertheless, Protestants made up an important minority of members and supporters throughout the period under review. Perhaps no group of Protestant revivalists is better known than those who were members of the Craobh na gCúig gCúigí, or Branch of the Five Provinces, in Dublin. Founded in 1904 by Nelly O'Brien, an Anglican and a granddaughter of the Young Irelander William Smith O'Brien, the branch included a significant proportion of non-Catholic members. Among them were Margaret and Sadhbh Trench, near relations of the former archbishop of Dublin; the artist Lily Williams; and Lil Nic Dhonnachadha, who in later years became principal of Coláiste Móibhí, the training college for Protestant primary school teachers.[141] In fact, contemporaries believed that the branch was composed almost entirely of Protestants, and some referred to it rather derisively as "the Branch of the Five Protestants."[142] When, however, its work was lauded by a Catholic priest in County Cork in 1907 as a worthy example for nationally minded Protestants, the former president of the branch, T. W. Rolleston, stated flatly in a letter to the *Freeman's Journal* that "the branch never was a Protestant branch in my time, and I am sure that it is not so now. I believe Catholics predominate in membership. Certainly, I do not know any Protestant member who would not have strongly objected to such a proceeding as the formation of a Protestant branch of the League."[143]

What had in all likelihood inspired the Cork priest's comments were press reports about an ongoing informal effort to recruit Protestants into the revival. This "Gaelic Mission to Protestants" met in a room provided by the *craobh*, hence the confusion with the branch itself.[144] The mission was led by several Protestant republicans, including George Irvine, Seamus Deakon, Sean O'Casey, and Ernest Blythe. At the time even D. P. Moran gave the mission some favorable coverage in the *Leader*.[145] O'Casey later maintained that their efforts quickly came to naught after the League leadership expressed concern that they were introducing sectarianism into the revival, though I have found no evidence to corroborate O'Casey's claim.[146] Alternatively, Blythe has suggested that the mission disintegrated after some of its own members objected to the tone of "boastful advertising" about their work in essays submitted by one of their number, Máire de Faoite, to the *Irish Peasant*.[147]

In spite of its relatively quick demise, the mission did achieve some notable successes, and several of its participants continued to press for a more liberal attitude toward the language among city Protestants. For example, in 1905 they convinced the rector of St. Kevin's Church to hold the first Gaelic-language St. Patrick's Day service in an Anglican parish.[148] And in 1914, Irvine and O'Brien were among the Gaelic Leaguers who founded the Irish Guild of the Church (or An Cumann Gaodhalach na h-Eaglaise) to encourage Irish-language services within the Church of Ireland.[149]

Aside from Hyde, the best-known Protestant advocate of the Gaelic cause was the Rev. J. O. Hannay, Anglican rector of Westport, Co. Mayo, but his association with the movement has been read as confirmation of growing religious intolerance within the League.[150] Beginning in 1904, Hannay displayed genuine enthusiasm for the movement, defending the League to his doubting co-religionists in numerous articles and letters to the editor.[151] The organization gratefully acknowledged his support by co-opting him onto the Coiste Gnótha in 1905 and reelecting him in 1906. At a meeting of the Branch of the Five Provinces in January 1906 he reciprocated their affection by describing the League as an organization in which "men and women of different creeds meet in friendliness; where priest and parson love one another—why, the golden age when lion and lamb feed together is nothing to this."[152] When, however, it was revealed just days later that Hannay had been pursuing another avocation (i.e., writing novels under the pseudonym George Birmingham), he found himself surrounded by biting criticism from Catholic priests and lay people who took offense at his portrayals of small-town life.[153]

Then, at the end of September, the chairman of a festival planning-meeting at Claremorris (Canon T. F. Macken, a parish priest from Tuam) sought to exclude Hannay for having violated "a higher constitution" than that of the nonsectarian Gaelic League. Although Irish-Irelanders (including another priest in attendance) rushed to Hannay's defense, the Coiste Gnótha delayed censuring Macken after committee member Stephen Gwynn defended his action. This move incensed Hannay, who was convinced that his fellow Protestant Gwynn had based his stance less on a belief in the propriety of Macken's deed than on a desire not to upset Connacht priests while running for parliament in County Galway. Hannay himself chose not run for reelection to the Coiste Gnótha in 1907, and he expressed the concern that "some of its leaders are becoming cowardly and truckling to priests and politicians."[154]

These incidents did *not* signal his complete disassociation from the revival, however. In his next novel *Benedict Kavanagh* (which appeared in

1907), Hannay not only chided his detractors in a brief foreword, but he also created an episodic tale in which the Protestant hero ultimately faced a choice between devotion to Irish nationalism or to the Conservative politics of his mother's family. Critically, his flirtation with nationalism comes after a brief association with the Gaelic League, and his guide is a young priest, Fr. Lawrence O'Meara.[155] Furthermore, in the midst of the Claremorris controversy, when the *Church of Ireland Gazette* opined that the event had marked a "strong confirmation of their fears concerning the Gaelic League," Hannay rebutted their charge and denied that Macken represented the League mainstream.[156] Most significantly, he also asserted that Protestant interest in the revival was growing: "A very large number of the clergy and laity of the Church of Ireland are now taking a sympathetic interest in the Gaelic League, and the number of Protestant members of the League is rapidly increasing."[157]

Whether this opinion can be substantiated is debatable, but there is considerable evidence that Protestants had been interested in the language movement prior to 1906 and remained so after that date. I have already noted a few individuals who had played leadership roles in Belfast and Derry, and the language movement in the north retained a Protestant presence well past the turn of the century. For example, a number of artists and journalists who shaped the Ulster cultural "renaissance" joined the Belfast League in the late 1890s.[158] Among the best known were James H. Cousins, Joseph Campbell, Robert Lynd, and Alice Milligan, the last of whom gave the League its first regular coverage in the monthly newspaper, the *Shan Van Vocht*.[159] The Quaker Bulmer Hobson, a founder of the Ulster Literary Theatre and (later) a key organizer of the republican movement, also served as the secretary of the Belfast district committee and encouraged Gaelic games in local *craobhacha*.[160]

Although these prominent individuals tended to support some variety of nationalist politics and were therefore not representative of the Protestant population of Belfast (or of Ireland generally), it should also be recognized that not all Protestants who patronized Gaelic activities were nationalists. In chapter 1, I alluded to Robert Lindsay Crawford, editor of the *Irish Protestant* and from 1903 to 1908 the Imperial Grand Master of the Independent Orange Order. In 1905, he editorialized that the language movement was "the awakening of Irishmen to the needs of their country and to their responsibilities as citizens. Protestant Ulster could not consistently object to the published aims and objects of the Gaelic League."[161]

Other Protestants also found constructive ways to support the revival and to mix with their Catholic neighbors. We have seen that some created alternative Gaelic societies, such as the College Gaelic Society in Queen's College,[162] and still others participated in public functions, such as feise-anna, which provided a neutral social ground on which curiosity seekers could tread without transgressing community taboos. For instance, beginning in 1904, when the branches of Belfast and County Antrim started the Feis of the Nine Glens, Protestants and Catholics mixed cordially each year.[163] In 1905, Hyde told a New York audience of still another festival that had taken place at Toomebridge: "Under our aegis Catholic and Orangeman came into that place in a spirit of brotherhood unexampled in that part of the world ever before, and I could not tell which was the most numerous at it."[164] Similar reports from locales as disparate as Clones, Newry, and Tralee stated that Protestants made up sizeable portions of the crowds addressed by League officials or attending concerts and prize ceremonies.[165] In keeping with Hannay's optimistic assessment, the same 1908 survey of Dublin schools mentioned earlier indicated that "the teachers in many of the Protestant schools and the managers of some are favorable to the language."[166] And in County Clare in 1911 the ubiquitous Nelly O'Brien played the central role in bringing together Catholics and Protestants from Kilrush and Kilkee to found the Gaelic summer college at Carrigaholt.[167]

Thus, although doubts about the language movement persisted for many Protestants in Ireland, Protestant involvement with the Irish-Ireland campaign was clearly more complicated than previous accounts have recognized. To be sure, Catholics made up the vast majority of Gaelic League members: Dinneen estimated in 1906 that Catholics constituted "probably 95 percent" of the League.[168] At the same time some Protestants were active and committed members into the 1910s, while others supported local League activities as patrons or joined parallel organizations that were less suspect in the eyes of their own communities.

Of course, the most important constituency to which the League appealed was the Irish-speaking population concentrated on the western and southern seaboards of the island. Gaelic Leaguers successfully established high concentrations of branches in counties such as Cork, Kerry, Donegal, Clare, Galway, and Mayo, all of which had large numbers of Gaelic-speakers, though most of these foundations did not originate with local people. In the main they resulted from a combination of unofficial visits by enthusiasts from larger communities, such as Dublin, and of the official efforts of League employees who prosyletized on behalf of the language.[169]

The League hired Concannon as its first *timire* (or organizer) at the end of 1898, but the scope of his task encouraged the Coiste Gnótha to expand its staff shortly after the turn of the century.[170] By 1905 the executive had hired eleven full-time *timirí* who were each to shepherd branches in a given county or region of Ireland. According to *Fáinne an Lae*, the *timirí* were to "form Irish classes and branches of the Gaelic League, to teach suitable persons to read Irish with a view to their carrying on Irish classes, to canvass for the support for the movement of the clergy, professional gentlemen, merchants, and other leading persons of each district visited, and to distribute Irish literature."[171] Besides promoting general goodwill toward the language, therefore, Concannon and his compatriots were to put MacNeill's program of expansion via local notables into practice throughout the Gaeltacht. The pressure of time precluded them from spending more than a few weeks in any particular locality, however, and local district councils therefore began hiring traveling teachers (or *muinteoirí táistil*) to concentrate on smaller areas. These men and women were paid through a combination of funds from local and national sources, and by 1908 there were 111 traveling teachers working throughout the island.[172] The League considered the efforts of the *timirí* and *muinteoirí* to be so vital that nearly half of the annual outlay of the central executive went toward their expenses.[173]

Organizers and traveling teachers engaged in the most grueling and indeed heroic work of the revival. At salaries ranging from as little as £50 a year for some teachers to £150 for a *timire,* they traveled enormous distances on foot or on bicycles every week. Most teachers, for example, covered territories of about 100 square miles to teach in the national schools during the day and in League branches each night.[174] The mundanities of their work are reflected in the records left behind by some former organizers and teachers. For example, in the correspondence of Liam Ó Buachalla of Banteer, Co. Cork, one finds letters and postcards between the teacher and several companies discussing his purchase of cycling capes and leggings for himself and junction bolts and (multiple) new saddles for his bicycle.[175] Likewise, Pádraig Ó Fathaigh, who taught in southern County Galway, spent countless hours pedaling his routes after dark on the poorly maintained roads through the Aughty Mountains.[176] Such effort inspired O'Casey to extol those who took to the roads with "backs bent, eyes gleaming, hands asweat or frozen on the handlebar, their feet going round endlessly on a glorious treadmill, rushing here, dashing there, to teach a class, to help found a new branch, spreading the Irish as a tree sends forth its pollen."[177]

One can surmise that the League intended its staff to project a familiar, yet respectable image to Irish-speaking audiences. Advertisements for organizing positions called for individuals who were fluent speakers and writers of Irish, able to "stand their ground" in public disputations about the need to revive the language. According to one expert, the League laid particular stress on a candidate's ability to encourage others to work on behalf of the language.[178] Of the twenty-two men who served as *timirí* between 1899 and 1915, fifteen of them (63 percent) had grown up in Irish-speaking homes, and exactly the same number grew up on farms, either as the son of a farmer or of a farm laborer. Two others were the children of shopkeepers; and others were, respectively, the sons of a baker, a game warden, a shoemaker, and a laborer on a fishing boat. Thirteen of them (57 percent) showed signs of upward mobility, either because they had toiled outside of Ireland prior to working as an organizer or because they had pursued educational opportunities or (prior) careers of higher status than their parents.[179] Impressionistic evidence suggests that traveling teachers tended to come from farming backgrounds, and they often taught in or near their home localities.[180] Possessing substantial familiarity with their neighborhoods, these men and women usually received their certification to teach Irish from one of the nearly twenty Gaelic summer colleges established by the League after 1904.[181]

Both official and unofficial visitors to the Gaeltacht faced generations of ingrained ambivalence about the language. Thus, although organizers encountered enthusiastic crowds at public meetings, they also reported continually confronting a generalized indifference toward Gaelic. Like all branches throughout the country, Gaeltacht *craobhacha* often fell to naught shortly after they had been founded. Indeed, when the League hired two organizers in 1901 to revisit areas worked by Concannon in the preceding year, both Peadar Ó hAnnracháin and Pádraig Ó Maille noted that the people they met had taken few practical steps to follow up on their predecessor's spadework.[182] These reports so troubled the national congress of May 1902 that the League hired four more *timirí* in the autumn.[183] What is remarkable in light of these concerns is the net growth of the League in the Gaeltacht in spite of branch atrophy. In the eleven counties visited by Concannon between 1898 and 1902, the number of branches had increased from 37 to 173.[184]

Even if branch foundations were not permanent, organizers and holiday visitors played a vital role in fostering revival in the Gaeltacht. For example, when the playwright J. M. Synge visited County Mayo as a reporter for the *Manchester Guardian* in 1905, he discovered a number of branches founded by Ó Maille. Synge recorded that the branch at Gweesalia (near Belmullet) received especially strong support from the local people because its classes and ceilidhs provided them with welcome entertainment. He claimed, moreover, that "for the present the Gaelic League is probably doing more than any other movement to check" emigration from the region.[185] Meanwhile, on Achill Island, where the branch had attracted broad support in 1899 and 1900, residents relied on outsiders to reinvigorate and sustain their spirits. In May 1911, for instance, an islander wrote to *An Claidheamh Soluis* that indifference had overtaken former members in the preceding summer and that "the cause was nearly lost" until two "young men from the south" energized them.[186] "Following up their success," she added, "the Gaelic League wisely sent us down a man who has kept alive the flame they revived in our hearts and in our midst. Gaelic classes, Gaelic dances, concerts, and plays are following each other, and now we are building for ourselves a Gaelic hall. There is no limit to our ambition."[187]

Nevertheless, even when enthusiasts successfully overcame apathy and suspicion to establish a presence in the Gaeltacht, two structural blocks undermined their efforts to sustain Irish as the spoken language. First, parental concerns over the economic conditions in the Irish-speaking districts dampened their enthusiasm for the revival. As we have seen, parents wanted their children to learn English in order to overcome the ingrained social stigma that Irish-speakers were poor and backward. In one case noted by Ó hAnnracháin, a man who was solicited for a small donation to the Language Fund offered to pay double that amount if his children could be kept out of all Gaelic classes![188] Fundamentally, however, Irish-speaking parents pushed children to learn English because they depended financially on the children succeeding as emigrants or as migrant workers. In the early years of the twentieth century the government had calculated that a subsistence allowance for a family of five could only be achieved on holdings with rateable valuations of at least £10 per annum. But the overwhelming proportion of farm holdings in the Gaeltacht did not meet this standard: fully half of all holdings in counties Donegal and Mayo were rated at below £4 per annum, and in the poor-law unions of Oughterard, Co. Galway, and Belmullet, Co. Mayo, three-fourths of the holdings were rated below £4.[189] Remittances and the earnings of migratory harvesters were all that kept many families solvent. Paul-Dubois reported in 1907 that half of the amount due for rents from the 3,300 families in the Clifden union came from "American letters" alone.[190] And when MacColuim, the Gaelic League's chief organizer for Munster, interviewed families in the townlands on Bolus Head, Co. Kerry, he found that "they look upon education in English as essential to the advancement of their children in life, emigration to America being almost the only outlook here as in other parts of Iveragh. It must be borne in mind that nearly every household is depending to a large extent on relatives in America for sustenance."[191] As noted in chapter 1, Connacht and Munster contributed disproportionately to turn-of-the-century emigration. In 1901, when their combined populations represented 42 percent of the total Irish population, almost 70 percent of emigrants came from these two provinces.[192]

And League observers remained acutely aware of this continuing phenomenon. When the 1911 census books appeared in 1912, *An Claidheamh Soluis* repeatedly referred to the "decimation" of the Irish-speaking population between the ages of 18 and 30 wrought by emigration.[193]

A second structural block related directly to the manner in which the League established itself in the Gaeltacht. Its reliance on notables significantly hampered the ability of the organization to appeal to those who spoke Irish as their everyday language by overemphasizing branch formation in towns and villages. The vast majority of Gaeltacht branches were located in communities of 1,000 or fewer inhabitants, but these communities were important commercial centers: nearly 73 percent of the branches in the congested counties were in localities that held markets or fairs.[194] Although such centers were intimately connected to their surrounding townlands through kinship and trading relationships, these very contacts were laden with tension.[195] For example, villagers were more likely to be habitual English-speakers than were farmers or laborers;[196] shopkeepers often had exploitative lending relationships with their rural customers, and in rural Connacht they also competed for grazing land with their smallholding neighbors;[197] and most parish priests—even those who paid lip service to the revival—continued in practice to discourage traditional culture in the daily lives of their parishioners.[198] In short, by looking to such "representative" men, the League worked at cross-purposes.

This situation inspired considerable debate within revivalist circles. In 1902 and 1903 the contributor of the "Mayo Notes" column to *An Claidheamh Soluis* repeatedly complained about the failure of the organization to move outside of the towns and penetrate the countryside.[199] Later in that same year, Patrick Mac Suibhne, an activist from the Waterford Gaeltacht who had moved to Fermoy, also objected to this phenomenon. In particular, he denigrated the work of the *timire* Donncha Ó Murchú near Dunmanway. According to Mac Suibhne, the *timire* refused to visit "the real Gaels in the country parts," preferring to remain in Dunmanway, which, "like most of the towns, is hopeless at present for the realization of Irish ideals."[200] Mac Suibhne dismissed the local leaders as "*stáigíní*" (worthless creatures) "who would be against the work in any event and who shall never be but a useless force in Irish-Ireland."[201]

On the other hand, the Coiste Gnótha remained committed to appealing to the Gaeltacht through town and village gateways. Dinneen, who complained at times that average Gaelic Leaguers were not interested enough in the Gaeltacht, summarized the prevailing sentiment on the executive. Addressing a small audience in Waterford city in December 1902, Dinneen insisted that "the real battle for the language" *needed* to be fought in "borderlands like Waterford": "Show me some conquered territory, show me a town or a village, one small spot of land to which Irish speech has been restored, and I will admit that your movement is making progress."[202] As late as November 1905, Dinneen repeated his stance at Dungarvan, saying that the real need was for "towns to become Irish," so that they could serve as bridges to the countryside.[203]

CONCLUSION

The issues of how to utilize the *timirí* and how to appeal effectively in the Gaeltacht remained contentious throughout the period under review,[204] and they assumed added piquancy when the 1911 census revealed that the number of Irish-speakers had declined significantly since 1901. In several Gaeltacht counties the percentage decline in the number of Irish-speakers was more than double that for the general population.[205] League observers, however, poured over the census data for signs that their work had borne some fruit, and they did find small pockets of improvement in a few regions where they had expended considerable energy and expense. Thus, although County Galway had experienced an overall decrease in the number and percentage of Irish-speakers, the percentage actually increased slightly around Oughterard, where more than 86 percent of the population continued to use the language.[206] Similarly, while County Mayo witnessed a significant fall in the number and percentage of Irish-speakers, the Belmullet rural district increased its population by 501 inhabitants and its Irish-speaking cohort by 460.[207]

The executive committee responded to the census data by establishing a special committee to examine what could be done to prevent further "decay" in the Gaeltacht, but because of its increasingly precarious financial condition the League was unable to expend even the same amount of resources that it had disbursed a few years previously.[208] Since 1910 austerity measures had led to the firing of four organizers, and League coffers remained depleted as the number of active branches continued the decline that had started in 1908.[209] Even if the organization had developed a coherent plan to save the Gaeltacht, it would not have had the resources to carry out such a program on its own.

Meanwhile, numerous counties and urban areas in English-speaking parts of the island reported higher numbers of people claiming a knowledge of Irish. Significantly, several northern areas—including Belfast, Newry, and the counties of Antrim, Down, Tyrone, and Fermanagh—recorded more Irish-speakers in 1911 than in 1901. Belfast alone reported an increase of more than 4,000 speakers, and the data indicated that the growth had taken place across the age spectrum. Dublin city reported more than 2,400 additional speakers in 1911, and in Limerick city over 900 more people reported the ability to speak Irish.[210] Outside of Belfast and County Antrim growth tended to be concentrated among school-aged children.[211] There is, of course, no means by which to test the fluency of any of these new "speakers," but because people self-reported their languages, and because most of the individuals studying Irish through the League received only a rudimentary introduction to the language, it is likely that many of these "speakers" were more enthusiastic than able.

Numbers alone would therefore suggest that the Gaelic League had failed in its first two decades of existence: fewer native Irish-speakers resided on the island, and most of the (comparatively) few new speakers were unable to express anything beyond basic thoughts through spoken Irish. Two things, however, should be recognized about these data. First, they do not take account of the underreporting of Irish-speakers. In spite of revivalist efforts to instill pride in one's ability to speak the native language, many Irish-speakers remained reluctant to acknowledge their familiarity with Irish to authority figures, such as the policemen who acted as census enumerators. One could potentially add to this "underreported" number those in the English-speaking districts who had developed a passing familiarity with the language through the revival, but who chose in all honesty not to report themselves as able to use both Irish and English. Second, the raw census data do not include those young people who had learned something of the language since 1893 but who had emigrated prior to the 1911 census. Whether or not their presence would have led to a more positive impression of the revivalists' efforts is a matter for conjecture. But since school-aged children accounted for most of the reported increases among Irish-speakers in 1911, and since more than 80 percent of Irish emigrants in this era were between the ages of 15 and 35 (i.e., in the immediate postschool years), it is likely that some measurable increase would have appeared in a revised census.

Finally, and most important, census data alone cannot depict the changing attitudes and opinions of Irish people toward the Irish language that the Gaelic revival fostered. As we have seen, hundreds of thousands of Irish men and women participated in the revival, at least for a short period of time. They came from a broader range of social classes and religious backgrounds than has previously been appreciated, and many of them appeared to be upwardly mobile, pursuing educations and careers that would raise their status above that of their parents. To be sure, their involvement was often limited to brief membership in a Gaelic League branch, followed by extended periods of socializing at League functions. Still, even if they did not fully appreciate what revivalist ideologues called "their duty to the language," their ongoing engagement with the League and their willingness to incorporate Gaelicism into their lives suggest that the language had attained some lasting meaning and importance for them.

4

Cooperating with the Cooperators
Branch Activities and the Regeneration of Ireland

OBJECTS

1. The preservation of Irish as the national language of Ireland, and the extension of its use as a spoken tongue.

2. The study and publication of existing Irish literature, and the cultivation of a modern literature in Irish.[1]

One way to assess the varied symbolic meanings attached to the language is to look at the intensive culture that Gaelic revivalists created for themselves and their neighbors. In their efforts to increase public appreciation of Irish, activists established *craobhacha* throughout Ireland, and the staples of branch meetings were relatively innocuous, simple pastimes. Typical League members rarely learned more than a smattering of Irish, and in Pearse's words they had "no adequate, accurate, coherent idea of the philosophy of the movement."[2] This incoherence was an inevitable outcome of two factors. First, as seen in the previous chapter, there was constant membership turnover within branches. People joined and studied Irish actively for only short periods of time, and thereafter they turned up occasionally for social activities or lectures on topics of interest to them. Leaders at both the national and the local level recognized this tendency, and although it remained a source of concern to some of them, they also saw it as the inevitable outcome of the voluntary nature of the movement. In later years, Hyde recalled that O'Hickey—who chaired the majority of executive committee meetings during the years of rapid expansion—had laid particular stress on winning recruits at almost any cost: "We are trying to get hold of public opinion, he used to say, and every recruit is of value. We must do nothing to drive away or frighten away anybody."[3] The second, related factor was that the League welcomed branches that formed within other organizations. This open-door policy had beneficial effects. In the case of the Belfast Naturalists' Field Club, for instance, it brought together members who came from different religious backgrounds in an amicable setting. At the same time, this stratagem exacerbated the ever-present possibility that members joined the League for some reason other than the preservation of Irish as a spoken language.

Given the role played by former revivalists in the foundation of the Irish state, it is perhaps understandable that we know a good deal about some who saw the language as a tool in their effort to achieve political independence. It is simplistic, however, to assume that one's political outlook was the most significant factor in determining one's engagement with the revival. In looking at the issues discussed within branches as well as the activities pursued by branch members it becomes apparent that the Gaelic revival achieved its widest support not because revivalists longed for *political* independence, but rather because they sought *personal* independence.

"THEY GATHERED NIGHT AFTER NIGHT"

In order to justify their movement, Gaelic revivalists deployed a mixture of emotional and intellectual appeals. In addition to making patriotic calls to interest oneself in the "grand old tongue," revivalists claimed to address more pragmatic concerns that affected most young people in Ireland and that had a strong appeal to those who were particularly vulnerable to a decline in social status and those who were most likely to emigrate. In effect, having internalized the British Victorian image of themselves as personally and collectively dependent upon the predominant partner in the United Kingdom, Irish revivalists pressed for a new national self-image with a moralistic emphasis on character-building through sobriety and industry.[4] Temperance advocates, industrial revivalists, and agricultural cooperators—many of whom were only tangentially interested in the linguistic aims of the League—became its allies, and the Irish-Ireland

movement came to encompass broader concerns than linguistic nationalism alone.

But if this process was evident at a leadership level, as Mathews and
Biletz have argued, it was even more apparent among the average Gaelic
Leaguers discussed in the preceding chapter.[5] From late September until
the end of April, League branches engaged in their most intensive study
of the language and traditional culture in what the organization called its
"indoor" or "quiet" season.[6] In the early days of the movement, language
classes were necessarily informal because of the dearth of trained language teachers. As Ryan described the situation:

> Sometimes there would be a native speaker or two or several at work in
> such a place, and consequently, after some practice and effort a possible
> teacher or two. Or a primary schoolmaster or a young priest, fresh from
> Maynooth and anxious to be worthy of Fr. O'Growney, would take up
> the work of class instruction. Very often, a young man or woman boldly
> took up the O'Growney textbooks, ploughed away for a time at the les-
> sons with the aid of the pronunciation "keys," and then faced a class and
> took it over the same stages. Any old Irish speaker in the neighborhood
> or within walking distance or driving distance, who could be got to cor-
> rect amateur pronunciation and repeat greetings, blessings, proverbs,
> songs, and so on, was a godsend.[7]

Over time classes became both livelier and more professional. With
the advent of the Gaelic summer colleges, instructors received specialized
training in pedagogy, pronunciation, history, literature, music, and dance.[8]
They returned to their branches better prepared and more enthusiastic to
teach. As a graduate of the Connacht Irish College described her experience, it was "one of those times when the soul is stirred to its very depths
and ready to dare all to achieve its ends."[9] League leaders encouraged
teachers attending the colleges to incorporate "simple Irish amusements"
like dances and songs into their classes throughout the year.[10] Endorsing
this practice in 1899, MacNeill reported that "we have heard some of the
members declare that they never spent a more pleasurable or profitable
time than they did at the classes and meetings of their branches during
last winter and spring."[11]

Depending on the interest of their members, individual branches developed varied programs of intellectual and social events outside of their weekly language classes. The former vice president of the Cork Gaelic League, John J. Horgan, recalled that history lectures, dancing, and music were favored pastimes for members throughout the country: "In small halls in back lanes and in remote country schoolhouses and barns they gathered night after night to nourish themselves at the roots of Gaelic culture."[12] Larger *craobhacha*, such as the Central and Keating branches in Dublin, organized lecture series and debates on literary, historical, and contemporary topics.[13] Such sessions could be entertaining and even confrontational. Horgan, who offered a history course in the Cork branch, remembered that each lecture "had to be carefully prepared, sources examined and references checked, for my pupils were both adult and critical, often with views or theories of their own."[14] To be sure, branch discussions did sometimes address political questions. Thus, during the Boer War the teacher in the Michael Dwyer branch in Dublin read newspaper accounts about the conflict and led discussions in Gaelic about the war. The Dwyers were, however, one of the most politicized branches of the League in 1900: they met in the rooms of the Celtic Literary Society, one of many clubs from which the IRB recruited new members, and they named their branch after a commander of the United Irishmen from County Wicklow.[15] Smaller provincial branches also organized lectures, but they occurred more sporadically, and weekly or monthly ceilidhs were their social mainstays. Given the reliance on clerical presidents in country branches, however, such activities were sometimes subject to strict limitations. For instance, the parish priest of Banteer told the traveling teacher of his district, "I *cannot* allow any entertainment in schools during *Lent*. You can have it after Easter."[16]

What becomes apparent through branch records is that these activities that were intended originally to augment language work became the normal mode of participation for most League members. By 1906 two frequent contributors to the *Leader* acknowledged openly what many knew from personal experience: adult Gaelic Leaguers were not learning the language. In an essay entitled "Confessions of an O'Growneyite," Arthur Clery spoke for many when he admitted to his own "modest learning" after several years of intermittent study.[17] Over the next two weeks in the aptly titled series "The Demi-Semi-Gael," "Marbhan" declared that it had been unrealistic to expect adults to learn idiomatic Irish.[18] Marbhan stated bluntly that League branches in the English-speaking districts had been wrong to concentrate their attention on adults, referring to this focus as "mere propagandism."[19] For the movement to have any lasting effect, he argued, it had to interest children in "Irishism."[20]

In practice, provincial leaders tacitly encouraged "mere propagandism" by adopting a blasé attitude about Gaelic Leaguers learning the language. A particularly glaring case occurred at Ballinasloe in 1903, where a member of the governing committee of the St. Grellan's branch proposed that committee members lead by example and attend the Irish classes regularly. If they missed more than three consecutive class meetings, the motion stipulated, they would forfeit their spot on the committee.[21] But when this rather modest proposal came up for consideration, it ran into stiff opposition. In fact, committee members endorsed an amendment that allowed them to skip language classes altogether and that stipulated that each future committee meeting would begin with a half-hour discussion about the language movement. The only penalty for missing these discussions would be the imposition of a nominal fine of 1d.[22] Of all the items discussed by the committee in its first five months of operation, language tuition was clearly secondary. Instead, they subscribed to several nationalist and Irish-Ireland newspapers; they sponsored a concert featuring the Gaelic harpist Owen Lloyd of Dublin; they established an active industrial subcommittee that discussed the business climate in Ballinasloe on a weekly basis; they sponsored a local football team and affiliated their branch with the Gaelic Athletic Association; they voted to allow games of chess and draughts in their classroom; and they sponsored a lecture series on "first aids and ambulence [sic] work."[23]

Although this example indicates the passive reinforcement of the general members' attitudes, other provincial activists openly acknowledged their reluctance to push for English-speaking adults to learn Irish. In a speech to a Dublin gathering of the United Irish League, Canon James MacFadden from County Donegal stated categorically that "every person calling himself an Irishman ought to know some Irish." But, added this member of the Coiste Gnótha, "It was not to be expected that those of advanced years who had not learned Irish in their youth would learn it now."[24] MacFadden encouraged adults to learn as much Irish as they wished, and like Marbhan, he thought that intensive language instruction should take place in the schools. Moreover, he believed that economic concerns, such as the encouragement of cottage industries and the settlement of outstanding tenant-rights claims, deserved equal attention.[25] Similarly, in 1910, Horgan told a festival crowd at Kilkenny that the language movement brought young and old together, but that older members should only feel obligated "to see their children were taught Irish, and to study Irish history, and to support Irish industries themselves."[26] Hence, both MacFadden and Horgan offered interpretations of what qualified as a sound Irish-Ireland stance that deemphasized the speaking of Irish and elevated participation through other means, such as enjoying Gaelic entertainments or working for other causes.

"IT IS OUTSIDE THEIR OBJECTS"

Recognition that local activists held such heterodox opinions about their work actually highlights several interrelated themes that explain both the appeal and growth of the language movement. Gaelic Leaguers, for example, sought to alleviate the negative impacts that the social vacuum discussed in chapter 1 had on provincial Ireland. In particular, they worried that economic and social stagnation encouraged alcohol abuse. Typical Irish villages, according to Dinneen, were "the dullest place[s] in the world, with no library or reading room, no amusements of a rational or national kind: nothing but public houses and the accompanying evil."[27] This slap at pubs was hardly overstated. In the half century since the famine the aggregate number of licensed houses in Ireland had doubled to nearly 30,000, but the population was more than cut in half.[28] In 1905 there was about one public house for every 146 people in Ireland, and in some smaller communities the ratio was even lower. Paul-Dubois reported, for instance, that there were ten pubs in the village of Mullagh, Co. Clare, a community with only 179 inhabitants.[29] Annually, Irish men and women spent an estimated £13 to £15 million on beer and whiskey, more than a third of which went into the imperial exchequer through taxation.[30]

Irish-Irelanders considered such spending wasteful and ultimately unpatriotic. Using rhetoric that had been common in Ireland since the report of the Financial Relations Commission in 1896 had bolstered nationalist claims that Ireland was overtaxed, the Portarlington protagonist P. T. MacGinley argued that the tax of five pence on the shilling on alcohol going "into the coffers of John Bull" "gives us a mighty poor return."[31] Meanwhile, Moran regularly denounced the economic and political power of brewers, distillers, and publicans within Ireland. One of his favorite targets was the Licensed Grocers' and Vintners' Protection Association, which controlled nearly one-third of the Dublin city corporation.[32] With his special gift for double entendre Moran dubbed the drink industry "King Bung," to reflect its political importance and his low opinion of those who profited from alcohol.[33]

Philosophically, then, temperance advocates and total abstainers saw Irish-Irelanders as being of like mind in the effort to curb the attractions of the drinking culture. In practice, moreover, the Gaelic movement openly claimed to encourage temperate behavior. MacGinley asserted in 1901 that "the work of the Gaelic League makes for temperance" because it gave members something constructive to do, and it espoused "high national and public ideals which are quite incompatible with the sordidness of drink."[34] A League brochure prepared as part of a fund-raising appeal in 1912 also stated unequivocally that "the language movement promotes temperance. On this everyone—the clergy who have long labored in this field of work, the police, the publican, the employer of labor—are agreed."[35] According to the text, all League functions, from business meetings to ceilidhs and festivals, were officially dry affairs.[36]

MacGinley also had highlighted another key point, which was that many of the younger men and women who joined the League in its early years had been reared during a period of temperance activism.[37] Beginning in the 1880s a popular Catholic religious revival bolstered the efforts of total abstainers: between 1889 and 1891 they had secured a quarter of a million pledges.[38] According to MacGinley, several of the Catholic bishops also had made it a standard practice to administer the pledge to children at their confirmations.[39] At the heart of this burgeoning movement was a Jesuit priest, Fr. James A. Cullen, whose temperance catechism sold 60,000 copies in 1892 alone. His work inspired the formation of the Pioneer Total Abstinence Association in 1901, which eventually claimed members all over the English-speaking world.[40] In a parallel crusade the Capuchin fathers administered a million abstinence pledges of their own between 1905 and 1911.[41] Thus, as MacGinley concluded, the League was "tapping a great sober population, and with its own tacit teaching, who knows but we are working toward a sober as well as an Irish Ireland."[42]

Temperance and total abstinence clubs in localities throughout the country took advantage of the open-door policy of the League by starting language classes and affiliating as branches. For instance, the *craobhacha* in Loughrea and Ballinasloe were headquartered respectively in total abstinence and temperance halls. Meanwhile in 1899 in Limerick, Gaelic Leaguers encouraged the formation of language classes in the St. John's Temperance Hall and the St. Michael's Temperance Hall, and in Dublin the members of St. Teresa's Total Abstinence Hall established a branch of their own the following year.[43] In Waterford a language class at the city temperance hall regularly drew 100 students, and the temperance club in Blackrock, Co. Dublin, reportedly was "at the heart" of the Gaelic movement in that suburban community.[44]

The relationship between temperance advocates and the Gaelic revival, however, was complex for several reasons. To begin with, contra MacGinley, many Gaelic Leaguers did not abstain from imbibing. In fact, when Hyde and Fr. O'Growney lunched together for the first time in 1892, they toasted their new partnership with champagne.[45] Even if official functions were dry, gatherings before and after meetings were not. Thus in 1900 seven priests in Ballina entertained Hyde before taking him to a League meeting, and their three-hour meal began with champagne and ended with whiskey punch! Hyde told Lady Gregory about the dinner the next day, and when he boasted that he may afterward have made the best speech of his life, she chided him that he had not yet seen it in print.[46] After gatherings of Dublin's Keating branch, members frequented the tobacco shop *An Stad* owned by Cathal MacGarvey, where pints of Guinness accompanied their conversations and songs.[47] O'Casey also recalled postmeeting talks in which he and other politically minded Leaguers emptied "glasses at a gulp" and groused about what they considered to be the occasional truckling of leaders like Hyde to government officials and priests.[48] And W. P. Ryan recorded primly that hundreds of the spectators from the Letterkenny feis in 1907—most of whom were members of the Ancient Order of Hibernians—drank enough after the event that "their conduct on the homeward way was not edifying."[49] Indeed, the convivial behavior of some Gaelic Leaguers themselves was known to upset their more abstemious fellows: in 1905 a dispute between the Lusk and Swords branches, which was rooted in clashes between teetotalers and members who drank, threatened to dissolve the Fingal *coiste ceanntair* in north County Dublin. Eventually, MacNeill intervened and smoothed over their differences enough to recreate an uneasy working partnership in the district.[50]

Although the Gaelic League courted Catholic temperance advocates, an incident from 1902 demonstrates that the organization also worked to remain true to its nonsectarian ideals. Prior to the Ard-Fheis, Gaelic Leaguers from Enniscorthy, Co. Wexford, had sent a circular to all branches asking their delegates to endorse the St. Patrick's Anti-Treating League at the national congress.[51] Established by clergymen in the diocese of Ferns, the Anti-Treating League sought to end the practice of "standing rounds," in which each member of a group of pub patrons purchased drinks for one another in turn. Antitreaters couched their appeal in terms that corresponded to Moran's and MacGinley's antidrink justifications, arguing that their program checked intemperance, cut "our extravagant expenditure on drink," and "reduce[d] our self-imposed yearly tribute to the English exchequer."[52] Some Gaelic Leaguers, however, objected that the St. Patrick's League was a Catholic body that targeted "the sin of intemperance."[53] In a letter to *An Claidheamh Soluis* a delegate named Diarmuid Ó Cruadhlaoich asked pointedly, "What has the Gaelic League to do with sin, and why is it proposed to incorporate this sectarian association, for Catholics are only a sect even in the 'Island of Saints and Scholars,' into the Gaelic League?"[54] In the event, a majority at the congress adopted a compromise position, agreeing that the Gaelic League could not endorse the St. Patrick's League specifically but expressing support for those who opposed the treating custom.[55]

The antitreating movement also received a qualified endorsement from Eoin MacNeill when the issue briefly resurfaced a few months later.[56] Careful not to overstep League rules, he cautioned that it was not "competent" for branches "to bind their members to become anti-treaters. It is outside their objects, and it would amount to spreading the anti-treating movement by a kind of compulsion."[57] Nevertheless, MacNeill believed that branches could adopt a resolution akin to the one passed at the Ard-Fheis, and that individual members could use "their position to spread the movement among their associates and their prestige as Gaelic Leaguers to spread it among the general public."[58] MacNeill, who was an antitreater, then asserted that there was a nationalist justification for Irish men and women to oppose the custom: it was not a native practice but an import from Britain. Claiming that "documentary evidence" backed his stance, MacNeill wrote that

> the custom of treating was established in Ireland by the English settlers—and not by the brave Normans, but by the planter hordes who came over in later times. It will therefore be a step in the direction of Irish-Ireland when we succeed to any degree in getting rid of this foreign custom. To accept conquest is bad enough, but what can be meaner than to accept the vices of the conqueror?[59]

His distinction between "brave Normans" and "planter hordes" could be read as a distinction between Catholic and Protestant settlers, thus giving his interpretation a sectarian coloring as well.

Still, as the secretary of the St. Patrick's League pointed out in the last item of public correspondence on this question in December 1902, temperance and total abstinence campaigns drew support across the sectarian divide in Ireland.[60] And the Gaelic revival served as a connecting point between Catholic and nonsectarian organizations at the turn of the century. For example, the antitreaters from Wexford were so interested in appealing to Irish-Irelanders that they followed the advice of "certain prominent members of the Gaelic League" and issued two sets of rules, one for Catholic parochial branches and one for other organizations "who think they can do a good service to Ireland by promoting the anti-treating movement within the range of their influence."[61] Other nonsectarian bodies, such as the Quaker-dominated Dublin Total Abstinence Society (DTAS) and the Irish Association for the Prevention of Intemperance (IAPI), also took part in certain Gaelic League campaigns and functions, such as the annual Language Week procession in Dublin, which is examined in chapter 6.[62] Thus, although it is accurate to discuss the expansion of temperance efforts generally in the context of a Catholic revival, one must also recognize that the opposition of language revivalists to the drink industry lent them caché with Protestants as well as Catholics.

"THE LIMERICK BRANCH HAS SWEPT THE FIELD"

Perhaps no single campaign better illustrates the cross-creed appeal of the Irish-Ireland campaign for public respectability—and the limits of its impact—than the effort of Gaelic Leaguers to make St. Patrick's Day a civic holiday. Although Irish Americans already had celebrated "the national day" for generations, this aspect of what was traditionally a church holiday was a relatively new phenomenon in Ireland. Prior to the twentieth century only two popular practices were associated with 17 March: the wearing of an emblem or symbol (usually a cross or a shamrock), and the public drunkenness known popularly as the "drowning of the shamrock."[63] According to one expert on Irish popular culture, "St. Patrick's Day was the only day during Lent when people were free to eat and drink their fill."[64] And it was this latter custom that prompted the crusade that started in 1902 and emphasized nationality and temperance.

The campaign began in Limerick and mushroomed into a nationwide effort. Fr. Timothy Lee, the president of the Limerick branch, proposed in February 1902 that St. Patrick's Day be treated as a civic holiday.[65] In starting the agitation, Lee declared it a "national disgrace" that foreigners had instituted bank holidays in Ireland while "Irish holidays" went unobserved.[66] Moran observed that Limerick "deserved well of the country" for its St. Patrick's Day efforts:

> We clamor for a Home Rule we have not got, and yet we willingly throw over St. Patrick's Day as a national holiday and adopt some holiday made

in London. There should be a general movement throughout Ireland for the observance of St. Patrick's Day as a lay holiday, and if it is objected that this, with the bank holidays, cuts too much into work, let one of the bank holidays be thrown overboard.[67]

Lee hoped to pressure businesses and especially public houses within the corporate limits of the city to remain closed on 17 March. If a total closure could not be achieved, his secondary goal was for businesses to close early, as they did on Sundays.

Within weeks of his call the Limerick branch had solicited the cooperation of many of the clubs and trade associations in the city. In addition to another League branch (the St. Mary's branch), those pledging their support included the Drapers' Club, the Mechanics' Institute Delegate Board, the Pork Butchers' Society, the Shop Assistants' Union, the Catholic Literary Institute, the Limerick Typographical Society, the Young Ireland Society, the Irish National Foresters, the Oddfellows' Club, the Daughters of Erin, and St. Michael's Temperance Society.[68] Given that the members of these organizations came largely from the same social strata that were often present in League branches, it is likely that the Limerick branch had some overlapping memberships with them. It is also quite probable that the prospect of encouraging a work stoppage led many of these societies to participate in the agitation. But it should not be forgotten that the League had been active in the city for several years before 1902 and was capable of arousing public interest. (In the preceding January, for example, the Limerick branch had hosted two nights of sold-out concerts at the Atheneum Theatre, each of which included propagandist speeches by Lee.)[69] Thus, they brought a sizable popular force to bear on Limerick's business community to recognize St. Patick's Day as a holiday.

The campaign led to a number of early closures but not to a complete shutdown of business. Nevertheless, Moran reveled that "the Limerick branch of the Gaelic League has swept the field."[70] In spite of resistance from the large drapery houses in Limerick, some 90 percent of the smaller shops and at least three of the larger stores agreed to adopt Sunday hours. According to the *Leader*, "only three houses of any note" had not "fallen in line." Moreover, several pubs agreed to close entirely, "and the rest are to close at least as on Sundays."[71] This campaign engendered even more public interest in other League activities. Later in that same year the Limerick branch hosted an open-air concert attended by 6,000 people. During his address to the crowd on that occasion Lee declared that wherever the influence of the League extended, "it made Irishmen more self-reliant, more self-respecting, more thoughtful. It put fire and strength into Irish veins and made new activity throughout the whole country."[72]

In the following year League branches in nearly every county encouraged voluntary St. Patrick's Day closings. And since the national executive had instituted its major fund-raising appeal (the so-called Irish Language Week) to coincide with the week of St. Patrick's Day, Gaelic League parades and entertainments became a staple of the secular activities in many villages and towns. These public festivities never achieved their entire objective when it came to discouraging the drowning of the shamrock. Pubs usually remained open to service the crowds attending parades and speeches (much to the frustration of Irish-Ireland temperance partisans), and those participating in the public observances of the holiday did not always share or understand the convictions of their League sponsors. Thus, in 1903 the St. Patrick's celebration in Cork began with an Irish sermon and a procession organized by the local trade associations. An observer reported to the *Leader* that

> most of those who were "in" the procession were not "of" it, and it didn't appear as if the long army of processionists had any deep, settled conviction to make them hold up their heads like free men or put down the foot *go daingion* [firmly, or with conviction]![73]

The procession ended in a square at Warren's Place, where the crowd heard speeches by League representatives and then passed resolutions that "tended Irish-Irelandwards." Still, according to the report, local publicans disrupted the seriousness of the occasion:

> Bung, being ever solicitous of the corporal wants of his clients, threw open his doors to give drink to the thirsty. It is humiliating to have to admit, now that the people are trying to pull themselves together, that

there was more drunkenness in Cork this past St. Patrick's Day than there was any Patrick's Day for years back.[74]

In spite of such incidents, the League received considerable credit from temperance and abstinence advocates for its St. Patrick's Day campaigns. In February 1904, for instance, the IAPI acknowledged that the Gaelic League had played the primary role in "inducing the voluntary closure" of 425 of the 918 pubs in Dublin in the preceding year. Unlike the Cork example, the IAPI also reported that cases of public drunkenness in Dublin had been more than cut in half in 1903.[75] By 1908 *An Claidheamh Soluis* crowed that "the festival is so firmly established as one of the three or four central events of the year—ranking only behind Christmas and Easter as a day of religious, civic, and social solemnity—that we find it difficult to realize that its institution as a national festival in the true sense is as recent as it is."[76] And in that same year the *Freeman's Journal* anticipated what it termed "the ceremonial observance of St. Patrick's day as a half-holiday" taking place "wherever the Gaelic League is in operation."[77]

"AN AGE OF COMMERCE AND INDUSTRY"

Just as revivalists sought to alleviate social stagnation through promoting safe and sober entertainments, so too they focused considerable attention on what they considered to be the other major cause of emigration—the lack of adequate employment, especially in the Irish-speaking districts. As discussed in chapter 1, craft work and the traditional industries in many inland towns were particularly vulnerable to disruption as the Irish economy became more firmly attached to the British and world economies. The threat posed by international markets led several Irish-Ireland ideologues to discuss the economic implications of the revival. For instance, Hutchinson has identified Moran and Griffith as the two chief articulators of the Irish-Ireland call to revive and support native industry, and he is clearly accurate in seeing their propagandist work as critical to the popularization of the Gaelic revival, especially in the towns.[78] Beginning in 1899 and 1900 respectively, Griffith and Moran provided constant platforms via their newspapers in support of Irish-made goods.

These "Buy Irish" efforts were both offensive and defensive in character. In the first instance both men promoted the work of Irish manufacturers and small businessmen through articles about successful enterprises. Moran also chided Irish manufacturers for not adopting modern advertising techniques, dubbing them "Dark Brothers" for their apparent desire not to make the public aware of their products.[79] At the same time, both men advocated some form of protectionism. Griffith, inspired by the German economist Friedrich List, advocated the erection of tariff walls by a future Irish government to foster native industry, and Moran pressed for voluntary protection, instructing his readers to buy Irish goods only when they were "as good and as cheap" as those of their foreign competitors.[80]

But one should be cautious about distinguishing between the emphasis on town-centered industrial advance in the *Leader* and the *United Irishman* and what Hutchinson describes as the peasant-centered romanticism of other revivalists, including Hyde and MacNeill.[81] Indeed, most Gaelic Leaguers recognized agriculture as the primary industry of Ireland, and in discussions about manufacturing, they focused their attention on smaller industries because they believed that such operations *augmented* a farm-based economy.[82] But even rural advocates such as MacFadden acknowledged that "manufacturing industries on a large scale were required in large cities and towns."[83]

Also, to equate statements that emphasized the "Celtic characteristics" of the Irish people with an inherent aversion to "modern" thinking does not allow for the possibility that there could be more than one path to modernity.[84] MacNeill in particular spoke almost as pointedly to "modern" concerns as did Griffith and Moran, reminding Irish-Irelanders that the twentieth century was "an economic age, an age of commerce and industry."[85] "Irish writers," he continued, "ought to study and write about the economic concerns of Ireland. If they write clearly, thoughtfully, and to the point, they need not have the least fear that people will get tired of them."[86] He recognized, as well, that the Irish language needed to be updated, so that native Irish speakers could discuss the issues and items of their everyday lives:

The absence of current terms for daily needs also weighs heavily on the minds of the native Irish-speaking population and produces a silent prejudice in them against their own language. "Ara, what's the good of it" is not always evidence of a failure to understand the national importance of a national language—does not always betoken servility or want of patriotic spirit. People must talk about the things they think about, and if a lot of these things have not names excepted [sic] between man and man in the native language, people will talk a language that can at least be understood.[87]

Thus, as he told the Central branch of the League in 1905, "Irish, unless it can express Ireland in all her moods, must die; and an effort should at once be made by some of our capable writers to bring the language, as far as material things are concerned, up to date."[88]

Although there can be no question that Moran and Griffith significantly aided in the creation of an "imagined" Irish-Ireland community through the circulation of their newspapers, neither man advocated positions that were particularly original in Irish society or even in Gaelic circles.[89] As Maume has noted, the "producerist" emphasis in their economic writings reflected a preference for small-business owners and the "traditional resistance of the trades to importing goods which could be supplied locally."[90] As seen in chapter 3, both artisans and small-business persons were active in the Gaelic revival from its foundation, and one finds that Gaelic League branches were already discussing economic questions from the small producer's perspective before either journalist founded his paper. As *An Claidheamh Soluis* told its readers in 1899, the Ard-Fheis of that year had endorsed a call for all branches to patronize local industries: "Even little industries which employ only one or two people should be noticed. In this connection we *again* remind our readers of the duty which lies upon them of supporting native manufactures."[91] Then, in a moment of self-promotion that is telling about the sentiments of League members, the paper added, "We appeal to the conductors of such industries to make us their chief advertising medium, for our readers are only too anxious to cooperate in an industrial as well as a language revival."[92]

Gaelic Leaguers offered two main justifications for their intense interest in Irish industries. First, they believed that their work on behalf of the language could not succeed unless native Irish-speakers stopped emigrating. In a leading article in 1901 entitled "Language and Industry," *An Claidheamh Soluis* referred to the continuing net outflow and asked plaintively, "Where, then, are we to find fathers and mothers for our new Irish-speaking generation? The youngest and strongest are going from us. None are left but the old, who will soon be at rest; and the young, who are growing up with no knowledge of their native language. To bring victory to the Gaelic League we must keep our people at home in the Irish-speaking districts and stop the frightful exodus of the best brain and bone in the country."[93] Thus, new opportunities were needed at home to prevent the otherwise inevitable drain of talent abroad.

Second, League activists in the English-speaking districts felt the need to refute the so-called "bread-and-butter" argument against learning Irish, that is, that studying the language would not result in any (material) benefit to the country.[94] In answer, they argued that national revivals elsewhere in Europe had taught them that language and industrial movements inevitably went hand in hand. Such claims would rarely be based upon more than the apparent coincidence of the heightened interest in a local vernacular and expanded trade. But from these unsystematic observations, they constructed a case that stressed the "increased mental agility" one developed through acquiring a second language and the intensification of patriotic sentiment that a native vernacular aroused.[95]

The League perpetuated these supposed links through its own publications and propagandist addresses. In a pamphlet in 1901, for example, Ryan outlined several "lessons" that he had adduced from studying other language revivals, including "the fine material and spiritual energy that results as they advance; the large and heartening opportunities that come forth for native power and talent, once the people, through the illumining [*sic*] and creative force of the language and all that it enshrines, are filled with the ideal of making the most of their land and their place in the onward movement of the world; how industry growing spacious brings social prosperity, and art becoming beautiful gives the nation new distinction; how speedily the language fits itself to modern life."[96] Similarly, Hyde and Dr. J. P. Henry told a crowd of almost 8,000 people meeting at Templeboy, Co. Sligo, that revivals in Wales, Bohemia, Belgium, and Finland "had in each case been followed by an industrial revival."[97] Henry then "appealed to the people to go back to the old tongue, music, customs, and names, and to support their manufactures, and then Ireland would retain her title to be called a nation."[98]

Exhortations to patronize native enterprises became almost as frequent within League branches as calls to speak Irish. In some cases these calls took on a generic quality. For instance, in May 1900 the St. Kevin's branch in Dublin sponsored a lecture about cottage industries at which the speaker pointed out that such operations would benefit small farmers.[99] In the following month in Cork, as Gaelic Leaguers prepared for the upcoming Munster feis, they determined to solicit subscriptions from the local "industrial and commercial class" on the grounds that the "industrial and language movements are so closely allied."[100] And four months later, the Dublin Central branch held a debate about what constituted the proper dress for Irish-Irelanders to wear, and according to the Leader, the only point on which all agreed was that the clothes should be made in Ireland.[101]

At the same time certain branches focused their attention on specific industries in their districts. Thus in Galway in 1901, when the branch president reminded members that they ought "as far as possible" to support Irish manufactures, a Mr. Hunt recommended that his fellow members who smoked tobacco purchase only Irish-made matches, "which would help to increase the match industry in the city."[102] In November 1904 the coiste ceanntair on the Dingle peninsula discussed the hope that fishing companies would hire more native Irish-speakers. Recognizing that "well over a thousand persons in the neighborhood" already worked as commercial fishermen, the committee expressed its hope that fishing companies might be "further developed."[103] Anticipating the annual exodus of young men for America, the chairman suggested that "it would be well to ascertain whether a number of the would-be emigrants were anxious to remain in Ireland if they got employment," so that they could be directed to any potential local employer.[104]

Gradually, the central executive moved to coordinate these disparate efforts. Carrying this sentiment into action, delegates at the Ard-Fheis in 1902 voted to create an industrial subcommittee made up of members of the national executive and outside experts. Among those approached to join were Moran, Griffith, and Fr. T. A. Finlay, S.J., the vice president of the Irish Agricultural Organisation Society (IAOS), which sponsored agricultural cooperatives and cooperative banks throughout the country. The industrial subcommittee first met in July 1902.[105]

For all their good intensions the members of the subcommittee were often frustrated in their efforts. Hence, in their first year of operation they contacted League branches encouraging them to establish local industrial subcommittees. When they asked branch secretaries to forward the names of subcommittee members, however, they received almost no information in return.[106] The members at Ballinasloe, we have seen, did form a subcommittee, and they were not a singular case, but the lack of response to the national subcommittee suggests that they were exceptional. Similarly, the Ard-Fheis of 1903 directed the industrial subcommittee to establish an "employment bureau" for Irish-speakers through the pages of the League newspaper. Almost immediately after the congress, subcommittee members wrote to manufacturers to see who would be willing to hire workers with the facility to speak Irish. In the first month after they made their appeal, only one company—a farm implements maker in Wexford—had responded.[107] The employment-bureau column did appear for a few months in *An Claidheamh Soluis,* beginning in August 1903, but it never publicized a significant number of places.[108]

"WE ARE DOING THIS PURELY ON COMMERCIAL GROUNDS"

Gaelic enthusiasts did, nevertheless, make tangible contributions toward invigorating Irish industry. Among the most important were several attempts to found manufacturing concerns in localities around the country. Often these enterprises were quixotic, reflecting enthusiasm rather than business acumen. For instance, one of the more prominent Gaelic Leaguers was John P. Boland, the Oxford-educated heir to the Boland's Bakery and Mills in Dublin. After being elected to parliament to represent south Kerry in 1900, he and his family rented Daniel O'Connell's ancestral home at Derrynane, so that Boland could be closer to his constituents when not in London.[109] A frequent visitor to League branches in the area, he helped to organize one of the first industrial exhibitions at the provincial festival at Glenbeigh in 1903, and he contributed articles to *An Claidheamh Soluis* promoting manufacturers in County Kerry.[110] Boland also invested considerable sums of his own money in founding several unprofitable businesses. At one point he attempted to establish a timber operation by planting sapplings at Derrynane, but as his daughter Bridget recalled, the soil proved too shallow and "goats ate the tops off his new plantations."[111] On another occasion he hoped to set up a lace-making cottage industry to supply orders for well-to-do acquaintances in London. By the time that he had "collected boxes and chests and crates of Irish lace of every kind," it was no longer in fashion, and no one purchased his product. According to his daughter, "We ended up with enough to dress a nation in our own London attics. My mother edged everything she could think of with it, and we certainly had very wonderful tablecloths, but cottage industry there was none."[112]

Elsewhere, however, revivalists were somewhat more successful. In Galway, for example, Fr. Peter Dooley spearheaded the establishment of the Galway Woollen Industry, which according to *An Claidheamh Soluis* was conducted on Irish-Ireland lines: "The hereditary skill of Galway women in spinning and weaving is made use of and encouraged; traditional patterns are reproduced; native wool used almost exclusively; the soap is Irish-made, as are the dyes as far as possible."[113] After less than eight years in operation Galway Woollens employed almost eighty workers and had seen its original stock value increase by 50 percent.[114]

Meanwhile, Andrew O'Shaughnessy, a creamery owner from Newmarket, purchased the out-of-date woollen mill at Dripsey, Co. Cork, and refitted it with modern machinery. O'Shaughnessy then brought in Liam Cronin, a Gaelic Leaguer who had previously been active in County Meath and Cork city, to serve as manager of his plant.[115] Two things made the Dripsey Woollen Mills important symbolically for Irish-Irelanders. First, O'Shaughnessy and Cronin determined to hire only workers who understood Gaelic.[116] In a letter to national school teachers in County Cork they explained:

> We are doing this purely on commercial grounds. Irish correspondence is now very general, and we receive and dispatch daily several letters

entirely or partly in Irish. Irish will not be confined to the offices. This will cause a general use of Irish in mill tickets, mill books, parcel tickets, etc., making it necessary for our employees in every department to read and write the language. We are determined to keep in the first rank of the industrial movement.[117]

This final point was equally important for revivalists, and in its first several years of operation the Dripsey Mills prospered. According to a report from the *Irish Peasant* in 1906, "Every cottage within a radius of two miles of the woollen mills is tenanted by active mill employees," and the wages for weavers had increased by 33 percent in "a comparatively short period."[118]

A still larger operation opened in April 1906. The Kilkenny Woollen Mills was the brainchild of Captain Otway Cuffe, the local president of the League and a prominent unionist. An article previewing the work noted that Cuffe drew upon the local "historical associations which give the project a peculiar interest": as recently as the 1840s, the Kilkenny region had had a thriving woollen industry with more than 4,000 hands employed at twenty-one different mills.[119] Before proceeding, he enlisted the support of his fellow Leaguers and other townspeople. A particularly attractive feature of the project was that it would include profit-sharing and pensions for the workers.[120] Using £15,000 raised through the sale of stock to 560 shareholders (including many working people from the city), Cuffe then purchased and refitted an abandoned mill at Greenvale, about a mile and a half from the Kilkenny town center.[121] When the works opened formally on 16 April 1906, the guests of honor were James Bryce, the chief secretary of Ireland, Stephen Gwynn, representing the Coiste Gnótha, and the earl and countess of Desart, Cuffe's brother and sister-in-law.[122]

Throughout the public speeches on that day the League received ample credit for its role in inspiring the project. Cuffe told the audience that "the enterprise was the outcome of the Gaelic League movement and the industrial movement." "Let others learn the same lesson of self-reliance that they had learned in Kilkenny," he concluded, "and then the future of Ireland would be secure."[123] Another local League officer, T. W.

O'Hanrahan, noted that "almost all the directors of the company were members of the Gaelic League."[124] And when Lady Desart started the machinery to open the mill formally, she offered a blessing in Irish: "Go mbuanniughid Dia gach aoinne agus gach aon rud a baineann less [*sic*] an muileann seo" ["May God prosper every person and every thing connected with this mill."][125] Until the 1940s, when a flood damaged the mill and destroyed a bridge connecting the workers' quarters to the factory, the Kilkenny Woollen Mills continued to operate.

Gaelic Leaguers were instrumental in another context in placing Irish manufactures quite literally before the public: they participated in the foundation of the Irish Industrial Development Association (IIDA).[126] The inaugural meeting of the IIDA took place in November 1905 in Cork, where two years earlier a group of young republican nationalists, one of whom was the secretary of the Cork *coiste ceanntair* of the League, had organized the first local Industrial Development Association on the island.[127] Their idea had been to promote industry in Cork by drawing together any interested members of the public regardless of their political affiliation. Members of the IIDA pledged to buy Irish-made goods whenever possible; they gathered data on local industries and natural resources; they approached shopkeepers about carrying Irish-made products in their stores and displaying them prominently in their windows; and they sponsored exhibitions of locally produced goods.[128] The Cork endeavor inspired the formation of similar committees in Dublin, Galway, Limerick, Belfast, and Derry as well as in smaller towns across Ireland. According to the *Irish Independent* in 1905, many of these local industrial associations were outgrowths of existing Gaelic League industrial subcommittees.[129] In fact, the Dublin *coiste ceanntair* had called the meeting at which the IIDA constituted itself in Dublin, and the president of the League in Galway led the effort to found the IIDA in that city.[130]

When representatives from these local committees met at Cork in November 1905, their most significant action was to take the initial steps toward creating an Irish national trademark, the first of its kind in the world.[131] At the center of the effort were League enthusiasts, such as Cuffe, Horgan, and Boland. Cuffe recommended that the trademark bear a Gaelic inscription, and over the course of the next several months a committee of the IIDA considered several potential designs.[132] Ultimately, they decided on a circular emblem bearing the motto *Déanta i hÉireann*, which translates simply as "Made in Ireland." Meanwhile, Horgan and Boland worked with the Board of Trade in London to register the trademark as the property of the IIDA, which began to issue licenses to use it on 1 January 1907.[133] Only companies that could authenticate that their products had been made by Irish workers were eligible for a license, and by 1920 more than 700 Irish manufacturers had received them.[134]

In general, the IIDA drew support from nationalists in southern Ireland, and Maume has remarked that most members of the association were small and medium-sized business owners (like Andrew O'Shaughnessy of the Dripsey Woollen Mills).[135] It is noteworthy, however, that the IIDA attracted the interest of a corps of liberal unionist landlords, including Lord Dunraven and Captain John Shawe-Taylor.[136] Moreover, at least some northerners were impressed by the efforts of the association: Lord Pirrie, owner of the great Harland and Wolff shipyards in Belfast, sent sympathetic apologies for not attending the IIDA conference at Galway in 1908, and the Belfast IDA hosted the 1909 conference.[137] Even the loyalist *Belfast News-Letter* declared that "the industrial revival is a fact, though much remains to be done, and the Industrial Devlopment Association is helping to do it. . . . An association which is striving to increase the material prosperity of Ireland may fairly appeal to the patriotism of the public to support it."[138]

Hence, the bulk of League industrial work in urban Ireland resulted from the interest and involvement of middle-class supporters. Nevertheless it is possible that at least some of the support for the language movement among lower-middle-class and working-class men and women arose because of the calls by Gaelic Leaguers to support home industries. Craft workers, who were threatened by factory-made goods and international competition, responded positively to the economic dimension of the Irish-Ireland movement. Thus one finds that a speaker at the Wellington Quay Workingmen's Club in Dublin, the home of one of the largest League branches in the city, adopted a Moranite line of reasoning in an address in 1903 entitled "Our Attitude Toward Our Irish Industries: A Plea for Voluntary Protection."[139] M. D. Clare appealled to "his countrymen to support their home products by purchasing all they possibly could of Irish manufacture and thus, by creating a larger industrial area, stay the tide of emigration that was rapidly depopulating the country."[140] Similarly, flour mill workers at Ringsend—employees of the firm owned by the Boland family—issued statements supporting the Irish industrial movement in 1903.[141] And as we have seen, when the League established a branch in the neighborhood in the following year, the members believed that it would "ameliorate" industrial conditions in this poor area of Dublin. Even leaders of the nascent Irish Labour Party, such as Thomas Johnson and William O'Brien, and socialist organizers, such as Seamus Hughes and James Larkin, joined League branches or supported the language revival. To be sure, their reading of the links between the language movement and industry were far from the norm in Gaelic circles. When Hughes proposed moving the League headquarters to Galway and establishing cooperative industries in the Irish-speaking districts rather than concentrating on a "purely scholastic program," *An Claidheamh Soluis* refused to publish his views. (Griffith, to his credit, published several pieces from Hughes.)[142] Some of the bitterness expressed in later years by O'Casey toward certain revivalists may in fact be rooted in the way that liberal, middle-class Leaguers marginalized these divergent views.[143] But what is interesting in the present context is that they were expressed or entertained at all.

"THE SAVING OF COUNTRY LIFE"

It would, moreover, be incorrect to claim that all Gaelic Leaguers focused their "industrial energies" on Irish manufactures, for they considered agriculture to be the primary industry in Ireland. Indeed, some speakers at the annual conferences of the IIDA made similar statements.[144] To be sure, many revivalists showed little more than a romanticized "big house" appreciation for the difficult living conditions in rural Ireland. But alongside these starry-eyed romantics were others who were aware of conditions in the countryside and who believed that improving them through agricultural "industry" was part of their revivalist mission.

From its first year in print, for instance, *An Claidheamh Soluis* carried stories about rural life that included columns about the plight of small farmers. Ranging from reports about the impact of bad weather on crops to statistical breakdowns of the uneven distribution of landholdings in County Mayo, these records showed a decided sympathy for small tillage farmers as opposed to the politically powerful grazing interests.[145] For instance, shortly after William O'Brien launched the United Irish League in 1898, his work to aid small farmers received favorable treatment in the Gaelic League weekly.[146] And in 1905, in a two-part article on the "Possibilities of Irish Industry," MacGinley argued that the most important things that could be done to improve the Irish economy were the full establishment of peasant proprietorship, the "replanting of the people on the grazing ranches, and the stimulation of tillage."[147] One also finds colorful accounts of cattle and horse fairs both in the Irish-language columns and in the published reports of *timirí*, who paid careful attention to the use of Irish in commercial exchanges in the villages and towns.[148]

Furthermore, as three brief examples from County Kerry indicate, language enthusiasts on the ground often mixed Gaelic propaganda with the pragmatic concerns of farmers. Thus in December 1905, when the League branch at Ardfert held a meeting to discuss the industrial revival, the chairman pointed out the illogical position of local pig farmers, who were "foolishly selling their bacon at 3d. or 4d. a pound and buying American or Russian bacon for their own use at 7d. a pound."[149] Meanwhile, that same year the technical committee of the Kerry County Council had hired Eibhlín Ní Dhuaghaill to serve as an itinerant dairy instructress. A convinced Gaelic Leaguer and the sister of popular revivalist author J. J. Doyle (*"Beirt Fhear"*), she reportedly peppered her lectures about the proper care and feeding of animals with Irish-Ireland appeals.[150] Most dramatically, in August 1903 the constabulary at Cloghane had witnessed *timire* Fíonán MacColuim promoting the first Dingle feis alongside Thomas O'Donnell, the member of parliament for west Kerry. Both men spoke in Irish about supporting the language campaign, but, according to the Royal Irish Constabulary, O'Donnell did so only after instructing the audience to form tenant committees that would settle all property sales with their landlords as a united body under the newly passed Wyndham Land Act.[151]

Further, many Gaelic Leaguers lived in the poorer parts of rural Ireland, and at least some of them worked to ameliorate their own situation through links with the cooperative movement. Spearheaded by the IAOS and following a self-help doctrine outlined by Sir Horace Plunkett, the cooperative movement attempted to "regenerate" Irish farmers materially and morally.[152] As we have seen, certain polemicist revivalists (O'Riordan and Moran among them) objected to Plunkett's *Ireland in the New Century* in 1904, but in practice Gaelic Leaguers and cooperators developed working partnerships throughout the period under review.[153] Fr. T. A. Finlay, the vice president of the IAOS, became a member of the industrial subcommittee of the League executive in 1902, and he was a frequent speaker on economic subjects at branch meetings, particularly in the north.[154] Hyde, meanwhile, was a proponent of cooperative banks run on the Raiffeisen system, and in 1900 he wrote a multi-part series in Irish for *An Claidheamh Soluis* explaining the benefits of these unlimited-liability enterprises for the people of the congested districts.[155] Several months later, the IAOS collected the articles into a pamphlet and distributed it at organizational meetings throughout the west of Ireland.[156] Periodically the League paper ran similar, if shorter commentaries lauding cooperative operations, such as stores, cottage industries, and banks for the Irish-speaking districts.[157] "The Irish Agricultural Organisation Society has set before itself the saving of country life," Pearse concluded in one such update. "And we look to it for assistance in the saving of the Gaeltacht."[158]

More important, numerous rural communities also looked at the two organizations as practical complements to each other. For instance, the president of the IAOS, Lord Monteagle, stated in his annual report in 1902 that Gaelic classes and ceilidhs were increasingly taking place in cooperative halls.[159] In his own neighborhood of Foynes, Co. Limerick, Monteagle had established a poultry society, built a clubhouse for his tenants, and erected a village library, while his daughter, the Gaelic enthusiast Mary Spring Rice, set up a Gaelic League branch that utilized the clubhouse. Together, they sponsored joint exhibitions of farm produce and local manufactures.[160] In counties Monaghan, Fermanagh, and Tyrone, Paul-Dubois observed that the establishment of League branches alongside cooperatives had lessened "the melancholy of country life by improving the condition of the cottage and by establishing libraries, classes, and lectures."[161] And in 1905 Synge noted a similar impact at Gweesalia, Co. Mayo, where he credited the League branch and a Raiffeisen bank with slowing emigration temporarily.[162]

Perhaps the most extensive crossover between the language and cooperative movements occurred in County Tyrone, first in the parish of Dromore and then in the parish of Kilskeery, where we have seen that Fr. Matthew Maguire was the key figure. In addition to managing several of the national schools and founding night schools for adults, he established the profitable lace-making enterprise known as St. Macartan's Home Industries Society.[163] In addition to reading, writing, arithmetic, and Irish and English history, local girls and young women also studied "domestic science," and the boys and young men took courses in horticulture. As part of their study, they planted and manured gardens next to the schools. In order to have these subjects taught, Maguire applied to the IAOS for aid. Through the personal financial assistance of Plunkett, Charlotte O'Conor-Eccles, an expert on cooperative movements in Europe, oversaw the domestic-economy classes and a program of home visitations in and around Dromore.[164] And in Kilskeery, according to a report from the *Leader*, the horticultural instructor not only taught in the schools but "gave advice to anyone who wanted it in the parish, and to a considerable extent his services were availed of."[165] Additionally, Maguire introduced regular ceilidhs and an enormous annual feis into the social life of both parishes. At Kilskeery he even hired prizewinning dancers to teach the language and dance classes.[166] Through it all the Irish-Ireland priest maintained that the language was "the soul of the whole scheme."[167]

Maguire was a devoted worker on behalf of the League, a man who served on the Coiste Gnótha for a number of years and whose work in County Tyrone was lauded as exemplary in Irish-Ireland circles.[168] In retrospect he was exemplary also because he encouraged the people of Dromore and Kilskeery to apply themselves to work far removed from the study of Irish. If Gaelic was "the soul" of his body of work, then the flesh and bone were made of lace, white-washed walls, and well-turned gardens.

CONCLUSION

In branches all across Ireland, Gaelic Leaguers shared similar pragmatic hopes, expressed in redemptive phrases but bearing little direct relationship to their ostensible goal of preserving Irish as a spoken language. Instead, they emphasized simple amusements, temperance, industrial development, and cooperation in addition to, or in lieu of, language study. Thus, as one Kerry activist told his branch in 1904, the language question was just the "immediate object" of the League, and it was "really but the paving of the way to its ultimate destination. The Gaelic League has for its ultimate and real aim the spiritual, material, and commercial freedom of our nation."[169]

5

The Grand Opportunity

Festivals and the Gaelic Revival

The weakness of our organization lies in our failure or partial failure to reach those who are not members of the Gaelic League. Public opinion is the lever by which we force matters forward. The stronger we make that opinion, the easier will be our work to perform.[1]

W hen Gaelic Leaguers moved out of their quiet season of branch activity to propagate their messages, they did so through public celebrations that presented the language as vital in itself and as vitalizing to the nation. Specialists in popular culture have studied communal celebrations as sites in which people construct and reconfigure images of the existing social order; thus, their insights are especially useful for understanding the way in which the assimilative process worked during the revival era. Manning, for example, has argued that the interplay between these images lends celebrations their special "piquancy and power" for both participants and spectators. Meanwhile, Turner has observed that people associate the cultural products of celebrations with the emotions and impressions they experienced during the events and that, over time, they invest these products with special meanings.[2]

There were two main types of League celebrations, feiseanna and processions, the latter of which will be the focus of chapter 6. The former included small local festivals and larger regional functions, and the feis season culminated in the national Oireachtas that brought together competitors from all parts of Ireland. Processions occurred in towns and cities throughout the island as well, but the most important one took place annually in Dublin. Beginning as a local affair, it grew to be the largest single event sponsored by the League, drawing national participation and press coverage and serving as a platform for various League causes. Those organizing the celebrations consciously highlighted the aims and achievements of the revival, and they involved people who were not active revivalists in an effort to entertain and enlighten their communities. Thus an examination of these events offers a unique perspective on the way that Gaelic Leaguers utilized existing symbols and media to a create an intensive culture that was both recognizable and appealing to the general public.

"RALLY THE IRISH NATION": THE FIRST OIREACHTAS

Prior to the founding of the Gaelic League, language enthusiasts such as Bourke and O'Growney wrote enviously about the popular (and elite) interest in the Welsh musical and literary festival, the Eisteddfod.[3] Not surprisingly, when representatives from the earliest League branches met in 1896 to discuss further coordinating their activities, they resolved to found a literary festival modeled after the Welsh event.[4] In announcing their project for 17 May 1897, the executive committee recognized that its fledgling organization did not yet possess the resources or members to "inaugurate any large or ambitious undertaking."[5] Indeed, they were so uncertain about the response to this initiative that they planned only one day of competitions, and they scheduled it to coincide with the opening of the Feis Ceoil, a four-day-long musical fete started in the preceding year by Gaelic sympathizers who had not included language events on their program.[6] Still, the executive hoped that the two occasions would complement one another and that "the large number of visitors" expected at the Feis Ceoil would also attend the literary function. Committee members played down expectations for their inaugural effort, though they intended to make the new festival an annual fixture, that they hoped would have a lasting impact on their fledgling movement. "The Oireachtas will," they pronounced hopefully,

> fix universal public attention on the Irish language movement; it will help in obliterating the dialectical differences and in fixing the literary

standard; it will make for the creation of a modern Irish literature; it will encourage and be a bond of union to all workers in the revival of Irish; and finally, it will rally the Irish nation for the maintenance of the national tongue.[7]

The first Oireachtas was indeed a fairly small affair, receiving only 103 submissions to its nine competitions.[8] Two-thirds of the entries (69 of the 103) were in just four essay competitions, and fully half of these (34 of the 103) came in a contest allowing submissions in Irish or in English.[9] This modest output reflected the limited impact that the revival had had in the four years since the foundation of the League—there were, after all, only forty-three League branches established as of 1897.[10] The profile of the competitors, so far as can be determined, suggests that they were representative of the early League membership as outlined in chapter 3. Only a third of the submissions (34) came from persons residing in counties with substantial Irish-speaking districts,[11] whereas a larger portion of the entries came from major urban areas—43 from Dublin, Belfast, or Cork. The *Gaelic Journal* was careful to point out that all addresses were merely the competitors' "present place of abode," suggesting that some were migrants to the cities. And among the prizewinners one finds Diarmuid Ó Foghludha and Pádraig Ó Séaghdha, both of whom were native-speaking civil servants from County Kerry who lived in Belfast at the time.[12] Six of the entries came from Maynooth, a sign of the early impact that O'Growney's pioneer efforts and O'Hickey's then-recent appointment were having within the college. (At least two of these entries came from a single student, John J. Hynes, who was "highly commended" in the essay and recitation competitions. Another Maynooth student, William Byrne, was also "highly commended" in the same essay competition.) Among the twenty individuals who won prizes or commendations for their entries, two were women—the poet and journalist Alice Milligan and the incoming secretary of the League Norma Borthwick.[13]

Apart from its lackluster number of entries, however, the first Oireachtas must be viewed as a success on two counts. First, the public face of the event was a decided triumph. Nearly 1,200 people attended the gala awards concert in the largest hall in Dublin, the Round Room of the Rotunda.[14]

City Councilor J. J. O'Meara presided, standing in for the lord mayor, who had taken ill, and among those seated on the platform were leaders of the League—such as Hyde, MacNeill, and Dr. Boyd of Belfast—as well as prominent public men, including the high sheriff of Dublin and Timothy Harrington, M.P. In a gesture of Celtic fraternity, T. H. Thomas, the Herald Bard of Wales, attended as well and brought greetings from the Eisteddfod. Over the course of the evening Hyde presented a specially composed ode on the Oireachtas as well as an address in Irish about the language movement, and the newly crowned champions recited their prizewinning essays, poems, and stories. Harpists and pipers further entertained the crowd with selections of Irish airs, and a vocal soloist accompanied by a specially selected choir debuted the prizewinning "rallying song" of the Gaelic League, "Go Mairidh ár nGaedhilg Slán."

Press opinions across the political spectrum were generally positive about the event. The nationalist *Irish Daily Independent* concluded that it had been "from every point of view a marked success," an opinion echoed virtually word for word by the unionist *Irish Times*. The *Freeman's Journal*, meanwhile, noted that the crowd consisted mainly of students and scholars of the language, who were "representative not merely of the district in which the meeting was held, but of all parts of Ireland—not only of the four provinces but of nearly all the counties. In that sense it was a great and important gathering, consisting of many elements likely to impress the people with the importance of acquiring a knowledge of the Gaelic language, or improving their acquaintance with it where they already speak it." The conservative *Daily Express* also referred to the student character of the audience in a backhanded fashion: "The songs and recitals in the vernacular proved most congenial to those who understood them, and interesting to those who know not what the words conveyed." Still, the *Express* heartily approved of the musical selections and declared that the entire "program was of a pleasing and novel character." The laborite *Irish Worker* congratulated the Gaelic League "on the eminently successful issue of their patriotic undertaking." "Such festivals," the *Worker* concluded, "will tend to stimulate thought and ultimately to wipe out the West British prejudices that have so long militated against the use of Irish as the language of the people." A London liberal weekly, the *Speaker*, reported that "the vitality of the Celtic temperament, as shown by the new movement in Ireland, is a phenomenon of far more than passing import." And the nationalist *Cork Examiner* called it "a marked development of the literary and musical spirit of nationalism now abroad."[15]

Not surprisingly, the most rapturous review came in the *Gaelic Journal* itself. After decrying the "retreat" of native culture during the eighteenth and nineteenth centuries, MacNeill claimed that the Oireachtas was an augury of better things to come:

> The significance of the celebrations that began on the 17th May lies in the fact that this national culture is brought back from its distant retreats and enthroned in the administrative centre of the nation. Let us hope that it is to enjoy no mere puppet-sovereignty. Such a reign would not last long. It is not what the people who supported the national festivals desire. The promoters of these festivals have a great opportunity. Let them not fail to realize it. Thoughtful onlookers have seen in these events the beginning of a new and honorable national life for Ireland. How great in after-days will be the honor of those who take an effective part in this regeneration![16]

The second reason why the initial Oireachtas must be seen as a success is that it became a model for the subsequent national and local festivals that have continued into the twenty-first century. As Ryan wrote later, the Oireachtas "brought a new 'note' into Irish life."[17] In the next few years the number of entries submitted to the national festival multiplied; for example, in 1901 the Oireachtas received more than 430 submissions.[18] Meanwhile, the first League-sponsored provincial festival occurred in March 1898 at Macroom, Co. Cork, and it included recitation, poetry, and musical competitions. *Fáinne an Lae* called the event a "rising," an evocative—if unconsciously humorous—description, since Macroom was one of the few locations at which members of the Fenian Brotherhood took up arms during the farcical insurrection of 1867.[19] In its glowing report on the Macroom feis, the *Cork Examiner* declared that "such a demonstration of the living potent strength of the Irish language was not witnessed in the south of Ireland for centuries, and with the exception of the Oireachtas in Dublin last year, it is doubtful if it was equaled in all Ireland in this or the preceding century."[20] In subsequent months, League branches sponsored "local festivals of the same nature as the Oireachtas" at Ballingeary and Ballyvourney in County Cork, and in the counties of Donegal, Monaghan, and Galway. Also, at the Feis Ceoil held in Belfast in May of that year, the local Gaelic League organized the entertainment for the last evening, "consisting of music, dances and *tableaux vivants*" portraying various scenes from Irish history.[21]

"WHAT ABOUT THE SPREAD OF THE LANGUAGE?"

After the turn of the century a regular series of festivals developed, starting in Wexford at Whitsuntide and continuing into September. It was not unusual for dozens of these functions to take place each summer: in 1907, for instance, the central Oireachtas committee sanctioned fifty-six local festivals.[22] Sometimes, six or more feiseanna occurred on the same weekend in different parts of the country, which entailed a great deal of coordination in order to assure adequate staffing.

Festivals linked local branches to the central executive in three very specific ways. First, national figures frequently served as judges and speakers at provincial affairs. League district councils and feis planners courted individuals like MacNeill to attend literally dozens of these functions.[23] Often those officers with strong ties to a region worked at festivals in their part of the country. Thus, O'Hickey, who was a priest of the diocese of Waterford and Lismore, attended festivals at Ardmore, Modeligo, and Dungarvan in 1899, and in 1901 he adjudicated four of the five major categories of competitions at the Feis na n-Deisi in Dungarvan.[24] Similarly, Ua Laoghaire, who lived in Castlelyons, Co. Cork, played a leading role in the Munster feis (Feis na Mumhan) as well as at smaller festivals, such as the one in Fermoy.[25]

Second, the Oireachtas brought provincial figures into the national spotlight. This worked on two levels. Administratively, the League scheduled its annual Ard-Fheis to coincide with the national festival, starting with the second Oireachtas in 1898. Thus, local representatives came together to decide on League policy amid the round of competitions and entertainments during the week. Further, the Oireachtas provided a showcase for provincial talent in its many competitions and for provincial activists who delivered odes and orations at the annual grand concert.[26] The Ard-Fheis tried to institutionalize this organic process by instituting graduated competitions in 1903, instructing the Oireachtas committee of the Coiste Gnótha to establish a schedule of contests in which local win-ners would compete in the same event at the next Oireachtas.[27] In practice the committee was to inspect and approve the entire program of the local festival in order for the winners of the specified competitions to qualify for the national event. When all such qualifications were met, the Oireach-tas committee provided local winners with travel expenses for the trip to Dublin and 10s. toward their upkeep during the week.[28]

The final way in which festivals drew local Leaguers closer to the national orbit related directly to this oversight function. Put simply, when festivals proliferated after 1900, the central body assumed greater control over local programs.[29] Three factors made this process necessary. First, with the number of festivals multiplying, scheduling became an issue. Because local organizers usually limited competitions to residents from the host county and perhaps a few neighboring counties, the number of competitors and the size of the audiences suffered when too many events took place on the same weekend in the same region.[30] Similarly, because feis planners called on national figures to serve as judges at their func-tions, there had to be some attempt to limit the number of events taking place on a single day in order to ensure adequate staffing. Thus, at the Ard-Fheis in 1903, delegates approved a resolution submitted by the Fer-moy activist Pádraig Mac Suibhne that "the dates of local feiseanna be fixed after consultation with the organization committee."[31] National of-ficials vigilantly watched over the activities of local committees to prevent conflicts and contacted them whenever troublesome overlaps appeared.[32] Securing judges remained problematic, however, leading some commit-tees to rely on willing students of the language, such as the Dubliner Seán T. Ó Ceallaigh, to adjudicate.[33] In a particularly forthright passage about the Dunmanway festival of 1908, Ó Ceallaigh acknowledged the difficulty of fulfilling his duties as a judge in the junior recitation competitions, and he outlined the test of stamina experienced by all judges regardless of their facility with Gaelic:

D'éist mé le paidreacha Gaeilge i rith an lae agus nuair a bhí gach páiste cloiste agam ba dheacair dom a dhéanamh amach cén duine ab fhearr orthu. Bhí orm ansin comórtas eile de mé chuid féin a chur ar siúl—ceisteanna a chur orthu i dtaobh a saoil, sa scoil agus sa bhaile, agus ansin m'aigne a dhéanamh suas faoin mbuachaill nó an cailín ar a mbronnfainn an duais. Geallaim duit go raibh an-áthas orm nuair a bhí Feis Dhún Maonmhaighe thart.

[I listened to the Irish prayers throughout the day, and when I had heard every child, it was hard for me to make out which person had been the best. Then there was another competition underway in which I took part—asking questions about their life, in school and at home, and then deciding upon which boy or girl to award the prize. I promise you that I was very happy when Feis Dunmanway was over.][34]

The second factor that facilitated the centralization process resulted from a modest apparent success of the movement, as it was becoming more common for organizations not affiliated with the revival to advertise an upcoming entertainment as a "feis." In April 1905 the executive committee of the League passed a resolution protesting against the use of the word "in connection with gatherings promoted in the interests of objects other than the propagation of the Irish language."[35] In its report about the resolution *An Claidheamh Soluis* acknowledged that the League had "no patent on the word, of course," and that the organization had "no means of preventing the use of the word by external bodies." It even stated that some non-League feiseanna had been helpful to the language movement; nonetheless, the paper called on branches and individual Leaguers not to patronize those feiseanna that aimed at promoting other causes and to make the Oireachtas committee aware of similar "unsanctioned" attempts to use the word.[36]

The issue festered throughout 1905 and came to a head at the national congress in 1906. Members of the Coiste Gnótha had been concerned enough about the issue that they passed another resolution in December 1905 seeking to disqualify individuals who had competed in "bogus" feiseanna from participating in licensed festivals for a period of three years.[37] Matters heated up the following June after the parish priest of Portarlington set up the unsanctioned "Bishopswood feis," discussed in chapter 2. At the national congress in August 1906, the O'More branch of Portarlington submitted a proposal "to include in the rules of the Gaelic League the resolution of the Coiste Gnótha of December 1905 in re [*sic*] the prevention of bogus feiseanna."[38] Pádraig Lynch—the Monasterevan supporter of the clerical faction in Portarlington—offered an amendment that would have tabled the O'More proposal for a year, but the congress rejected it and passed the original motion intact.[39] Immediately thereafter Fr. Lorcan O'Kieran from County Monaghan proposed a more specific amendment to the League rules vis-à-vis the sanctioning of feiseanna:

> To obviate all difficulty the Oireachtas committee recommend that they be empowered to issue a license for the holding of the feis, or any event in the nature of a feis, and a small fee (2s. 6d.) be charged for the authorization, and that any person competing at a feis not so authorized shall be ineligible to compete at any Gaelic League gathering for a period of three years.[40]

The Ard-Fheis adopted O'Kieran's proposal, with the only dissenter being Dinneen (who had also been the lone supporter of Lynch's earlier failed amendment). An uneasy truce between the two sides seems to have been reached, however, when the Dublin priest Fr. F. MacEnerney offered a motion reaffirming the organization's commitment to nonsectarianism and adding "as a corollary that any branch or individual initiating or sanctioning any violation of this principle in the Gaelic League is acting *ultra vires*."[41] Dinneen and MacGinley—the leader of the O'Mores—jointly seconded the motion, which passed by an overwhelming majority.[42]

MacEnerney's resolution points to the third critical factor motivating the central executive to assume greater control over provincial festivals: it was apparent that even "sanctioned" feiseanna did not always project the inclusive Gaelicism espoused by the leaders of the movement. For example, several festivals violated the "self-denying ordinances" of the League by instituting competitions in which only Catholics could participate in good conscience. Typically, these contests required children to answer questions about simple texts that were a part of the approved national-schools program and then to recite Catholic prayers in Irish (as at the Dunmanway feis at which Ó Ceallaigh adjudicated).[43] At the Feis na Mumhan in 1907 several competitions even required entrants to demonstrate familiarity with the Catholic catechism prepared by Ua Laoghaire in Irish.[44]

Equally troubling, some argued, the early festivals did not pay enough attention to the language—the ostensible reason for the existence of the League. In the summer of 1903 a correspondent to *An Claidheamh Soluis* tried to draw feis planners back to first principles. Citing "various feis programs" as evidence, P. J. O'Sullivan protested that "the Irish language is not at all being catered for as it should. Too much prominence is given to dancing and singing as compared with what the language gets. It is high time the case were reversed, otherwise Irish is doomed."[45] "We hear a great deal about the spread of the Gaelic League," he concluded, "but what about the spread of the language? The spread of the Gaelic League, it should be steadily borne in mind, does not always mean the spread of the Gaelic tongue. The sooner Gaelic Leaguers recognize this fact, the better for the safety of the Irish language."[46] Later in that same year, another portentous letter appeared from the League organizer for County Waterford, Pádraig Ó Cadhla.[47] After visiting several festivals, he and his superior MacColuim had concluded that "as a propagandist factor, the utility of feiseanna cannot be denied. But from the language point of view it is a question whether the feiseanna of the last year have given sufficient return for the amount of money expended on them."[48] The two *timirí* had drawn up a specimen program, which included forty-one competitions, more than half of which could be considered "language friendly": sixteen of them required speaking or writing in Irish and six others involved singing in the traditional *sean-nós* style.[49]

In 1907, the Oireachtas committee proposed new requirements for licensing festivals to address this ongoing concern. According to their report, the committee felt that festival planners allowed too many song and essay competitions in English. Furthermore, "where Catholic prayers are specified" in competitions, feis planners usually failed to "make provision for those of other creeds."[50] Significantly, the local delegates who attended the 1907 Ard-Fheis approved the proposed changes. Nevertheless, as we will see below, some festivals continued to submit programs that violated the terms of the Oireachtas committee.[51]

"FULL OF HOPE FOR THE FUTURE"

Although individual feiseanna developed their own unique characteristics, an examination of more than two dozen feis programs suggests that the efforts of the central executive to coordinate festival planning did bear some fruit.[52] Lasting anywhere from one day to a full week, most feiseanna followed the same basic format. During the day students from the host district and adult members of local branches competed for small monetary prizes or books; at night host committees sponsored concerts known as *aeríochtaí* or *scoruigheachtaí*.[53] At these spirited sessions, branch members or students from area schools typically performed short plays and musical numbers alongside local enthusiasts and nationally known Irish-Irelanders, who delivered addresses designed to stir up support for the movement.[54]

Such gatherings inspired the League faithful and gave them a sense that they and their neighbors were connected to something larger than themselves. In 1899, *An Claidheamh Soluis* compared the ancient festivals of Ireland with those of Greece and asserted that "common festivals have ever been a tie between individuals of a race."[55] Now, the paper said, "the ancient assemblies are revived in the Oireachtas. The festival is the rallying point of the movement. It affords a centre for the thought of all Irish-Ireland. It makes for social as well as for linguistic and literary unity."[56] Ryan later observed that it was difficult to recall whether the intellectual or the social side of Oireachtas week had been more appealing. "It was," he concluded, "wonderfully human and humanizing at any rate. The public functions and features were only part of the charm: *seanchas* (storytelling), song, and story went on in favorite centers until the sunrise."[57] When MacNeill visited the Connacht feis in 1900—an event attended by numerous League and political luminaries—he reported to his wife in a similar vein about his unofficial activities on its second day:

Today I mainly loafed about and spent some hours chatting with local brethren. There was a very nice young priest, Father Forde, staying at this hotel, a man of brains, though in no way conceited. He and the proprietor and I sat up till 3 ½ o'clock after the feis was over, chatting about everything.[58]

More generally, Ó Ceallaigh remarked about the numerous provincial feiseanna that he attended:

B'iontach an spiorad náisiúnta agus an spiorad Gaelach a bhí le tabhairt faoi deara in óg agus aosta ar na feiseanna go léir an uair ud. Bhí fonn ar gach duine an Ghaeilge a labhairt agus cúis na Gaeilge a chur ar aghaidh. Chuirfeadh sé ríméad ar chroí aon Éireannach an spiorad sin a fheiceáil.

[It was wonderful the national spirit and the Gaelic spirit that was given to young and old at all the festivals at that time. Everyone desired to speak in Irish and to put forward the language cause. It put joyous pride into any Irishman's heart to see that spirit.][59]

Recognizing the inspirational potential of such events, the executive committee endorsed their use as propagandist tools. In a lead article at the opening of the festival season in June 1900, *An Claidheamh Soluis* stated bluntly: "We cannot too fully emphasize the importance of these local feiseanna for spreading a knowledge of the movement and for creating a healthy public opinion in favor of the language. These feiseanna are one of the most effective weapons at the League's disposal and invariably result in great good to the movement."[60] Several years later, Pearse asserted that the League derived two major benefits from its festivals. First, they developed a wider public sympathy for the language cause. "When we have their sympathies," he suggested, "their acceptance of our more practical program will naturally follow."[61] Still, he considered the second benefit to be even more important:

If we can give to thousands of our people an interest in Irish places by taking them on summer excursions, and make them happier by providing for them healthy native entertainments, it should be our duty to do so even if they never became students of the language, for in giving people an interest in their country and in teaching them how to amuse themselves in an original and native fashion, we make them safe and useful members of the community.[62]

This claim provides considerable insight into the thinking that Irish-Ireland leaders passed on to League branches. Their aim was to popularize the ideas behind the language cause, not simply to recruit new members or even to encourage the speaking of the language. The appeals made by the League were, therefore, designed to "mobilize" their audiences through entertainments, not simply to educate them.[63]

But what kind of entertainment did these celebrations provide? Generally, the competitions themselves took place in at least eight major categories: the literary, in which schoolchildren or students from League classes answered questions about basic Irish texts; storytelling, a category that often included separate competitions for native-speaking and student contestants; recitation/oration, in which entrants addressed either a poem or a prose set-piece to the judges; essays, which included junior and senior competitions on historical subjects or contemporary questions; "collections," in which entrants put together lists of local place names in Gaelic or transcribed folktales or poems from a native speaker in their district; singing for individuals or for choirs; instrumental, which could include violin, tin whistle, or bagpipe events; and dancing, either as individuals or in groups. Occasionally, as at the Galway feis in 1906, there were also events in which competitors translated a short story from English into Irish, composed a song or poem in Irish, or wrote a one-act play in Irish.[64] Festival planners also imposed specific conditions on competitors. Most commonly, they restricted competitions to people who were natives or residents of the county or province in which the festival occurred. Also, it became almost universal that committees only allowed adults to compete if they wore clothes of Irish manufacture. Similarly, when adults opted to compete only in a musical or dancing event, many committees required that they display some elementary knowledge of Gaelic prior to competing.[65]

In order to create a more specific profile of those participating in provincial feis competitions, I have made an intensive examination of programs from six festivals: Feis na n-Deisi of 1901 in Dungarvan, Co. Waterford; Feis Íbh-Ráthaigh of 1904 in Cahirciveen, Co. Kerry; Feis Cholmáin of 1906 in Fermoy, Co. Cork; Feis Dhroichid na Banndan of 1906 in Bandon, Co. Cork; Feis Dhaingin Uí Chúise of 1906 in Dingle, Co. Kerry; and Feis na Gaillimhe of 1906 in Galway city. To a certain extent, the choice of these six festivals was determined by the specific material contained in the programs: each of these booklets contained lists of competitors' names, their rudimentary addresses, and the conditions for participating in a given event. This last item was particularly useful as a gauge of the relative age of competitors. I recognize that the data generated may not be representative of the entire country because of the heavy concentration of southern festivals in the sample. (Five of the six were held in Munster, and the other was in the largest community in Connacht.)

Still, in many respects these festivals took place in communities that were representative of the provincial League centers described in chapter 3. Each was in a town or city that served as a trade and information center in or near the Gaeltacht. The size of these communities varied considerably, but by turn-of-the-century Irish standards, all six were substantial. The smallest, according to the 1901 census, was Dingle, which still had a population of nearly 1,800 people. At the other extreme, Galway city had more than 13,400 residents in 1901.[66] Finally, with the exception of Bandon, each town also boasted a connection to at least one major figure of the revival.[67] And in the case of Bandon, its proximity to Cork city, Kinsale, and Dunmanway placed it on the route used regularly by League timirí since 1900.

When one excludes group competitions, such as four-hand reels and interschool vocabulary quizzes, one finds that these festivals drew a gross aggregate total of 1,564 individual entries. They ranged in size from a low of 73 entries at the Feis na n-Deisi in 1901 to a high of 424 entries at Feis Dhaingin Uí Chúise in 1906. Relatively few entries came in competitions that required contestants to adopt pseudonyms in order to insure the impartiality of those judging. If one excludes the pseudonymous entries from the aggregate total, one finds a net total of 1,493 individual entries.[68]

Of these, almost two-thirds (66 percent) came from males, and slightly more than one-third (34 percent) came from females.[69] That women and girls made up roughly a third of those entering feis competitions suggests the continuation of another trend discussed in chapter 3: women became more engaged in the movement after being largely absent from its ranks in its earliest days. In this context, it is noteworthy that the earliest festival in this sample, Feis na n-Deisi, had the lowest percentage of female entries (18 percent), but the percentage of female entries at the five later festivals was consistently much higher, ranging from 29 percent at Galway to 38 percent at Fermoy.[70]

Similarly, the age range of competitors mirrored that found in the general membership as well, though the evidence on this point is far from precise. Feis planners generally divided competitions only into "junior" and "adult" categories, and while some "junior" competitions did specify upper age limits for their entrants, these limits were not always consistent even at the same festival.[71] Recognizing this uncertainty, it is possible to offer a rough division of entrants indicating that approximately 60 percent could be classified as juniors and 40 percent as adults.[72] As compared to the simple gender breakdown, the division according to ages showed much wider differentiation at the five later festivals. For instance, the festival with the highest proportion of adult competitors was at Cahirciveen in 1904 (54 percent), while at Dingle two years later only 23 percent of the entrants were adults.[73]

What accounts for such a wide variance in the age structure of feis competitors? No doubt, part of the explanation is rooted in the specific design of the programs themselves. Simply put, the syllabus for Feis Íbh-Ráthaigh contained a higher number and proportion of contests aimed at adults than did Feis Dhaingin Uí Chúise—17 out of 29, as compared to 9 out of 30. To an extent, the Iveragh feis was exceptional, as most festival programs either had greater balance between the number of junior and adult events, or they included more competitions for juniors than for adults.[74] Another factor perhaps was the strength of the local Irish-Ireland organizations in a given community. Thus, although the League maintained a steady presence on the Dingle peninsula throughout the period under review (local enthusiasts even founded a summer college there in

1908), revivalists lamented their inability to retain a continuous enrollment of adults in Dingle and the neighboring Corkaguiney district.[75] At Cahirciveen, meanwhile, the secretary of the branch was Thomas MacDonagh O'Mahony, a county councillor and justice of the peace. He worked steadily with his committee to sustain League membership, and although they had greater success in attracting women and children to their classes than men, they kept the revival very much in the public eye.[76]

"LITTLE . . . HAS RISEN ABOVE THE PAINFULLY MEDIOCRE"

When one looks at the competitions themselves, four things become apparent. First, whether one focuses on provincial festivals or the Oireachtas, one finds that the number of entries existed in an inverse relationship with the sophistication of contestants' command of Gaelic. For example, at the Dingle feis in 1906 the three competitions with the highest number of entries were aimed at children and required them to answer questions about simple Irish primers or conversation books. They drew 32, 49, and 51 competitors.[77] Conversely, the nine competitions that required an advanced understanding of Irish, especially written Irish, brought in only from 1 to 7 entries.[78] Even at the Oireachtas, which attracted entries from some of the finest writers, speakers, and singers of the day, the most popular events did not involve speaking or writing Gaelic. In 1901, for example, the four largest competitions were in the instrumental and vocal music categories.[79] At the Ard-Fheis two years later, O'Farrelly echoed the complaints of Mac Coluim and Ó Cadhla that contestants paid too much attention to the musical side of the national festival, and she sponsored a proposal directing the Oireachtas committee to give primacy to the speaking and literary events.[80] Her action, however well intentioned, could not address the fundamental problem that faced committees hoping to attract large numbers of sophisticated competitors: most Gaelic Leaguers were merely eager beginners.

A second observation that suggests the limited command of Irish of many participants is that the quality of entries varied widely. Philip O'Leary is certainly correct to highlight the positive contribution of League festivals, especially the Oireachtas, in fostering the early works of some of the finest Gaelic writers and folklorists of the twentieth century.[81] At the same time, adjudicators often awarded prizes with profound reservations. For example, when Joseph O'Neill of Galway won the Oireachtas prize for best short drama in 1903, the judges seemed to recognize him more for his subject matter than for his Irish: "This is the old story of Deirdre told well in dramatic form. The language of the competitor is not nearly so good as that of many of the others, but as a drama, it deserves the prize."[82] In some instances judges simply decided not to award any prizes whatsoever. Thus, at the Oireachtas in 1901, three events concluded without a prizewinner.[83] In other cases adjudicators noted significant differences between the meritorious work of prizewinners and the mediocrity of the other competitors. Again in 1901, in the inaugural short drama contest, the judges considered the experiment a success because four of the ten submissions had been "well qualified to obtain a prize."[84] But they did not spare the feelings of the other contestants. They considered the submission from "Cormac Ua Connaill" to be "rather flat," while that from "*Ar Bórd*" was "rather silly" and displayed "no dramatic talent." Their critical knife cut deepest, however, when referring to the entry from "Cill Gobnatan": "Has this individual being [*sic*] playing pranks on us? He writes in pencil. Read it through to the last word expecting to find the point somewhere but failed. 0 marks."[85]

Third, although some essay competitions encouraged the development of philosophical discussions and literary criticism in Irish, the subjects of others—especially at provincial festivals—betrayed the likely nationalist political leanings of event planners. For instance, at the first Oireachtas two of the contests asked competitors to define "what is charity?" and "what is truth?" Five years later, Oireachtas essayists wrote about the literature of the seventeenth-century priest, poet, and scholar Geoffrey Keating, as well as about traveling in Wales, and in 1905 one competition asked for a discussion of Gaelic poets and poetry from the eighteenth century.[86] By contrast, local festivals featured essays on historical subjects that either deemphasized the presence of foreigners in Ireland or focused on evocative patriotic figures from the nationalist pantheon.[87] For example, at the Iveragh feis in 1904, competition no. 2 asked for the best Irish essay about any of several figures—Brian Boru, Eoghan Ruadh Ó Néill, Patrick Sarsfield, and Daniel O'Connell.[88] At Dingle two years later, three contestants wrote essays about the impact of O'Connell's "work on the traits and nationality of the Irish."[89] (One wonders whether any of their essays referred to the Liberator's celebrated aversion to the use of spoken Irish.)

Perhaps the most common theme evident in these contests, however, was the very same desire expressed so frequently in regular branch activity, the yearning to invigorate industry and agriculture, thus reinforcing the economic ideals espoused by the League and organizations like the IAOS. Occasionally these competitions also took on a politicized character, as at Listowel in 1910, when writers were asked to address the "advantages of tillage over grazing."[90] Significantly, this festival came at the tail end of the so-called Ranch War, in which small farmers and agricultural laborers had pushed unsuccessfully for the nationalist parliamentary party to advocate the break-up of large grazing farms in favor of more labor-intensive tillage plots as a way to halt emigration.[91] It also reiterated a theme that, as seen in chapter 4, had appeared periodically in the Gaelic press. More commonly, contests with economic themes tended to focus on proactive ways to bolster Irish agriculture and industry that did not challenge existing power structures. For instance, the president of the IAOS, Lord Monteagle, sponsored a competition at the Munster feis in 1902 that asked competitors to write about "Na Buntáiste Chómhpháirteachais Oibre" ["The Advantages of Cooperation"].[92] Subsequently, the society published the prizewinning essay along with a translation by the Gaelic Leaguer Mary Spring Rice, Monteagle's daughter.[93] On the national stage the Oireachtas sponsored numerous competitions for collecting technical terms related to specific industries, as well as essay contests with topics such as "the necessity for supporting the revival of Irish industries," "industrial cooperation in Ireland," "the decay of Irish industries with suggestions for their revival," "agricultural cooperation," and "cottage industries suited to Ireland and the best ways to encourage them."[94]

Around 1904, many larger feiseanna went still further, adding industrial exhibitions to their competitions. Exhibitions ranged from small displays of the products of local industrial schools and home crafts to elaborate shows of cottage industries and factory-produced wares. One of the first large-scale attempts at an industrial display came at the inaugural

Feis na nGleann (or Feis of the Nine Glens) in County Antrim in 1904. With awards for items such as the best ball of home-spun Irish wool, the best pair of boots or shoes, and the best ironwork made by a blacksmith, it drew entries from virtually every town and village in northeast Antrim. Sir Horace Plunkett, then vice president of the Department of Agriculture and Technical Instruction, and Evelyn Gleeson, a founder of the Dun Emer Guild and Industries, both expressed their astonishment at the interest in and quality of the exhibition. According to Plunkett, "Miss Gleeson had told him that by any standard of comparison the industries which she had been inspecting that day possessed extraordinarily high merit and were full of hope for the future."[95]

The most consistently impressive industrial show, however, took place at the annual Wexford festival, which attracted exhibitors in as many as sixteen different categories from "fine arts and technical school products" to farm implements and craft works. The number of displays warranted detailed listings in the feis programs and multiple exhibit halls to accommodate all entries. In 1905 the Wexford exhibition featured 447 individual displays, and in 1908 the "manufacturers' exhibits" alone included products from thirty-five companies from Enniscorthy, New Ross, Wexford town, Dublin, Cork, Kilkenny, Carlow, and Waterford.[96] One reason for the success of festival exhibitions in securing entries was that, unlike musical or dance competitions, industrial exhibitions did not require participants to show any familiarity with Gaelic.[97] At the same time, exhibitors displayed their wares with an eye toward capturing the potential market of revivalists. At Wexford, for example, all competitors were to state the prices at which their samples could be purchased, and after 1907, entries were either to bear the Irish trademark or to carry a guarantee that the article had been made in Ireland.[98]

For those attending feiseanna, of course, the competitions made up only one part of the experience. Another feature garnered at least as much interest from festival crowds and competitors alike, and these were the *aeríochtaí* (or "grand concerts"). These affairs deserve more extensive examination in their own right, but here I would highlight two aspects of them. First, feis concerts provided showcases for professional and semi-professional performers whose expertise in traditional music and dance were not in demand in music halls or metropolitan theatres. Individuals such as the celebrated Dublin harpist Owen Lloyd were fixtures at many larger events, and they became well known throughout the ranks of Irish-Ireland. (At one concert in Glasgow in 1901, Lloyd's very appearance on the platform brought "a loud outburst of cheering.")[99] Equally important, provincial and Oireachtas concerts allowed festival prizewinners to exhibit their talents before their neighbors, literally bringing home the point that the cultural aspirations of the language movement were not simply a Dublin phenomenon.

Second, as important as it was to involve local amateurs, festival concerts exposed the weaknesses of the movement as well as its strengths. For those activists hoping to create a viable native alternative to existing popular entertainments, the one-act plays and short dramas that were a common feature at *aeríochtaí* proved to be a chastening reminder of how far the movement still had to go. Works by Hyde, MacGinley, Dinneen, and Ua Laoghaire were among the most popular with feis planners.[100] But as Yeats pointed out, many of these pieces would have presented staging difficulties for professionals, much less for amateurs, since they required multiple scene changes that disrupted the emotional and narrative impact of the productions.[101] Moreover, cast members frequently could not speak their lines fluently and naturally, providing painful evidence that enthusiasm for the language did not always result in the ability to use it. Hyde attempted to counter such difficulties by adopting a simple strategy: he set the action of his plays in familiar crowd settings (such as a kitchen or a schoolroom), so that they included many participants but only a limited number of principal (speaking) performers.[102] But such tactics could not overcome the lack of preparation and poor stage management that were endemic to productions put on by people who attended rehearsals intermittently after a full day at work.[103] Thus, when the Galway League performed Hyde's comedy *An Cleamhnas* (*The Match*) at their 1903 feis after only two rehearsals, Yeats found it to be "the worst [production] I ever saw." Three years later, Pearse acknowledged that "we have hitherto got very little acting in Irish that has risen above the painfully mediocre."[104]

Meanwhile, local singers and musicians who performed at provincial festivals relied on a repertoire of Gaelic and Anglo-Irish songs, the latter of which were familiar to performers and audiences alike. For instance, the evening entertainment at the County Wexford feis in 1908 featured a "grand promenade and torchlight tattoo," which included one band of pipers, two brass bands, and three fife and drum corps playing under the glare of 200 torches and a string of colored lights.[105] In addition to performing a series of well-known tunes such as "The Lily of Killarney," "The Wearing of the Green," and the locally significant "The Boys of Wexford," the massed brass and reed bands concluded the evening with a rendering of the unofficial nationalist anthem "God Save Ireland."[106] Similarly, the second half of the grand concert at the Munster feis of 1910 interspersed demonstrations of a four-hand reel and the uilleann pipes among an orchestral arrangement called "Erin Fantasia," an organ solo(!), and renditions of the airs "Steep Galtymore" and "The Green Isle of Erin."[107] In short, festival concerts were often little more than green-glossed versions of the respectable Anglo-Irish entertainments that were the targets of derisive comments from Irish-Ireland purists.

"COMPELLED BY SUPERIOR AUTHORITY"

In general terms, then, feiseanna did provide a new note to social life in communities across Ireland, albeit one that shared more with its cultural rival than contemporary Irish-Irelanders would have wished to acknowledge. But two questions remain: Did League festivals appeal to all creeds and classes? And did they find an audience? In order to answer these questions, it might again be useful to look intensively at a few individual festivals.

To begin with, there can be little doubt that certain festivals attracted the sympathy of local elites as well as the interest of people lower down the social scale. A significant indicator of elite interest is that some aristocrats, justices of the peace, landlords, and professionals served as the patrons or hosts of various feiseanna. In 1904, for instance, when disagreements among Cork Gaelic Leaguers forced the regional Feis na Mumhan to move to County Kerry,[108] the aged Earl of Kenmare opened his demesne to serve as the site of the festival. In the following year his son and heir repeated the gesture.[109] In 1907, after the feis had returned to Cork, local organizers secured donations of special prizes from the bishops of Cork, Cloyne, Kerry, and Waterford and Lismore. They also established a "general committee" to add prestige to their work. Among those lending their names to the effort were two members of parliament, the lord mayor and high sheriff of Cork city as well as two aldermen and two justices of the peace, four medical doctors, four lawyers, four Catholic priests, a Protestant minister, and the president and three professors from University College, Cork.[110] Like the priest-presidents of League branches, however, such patrons apparently did little more than offer modest subscriptions to the feis coffers and attend the event. Thus, aside from opening his grounds in Killarney and offering a £5 subscription, there is no sign that the Earl of Kenmare showed much interest in the progress of the language revival.[111]

There were, however, some elites who were more actively engaged. For instance at Foynes, Co. Limerick, Mary Spring Rice annually hosted the "Feis na Sionainne" ("Shannon Festival") on the Monteagle estate. In addition to contingents of Gaelic Leaguers from Limerick city and county, she attracted other Protestant nationalists such as Alice Stopford Green and Nelly O'Brien, as well as sympathetic peers like Lord Castletown.[112] Elsewhere, the whiggish Catholic landlord Sir Henry Bellingham of Castlebellingham, Co. Louth, helped to establish the County Louth feis in 1902.[113] Letters to *An Claidheamh Soluis* at the time questioned whether his involvement had been motivated by a desire to prevent more radical Leaguers—possibly from Dundalk—from controlling the festival, but his continuing active support of the feis throughout the early 1900s indicated his genuine interest in the movement. We can surmise that at least part of his commitment stemmed from a belief that the widespread study of Gaelic improved the Irish economy by creating "more vigorous and capable people." This had been the thrust of a speech given at the feis in 1908 by the president of the League in Kilkenny, the Hon. Otway Cuffe, himself the brother of Lord Desart, which Bellingham endorsed heartily from the platform.[114]

Given the nature of the available sources, it is impossible to be precise about the social strata from which festivals drew financial support. Nevertheless, a cursory review of subscription lists indicates that individuals from the strata common in League membership rolls were represented and that those elites who did take leadership roles may have influenced a few of their acquaintances to participate as well.[115] In the published records that I have examined, donations ranged from a high of £10 to a low of 6 pence, though some individuals perhaps gave even smaller amounts through League branches that subscribed en masse.[116] The report containing the best information with regard to the social status of contributors comes from the Munster feis of 1904. Nearly all of the individual contributors hailed from County Kerry, a rare occurrence for this traditionally Cork-based festival, but it was a logical result of the disputes alluded to above.[117] The vast majority of individual donors made very small gifts: 155 of the 191 contributions (81 percent) were for 10s. or less. In addition to the Earl of Kenmare, aristocratic contributors included the Marquess of Waterford and Lady Castlerosse, though their gifts of £2 apiece were far from princely. Meanwhile the leader of the Irish parliamentary party, John Redmond, also made a rare appearance on a festival subscription list, giving £1 10s., while his colleague J. P. Boland gave £1. Other local notables identifiable from the published report included two doctors, one solicitor, one registered magistrate, one justice of the peace, and three drapers from Killarney. Additionally seventeen priests and nuns gave to the festival, though a noteworthy absentee from the list of clerical contributors was the bishop of Kerry, who had a prickly relationship with language enthusiasts. Not surprisingly, the bulk of identifiable contributors came from those strata most associated with League membership— the black-coated workers of the lower-middle classes. They included nine national school teachers, two bank clerks and the clerk of the Killarney poor law union, two traveling Irish teachers and an itinerant dairy instructress employed by the Department of Agriculture and Technical Instruction, one printer, and fourteen draper's assistants. There were a further fourteen individuals who listed themselves as "from Meaghar's boot factory," who presumably could be classed as shop assistants, skilled or semiskilled workers.[118]

Overwhelmingly, those planning and attending League feiseanna were Catholics, and there were two celebrated cases in which the local notables in charge of festivals violated the nonsectarian intent of the organization. The first incident occurred at the County Donegal feis in June 1908. The feis committee, which consisted mainly of priests, had scheduled their function to coincide with the Catholic feast of Saints Peter and Paul at the remote Rock of Doon, the site of an annual pilgrimage. They had not, however, informed the Oireachtas committee about the program for their full day of activities. According to Ryan, the feis "proved to be largely a religious service and demonstration. It was begun with high mass on the Rock, there was a sermon, and certain subsequent addresses were like sermons. The bishop of Raphoe, Dr. [Patrick] O'Donnell, the great power in Donegal affairs, was present in state, and preached or spoke; there were several priests and a multitude of people. The Gaelic competitions, when they came, were badly arranged and managed."[119] Ryan, who was a member of the Oireachtas committee, objected strenuously to the feis because "through Feis Thir Chonaill a million and a half Irish Protestants and Presbyterians were notified that, so far as certain Irish priests are concerned, they are not wanted in the Gaelic League."[120] At least one Protestant had attended the feis, however, and this was the prominent Belfast Leaguer Francis Joseph Bigger, who presided jointly with Bishop O'Donnell. He defended the action of the Donegal clergy as a pragmatic way to retain the institution of the pilgrimage and to ensure that thousands would attend the festival. He also denied that any ill will existed at the feis itself: "All the speakers expressed entire satisfaction at this union of Irishmen in a common cause. Nothing could have been more perfect, more complete, more harmonious."[121] It is unclear whether Bigger wrote in the belief that a percentage of the crowd was Protestant or whether he was incredibly naive about the ripple effect that this public linking of a feis with the Catholic church might have among Irish Protestants generally. But the Oireachtas committee had no doubt that the local planners had openly violated League policy. When the preliminary program for 1909 Donegal feis came before the committee and appeared to be substantially unchanged, the committee refused to license it.[122]

This decision exacerbated growing tensions between the League executive and the clergy in County Donegal, especially O'Donnell,[123] yet the refusal may also have caught him somewhat by surprise. A native speaker of Irish and an early adherent of the League, the bishop previously had held entertainments to benefit the Catholic church that incorporated appeals on behalf of the League as well. Most famously, in 1898 he sponsored an *aonach* (fair) at Letterkenny for the dual purposes of raising funds for a new cathedral and of encouraging the language movement.[124] Among the prominent Gaelic Leaguers in attendance on that occasion were Hyde and Milligan, an Anglican and a Methodist respectively.[125]

Whether or not the 1909 decision had been a surprise, it hardened O'Donnell's increasing dissatisfaction with the League over the role of priests in Irish affairs. In April 1909, the bishop founded his own clerical language organization, Crann Eithne, which remained under his personal control. Also, shortly after the League action he started working energetically, if quietly, to oppose the revivalists' demand for compulsory Irish. It is worth noting, for instance, that MacFadden—who was a Donegal priest and a member of the Gaelic League executive—had intended to propose a resolution in favor of compulsory Irish at the national convention of the United Irish League (UIL) in February 1909, but he withdrew it at the end of January, reportedly because he was "compelled by superior authority."[126]

The second festival that blatantly violated the League constitution also took place in 1908 at Killarney.[127] The circumstances bore a striking similarity to the Donegal feis and the Letterkenny *aonach* of 1898: "Feis na n-Airne" was to be "held in connection with the Killarney Fete and Fancy Fair," the proceeds from which aided the construction of a new cathedral for the diocese of Kerry.[128] Retrospectively, the incident abounded in ironies: revivalists considered Bishop John Mangan of Kerry at best a lukewarm advocate of the language movement;[129] and two of the most respected members of the League—Fr. Cathaoir Ó Braonáin and Fionán MacColuim—were complicit in the event. Ó Braonáin, the passionate leader of the League in Killarney and a member of the Coiste Gnótha, had learned to speak Irish fluently and objected strenuously when professing revivalists did not regularly use the language.[130] He had started an annual feis in 1902, at which, according to the *Peasant and Irish Ireland*, Killarney "woke up to the fact of the Gaelic revival,"[131] and when the Munster feis moved temporarily to Killarney in 1904, he had spearheaded the planning committee. It is perhaps indicative of Ó Braonáin's strong sense of propriety in League dealings that the organizers advertised their feis only as taking place "in connection" with the "fete." (In 1903, Ó Braonáin had informed MacColuim that Killarney Leaguers would "not be able to send anything great this year" to the Language Fund because they felt that their contributions the previous year had not been acknowledged adequately in published reports.[132] Two years later, he berated Hyde at an executive committee meeting because he felt that the League president had wronged the Kerry-born journalist J. J. O'Kelly.)[133] In spite of their sleight of hand, however, Killarney Leaguers did not receive an official license for the feis.[134]

League officials in Dublin still did not fully appreciate the connection between the feis and the cathedral fund until word reached the capital after the event. *An Claidheamh Soluis* carried a colorless report about the event, including only very brief statements made by Bishop Mangan and Canon Peadar Ua Laoghaire about the importance of teaching Irish and speaking it in people's homes.[135] Meanwhile, Ryan in the *Peasant and Irish Ireland* openly accused the Killarney Leaguers of duplicity and demanded a full explanation.[136] That explanation came from MacColuim, the leading paid representative of the League executive in the south of Ireland. He had attended the feis in his capacity as organizer, and his letter to the Oireachtas committee could hardly have pleased those present. At the time, he claimed that he had assumed that the feis had been licensed because it had been listed among upcoming "fixtures" in *An Claidheamh Soluis*.[137] In a published account four years later, Ryan included the detail that MacColuim had also "thought it good policy to go out of one's way once in a while to befriend a bishop."[138]

Of the two statements—neither one of which would soothe those, like Ryan, with deep suspicions about clerical power in Ireland—the second rings truer. MacColuim knew ahead of time what the local members had intended: his extant papers include a draft of the poster and syllabus for the feis with an undated letter attached to it stating that the feis was "in conjunction with the bishop's efforts to raise money for the Killarney cathedral fund."[139] Aware of Mangan's equivocal support of the revival, MacColuim may have hoped to draw the bishop closer to the Irish-Ireland fold by aiding the feis. But the Oireachtas committee and the Coiste Gnótha recognized his and the Killarney Leaguers' actions as unconstitutional.

Ultimately, the executive censured MacColuim and suspended the Killarney branch.

Both the Killarney and Donegal feiseanna of 1908 highlight several things about the relationship between central League authorities and provincial committees. Although the oversight function of the League was effective only after the fact, the executive did act against the Donegal and Killarney committees, in practice reaffirming the commitment to the nonsectarian ideals of the League. Nevertheless, local committees retained a substantial amount of autonomy in spite of the centripetal impulses of the League organization. Thus the potential continued to exist that League functions could be utilized for purposes other than those approved at the annual national congresses. In these two instances the offending parties happened to be Catholic priests and complicit lay persons.

"A COMMON PLATFORM"

In spite of such incidents, Irish Protestants displayed their continuing interest in League festivals, particularly in the north. No feis better exemplified the efforts of the League to draw together Protestants and Catholics than the Feis of the Nine Glens in County Antrim. Recall that the few early language enthusiasts in northeast Antrim had to overcome clerical fears that the movement was a Protestant proselytizing mission and that one factor contributing to these fears had been the involvement of several women from Protestant landed families.[140] According to John Clark, the traveling teacher for the region, the principal officers of the feis committee were "Protestant imperialists."[141] Whether one can accept Clark's judgment is open to question. One of those he expressed initial doubts about was Sir Roger Casement, whose overture to Clark in 1904 was met initially with disbelief because the Casements "were considered tyrants in the old days."[142] At the same time, one of the most active members of the committee was Margaret Dobbs, whose association with the feis began in 1904 and continued unabated into the 1940s.[143] In her case Clark was not far off the mark: Dobbs appears to have remained a unionist throughout her life, and her brother even participated in the loyalist gun-running at Larne, Co. Antrim, in 1914.[144]

Yet to judge by the guests assembled on the platform at the first feis in 1904, Dobbs and her committee had indeed attracted an impressive mix of creeds and political ideologies. In addition to the Catholic vice president of the League, Eoin MacNeill, the principal speaker was Sir Horace Plunkett, a southern unionist and the son of a peer. Also in attendance were the Belfast Protestant nationalist F. J. Bigger, the Protestant unionist president of the League in Kilkenny, Captain Otway Cuffe, and the Protestant Home Ruler Stephen Gwynn. The most surprising guests on the dais, however, were two well-known northern Protestants—Sir Hugh Smiley, J.P., the chairman of the *Northern Whig* newspaper, and Sir Daniel Dixon, the timber and shipping merchant who was lord mayor of Belfast on several occasions in the 1890s and early 1900s and who would win a contentious parliamentary by-election in 1905 on a staunchly Conservative anti–Home Rule platform. In a moment of rhetorical self-congratulation *An Claidheamh Soluis* concluded its report of the event with a question: "What other movement could collect on a public platform men representative of such widely different spheres of thought and action?"[145]

The choice of Plunkett as principal speaker is interesting in its own right. Only months before, his book *Ireland in the New Century* had riled many Irish-Irelanders, but their reactions did not dissuade Plunkett from mixing with Gaelic revivalists. Instead, he took to the podium in early July and described the Gaelic League as providing "a common platform on which every man who wished well to Ireland and was ready to help Ireland could meet and work shoulder to shoulder until they had elevated Ireland to the condition to which, if he knew their minds, they intended to elevate her."[146]

Catholics and Protestants alike attended the Glens festival in great numbers. According to an account written at the time by MacNeill, the feis was the "largest rural feis" he had yet seen, and he specially noted that there was "a large attendance of the local 'landocracy,' whose traditions were often anything but harmonious with the ideals of the feis."[147] The program featured 120 competitions, including contests in language proficiency, dancing, singing, athletics, and the aforementioned industrial exhibition. Another contemporary report, from the Belfast nationalist newspaper the *Irish Weekly*, described the scene at the various venues:

"Upon a wooden platform in the open field a stalwart young Glensman is reciting Stephen Gwynn's 'Song of Defeat'; at another platform *buachaillí* and *cailíní* (boys and girls) are dancing to the strains of pipe and fidil [*sic*]; in a quiet corner the story-telling competitions are going on, the competitors being apparently oblivious of the distractions around them; and from the large hall comes the sound of a Gaelic chorus, sung by a Glen choir."[148] MacNeill saw excited spectators at each location but claimed that the dance competitions attracted the largest following. "It was impossible," he declared, "to get a look in at the dancing unless perhaps you came there the night before, for from ten o'clock till six the platform was surrounded by a dense crowd."[149] As the *Irish Weekly* concluded, "In point of numbers alone there can be no doubt that the Feis of the Nine Glens of Antrim held at Glenariff last weekend has proved a success."[150]

It also was not an isolated success. In view of the attendance at other provincial feiseanna, a market clearly existed for the public entertainments presented by the League, "native" or otherwise. Accurate estimates of crowd sizes are difficult to find, as typical reports in the Irish-Ireland press merely stated that "the people in their thousands" gathered; however, occasional comments in constabulary, press, and organizers' reports indicate that such claims were not idle boasts. For example, in July 1902 the police recorded that "about 7,500 people were present" at the "carnival" organized by the League in Wexford town; in the following month "about 7,000 people with bands" took part in the feis at Omeath, Co. Louth; and in September "upwards of 10,000" witnessed the festival at Newcastle, Co. Down.[151] In 1903, *An Claidheamh Soluis* reported that a feis at Youghal, Co. Cork, drew a crowd of 5,000 spectators, and MacColuim estimated that 2,000 people had attended the first day of the feis at Dingle, with the crowd swelling to nearly 5,000 on the second day.[152] In 1907, according to the *Leader*, the inaugural feis at Kilskeery, Co. Tyrone, attracted nearly 3,000 entrants to its various competitions.[153] Meanwhile, "thousands" gathered from Tipperary and surrounding counties for the annual feis organized by Fr. Matthew Ryan at Knockavilla. According to League *timire* Séamas Ó h-Eochaidh, "Ba chosamhla le Oireachtas ná le feis é. Níor spáráil an t-Ath. Maitiú bocht, ór ná airgead ar an nGaedhilg." ["It was more like the Oireachtas than a feis. Poor Fr. Matthew did not spare gold or money on the Irish language."][154]

One must balance such large-scale affairs against other, less numerically successful efforts. For instance, the Scots enthusiast E. C. Carmichael reported to his countrymen from the Feis Connacht in 1901 that only about five hundred people attended the competitions during the day.[155] Carmichael was, however, surprised that there was *any* audience at 10 in the morning, and he considered their presence a sign of intense interest. He also asserted that the "great majority of them were evidently Gaelic-speaking, for they laughed at the proper places, and that is the great test of knowledge of a language."[156] Although he did not estimate further, he said that the concert in the evening was a more crowded affair, at which, "if possible, the audiences were more sympathetic and enthusiastic than during the day."[157]

Another feis that consistently drew lukewarm interest was the Dublin festival. On the surface this fact might seem surprising because the city was the hub of the movement, and it contained the highest concentration of League branches in Ireland. In 1902, there had been as many as fifty-four branches in metropolitan Dublin, and as late as 1908, there were still more than thirty affiliated branches in the city.[158] Nevertheless, the number of entries to the feis competitions never approached what festival planners had hoped for, and the audiences at the festival concerts generally were not as large as the ones found in the countryside or especially at the Oireachtas.[159] To be sure, Dubliners had more entertainment options to attract them away from League-sponsored activities than did the residents of most provincial towns and villages, but another explanation for the apparent lack of interest among Dubliners in a local festival was that the League may already have saturated its market with its regular round of concerts, speeches, entertainments, and excursions. In June 1904, for instance, three Dublin-area branches held concerts on successive weekends, and a fourth organized a trip for its members to Limerick, so that they could attend the Thomond feis.[160] Further, because the Oireachtas was held in June or August each year, many Dublin enthusiasts focused attention on the national festival rather than a local event.[161] Thus, the *Freeman's Journal* concluded in 1906 that "some of the county feiseanna exceed it [the Dublin feis] in relative importance inasmuch as they excite intense interest amongst all classes of the people and are events of outstanding importance in the life of the whole locality."[162]

CONCLUSION

That importance was also not merely a fleeting phenomenon. For those competing, they devoted weeks (and in some cases months) to preparation, planning, rehearsal, memorization, and study that was both personal and shared. As Ryan recalled of feiseanna generally, they "bring to a head the quiet work of many months in branch classes, schools, homes, and sometimes workshops and gardens."[163] For those in the audience, the anticipation of what they would see and hear must also be taken into account. MacNeill found the excitement before the Feis of the Nine Glens to be almost palpable:

> For months before, the feis was the one thing talked about "all over the Nine Glens." The night before the feis, I stayed in Glenarm, where I was born, twelve miles from Waterfoot. The driver who brought me from Larne said, "There'll be more people in Waterfoot the morrow than ever was in it since the world was made." The next morning Glenarm was in the street before six o'clock, yoking up and filing vehicles. The coast road was one long procession of cars and bicycles. Three hundred people out of the thousand that live in Glenarm were on the road. The shops were closed and a general holiday was in force. Every side road swelled the crowd. From Ballymena seven hundred persons came down over the mountain. From the island of *Reachra* [Rathlin] on the north came a steamer full of people. The other northern districts sent their contingents at the same rate. The steam yachts and motor cars of the wealthy were also to the fore. An old friend—we are all cousins in the Glens—joined the stream when we passed Carnloch—and, hardly waiting to pass a greeting after years of severance, said with delight "This will be the greatest day we ever had in the Glens."[164]

On the eve of the Wexford festival in 1912 the *Enniscorthy Echo* reported in a similar vein that "the feis atmosphere is found all over the place, not alone in the streets but permeating every home in the land from the wealthy mansion to the humblest cabin."[165]

Several conclusions emerge from this discussion. First, the line between League "members" and the "general public" blurred considerably during festivals. Because individuals moved into and out of the official ranks of the League without fully disengaging from the revival, their ongoing participation as competitors or audience members at festivals was an important link to the revivalist cultural ethos. Second, because feis organizers generally worked to maintain the League's self-denying ordinances, festivals served as intensive models of what an Irish-Ireland community could be, bringing "all creeds and all classes" together in relatively peaceful and interesting settings, if only for a brief few days. Third, as noted in chapter 4, the people designing these public functions had a variety of understandings of the revival, and, not surprisingly, they emphasized this variety in their appeals to the public. Essay competitions and *aeríochtaí* drew attention to local issues while appropriating aspects of the prevailing Anglo-Irish culture and grafting them into the Irish-Ireland repertoire.

Last, in relying on local notables to play key roles in festival planning, Gaelic enthusiasts opened themselves up to the possibility that their call for inclusive Gaelicism would be lost. One's engagement with the language, therefore, depended as much upon one's belief that the revival addressed everyday local concerns as it did upon whether one could use more than a simple Gaelic greeting. Ultimately, in reaching out to Irish men and women through public celebrations, the League secured for the Gaelic language a stylized symbolic place in twentieth-century Irish society, but it did so at the cost of deemphasizing the primary mission of the revival. As a result, although the cultural products of revivalist festivals made support for "the language" a mnemonic for national advance on a number of fronts, they did so at the expense of incorporating the Irish language into everyday life.

6

The March of a Nation
Dublin's Language Processions

On the day of the language procession the stranger might be pardoned for
thinking that a passion for Irish is the one great obsession of Dublin.[1]

Although Dublin Leaguers failed to create a large local feis to complement the Oireachtas, it was not because of an inability to stage
imposing public celebrations. Indeed, consistently the largest and most
anticipated event on the League calendar was the city's annual language
procession. Between 1902 and 1913 the Dublin district council sponsored
eleven of these events, which served two purposes. On a mundane level,
the procession was the centerpiece for the district council's collection for
the National Language Fund and kicked off the local observance of the
League's fund-raising scheme, Irish Language Week. (Local representatives took in coins from the people who gathered to watch the procession
and then fanned out in subsequent days to perform house-to-house collections throughout Dublin.)[2] Equally important, the procession placed
the language cause before crowds that regularly grew to the hundreds
of thousands.[3]

"THE VASTNESS OF THE MULTITUDE ASTOUNDED"

Dublin Leaguers and their supporters hoped that an annual spectacle
would increase awareness of the language movement among the residents
of the city. Moran endorsed the idea in 1902 because the movement had
"need of imposing demonstrations now and then to strike the attention

of the unconverted and put new hope and grit into the revivalists."[4] In later years the organization subcommittee of the district council—which took charge of planning the procession—mixed conversations about how to create entertaining and instructive displays with discussions about halting the decline in League membership. These interests overlapped most often when the subcommittee discussed support of Irish industries. For example, during the earliest conversations about Language Week for 1906, the subcommittee recommended that "the best means of extending the membership and influence of the League in Dublin" would be for all branches in the district to endorse a resolution that "only firms employing Irish and trade union labor be allowed to tender for Gaelic League contracts."[5] Subcommittee members agreed two months later that special attention should be paid to expanding the industrial component of the procession, and they decided to contact local manufacturers to enlist their participation by "pointing out the advantages of exhibiting in the procession."[6] In February 1906, when they issued their invitation to march, the Dublin Leaguers made clear that bread and butter concerns were on a virtual par with their efforts in the Gaeltacht: "The claims of the Gaelic League to the sympathy and cooperation of all classes of the citizens are undeniable. Besides working unceasingly for the preservation of the language in the Irish-speaking districts, and endeavoring to restore it as a spoken tongue throughout the length and breadth of Ireland, it labors strenuously for the encouragement and support of our languishing native industries."[7]

In sheer scale the processions succeeded enormously in creating Moran's "imposing demonstrations." Still, determining their precise size remains problematic at best. As Gary Owens has discussed in his study of Daniel O'Connell's "monster meetings," too ready an acceptance of counts offered by partisan press sources often leads to overestimation.[8] Indeed, if one were to rely uncritically on the most partisan of sources—*An Claidheamh Soluis*—one might think that the language processions grew continuously throughout the decade under review. Police records can serve as a check on overestimation, but their usefulness in this context is limited on two counts. In the first place, the files of the Crime Special Branch Division of the Dublin Metropolitan Police are incomplete for the relevant years. Second, as any perusal of these records indicates, the branch made its estimates based on a combination of first-hand observations *and* inspection of the same press reports on which the historian relies! Thus, as a further check on overestimation, I have paid particular attention to another indicator of relative growth and decline, that being the time it took processionists to pass a given point.

By this measure the number of marchers seems to have increased between 1902 and 1904, remained roughly at the same level until 1906, and then declined after the procession was moved to a later point in the calendar year. In 1903, for example, *An Claidheamh Soluis* reported that marchers filed steadily past the O'Connell Monument for "two long hours"; however, the *Leader* claimed that the same processionists "marched past for an hour and a half."[9] In 1904, when Gaelic Leaguers said the event was even bigger than in the preceding year, the *Irish Times* reported that it again took about an hour and a half to pass a given point, a figure that the same source repeated in 1906.[10] But by 1909, 1910, and 1911, numbers had dwindled, and the procession lasted for slightly less than one hour, implying that the number marching was perhaps only one-half to two-thirds of its size in earlier years.[11]

The largest specific figures reported by *An Claidheamh Soluis* were 45,000 marchers and 200,000 onlookers for 1905. Although the reporter for the *Irish Independent* acknowledged that the 1909 procession itself was smaller than in previous years, he claimed that the number of spectators had actually increased to nearly half a million.[12] Such numbers are almost certainly exaggerated. Fortunately, police records do give a starting point for comparison. The only figures that they specifically include for the processions were 18,000 marchers for the 1902 procession and 10,000 for 1911. But the impressionistic comments made by police observers corroborate the general pattern of growth and decline indicated in the march times above, that is, that the processions increased in size until the middle of the decade before tailing off in later years.[13] If one assumes that processionists moved at approximately the same pace each year, it may be possible to extrapolate back to those larger processions using the 1911 figure as a basis of comparison. Thus, if 10,000 marchers took fifty minutes to pass a given point, it is reasonable to assume that the earlier processions included *at least* 20,000 to 25,000 marchers.[14] And even if the crowd estimates of 200,000 for the procession of 1905 and 500,000 for that of 1909 were wildly exaggerated, they suggest (conservatively) that from one-quarter to one-half of the population of metropolitan Dublin participated in the language processions at some point during the decade either as a marcher or as a spectator—a figure that dwarfed any festival crowd.[15]

Over the years several individuals played key roles in bringing the processions to fruition, the most important of whom were Patrick Ingoldsby and Michael O'Hanrahan. Ingoldsby, who was known in League circles by his Gaelic name, Pádraic Mac Giolla Iosa, served as secretary of the organization and collection subcommittees of the district council from 1905 until 1909 and spent several months each year overseeing every aspect of the production.[16] Among his duties, he contacted all platform speakers and organizations which marched; met with representatives of these bodies to discuss the purpose and logistics of the procession; made arrangements for whatever permits were necessary to hold public meetings; maintained a group of press stewards to inform local newspapers about all aspects of the procession; and set up a corps of marshals to coordinate the celebrants' movements and to keep order along the two- to three-mile long parade route.[17] O'Hanrahan—who would be executed in 1916 for his role in the Easter rebellion—gained notoriety as one of Ingoldsby's "fellow laborers," and his particular specialty was in promoting the event.[18] It is a sign of the high regard in which he was held that the district council placed O'Hanrahan in charge of promotion in 1909, for that was the year in which the council used the procession as a nationwide demonstration of solidarity during the campaign to make Irish a compulsory subject in the National University. The work was especially complicated in Ulster where, although the Great Northern Railway had agreed to provide special excursion trains for northern Gaels traveling to Dublin, the railway would not agree to promote their reduced rates. Within ten days of the procession O'Hanrahan oversaw the production and distribution of 1,000 posters to stations throughout the north.[19]

Generally, marshals gathered processionists into seven sections intended to represent various facets of Dublin life: the language movement, Gaelic athletic clubs, educational organizations and student groups, temperance advocates, local industries, friendly and trades societies, and last, political bodies. As the advance report for the 1903 procession made clear, the arrangement of processionists was quite intentional:

> Fifty Dublin craobhacha, led by the Coiste Gnótha, will form the vanguard. Tableaux representative of ancient heroes, of *Éire* presiding over the *Cúig Cúigí*, of Conradh na Gaeilge instructing youth, and similar subjects, will be displayed in this section; but the most significant tableau for those who have eyes to see will be the fifty city branches leading the remainder of the citizens.[20]

The organization subcommittee therefore placed the language movement in the forefront of society in the capital. They described the hurling teams and other Gaelic athletes as "Dublin's sinew" and the schoolchildren as "Dublin's hope." Perhaps most significantly, they placed the various political organizations at the end of the procession, so that they could "make their obeisance" to the language movement: "The local elective bodies will pay homage to Irish-Ireland and bring up the rear."[21] In short, politics was to serve culture rather than the reverse.

Scattered throughout the assembly were Gaelic pipers, temperance and trade-society bands, and tableaux recalling events in Irish history and commenting on contemporary issues. Marchers usually dressed in costume, or they wore colored sashes and badges emblematic of their organizations. They also carried banners advocating their specific causes—often in Irish and in English, so that the assembled crowds, most of whom had little or no knowledge of Irish, could comprehend their messages.

The effect created on these occasions was a stirring blend of colorful sights and deafening sounds that left lasting impressions on those who witnessed them. Indeed, the third segment of O'Casey's multivolume autobiography referred to the processions in its very title, *Drums under the Windows*. After nearly four decades he recalled the processions as "the power germinal that thrilled the sunny air with drum-beat and bugle-call."[22] Together with the crowds lining the streets and filling the windows along the route, the marchers formed what another observer described as a "lengthening chain of life and color that passed before us":

> Four deep they were, and mingling with them and following them 'midst
> blaze of green and patches of banner coloring came bands—bands whose
> drum beats filled the air and ricocheted in volleys against adjacent build-
> ings and music that was of the past but filled one with the present.[23]

Two years later, the same commentator declared that witnessing the procession had "stunned the mind" because "the vastness of the multitude
astounded one."[24]

After winding through the city, processionists and onlookers gathered at demonstrations to hear addresses from Gaelic League officers, city
officials, and clergy. The site for these speeches varied, depending on the
route that was followed. Most often, they took place in the large open-
air marketplace at Smithfield, near both the heart of the city's depressed
metal-working trades and the seat of legal education, the King's Inns. In
1908, however, the demonstration occurred in the Phoenix Park, home of
the British viceroy; and in 1909 it met at the north end of O'Connell Street,
just outside the Gaelic League offices, where the gathering crowd over-
flowed into the side streets.[25]

Like the processions, these demonstrations were highly stylized, cho-
reographed affairs. Before any speeches were delivered:

> League branches will be ranged on either side of the platform. The Gaelic
> athletic section will form a hollow square in front of the platform, and
> this space will be occupied by the educational section. The choruses—
> "Dóchas" and "Go Máiridh ár nGaedhilg Slán"—will be sung by the craob-
> hacha, schools, colleges, clubs, etc.[26]

Clearly, the organizers wanted to infuse the demonstrations with symbolic
overtones, ranging the language enthusiasts and their athletic counterparts around the student marchers, welcoming "Dublin's hope" in song
into a Gaelic ceremony. Furthermore, the two songs evoked the mission
of the League. The title "Dóchas" literally means "hope," while that of Ó
Foghludha's Oireachtas prizewinner—"Go Mairidh ár nGaedhilg Slán"—
translates roughly as "Long Life and Health to Our Irish Language." "Go
Mairidh" summed up in its refrain the sentiment that League purists hoped

to instill in the rising generation: "Moch, mall, thoir, thall, ná labhram acht Gaedhilg bhláith. . . . Moch, mall, thoir, thall, ná labhram acht Gaedhilg bhláith." ["Early, late, east, beyond, I will only speak beautiful Irish. . . . Early, late, east, beyond, I will only speak beautiful Irish."][27] In 1907, to ensure that the participants would know the words of these songs, the organizers printed and distributed 5,000 copies of each song through League branches and local schools.[28] According to one report, the collective enthusiasm of the crowd as it sang was "almost unnerving": "It rent the skies with its boomings and rolled with long-sounding echoes over the housetops."[29]

"IT WAS NOT LOVE OF THE LANGUAGE BUT HATRED OF THE TAXI"

The contact of the organization subcommittee with groups that wished to march gives some indication of how the League disseminated its message and how different sectors of the city population understood those aims. These contacts were three-tiered in approach. First, it was standard practice to send out circular letters inviting participation from schools, trades, and other organizations.[30] Then, the subcommittee followed up these invitations by sending representatives to meet with larger bodies, such as the Dublin Trades Council.[31] Last, subcommittee members sponsored public meetings, which were specifically intended to instruct participants about the justifications for and logistics of the procession.

At one such meeting in September 1908, 180 delegates attended from dozens of organizations. They represented numerous Gaelic League branches, temperance organizations, clubs, and trade societies. Most of the club delegates came from chapters of the Irish National Foresters (INF) (a nationalist friendly society) and the Wolfe Tone Memorial Committee.[32] Among the trades present were the Amalgamated Slaters and Tilers, the Mineral Water Operatives, the Drapers' Assistants, the Brassfounders, and the Bookbinders and Rulers unions. Also present was the secretary of the Operative Bakers' band.[33] The responses to statements made by Ingoldsby and by national secretary Pádraig Ó Dalaigh are instructive as to the delegates' understanding of the intentions of the League. Ó Dalaigh's speech highlighted many of the major goals of the revival, such as the need to maintain paid personnel in the Gaeltacht and to push for Irish to become an essential subject in the National University, both of which drew applause. But he also received applause when he said that "all Gaelic Leaguers considered themselves morally bound to support home manufacture."[34] Similarly, when Ingoldsby reported that he had received several commitments to take part in the industrial section of the procession, it prompted a "hear, hear" from the assembly.[35]

After the main addresses had concluded, a member of the Wolfe Tone Memorial Committee offered a resolution endorsing the call to the "citizens generally to render material and moral assistance in securing the success of Irish Language Week, and thus enable the Gaelic League to continue and still further develop its labors in the Irish-speaking districts and in the cause of the Irish language generally."[36] Among those who spoke in favor of the resolution were Fr. Angelus, O.S.F.C., president of the Father Mathew Temperance Hall, and Sean T. Ó Ceallaigh, who had been elected an alderman in the preceding January with significant backing from labor. Not surprisingly, Fr. Angelus said that he supported the League because it "was helping the temperance movement, and he thought he could claim that the temperance movement was helping the Gaelic League."[37] Ó Ceallaigh also supported the resolution, but he continued by denouncing "the ignorance of the public with regard to the question of buying Irish goods." He suggested that members of the Gaelic League "should go out to the street corners and talk to the people and educate them on this question."[38] Thus, these representatives understood the intent of the procession through its relationship to causes they already espoused. This does not mean that they viewed the linguistic message of the League as irrelevant in and of itself; rather, it indicates that, as processionists, they applied their own interpretations to the linguistic nationalism of the League. Hence, to cite Fr. Angelus again, both the language and temperance movements reinforced each other by working "for the elevation of the social and moral status of the Irish people."[39]

Certain processionists sought to advocate specific causes or organizations through their participation, and some even sought pride of place in the line of march. The INF, for example, considered withdrawing from the procession in 1906 because they felt that their contingents had not been visible enough in the friendly societies section in preceding years.[40] They remained concerned into 1907 and approached the organization subcommittee four months before the march in order to press for a more prominent space. The League accommodated them by moving the INF forces from the friendly societies section to the head of the industrial section, which was the second largest contingent of the procession.[41] After the same 1906 procession a mineral water manufacturer, Kernan and Company, protested to the subcommittee that press reports had failed to note their participation, suggesting that the procession had not provided them with the exposure they had expected. One can sense that their complaint rankled some members of the subcomittee, for the assistant secretary responded that "he had informed Messrs. Kernan that notwithstanding their failure to supply details [about their contingent], a full description of their exhibit had been supplied to the press by P. Mac Giolla Iosa and duly published in [the] daily papers of Monday [the] 12th which account they must have overlooked."[42]

Another example of a nonaffiliated organization "using" the procession occurred in 1910. With the advent of motor vehicles, automotive taxicabs already had become a reality in a few larger cities and towns in the United Kingdom, but in Dublin the horsedrawn car with its "jarvie" [driver] remained the staple form of transportation well into the twentieth century. Realizing that motorized transport posed a growing danger to their business, a large number of Dublin jarvies banded together into the Anti-Taxicab Association.[43] In September 1910 they brought their case into the language procession. Ryan recognized it as the first time that "cardrivers" had taken part.[44] Moran did as well, but he called it "a pure piece of exploiting the Gaelic League."[45] "Obviously and avowedly," he exclaimed, "it was not love of the language but hatred of the taxi that inspired them."[46] The report in An Claidheamh Soluis did not betray any anger at this "exploitation"; instead, the official organ of the League reported that the horses "added considerably to the picturesqueness of the procession."[47] Three years later, the Irish Women's Franchise League (IWFL) sent a contingent of a hundred women led by Hanna Sheehy-Skeffington to march. Occasionally, they met with boos from the crowd, but they also distributed pamphlets in Irish and in English about the issue of women's suffrage.[48] If neither the jarvies nor the members of the IWFL had any previous relationship to the language revival before joining in the processions, it is nonetheless worth noting that they considered the procession to be an effective venue from which to appeal to a large portion of the Dublin populace and that—in the case of the IWFL—they made their case in English *and* in Irish.

Of course, there were abuses of the occasion from time to time. Ironically, the most consistent abuses came from displays associated with one of the most prominent industrial supporters of the League—Boland's Bakery Company, one of whose directors was the parliamentarian and revivalist J. P. Boland. Moran complained in 1904 that the people riding on the Boland's exhibit had thrown small loaves of bread into the crowds lining the street. "This was in execrable taste," he declared. "We trust that next year, if this bakery company seeks to be permitted to join the procession, that a written undertaking will be obtained from it that such regrettable and ill-mannered conduct will not be indulged in."[49] Whether the League pursued such an undertaking is uncertain; yet in 1906 Ingoldsby did instruct the marshals that the "distribution of samples or exhibits during the course of the procession should be strictly forbidden," and that "any person infringing this regulation" should be removed from the ranks.[50] In spite of such efforts, incidents involving the Boland's vans continued to occur. Ryan complained that the tossing of loaves in 1908 set off a "scramble of the poor little street children" lining the route.[51] Whereas Moran—who advocated economic advancement by focusing his attention on capital—found such incidents simply "ill-mannered," Ryan—who was an advocate of labor and the poor—described the circumstance as "an indication of the deep and chronic distress which prevails in the city."[52] In the following year another scramble occurred, and according to the *Irish Independent,* the scene took on a tragicomic quality. This time the bread vans were stacked high with loaves held together "by means of light colored ribbons."[53] Gangs of "young roughs who [were] prompted by a spirit of devilry" followed the vans and tore away the ribbons: "From George's Street all round to O'Connell Street spectators were urged many to laughter and many to expressions of disgust at the unedifying spectacle of gangs of rowdies and women tearing and scratching in a wild scramble for lumps and loaves of the purloined broken bread." By the time that the van reached the reviewing platform midway up O'Connell Street, spectators witnessed the van driver "squatted on a huge square loaf boasting aloud that he was saving that for himself!"[54]

Such incidents have led Anton Großmann to suggest that the processions ceased to fulfill their responsibilities to the language cause. After viewing photographs of the 1908 procession, he discounted the event as having had its character altered specifically because displays in the industrial section advertised local bakeries and breweries.[55] But as the aforementioned discussions of the organization subcommittee suggest, and as Ingoldsby's published preview of the 1906 procession makes clear, the League included the industrial section "to convince the enormous concourse of spectators, as well as the readers of the newspaper accounts through the country, of the necessity of supporting the work of Irish hands and of seeking for and encouraging these manufactures."[56] Similarly, as Ingoldsby stated, trade-society tableaux exhibited "the particular work in which they [the trades] are employed." The procession, in his opinion, was meant to be "a striking object lesson in the support and fostering and extension of Irish manufacture."[57]

The industrial displays also hearkened back to the traditions of the early modern era, when incorporated guilds and their tradesmen displayed their wares during the triennial "riding the franchises" and the annual lord mayor's processions.[58] By adapting a familiar mode of public expression to their own ends, therefore, Dublin Gaelic Leaguers engaged in a process described by Alter as utilizing existing symbols "to convey a particular interpretation of the history of the country."[59] What Großmann took to be an aberration was in fact by design. The district council took a familiar mode of expression—which included displays by citizens not fully in touch with the language cause—and adapted it to promote the idea that the language was the thin end of a wedge that would open a path to the advance of education, art, and especially home industries.

"MANY AND SARCASTIC WERE THE COMMENTS"

One finds similar themes emphasized repeatedly in the tableaux presented by League branches in the language section. These allegorical scenes can be divided thematically into three main categories: historical; historical designed to comment on contemporary issues; and contemporary. Press accounts, including occasional photographs and drawings, as well as programs prepared by procession organizers give some insights into the content of the tableaux. Historical scenes were among the most popular, as branch members depicted well known figures from pre-Norman Ireland and encounters between heroes of the Irish past and their Anglo-Norman or English foes. Whether it was Shane O'Neill kneeling before Queen Elizabeth I, or Seathrún Céitinn (Geoffrey Keating) writing his *History of Ireland* while hiding in the Glen of Aherlow, these scenes were often anachronistic hodgepodges constructed from popular histories or the lectures prepared for League branches by autodidact members.[60] Still, tableaux could be quite evocative for their audiences. According to one account of the Keating scene, a small child was so frightened by the sight of red-coated soldiers looking for Keating that she watched the rest of the procession through "tear-dimmed eyes," saying repeatedly "I hope they won't find him."[61]

The second category also included historical figures, but these scenes appeared to be overt commentaries on the existing condition of the Irish language as well as on the uneven power relationship between state authorities and the language enthusiasts. For example, two of the high kings of Ireland portrayed in various years—Malachy II and Brian Boru—were popularly well known for having fought against Viking invaders.[62] The most militant of these three tableaux appeared in 1911 as the entry of the MacHale Branch, and it featured the aged Boru on horseback leading spear-toting troops toward the battle of Clontarf. Since the MacHale branch was one of the main centers of Irish Republican Brotherhood (IRB) activity in Dublin, it is logical to conclude that advanced nationalist politicians in the League sought to use the procession to present a stirring image to the crowd.[63] And one could read the inclusion of both warrior figures by League branches as a sign that militant revivalists had placed Gaelic on a par with two men recognized for repelling invasion, metaphorically carrying Thomas Davis's dictum about a nation's language being a nation's surest barrier to its logical conclusion.

Such a reading is superficial, however, and in the case of the Boru scene in 1911, problematic. A bannerette featuring "a rising sun bursting through a forest, with a cross-hilted sword flashing in the sun," preceded the MacHale tableau.[64] Although a dawn image might seem a self-evident reference to the republicans' ever-promised coming day, it could also have had at least two other specific meanings.[65] First, daybreak and the sword of light were symbols associated with the Gaelic League. Indeed, they were the literal translations of the titles of the two League newspapers *Fáinne an Lae* (Dawn of Day) and *An Claidheamh Soluis* (The Sword of Light). In this reading the branch might simply have been utilizing standard League imagery to imply that the forces of the revival were reawakening Ireland. A second reading is perhaps even more likely as an alternative in the context of Dublin in September 1911. At that time the sunburst symbol was associated most directly with the organ of mainstream constitutional nationalism, the *Freeman's Journal*, which featured a sunburst on its masthead.[66] Thus it is equally possible to read the apparently defiant march of the MacHales as a reference to the highly anticipated coming of the third Home Rule bill, which had become a virtual political certainty only weeks before the language procession with the passage of the Parliament Act.[67]

The final category of tableaux directly addressed contemporary issues associated with the revival. Some scenes were virtual advertisements for the League, ranging from straightforward depictions of the Gaelic summer colleges to allegories about what the League believed it was doing for Ireland.[68] Often the allegories involved two tableaux presenting contrasting images of what would happen if Ireland remained untouched by the language movement and what could happen when the movement revived "*Éire*." Thus in 1906 the Central branch presented two scenes relating to emigration. In the first, one saw a family of emigrants struggling abroad, "poverty-stricken and dejected in the midst of unsympathetic strangers"; in the other one saw an "Irish-Ireland home," comfortable and clean.[69] Similarly, in 1910 the Drumcondra and Central branches presented contrasting images of the "Start of the Gaelic League" and the "Results of the League's Work." In the Drumcondra tableau *Éire* laid "despondent and hopeless" until a boy dressed in a "national costume," featuring a shield and spear, awakened her "to energy, to hope and fearlessness."[70] Meanwhile, the Central branch showed "*Éire* enthroned, surrounded by industry, arts, agriculture, music, and guarded by the Gaelic League," represented this time by a grown man in the same "national" costume.[71]

Another type of contemporary scene focused on controversies involving Gaelic Leaguers. Natural targets for these types of tableaux were the National Board of Education and the Intermediate Board of Education, both of whose consistent reluctance to include Irish in the school curriculum had drawn fire from revivalists.[72] Similarly, publicans, who had resisted League calls for voluntary closure on St. Patrick's Day since 1902, were the subjects of a tableau in 1906. It portrayed a tavern filled with customers who were seated atop barrels bearing such inscriptions as "I'll close if my neighbors close," and "I'm as good an Irishman as any Gaelic Leaguer."[73] More generally, a scene with the theme of "Driving Back the Demon of Anglicization" appeared on two occasions. In both instances the "demon" appeared in the form of Mephistopheles with scrolls hanging from his cloak, representing foreign games, immoral literature, poverty, religious bigotry, and music halls, while a tweed-clad youth carrying a hurling stick faced him down. Ironically—given this mise-en-scène—Mephistopheles also carried "the usual insignia" (i.e., red robes, a horned cap, and a broad mustache);[74] therefore, his appearance mirrored that which had been popularized in the very music halls denounced by the League. And the crowds interacted with "the villain" in appropriate music-hall fashion: in 1907, according to the *Independent*, the "demon" had "a warm time of it, particularly when his moustache of a true Mephisophelean mold appeared to be in eminent danger of falling off."[75]

One of the most dramatic specific confrontations between the League and a government agency resulted in a memorable tableau in 1905. The issue revolved around the persistent trouble that Gaelic enthusiasts experienced when sending correspondence addressed in Irish. Since 1901 the post office had declared that unless a letter addressed in Irish originated from an Irish-speaking district, it was to be treated "as undeliverable and dealt with in the Returned Letter Office [in Dublin], just as it is understood that in Germany letters addressed in Polish are treated as undeliverable."[76] In practice local postal officials either returned letters to their point of origin or forwarded them to the Returned Letter Office for translation and possible delivery. The resultant delays aggravated Irish-Irelanders and prompted several letter-writing campaigns aimed at vexing local postmasters.[77] In spite of the inconvenience, the general volume of letters addressed in Irish had increased since 1901. Between 13 and 19 February 1905 alone, some 4,000 pieces of mail had arrived in Dublin, requiring four junior sorting clerks to spend fifty man-hours translating addresses.[78] The increased pressure on his staff led the Dublin postmaster, Charles Sanderson, to refuse any more correspondence addressed in Gaelic at the beginning of March, at the very time when the League planned to send out materials for the 1905 Language Fund collection to branches throughout the country.[79] Sanderson's decision so incensed Ó Dalaigh that he enlisted 200 Dublin Leaguers to accompany him to the post office, where they paid for the parcels one package at a time, putting a stop to ordinary business for more than an hour.[80]

In the following week at the procession a tableau bearing the legend "No Surrender to the GPO/Address All Letters and Parcels in Irish" received considerable attention in the nationalist press. Only two characters appeared in the scene—a Gaelic Leaguer carrying parcels addressed in Irish and a postal official refusing them one by one. Both the *Freeman* and the *Independent* claimed that onlookers responded enthusiastically to the scene throughout the length of the march, but the most fervent reaction took place as the wagon passed by the General Post Office itself. There the crowd "vigorously cheered" and according to the *Independent*, "many and sarcastic were the comments to be heard on all sides."[81] The progress then halted briefly, and bands in the vicinity of the General Post Office began playing the nationalist anthem "A Nation Once Again," which was sung by the entire language section of the procession.[82] Nevertheless, postal officials refused to change their policy, and the issue of delayed mail addressed in Irish remained a standing complaint among Irish-Irelanders until the foundation of the Irish Free State.[83]

"AN IRISH UNIVERSITY OR ELSE—"

The most impressive and sustained set of tableaux appeared in 1909, however, when the district council used the procession to demonstrate League unity for the campaign to make Irish compulsory in the National

University. Combining historical images with contemporary commentaries, League branches linked the apparently esoteric issue of a matriculation requirement directly to material advance for the nation as a whole. They also challenged the increasingly hard-line approach taken by the Catholic hierarchy toward "fair argument" on the issue.

Five of the largest Dublin branches opened the 1909 procession, led by the Central branch, which presented two tableaux. The first illustrated one of the most widely known moments in the history of early Irish education, with its portrayal of St. Columcille's appearance at the Convention of Druimceat.[84] For this sixth-century assembly Columcille, the founder of dozens of monasteries and schools in both Ireland and Scotland, had returned from missionary exile to defend his fellow bards from certain destruction. For centuries the bardic order had been respected and feared throughout Ireland because of the scholarship and rhetorical gifts displayed by its members. But their arrogant abuse of the right to free quarters had angered Irish chieftains, who met to determine their fate at Druimceat. Columcille attended the assembly blindfolded, so that he could uphold the letter of a penance he had received more than a decade earlier, prohibiting him from ever seeing his homeland again. He argued (successfully) that the bardic order ought to be spared, that the bards must submit to more stringent discipline, and that their schools be reformed and opened to the men of Ireland as "national literary colleges."[85] Just as the blindfolded missionary had protected the crafters of the language in another era, the League and its allies asserted that they were working to create a "national literary college" through compulsory Irish.

The second of the Central branch entries alluded to the story of Cinderella, like Mephistopheles a popular staple in music-hall repertoires. The scene featured four women, three of whom—dressed as Brittania, Germany, and France—were gathered around a table on which the fruits of learning rested. The fourth woman, robed as Ireland, sat "hungry and disconsolate" at the other end of the platform, and a banner over her head posed the question, "Is this the place that we are to give Irish in the new university?" According to the *Freeman's Journal*, the crowd admired the tableau both for the ladies' costumes and for the "general sympathy" raised "for poor Ireland."[86]

Next the MacHale and the Columcille branches highlighted the importance of the university senate's upcoming decision to the university itself. The MacHale tableau served as a cautionary tale about what the League believed would happen if the senate refused its demand and prompted local governments to withhold the money needed to fund student tuition. Under the banner "Students Wanted," a forlorn professor stood before a largely empty classroom. According to the *Independent*, "there was an air of loneliness about the affair, and the empty desks and the vacant and anxious look of the participants put a color into the design which spoke more strongly than words."[87] Meanwhile the Columcille branch presented the counter image of "New Universities with Irish," which featured a classroom overflowing with students. Significantly, the scene included foreign students in addition to Irish students in its projection of a proper university. Although the bulk of those watching the procession may not have understood the full significance of the tableau, the inclusion of students from abroad may well have been intended to answer episcopal fears that compulsory Irish would preclude foreigners from attending the National University of Ireland.

At the same time, the Father Anderson and Keating branches addressed the bread-and-butter side of the language requirement. The tableau from the Father Anderson branch was especially provocative, as it focused attention on "The Result of University Education without Irish." The Andersons depicted a desolate Ireland flooded with "imported foreign goods," such as cigarettes and "unwholesome literature," all of which were sold by a Jewish shopkeeper named "Soloman Isaacs."[88] The piquancy of this overtly anti-Semitic display cannot be fully appreciated, however, without reference to the subtitle of the tableau: "An Irish University or Else—." Recall that this was the title of the provocative pamphlet containing the letters written by O'Hickey during the early days of the compulsory-Irish controversy, and that his refusal to denounce the pamphlet had led the bishops to dismiss him from his chair at Maynooth in June 1909. In the two months leading up to the procession, these incidents had received considerable attention in the public press, much of it highly critical of the decision of the hierarchy.[89] Undoubtedly, many in the crowded streets were familiar with the issues involved. By linking the

O'Hickey affair to a flood of immoral literature and Jewish-brokered foreign goods, the Anderson branch played upon Catholic xenophobia and fears of financial ruin by suggesting that there would be severe economic and cultural consequences arising from the actions of the bishops.

There is a further item to note about the Anderson tableau. As we saw in chapter 2, not all members of the hierarchy opposed compulsory Irish. Most important among those attempting quietly to accommodate the League was Archbishop William Walsh of Dublin, who ultimately cast the deciding vote in favor of compulsion in 1910. Walsh's views on compulsory Irish were not known publicly until May 1910, but it is potentially significant that the Anderson branch was headquartered in the Church of the Immaculate Heart of Mary on City-quay in Dublin. This parish was one of three cathedral parishes in the city, whose pastor was Archbishop Walsh. It is not unreasonable to assume either that the tableau reflected his own disagreement with his august brethren or that the parishioners of Immaculate Heart were challenging their still-reticent pastor to act in the "national" interest.

If the Anderson branch concentrated on a negative decision by the University Senate, the Keating branch focused on the economic benefits that would accrue from a "proper treatment of Irish in the universities." Ireland, in its view, would be a "prosperous nation, with its industries in a flourishing condition." Even more important, according to the *Independent*, "the great point was effectively made that the country had secured a large and lucrative foreign trade."[90] In short, the Keatings countered the pessimism of the Anderson tableau with the message that students educated at a university with a language requirement would lead Ireland into an economically secure and self-confident future.

"A LIVING AND IMPORTANT FORCE"

It is also worth inquiring whether the League processions projected an image of the revival leading all citizens or whether it led only the Catholic citizenry. The minutes of the organization subcommittee make clear that League officials intended to remain true to their nonsectarian ideals.[91] To cite just one example from 1906, when the Rathmines Catholic

Young Men's Society asked whether they might advertise their magazine *The Catholic Young Man* while they marched, the organizers "unanimously decided that this could not be permitted."[92]

Official intent aside, however, the composition of most processions may have strengthened anxieties among non-Catholics about the true intentions of the League, just as did the O'Growney funeral procession. That the organization concerned in the last example was the "Catholic" Young Men's Society is telling. Indeed, if one looks at the friendly societies section of the processions, it is striking that the Protestant Young Men's Societies and Boys' Brigades do not appear, while numerous of their Catholic counterparts marched annually. By 1904, as we have seen, these bodies were joined by branches of the INF, who sought even greater exposure than they had originally received. Still later, as the Ancient Order of Hibernians (AOH) expanded from its northern heartland into southern Ireland, AOH contingents joined as well, creating a Catholic phalanx in the friendly societies section.[93]

At the same time, one finds a somewhat more diverse picture in the temperance sections. Nonsectarian temperance bodies, such as the Dublin Total Abstinence Society (DTAS) and the Irish Association for the Prevention of Intemperance, took part in the processions alongside more "purely" Catholic societies. For example, in 1906 both temperance groups decided to participate, with the DTAS providing its brass and reed band. Even in the temperance section, however, Catholic groups, including the Father Mathew Temperance Society run by the Capuchins in Church Street, formed the bulk of those marching, particularly in later years.[94]

Within the language section itself there were two obvious ways in which Protestant and unionist suspicions might have been aroused or exacerbated: the presence of priests at the head of League branches and as speakers at the post-procession demonstrations. We have seen that priests often served as the presidents or vice presidents of League branches, though this tendency was more prevalent in smaller towns and villages than in Dublin. As a gauge of the relatively modest presence of clerics, one can look again at the 1906 demonstration as exemplary. Of the forty-three branches which marched, thirty-three recorded the names of their officers in press reports; of these, fifteen were priests, five of whom marched with one branch. Among the twenty-three members of the Coiste Gnótha and the fifteen members of the Dublin district council marching, only one was a priest.[95] When one considers that more than 3,600 Gaelic Leaguers marched in the language section, sixteen priests would hardly seem significant. Looked at from the perspective of one who might already be concerned about clerical influence, however, the sight of priests leading roughly one-third of those 3,600 people might indeed be ominous.

One might conclude, therefore, that Protestants, including potential participants, had determined that the processions were not intended to be inclusive events. Although some may have reached that conclusion, one must recognize that another factor prevented sympathetic Protestants from joining these annual marches. That factor was timing. Since the processions were intended as the beginning of fund-raising efforts in the capital, Dublin Leaguers sought to reach the widest possible audience, and they scheduled the marches on Sunday afternoons when most working people in Dublin had the day off. Secular activities on Sundays, however, raised a systemic block keeping away many sympathetic Protestants. Evidence on this point is somewhat thin, but two incidents suggest that the League was aware of this difficulty and considered changing the date of the procession in order to meet Protestant desires.

First, in 1905 and 1906 the organization subcommittee invited both archbishops of Dublin to take part in the post-procession demonstration in Smithfield market. In 1905, Archbishop Walsh did speak at Smithfield, but his Anglican counterpart, Archbishop Peacocke, offered his regrets. In the following year, neither attended—Walsh because of illness, but Peacocke specifically for reasons of conscience. In a letter to the subcommittee he expressed his appreciation for their efforts on behalf of Irish industries and the temperance cause, but he observed that he would be "unable to accept the invitation, having conscientious objections to attending meetings other than religious ones on Sundays."[96] Second, in 1905, MacNeill had stated publicly that the League was considering moving the processions from Sunday to St. Patrick's Day itself, in part because "there were many manufacturers whose principles prevented them from taking part in a Sunday procession."[97] At the time, the League was engaged in efforts to have St. Patrick's Day declared a bank holiday, and the expectation appears to have been that the procession would take place on the holiday when all could gather in good conscience and without fear of reprisal at their place of employment.

When the date of the procession did change, however, the reason was quite literally more elemental. Writers in *An Claidheamh Soluis*, the *Leader*, and the *Peasant* commented on the cold and rainy conditions in 1906. "We have no doubt," declared Moran, "that many who took part in the great demonstration are now laid up with colds."[98] Such conditions also made it less likely that the audience would be large or would understand all the displays. According to Ryan, the weather took away from the "spectacular purpose" of the "Irish-Ireland pageant" because

> banners were obstreperous; the tableaux in the wind and rain rather failed of their effect; the fair and light-robed *cáilíní* shivering on the wind-swept cars seemed pathetically out of place.[99]

Wet weather posed a further difficulty: slick, dirty roads. Because the streets were paved with inexpensive macadamized stone, the subsoil tended to seep through to the surface when the streets became wet, making them even more uncomfortable for the processionists.[100] Moran cautioned that weather would be a danger every March: "Even if the rain keeps away, it is almost sure to be bitterly cold."[101] At a special meeting in April 1906, therefore, delegates from the Dublin branches decided to move the procession to June in 1907. After finding it difficult to coordinate the function at the beginning of the summer holiday season, they then moved it in 1908 to September in order to coincide with the opening of League classes around the city.[102]

Ryan complained in 1909 that the changes had been made "for special metropolitan reasons" and that the later collection in Dublin had had a deleterious effect on the Language Fund as a whole.[103] Contributions to the fund had been decreasing since their peak in 1905–6, reflecting the general decline in League membership. By 1909 many branches either made their collections later in the year or failed to submit their money altogether. According to Ryan, Gaelic Leaguers in the country pointed to the example of Dublin as having inspired their own delayed collections, and he "urged a readjustment" in the capital:

> Doubtless, the Dublin *coiste ceanntair* has good grounds for its own position and attitude, to which it steadfastly adheres, despite the criticism and the complaints. But the fact remains that the general interests of the movement are being retarded instead of being advanced.[104]

Eventually, in 1913, Dubliners did schedule their Language Week for March. With each move, however, the district council also perpetuated the systemic problem of Sunday processions, finding it more pragmatic to make the event available to the largest potential audience, even if it barred interested Protestants from participating.

An indicator of growing curiosity about the revival among Dublin Protestants is the treatment of the procession in the unionist press. Protestants were not the sole readers of unionist newspapers, of course, but because most unionists were Protestants, the unionist press is a potential source of information about Protestant opinion. Unionist dailies generally downplayed the first procession in 1902. The *Evening Mail* took one of the hardest stances against the language campaign, seeing it as "only another side of the eternal political agitation with which this land is cursed." Referring specifically to the procession, the *Mail* concluded:

> It is nationalist, not national, and we are inclined to regret the fact. If we could believe that yesterday's procession was not, after all, a political demonstration and that "God Save Ireland" was a pious aspiration rather than a fierce battle-shout, we would be heartily glad; but it would be unwise, we think, to accept the demonstration in this light.[105]

The *Irish Times* meanwhile provided a brief report (one-half column in length) about the first procession, which Moran described as "carefully censored and colorless news." And the *Daily Express* gave it only slightly more play (a full column of news and a brief editorial notice).[106]

The continuing presence of the League and the growth of the procession prompted a gradual change in attitude. The length of the news reports in unionist papers increased, as they utilized materials offered by League press stewards, and editorial articles discussed the significance of the procession. After the procession in 1904, for example, the *Irish Times* stated in a leading article that "the Gaelic League deserves immense credit for this achievement, which proves that its organizing powers are of no ordinary kind."[107] Two years later, the same newspaper was even more emphatic in its recognition of the procession:

> The Gaelic League is a living and important force in Ireland. Nobody can deny that fact who watched its great annual procession pass yesterday through the streets of Dublin. For a full hour and a half the procession flowed past a given point, and its comprehensive elements included energies—educational, industrial, artistic, literary, and athletic—which play a large part in the life of Ireland.[108]

In citing this editorial, I am not suggesting that all unionists agreed with the *Irish Times* or even that sympathetic unionists agreed with the effort to revive spoken Gaelic as an everyday medium of communication. Rather, what these comments indicate is that the leading organ of the unionist press recognized the language procession as an event that had become significant in the life of the Irish capital, and, by extension, it recognized the revival as "a living and important force."

CONCLUSION

Such evidence might tempt one to conclude, along with the editorial writer of *An Claidheamh Soluis,* that the Gaelic League had "struck deep roots in the capital" by the time of the 1910 procession.[109] Another contemporary observer, however, offered a more measured assessment of its impact. The attorney William Dawson witnessed the great excitement generated by the annual celebration, and he declared in 1912 that "on the day of the language procession the stranger might be pardoned for thinking that a passion for Irish is the one great obsession of Dublin."[110] But he believed that "what strikes the observer most about the influence of the League in your city is that it runs, so to speak, in a parallel stream to the broad river of Dublin life."[111] Such a conclusion echoed Ryan's oft-expressed opinion, chastening the overly optimistic with the comment that "one great gala day is very interesting and striking so far as it goes, but it is not enough to affect the imagination and open the purse-strings."[112]

Similar cautionary notes should be struck when reflecting on the significance of all major Irish-Ireland entertainments. Yet Dawson's image of parallel streams does not convey the situation fully. As in the case of provincial feiseanna, the Gaelic processions appropriated aspects of preexisting traditions and the prevailing Anglo-Irish culture of the capital and grafted them into the Irish-Ireland repertoire, creating a tributary, if not a parallel, stream. Moreover, just as festival participants expended a great deal of time and energy to prepare for their brief moment in the spotlight, so too have we seen that procession planners spent months contacting potential participants, raising awareness, and distributing information about their event.

Still, anticipation and excitement about the processions could be sustained only as long as local Gaelic Leaguers presented the kind of events which entertained and impressed the public, a prospect that proved increasingly difficult after 1906. As the number of branches waned in the capital, the size of processions declined as well. By 1911 even *An Claidheamh Soluis* acknowledged that the tableaux in the language section were "not so numerous as one would wish."[113] And in 1913, when the district council attempted to reinstitute the procession on short notice, only ten area branches mustered, none of which had had time to put together a tableau.[114]

As long as they remained a viable means of public appeal, the language processions provided revivalists with a unique way to bring their cause into the streets of the capital. By drawing on traditions of civic pageantry, the League addressed Dubliners through a familiar medium that allowed unions and trade societies, temperance organizations, friendly societies, and other advocacy groups to align themselves opportunistically with the language cause. In practice, therefore, preexisting associational networks, the socioeconomic conditions of the city, the condition of the League as an organization, and the spectacle of the processions themselves all combined to affect how people interpreted and internalized the League's linguistic nationalism.

Conclusion

The Gaelic League, which was really a delightful body of men and women so long as it was actuated by only one desire, that of restoring the Irish language, began to lose its charm when it became powerful. It was then worth capturing, and people, notoriously Griffiths [sic], set about to do so.[1]

D ouglas Hyde penned these words in April 1918 as he lay in bed, ill and somewhat despondent at the takeover of the Gaelic League by republican forces three years earlier at the Ard-Fheis in Dundalk. Past disagreements with Arthur Griffith—and the latter's growing affiliation with those involved in the takeover—led Hyde to ascribe the action unfairly to Griffith rather than to the IRB. In the nearly fifteen years since the great procession that welcomed O'Growney's remains back from the United States, Hyde had seen the small society they had fostered with their friend MacNeill become the most important body at the heart of the Gaelic revival. Hundreds of thousands had joined—and left—its ranks, many of them drawn through O'Growney's *Simple Lessons* to a new sense of themselves. Through their branch activities, concerts, festivals, and processions, they had shared their excitement and their belief in the promise of a more prosperous Ireland with their neighbors. But now the League had been turned to political ends, advocating a free Ireland as well as a Gaelic one, and some of its most devoted workers were either dead, such as Patrick Pearse and Thomas Ashe, or under constant surveillance, like Seán Ó Murthuile, because of their open defiance of Ireland's continued incorporation in the United Kingdom.

Of course, as seen in chapter 1, the League had always been subjected to entryist tactics. As early as the 1890s, political factions, especially those associated with advanced nationalist politics, sought to control its resources for their own ends. In retrospect, two things leant special significance to the IRB attempt in 1915. First, and most obviously, it had succeeded. Hyde and others committed to the nonpolitical stance of the League resigned their positions on the Coiste Gnótha in the months prior to the Easter Rising, when it became clear that they were no longer welcome. Three years on, however, Hyde speculated that the link with politics might eventually benefit the language cause:

> This section of the nation has now definitely placed the language in the very forefront of its program, and for very shame's sake cannot withdraw from its own professions. Though I must say I have noticed very little enthusiasm on the part of the Volunteers proper to help us out in our language campaign . . . it is quite possible however in spite of this that it may prove that the language has really been best served by the extreme party confiscating it for themselves as their own particular asset.[2]

In the short run this analysis seems to have been on the mark. At the time of the Dundalk congress, the League had dwindled in size to a mere 262 branches, but it expanded rapidly after the Rising to more than 550 *craobhacha* in 1918. Much of this growth could, no doubt, be attributed to the association of the League with those pushing the separatist program. Crown authorities noted these close connections as well, and just three months after Hyde proffered his conclusion, Dublin Castle declared the Gaelic League a "dangerous" body.[3]

But there is a second reason that the takeover has been seen as significant: that is, the status that the Irish language attained among the leaders of the revolutionary and immediate postcolonial eras. In 1919, for instance, one of Hyde's successors as president of the League, J. J. O'Kelly ("Sceilg"), served in the first *Dáil Éireann* as minister for the short-lived Department of the National Language. After 1922, the Irish Free State embraced the language as its central cultural component, with successive governments in the interwar years encouraging the use of Irish in public life, at least in a ceremonial fashion. Native speakers of Irish became possibly even more the objects of cultural reification than they had been for those early revivalists taking summer trips to "the West."[4] In effect, they were valued more as artifacts than as living beings—they were to educate and inoculate the rest of their fellow citizens from the lingering danger of Anglicization in a state in which more than 90 percent of the residents were native speakers of English. All the while, the economic and sociocultural stresses faced by residents of the Gaeltacht proved equally effective as impediments to the preservation of the language in daily life as they had before independence.

Politicians had greater success in changing educational norms, if not educational performance, reversing the policy of the nineteenth-century national school system by mandating the incorporation of Irish in the elementary and intermediate school curricula. This emphasis placed the primary onus for Gaelicizing the new Ireland on the young and their teachers. There was stridency in these official positions, so much so that figures such as Ernest Blythe and Tomás Ó Deirg—respectively, the Minister for Finance in the Cumann na nGaedheal government of the 1920s and the Minister for Education under Fianna Fáil in the 1930s and 1940s—angered contemporary (and later) critics, including the Irish National Teachers Organization (INTO) because improved proficiency in Irish was placed ahead of mastering other subjects, including mathematics, English, and rural sciences.[5] One irony of alienating groups such as the INTO was that, as seen in chapters 2 and 3, teachers had been among the most active proponents of Irish in the schools prior to independence. In spite of managerial and governmental reluctance to provide them with training and support, some 40 percent of teachers in the Free State were already certified to teach through the medium of Irish in the spring of 1922, having taken advantage of the voluntary summer colleges founded by the Gaelic League during the height of the revival. Of course, this meant that 60 percent of the teaching staff were *not* initially certified when the curricular policy was promulgated, and even when more attained their accreditation, it did not guarantee a high caliber of teaching through the medium of Irish.[6]

But there is another point that should not be lost when discussing the incorporation of the language into revolutionary and postcolonial policy. Hyde's assessment of the transformation of the League masks two essential facts established in the present study. First, the membership (let alone the leadership) of the organization in 1918 was emphatically not the same as that which had existed when the League recorded its highest number of branches in 1906. Hundreds of *craobhacha* had ceased to function in those years, and individual membership had turned over as well. The influx and outflow of individuals described in chapter 3 continued right up through the years of the Great War, such that League activity throughout provincial Ireland waxed and waned.[7] Second, and emerging out of this constant turnover, members had never been "actuated by only one desire."

Here Hyde was making the same type of mistaken assumption that Frank Gallagher would in his famous account of the Irish War of Independence, *The Four Glorious Years*.[8] After 1916 the tide of public opinion in Ireland was indeed shifting toward what is often called advanced nationalism or, in the context of that time, "Sinn Féinism." But what precisely this meant varied depending on local circumstances. It could mean that one wanted an independent republic, or that one still wanted Home Rule but that Redmond's party looked spent in comparison to the dynamism of de Valera's associates, or that one wanted further land reform than had been provided by earlier land acts. More than likely it meant that one opposed conscription into the British army and the measures of "mild coercion" that the government was introducing, including the proscription on public meetings of the Gaelic League.[9] Thus, just as those who would fight against Crown forces were actuated by multiple understandings of what Irish freedom and democracy might mean—understandings that would result in the blood-soaked fissures of civil war—so too had Gaelic revivalists joined in the language campaign for a multiplicity of reasons.[10]

Recognizing this fact should not lead one to dismiss the Irish language as unimportant to League members or, indeed, to the people to whom they appealed. The willingness of ordinary men and women to challenge powerful local figures (including their priests), the ready audiences for festivals and processions, and especially the enormous interest generated by the compulsory Irish campaign, all indicate that a significant portion of the Irish public believed that the language deserved to be a central symbol of Irishness by 1910. The question of why they had come to believe in its importance remains to be answered.

On one level, there can be little question that part of the answer lies in the number of people exposed directly to revivalist propaganda through League branches. The membership of the organization was in fact larger than any single-year total would indicate, and it was also considerably broader than has hitherto been appreciated. From its very first year the League included members who were largely representative of the Irish urban middle classes, though it also attracted a fair number of rural members from the ranks of farmers and farm laborers. As it grew in size, the League also attracted the interest of a relatively small number of laborers in cities such as Dublin, Belfast, and Derry, though the vast majority of the members continued to come from the middle classes, including especially the black-coated workers of the lower-middle classes. Indeed, one of the most important findings of the present work is that black-coated workers made up the largest proportion of League membership as early as 1894, thus refuting the notion that the League became radicalized only after the lower-middle classes predominated. In fact, they had always predominated, even in the most liberal phase of League activity.

Furthermore, contrary to received notions that Protestants withdrew from the League shortly after 1900, a significant—if small—percentage of the membership was made up of Protestants. Equally important, we have seen that many Protestants who were not members of the League expressed an interest in its overarching goals, either through a cognate organization, such as the Gaelic Society at Queen's College, Belfast, or by supporting other movements, such as the temperance movement, which allied with the language revival. To be sure, those Protestants who participated actively in the League were exceptional in some way. Specifically, most appear to have been political nationalists, an increasingly lonely minority among Irish Protestants after 1900. Still, their presence should not be overlooked when assessing the appeal of the movement.

The one significant constituency that the League failed to enlist in great numbers was the native-speaking population of the west and the south. In part, they stayed away because the traveling organizers of the

League called upon town-based local notables to take charge of Gael-tacht branches. Ingrained frictions between town dwellers and their rural neighbors dampened the enthusiasm of men and women from the countryside who continued to use the language but who remained skeptical about the intentions of the revival. Even more important was the utter distress faced by Irish-speaking families in the west and south of Ireland, whose greatest natural resource continued to be the children they raised to emigrate. In both respects, these failings prefigured the policy shortcomings of the Free State and Republic alluded to above.

The men and women who joined the revival were both aspiring and wary. Among the farmers, clerks, teachers, and shop assistants in the ordinary membership, and in the more elite corps of League executive members, we have seen that there were people who were rising above the station of their parents, as well as a disproportionate number of migrants into the metropolitan population. They were also intensely aware that their contemporaries continued to leave Ireland because they found its culture stultified and its economic potential unfulfilled. Revivalists addressed the former problem through their language classes, lectures, concerts, dances, and festivals. They attacked the latter through their championing of Irish industry, including agriculture; their founding of small businesses and advocacy groups; and their creation of the world's first national trademark.

As seen in chapter 4, however, revivalists were not universally committed to Griffithite economic thought. To be sure, many Irish-Irelanders were protectionists, but others were free traders interested in supporting homemade products that were "as good and cheap" as imports. Still others were "cooperators," and a small number were socialists. Regardless of their approach to matters economic, they shared the expectation—millennial perhaps—that the creation of an Irish-Ireland would bring greater prosperity and wider opportunities than existed in the Anglicized Ireland they knew. It is possible—though this point would require significant further research—that the lackluster economic performance under both the Cumann na nGaedheal–led and Fianna Fáil–led governments in the interwar years may actually have undercut support for state-initiated efforts to preserve and extend the use of Irish. In short, economic stagnation may well have undermined one of the pre-independence justifications for preserving the language.[11]

The very existence of a meeting place in a town or village (outside of a public house or shebeen) at which people of all ages could enjoy participatory entertainment was an exciting, if not entirely novel, concession to the transformations in popular culture that had occurred since the famine.[12] But as shown in chapters 5 and 6, the claims of language enthusiasts that these entertainments were entirely native in character were overstated. They borrowed from well-known cultural forms—including Anglo-Irish and English models—just as they drew from traditional Gaelic culture. Recognizing this fact does not diminish the development of these new Irish entertainments; rather, it highlights the ability of ordinary men and women to adapt market-driven cultural forms in order to fashion their own productions. Thus, even if Oireachtas and feis competitions produced "rather silly" or derivative works, they also nurtured the early talents of those, such as Padraig Ó Conaire, who helped to establish modern literature in the Irish language.

The preceding examination of the Gaelic revival argues, therefore, for a substantial revision of its place in modern Irish history. The belief that the movement was a monocular, peasant-centered foretaste of the provincialized culture of the Irish Free State and Republic must be qualified. To be sure, there were many who considered the language a bulwark against the encroaching secularism and modernism they saw as inherent in Anglicization, and such rhetoric echoed through policy and propagandist statements for generations. But the cultural practices embraced by the majority of people on the island before Sinn Féin even emerged as a viable challenger to the Irish parliamentary party suggest that many also understood the revival as a bridge to modernity. They learned their "cupla focail," but to the dismay of ideologues such as Pearse they lacked an "adequate, accurate, coherent idea of the philosophy of the movement." Instead, they enjoyed the pastimes they created for themselves rather than progressing beyond the first volume of O'Growney's *Simple Lessons,* or they engaged in temperance, industrial, and cooperative campaigns, claiming inspiration from the language and believing all the while that they were contributing to its preservation. And this belief was no delusion; it was a result of the assimilative process whereby revivalists—and Irish society more generally—grasped "preserving the language" as a notional meta-concept, open to multiple understandings, only one of which required a personal commitment to acquire a speaking knowledge of Irish.

ABBREVIATIONS

NOTES

GLOSSARY

BIBLIOGRAPHY

INDEX

Abbreviations

ACS	*An Claidheamh Soluis*
CO 904	Colonial Office Papers, Series 904
CCCA	Cork City and County Archives
CSB	Crime Special Branch
DMP	Dublin Metropolitan Police
EMP	Eoin MacNeill Papers
FL	*Fáinne an Lae*
FMP	Fionán MacColuim Papers
FJ	*Freeman's Journal*
GJ	*Gaelic Journal/Irisleabhar na Gaedhilge*
MCR	Inspector General's Monthly Confidential Report
IH	*Irish Homestead*
II	*Irish Independent*
INP	*Irish Nation and the Peasant*
IP	*Irish Peasant*
IT	*Irish Times*
JGP	John Glynn Papers
LMOF	Letters of Abbot Maurus Ó Faoláin
MMA	Mount Melleray Abbey
NAI	National Archives of Ireland
NLI	National Library of Ireland
PII	*Peasant and Irish Ireland*
RIC	Royal Irish Constabulary
SVV	*Shan Van Vocht*
SF	*Sinn Féin*
UCD	University College Dublin
UI	*United Irishman*
WPRP	W. P. Ryan Papers

Notes

INTRODUCTION

1. "Brian na Banban" (Brian O'Higgins, pseud.), in the *Leinster Leader*, quoted in *ACS*, 27 May 1911.

2. For example, see Ciaran Brady, ed., *Interpreting Irish History: The Debate on Historical Revisionism, 1938–1994* (Dublin: Irish Academic Press, 1994); and D. George Boyce and Alan O'Day, eds., *The Making of Modern Irish History: Revisionism and the Revisionist Controversy* (London: Routledge, 1996). More recently, Daly has provided a stimulating discussion of the controversy and its aftermath. See Mary E. Daly, "Forty Shades of Grey? Irish Historiography and the Challenges of Multidisciplinarity," in *Ireland Beyond Boundaries: Mapping Irish Studies in the Twenty-First Century*, ed. Liam Harte and Yvonne Whelan (London: Pluto Press, 2007).

3. For examples of more general treatments, see F. S. L. Lyons, *Ireland since the Famine* (London: Fontana Paperbacks, 1973); Oliver MacDonagh, *States of Mind: A Study of the Anglo-Irish Conflict, 1780–1980* (London: Allen and Unwin, 1983); R. V. Comerford, "Nation, Nationalism, and the Irish Language," in *Perspectives on Irish Nationalism*, ed. Thomas E. Hachey and Lawrence J. McCaffrey (Lexington: Univ. Press of Kentucky, 1989); Donal McCartney, "Hyde, D. P. Moran, and Irish-Ireland," in *Leaders and Men of the Easter Rising: Dublin 1916*, ed. F. X. Martin (Ithaca, N.Y.: Cornell Univ. Press, 1967); and Donal McCartney, "MacNeill and Irish-Ireland," in *The Scholar Revolutionary: Eoin MacNeill*, ed. F. X. Martin and F. J. Byrne (Shannon: Irish Univ. Press, 1967). Examples of more sophisticated treatments include Tom Garvin, *Nationalist Revolutionaries in Ireland, 1858–1928* (Oxford: Clarendon Press, 1987), and John Hutchinson, *The Dynamics of Cultural Nationalism: The Gaelic Revival and the Creation of the Irish Nation State* (London: Allen and Unwin, 1987). See also three useful unpublished doctoral theses: Martin J. Waters, "W. P. Ryan and the Irish-Ireland Movement" (Ph.D. diss., Univ. of Connecticut, 1970); Shane O'Neill, "The Politics of Culture in Ireland, 1899–1910" (D.Phil. diss., Oxford Univ., 1982); and Frank Biletz, "The Boundaries of Irish National Identity, 1890–1912" (Ph.D. diss., Univ. of Chicago, 1994). See also Timothy G. McMahon, "The Gaelic League and the Irish-Ireland Movement" (master's thesis, Univ. of Wisconsin-Madison, 1994); and Timothy G. McMahon, "The Social Bases of the Gaelic Revival, 1893–1910" (Ph.D. diss., Univ. of Wisconsin-Madison, 2001).

4. John Hutchinson, "Irish Nationalism," in *The Making of Modern Irish History: Revisionism and the Revisionist Controversy*, ed. D. George Boyce and Alan O'Day (London: Routledge, 1996), 117.

5. [Eoin MacNeill], "The Gaelic League," *GJ*, 4 (Nov. 1893), 226. The article was unattributed in the original.

6. See Pádraig Ó Fearáil, *The Story of Conradh na Gaeilge* (Dublin: An Clódhanna Teoranta, 1975). Also, Ó hAilín and Ó Tuama provide useful introductions to the League. See Tomás Ó hAilín, "Irish Revival Movements," in *A View of the Irish Language*, ed. Brian Ó Cuiv (Dublin: Stationery Office, 1969), and Seán Ó Tuama, ed., *The Gaelic League Idea* (Cork: Mercier Press, 1972).

7. MacDonagh, *States of Mind*, 112. See also Garvin, *Nationalist Revolutionaries*, 78–107; Tom Garvin, *The Evolution of Irish National Politics* (New York: Holmes and Meier, 1981); and Tom Garvin, "Priests and Patriots: Irish Separatism and Fear of the Modern, 1890–1914," *Irish Historical Studies* 25 (May 1986): 67–81. Comerford, meanwhile, provides a somewhat different view of the impact of the Gaelic revival on the later Irish states. See Comerford, "Nation, Nationalism," 20–41; and R. V. Comerford, *Ireland: Inventing the Nation* (London: Hodder Arnold, 2003), 121–52. Finally, Boyce and Foster present opposing views on the political role of Gaelic revivalists from the fall of Parnell until the third Home Rule bill. See D. George Boyce, *Nationalism in Ireland* (London: Routledge, 1991), chap. 8; and R. F. Foster, "Anglo-Irish Literature, Gaelic Nationalism, and Irish Politics in the 1890s," in *Ireland after the Union: Proceedings of the Second Joint Meeting of the Royal Irish Academy and the British Academy, London, 1986* (Oxford: Oxford Univ. Press, 1989).

8. Patrick O'Farrell, *Ireland's English Question: Anglo-Irish Relations, 1534–1970* (New York: Schocken Books, 1971). Lyons repeats and develops several themes from O'Farrell and has been extremely influential on the cultural roots of division in turn-of-the-century Ireland. See F. S. L. Lyons, *Culture and Anarchy in Ireland, 1890–1939* (Oxford: Clarendon Press, 1979), chaps. 2 and 3. Hutchinson's research provides an in-depth look at the Gaelic revival and the interplay between cultural and political developments at the turn of the century. See Hutchinson, *Dynamics*, passim. Brown's work is the most important treatment of the culture of postindependence Ireland. See Terence Brown, *Ireland: A Social and Cultural History, 1922 to the Present* (Ithaca, N.Y.: Cornell Univ. Press, 1985).

9. Garvin, *Nationalist Revolutionaries*, 7.

10. Ibid., 22.

11. Hutchinson, *Dynamics*, 244. See also Anthony D. Smith, *Nationalism in the Twentieth Century* (New York: New York Univ. Press, 1979); Anthony D. Smith, *The Ethnic Revival* (Cambridge: Cambridge Univ. Press, 1981); Anthony D. Smith, *The Ethnic Origins of Nations* (New York: Basil Blackwell, 1986); Anthony D. Smith, *National Identity* (Reno: Univ. of Nevada Press, 1991).

12. Smith, *Ethnic Revival*, 103; Hutchinson, *Dynamics*, 244.

13. Hutchinson, *Dynamics*, chaps. 7 and 8.

14. The lack of support among legal and medical professionals was a frequent topic in the Gaelic press, though there were significant examples of both lawyers and doctors in League ranks. For example, see the letter from Eamonn Ceannt in *ACS*, 8 Aug. 1908. See also *Leader*, 2, 9, 16 Mar. 1907.

15. Peter Murray, "Irish Cultural Nationalism in the United Kingdom State: Politics and the Gaelic League, 1900–18," *Irish Political Studies* 8 (1993): 56–57. Indeed, it is ironic that the individuals named by Hutchinson as university graduates who were associated with the revival had all received positions or, in the case of Mary Butler, chose to adopt a domestic lifestyle rather than a professional one. See Hutchinson, *Dynamics*, 269.

16. Hutchinson does include considerable census data in order to establish that more of the Irish population was educated by 1900 than could find positions in the professions and the civil service, but aside from references to a handful of League leaders, he does not specifically address the wider membership.

17. P. J. Mathews, *Revival: The Abbey Theatre, Sinn Féin, the Gaelic League, and the Co-operative Movement* (Notre Dame, Ind.: Univ. of Notre Dame Press, 2003); Philip O'Leary, *The Prose Literature of the Gaelic Revival, 1881–1921: Ideology and Innovation* (University Park: Pennsylvania State Univ. Press, 1994); and Philip O'Leary, *Gaelic Prose in the Irish Free State, 1922–1939* (Dublin: University College Dublin Press, 2004).

18. Louis A. Paul-Dubois, *Contemporary Ireland*, with an introduction by Tom Kettle (Dublin: Maunsel and Co., 1911), 167–68. See also Foster's account of the impression created by the young W. B. Yeats when he moved into London clubs after having cut his teeth in the more virulent atmosphere of Dublin debating clubs in R. F. Foster, *W. B. Yeats: A Life, Vol. I, The Apprentice Mage* (Oxford: Oxford Univ. Press, 1997), 64; Dominic Daly, *The Young Douglas Hyde: The Dawn of the Irish Revolution and Renaissance, 1874–1893* (Dublin: Irish Univ. Press, 1974), 154–55.

19. The *Leader* actually had a wider circulation than did Griffith's *United Irishman* up until at least 1905. It lost favor with some Irish-Irelanders, however, because of Moran's advocacy of the Crown link, which is suggestive of the political makeup of the Irish-Ireland reading public. For a useful introduction to Moran's career, see Patrick Maume, *D. P. Moran* (Dundalk: Dundalgan Press, 1995). On the circulation of *The Leader* and the *United Irishman*, see P. S. O'Hegarty, *A History of Ireland under the Union, 1801 to 1922: With an Epilogue Carrying the Story down to the Acceptance in 1927 by de Valera of the Anglo-Irish Treaty of 1921* (New York: Kraus, 1969), 615.

20. Robert Hogan, Richard Burnham, and Daniel P. Poteet, *The Modern Irish Drama: A Documentary History, IV: The Rise of the Realists, 1910–1915* (Dublin: Dolmen Press, 1979), 68. O'Leary, *Prose Literature*, 318–19. Along similar lines, Pearse moved a vote of thanks to Yeats for speaking to the Gaelic League Central branch in 1910. Although their relationship could be prickly, Yeats and Pearse clearly respected one another, as evidenced by Yeats's staging the premier of Rabindranath Tagore's play *The Post Office* along with Pearse's short Irish drama *An Rí* at the Abbey Theatre to raise money for Pearse's school, St. Enda's. See

R. F. Foster, *W. B. Yeats*, 469–73; Ruth Dudley Edwards, *Patrick Pearse: The Triumph of Failure* (London: Gollancz, 1977), 171–72; *SF*, 12 Mar. 1910; *ACS*, 19 Mar. 1910.

21. Miroslav Hroch, *Social Preconditions of National Revival in Europe: A Comparative Analysis of the Social Composition of Patriotic Groups among the Smaller European Nations* (New York: Columbia Univ. Press, 2000), 22–24.

22. For example, see Hans Kohn, *The Idea of Nationalism: A Study in Its Origins and Background* (New York: Macmillan, 1944); Carlton J. H. Hayes, *The Historical Evolution of Modern Nationalism* (New York: Russell and Russell, 1968).

23. "Notional" in this sense differs from its use by Daly, who described it as the use of "ritualized aspirational slogans." Although the assimilative process described here may result in such slogans, it is the process through which a person understands concepts and relates them to one's own life experience. It is similar to what the French describe as "bricolage," that is, constructing something from whatever parts are available. Cf. G. Daly, "On Formulating National Goals," in *Ireland in the Year 2000: Towards a National Strategy: Issues and Perspectives; Proceedings of a Colloquy, Kilkea Castle, February 1983* (Dublin: An Foras Forbatha, 1983), 29–30.

24. Just as Turner has demonstrated that celebratory symbols can be read in multiple ways, so too can various types of texts from newspapers to books to political tracts. What makes this insight particularly important to the Gaelic revival is that the public became acquainted with revivalist thought through public celebration. Cf. Victor Turner, *Celebration: Studies in Festivity and Ritual* (Washington, D.C.: Smithsonian Institution Press, 1982), 16.

25. For example, see Mike Cronin and Daryl Adair, *The Wearing of the Green: A History of St. Patrick's Day* (London: Routledge, 2002); Brian Walker, "Public Holidays, Commemoration and Identity in Ireland, North and South, 1920–1960," in *De Valera's Irelands*, ed. Gabriel Doherty and Dermot Keogh (Cork: Mercier Press, 2003); Brian Walker, *Dancing to History's Tune: History, Myth and Politics in Ireland* (Belfast: Institute of Irish Studies, 1996); Gary Owens, "Constructing the Repeal Spectacle: Monster Meetings and People Power in Pre-Famine Ireland," in *People Power: Proceedings of the Third Annual Daniel O'Connell Workshop*, ed. Maurice O'Connell (Dublin: Institute of Public Administration, 1993); and Gary Owens, "Nationalism without Words: Symbolism and Ritual Behavior in the Repeal 'Monster Meetings' of 1843–5," in *Irish Popular Culture, 1650–1850*, ed. James S. Donnelly Jr. and Kerby A. Miller (Dublin: Irish Academic Press, 1999). For an influential early study of the use of festivals in France, see Mona Ozouf, *Festivals and the French Revolution*, trans. Alan Sheridan (Cambridge, Mass.: Harvard Univ. Press, 1988).

26. Turner, chap. 1; Clifford Geertz, *The Interpretation of Culture* (New York: Basic Books, 1973); Ray B. Browne and Michael T. Marsden, eds., *The Cultures of Celebration* (Bowling Green, Ohio: Bowling Green State Univ. Popular Press, 1994); and Frank E. Manning, ed., *The Celebration of Society: Perspectives on Contemporary Cultural Performance* (Bowling Green, Ohio: Bowling Green State Univ. Popular Press, 1983).

27. Turner, 16.

1. THE STRANGE CASE OF O'GROWNEY'S BONES

1. *FJ*, 28 Sept. 1903.

2. Planning for the transfer started almost as soon as he died in October 1899, but the final arrangements were not completed until early 1903. See Agnes O'Farrelly, ed., *Leabhar an Athar Eoghan/The O'Growney Memorial Volume* (Dublin: M. H. Gill and Son, 1904), parts 1 and 2.

3. Ibid. See also Patrick J. Corish, *Maynooth: 1795–1995* (Dublin: Gill and Macmillan, 1995), 287–88.

4. O'Farrelly, *Leabhar*, 69; NAI, DMP CSB 1903/28,965/S., Precis for September 1903. At one point, the front of the procession was entering Rutland (now Parnell) Square while the contingents stretched back through Britain Street, Capel Street, Parliament Street, Dame Street, College Green, Westmoreland Street, and onto the O'Connell Bridge.

5. *FJ*, 27 Sept. 1903.

6. Ibid.

7. Mathews, 6–12.

8. Eugene O'Growney, *Simple Lessons in Irish; Giving the Pronunciation of Each Word*, Part 1 (Dublin: Gaelic League, 1903), frontispiece.

9. *ACS*, 4 Nov. 1899.

10. Quoted in *The Workshop of Daedalus: James Joyce and the Raw Materials for* A Portrait of the Artist as a Young Man, ed. Robert Scholes and Richard Kain (Evanston, IL: Northwestern Univ. Press, 1965), 161.

11. Most of the priests marched with Gaelic League branches, though two members of the League executive marched with that contingent, four accompanied the official Maynooth contingent, two had been sent from America as pallbearers, and ten others were seminary classmates of O'Growney's. Even if one assumes that two priests accompanied each of the thirty-seven League branches, the total number of priests marching would have been ninety-two. For the purposes of the ratio, I have rounded this figure to 100, thus rendering a ratio of 1 in 60.

12. Michael J. F. McCarthy, *Priests and People in Ireland* (Dublin: Hodges and Figgis, 1903), 448.

13. Lyons, *Culture and Anarchy*, chap. 3; Hutchinson, *Dynamics*, 175–90; Boyce, *Nationalism*, 242–43; Garvin, *Nationalist Revolutionaries*, 63–64, 81–83.

14. As early as January 1902, Constabulary sources in Galway and Special Branch members of the Dublin Metropolitan Police learned that American Fenians intended to remove O'Growney's remains to Maynooth. See NAI, RIC CSB 1902/26,355/S., Report for 16–31 Jan. 1902; and NAI, DMP CSB 1902/26,441/S., Precis for Feb. 1902. On the various contingents of the procession, see O'Farrelly, *Leabhar*, 44–46, 61–70; and *FJ*, 27 Sept. 1903.

15. Garvin, *Nationalist Revolutionaries*, 94–95.

16. *FJ*, 28 Sept. 1903.

17. For a discussion of the early development of the constitution of the League, see Timothy G. McMahon, "Gaelic League," chap. 4. See also Garvin, *Nationalist Revolutionaries*, 91–95.

18. In noting these difficulties, I echo concerns raised by O'Neill and Grote. See Shane O'Neill, "Politics of Culture," 43; Georg Grote, *Torn Between Politics and Culture, The Gaelic League, 1893–1993* (New York: Waxmann, 1994), 79–81.

19. NLI, MS 11,505 through MS 11,517 are letter books containing copies of official correspondence from secretary Pádraig Ó Dalaigh, treasurer Stiofán Báiréad, and other officials dating from 1902 through 1918.

20. Quoted in the *IP*, 21 Apr. 1906.

21. Michael Tierney, *Eoin MacNeill: Scholar and Man of Action, 1867–1945*, ed. F. X. Martin (Oxford: Clarendon Press, 1980), 54–55. MacNeill's brother Charles took over the secretarial responsibilities during his breakdown, and a series of volunteer secretaries performed those duties until the executive hired Ó Dalaigh to serve as a full-time secretary in 1901.

22. *ACS*, 20 June 1908.

23. D. P. Moran, *The Philosophy of Irish Ireland* (Dublin: James Duffy, 1905).

24. Emmet Larkin, *The Historical Dimensions of Irish Catholicism* (New York: Arno Press, 1976), 884.

25. MacDonagh, *States of Mind*, 104.

26. On the growth of Belfast, see C. E. B. Brett, "The Edwardian City: Belfast about 1900," in *Belfast: The Origin and Growth of an Industrial City*, ed. J. C. Beckett and R. E. Glasscock (London: British Broadcasting Corporation, 1967), 120. See also J. C. Beckett, ed., *Belfast: The Making of the City, 1800–1914* (Belfast: Appletree Press, 1983); Sybil Gribbon, *Edwardian Belfast: A Social Profile* (Belfast: Appletree Press, 1982); and A. C. Hepburn, *A Past Apart: Studies in the History of Catholic Belfast, 1850–1950* (Belfast: Ulster Historical Foundation, 1996).

27. Kennedy and Hoppen discuss the increase in urban population and the subsequent impact of towns and town interests on Irish politics. See Líam Kennedy, "Farmers, Traders, and Agricultural Politics in Pre-Independence Ireland," in *Irish Peasants: Violence and Unrest, 1780–1914*, ed. Samuel Clark and J. S. Donnelly Jr. (Madison: Univ. of Wisconsin Press, 1983), 341; and K. T. Hoppen, *Elections, Politics, and Society in Ireland, 1832–1885* (Oxford: Clarendon Press, 1984), chap. 6. Freeman points out, however, that the smaller the town, the worse it fared in maintaining population levels near to those at midcentury. See T. W. Freeman, "Irish Towns in the Eighteenth and Nineteenth Centuries," in *The Development of the Irish Town*, ed. R. A. Butlin (London: Croom Helm, 1977), 132–33.

28. Clark has argued, for instance, that laborers and cottiers constituted between 50 and 70 percent of the agricultural workforce before the famine, but in the 1880s they made up only about a third of the workforce. Lee has shown that the number of agricultural laborers fell by 40 percent during the famine period of 1845–1851, and they fell another 40 percent in the next sixty years. At the same time, the number of farmers fell at a much slower

rate, creating a relative increase in their power in the countryside. In the specific case of County Cork, for example, the number of laborers and household servants fell between 1841 and 1891 from 149,000 to 41,000, while the number of farmers fell only from 34,000 to 29,000. See Samuel Clark, "The Importance of Agrarian Classes: Agrarian Class Structure and Collective Action in Nineteenth-century Ireland," in *Ireland: Land, Politics, and People,* ed. P. J. Drudy (Cambridge: Cambridge Univ. Press, 1982), 14–19; J. J. Lee, *The Modernisation of Ireland* (Dublin: Gill and Macmillan, 1973), 2–3; James S. Donnelly Jr., *The Land and the People of Nineteenth-Century Cork: The Rural Economy and the Land Question* (London: Routledge and Kegan Paul, 1975), 229.

29. In County Cork, for example, only half as much land was tilled in 1891 as had been cultivated in 1851. See Donnelly, *Land and the People,* 133.

30. L. M. Cullen, *An Economic History of Ireland since 1660* (New York: Barnes and Noble Books, 1972), 146–47.

31. Ibid., 143. There were 428 miles of rail open in 1849, and by 1866 the total had reached 1,909 miles.

32. Ibid., 147.

33. Paul-Dubois, 301–04. See also MacDonagh, *States of Mind,* 104; and Comerford, "Nation, Nationalism," 21–23. See chapter 3 below.

34. These calculations are based on tables of population and emigration in *Thom's Official Directory of the United Kingdom of Great Britain and Ireland, for the Year 1905* (Dublin: Alexander Thom, 1905), 727–28. Hereafter this annual directory is cited as *Thom's,* with the year in parentheses.

35. The phrase comes from a pseudonymous letter that appeared in the *Irish Homestead* under the heading "Our Country Villages—Dull or Bright?" See "A.M.M.," in *IH,* 4 July 1903. See also another pseudonymous contribution from "Firín" in *IH,* 10 Oct. 1903. For a contemporary novelization of sterile town life, see Gerald O'Donovan, *Father Ralph* (Dingle: Brandon, 1993), 238–45, 270–71. See Elizabeth Malcolm, "Popular Recreation in Nineteenth-Century Ireland," in *Irish Culture and Nationalism, 1750–1950,* ed. Oliver MacDonagh, W. F. Mandle, and Pauric Travers (London: St. Martin's Press, 1983), 40–55. See also Hoppen, 423–35.

36. *Leader,* 21 Dec. 1901.

37. Cheryl Herr, *Joyce's Anatomy of Culture* (Urbana: Univ. of Illinois Press, 1986), 191–92.

38. Ibid., 110–12.

39. Ibid., 113.

40. For example, see *Leader,* 15 Sept. 1900; and Douglas Hyde, "The Necessity for De-Anglicising Ireland," in *The Revival of Irish Literature,* ed. Sir Charles Gavan Duffy (London: T. Fisher Unwin, 1894).

41. On Moran's view that parliamentary nationalism distracted from the more important need to save Irish civilization, see Timothy G. McMahon, "Cultural Nativism and Irish-Ireland: The *Leader* as a Source for Joyce's Ulysses," *Joyce Studies Annual 1996* (Austin: Univ. of Texas Press, 1996), 72–73.

42. R. F. Foster, "Anglo-Irish Literature," 61–63.

43. On the Parnellite split and its impact on the Irish parliamentary party, see F. S. L. Lyons, *The Irish Parliamentary Party, 1890–1910* (Westport, Conn.: Greenwood Press, 1975); F. S. L. Lyons, *John Dillon* (London: Routledge and Kegan Paul, 1968); Frank Callanan, *The Parnell Split, 1890–91* (Cork: Cork Univ. Press, 1992); Frank Callanan, *T. M. Healy* (Cork: Cork Univ. Press, 1996); Sally Warwick-Haller, *William O'Brien and the Irish Land War* (Dublin: Irish Academic Press, 1990); and Patrick Maume, *The Long Gestation: Irish Nationalist Life, 1891–1918* (New York: St. Martin's Press, 1999).

44. Leon Ó Broin, *Revolutionary Underground: The Irish Republican Brotherhood, 1858–1924* (Dublin: Gill and Macmillan, 1976), 132. For a negative view of senior Belfast IRB men in 1904, see Bulmer Hobson, *Ireland Yesterday and Tomorrow* (Tralee: Anvil Books, 1968), 35.

45. Paul Bew, *Ideology and the Irish Question* (Oxford: Clarendon Press, 1994), 3–4. The most comprehensive account of the development of the Ulster Unionist Party is in Alvin Jackson, *The Ulster Party: Irish Unionists in the House of Commons, 1884–1911* (Oxford: Clarendon Press, 1989). See also Brian M. Walker, *Ulster Politics: the Formative Years, 1868–86* (Belfast: Institute of Irish Studies, 1989).

46. Andrew Gailey, *Ireland and the Death of Kindness: The Experience of Constructive Unionism, 1890–1905* (Cork: Cork Univ. Press, 1987), 153–58. See also Alvin Jackson, "The Failure of Unionism in Dublin," *Irish Historical Studies* 26 (Nov. 1989): 376–95.

47. UCD, Dept. of Irish Folklore, MS SOD/4/X/1961 Douglas Hyde Memoir, 1918, 18–19. Hereafter cited as Hyde Memoir.

48. R. F. Foster, "Anglo-Irish Literature," 69.

49. Among the more prominent politicians associated with the revival were the parliamentarians Thomas O'Donnell, John P. Boland, and Stephen Gwynn, as well as the earliest presidents of Sinn Féin, Edward Martyn and John Sweetman.

50. Seán Ó Murthuile, organizer in Munster, and Colm Ó Gaora, a traveling teacher in Connemara, were both sworn into the IRB between 1912 and 1914, while Pádraig Ó Fathaigh, traveling teacher in south Galway, appears to have joined the IRB in the same period and to have introduced drill into his language classes in 1914. See Colm Ó Cearúil, *Aspail ar Son na Gaeilge: Timirí Chonradh na Gaeilge, 1899–1923* (Dublin: Conradh na Gaeilge, 1995), 139–40; Colm Ó Gaora, *Mise* (Dublin: Oifig an tSolátair, 1943), 115; and Timothy G. McMahon, ed., *Pádraig Ó Fathaigh's War of Independence: Recollections of a Galway Gaelic Leaguer* (Cork: Cork Univ. Press, 2000), 5. On the takeover see Garvin, *Nationalist Revolutionaries*, 97–98.

51. For instance, MacNeill warned the Society for the Preservation of the Irish Language about the political intriguer Henry Dixon and his unsuccessful efforts to influence the Gaelic League in 1898–1899. See Eoin MacNeill to Fr. [?] MacEnerney, 29 Apr. 1899, UCD Archives, MS LA1/G/42, EMP. Thomas Ashe was similarly frustrated in his efforts to recreate the League in the 1910s. See his correspondence with John Devoy in 1914, especially a letter dated 27 Apr. 1914 in *Devoy's Post Bag, Vol. II, 1880–1928*, ed. William O'Brien and Desmond Ryan, (Dublin: C. J. Fallon, 1953), 427. See also Ashe's comments about the

quiescence of the League on the question of partition in Sean Ó Luing, *I Die in a Good Cause: A Study of Thomas Ashe, Idealist and Revolutionary* (Tralee: Anvil Books, 1970), 63. In Dublin, radical nationalist and IRB activity was generally confined to two large branches, the Keating and MacHale branches. See Brian Patrick Murphy, "Father Peter Yorke's 'Turning of the Tide' (1899): The Strictly Cultural Nationalism of the Early Gaelic League," *Éire-Ireland* 23 (Spring 1988), 44; and Brian Patrick Murphy, *Patrick Pearse and the Lost Republican Ideal* (Dublin: James Duffy, 1991), 38–40; and Seán T. Ó Ceallaigh, *Seán T.: Scéal a Bheatha á Insint ag Seán T. Ó Ceallaigh*, ed. Proinsias Ó Conluain (Dublin: Foilseacháin Náisiúnta Teoranta, 1963), 50, 153–54.

52. CO 904/120, File 8582/S., RIC Inspector General's MCR for April 1915.

53. *Dublin Evening Mail*, 17 Mar. 1902, quoted in Maria Tymoczko, *The Irish Ulysses* (Berkeley: Univ. of California Press, 1994), 239. In 1904 a meeting of the Irish Unionist Alliance described the language movement in similar terms. See *ACS*, 23 Apr. 1904. There is also a contemporary fictional account that referred to the language movement as "a new form of the United Irish League, that [it] aimed at shooting landlords and extirpating Protestants." See George A. Birmingham [J. O. Hannay, pseud.], *Benedict Kavanagh* (London: Hodder and Stoughton, 1913), 59.

54. *ACS*, 16 Dec. 1911. See also Liam Andrews, "The Very Dogs in Belfast Will Bark in Irish: The Unionist Government and the Irish Language, 1921–43," in *The Irish Language in Northern Ireland*, ed. Aodán Mac Póilin (Belfast: Ultach Trust, 1997), 53.

55. *SVV*, 7 June 1897; George A. Birmingham [J. O. Hannay, pseud.], *An Irishman Looks at His World* (London: Hodder and Stoughton, 1919), 164.

56. Roger Blaney, *Presbyterians and the Irish Language* (Belfast: Ultach Trust, 1996), 181–82. Hamilton became vice-chancellor of Queen's when it attained university status in 1908. Blaney suggests that Hamilton may have severed ties to the society when the Gaelic League took its stand for Irish freedom in 1915.

57. Bew, *Ideology*, 84. See also *Parliamentary Debates*, 5th ser., vol. 42 (1912), cols. 1967–2026. On McNeill's importance to the construction of a unionist historiography, see Alvin Jackson, "Irish Unionism," in *The Making of Modern Irish History: Revisionism and the Revisionist Controversy*, ed. D. George Boyce and Alan O'Day (London: Routledge, 1996), 128.

58. On Boyd, see Gearóid Mac Giolla Domhnaigh, *Conradh na Gaeilge Chúige Uladh ag tús an 20údh chéid* (Monaghan: Comhaltas Uladh de Conradh na Gaeilge, 1995), 60. On Castletown, see Diarmuid Breathnach and Máire Ní Mhurchú, *1882–1982 Beathaisnéis a Dó* (Dublin: An Clóchamhar Teoranta, 1990), 59. On Crawford, see J. W. Boyle, "The Belfast Protestant Association and the Independent Orange Order, 1901–10," *Irish Historical Studies* 13 (Sept. 1962): 117–52; Maume, *Long Gestation*, 42–43, 101–2, 225; and *IP*, 5 Aug. 1906; *FJ*, 22 Jan. 1909.

59. Diarmid Ó Cobhthaigh, *Douglas Hyde* (Dublin: Maunsel, 1917), 55. J. O. Hannay, the Protestant rector of Westport, Co. Mayo, stated confidently in 1906 that unionists could join the League without fear of discrimination because of their politics. Later, however, he

asserted that it was doubtful whether many unionists belonged to the League because exposure to the League undercut their belief in the union and made them nationalists. Cf. J. O. Hannay, *Is the Gaelic League Political? A Lecture Delivered under the Auspices of the Branch of the Five Provinces on January 23rd, 1906* (Dublin: Gaelic League, 1906); Birmingham, *An Irishman Looks*, 164; and R. B. D. French, "J. O. Hannay and the Gaelic League," *Hermathena: A Dublin University Review* 52 (Spring 1966): 26–52.

60. Maume, *Long Gestation*, chap. 7. On the Ranch War in County Galway and its long-term effect on the rise of Sinn Féin, see Fergus Campbell, *Land and Revolution: Nationalist Politics in the West of Ireland, 1891–1921* (Oxford: Oxford Univ. Press, 2005); and Timothy G. McMahon, *Pádraig Ó Fathaigh's War*, 9. Unionist leaders walked a similar pragmatic tightrope between their more militant loyalist supporters and their more moderate Tory allies in Britain. See Andrews, 50–51.

61. Emmet Larkin, "The Devotional Revolution in Ireland, 1850–1875," *American Historical Review* 77 (Fall 1972): 649.

62. Ibid., 636.

63. Ibid., 644; Mary Peckham Magray, *The Transforming Power of the Nuns: Women, Religion, and Cultural Change in Ireland, 1750–1900* (Oxford: Oxford Univ. Press, 1998), 9; Census of Ireland 1901, quoted in *Thom's* (1905), 743.

64. The concept of "devotional revolution" has been questioned from several perspectives. For three useful discussions, see Timothy G. McMahon, "Religion and Popular Culture in Nineteenth-Century Ireland," *History Compass* 5 (2007): 845–64; John Newsinger, "The Catholic Church in Nineteenth-Century Ireland," *European History Quarterly* 25 (Apr. 1995): 247–67; and S. J. Connolly, *Religion and Society in Nineteenth-Century Ireland: Studies in Irish Economic and Social History,* 3 (Dundalk: Dundalgan Press, 1985), chap. 4. Of particular importance to the periodization and extent of devotional practices, see David W. Miller, "Irish Catholicism and the Great Famine," *Journal of Social History* 9 (1975): 81–98; David W. Miller, "Mass Attendance in Ireland in 1834," in *Piety and Power: Essays in Honour of Emmet Larkin,* ed. S. J. Brown and David W. Miller (Belfast: Institute of Irish Studies, 2000); David W. Miller, "Landscape and Religious Practice: A Study in Mass Attendance in Pre-Famine Ireland," *Éire-Ireland* 40 (Spring/Summer 2005): 90–106; Desmond Keenan, *The Catholic Church in Nineteenth-Century Ireland: A Sociological Study* (Dublin: Gill and Macmillan, 1983); S. J. Connolly, *Priests and People in Pre-Famine Ireland, 1780–1845* (Dublin: Gill and Macmillan, 1982); Patrick J. Corish, *The Irish Catholic Experience: A Historical Survey* (Dublin: Gill and Macmillan, 1985); Kevin Whelan, "The Catholic Church in County Tipperary, 1700–1900," in *Tipperary: History and Society,* ed. Willaim Nolan and Thomas G. McGrath (Templeogue, Co. Dublin: Geography Publications, 1985), 219; Kevin Whelan, "The Regional Impact of Catholicism, 1700–1850," in *Common Ground: Essays on the Historical Geography of Ireland: Presented to T. Jones Hughes,* ed. W. J. Smyth and Kevin Whelan (Cork: Cork Univ. Press, 1988); and Emmet Larkin, *The Pastoral Role of the Roman Catholic Church in Pre-Famine Ireland, 1750–1850* (Dublin: Four Courts Press, 2005).

65. Larkin, *Historical Dimensions*, 1254. The Maynooth grant stood at just over £8900 until 1845. Then, in an effort to discourage clerical support for O'Connell's repeal movement, the government nearly tripled the grant. See also Corish, *Maynooth*, 1–13.

66. In the act establishing the seminary (35 Geo. III, c. 21), the board of trustees was constituted of twenty-one people, four of whom were Protestant "high judges," six of whom were Catholic aristocrats and gentry, and only eleven of whom were ecclesiastics. Within four years, the judges ceased to serve as trustees, though they remained as "visitors" without much real say in the affairs of the college. Over time, and particularly after Paul Cullen became archbishop of Dublin in 1852, the bishops on the board dominated proceedings. By the mid-1870s, only one lay Catholic remained on a board of seventeen trustees. As there were twenty-eight bishops and only seventeen trustees, eleven bishops remained excluded from the board, despite repeated efforts to expand the board through new legislation. A working solution developed in the 1890s when the June and autumn meetings of the bishops took place at Maynooth, the June session coinciding with the trustees meeting. By then, however, the connection between "Maynooth" and "the bishops" had been cemented in the popular mind. For the composition of the board and attempts at expanding it, see Corish, *Maynooth*, 24–25, 150, 177–79.

67. Pius IX moved Cullen to the archdiocese of Dublin in 1852. He became a cardinal in 1866.

68. Larkin, *Historical Dimensions*, 648; Corish, *Maynooth*, 223, 251. See also the semi-autobiographical work by Gerald O'Donovan in which a parish priest grouses about the Maynooth faculty being "too busy keeping their eyes on bishoprics to do much work." See Gerald O'Donovan, 187–88.

69. David W. Miller, *Church, State, and Nation in Ireland, 1898–1921* (Dublin: Gill and Macmillan, 1973), 14.

70. Corish, *Maynooth*, 211.

71. Gerald O'Donovan, 174.

72. James O'Shea, *Priest, Politics, and Society in Post-Famine Ireland: A Study of County Tipperary, 1850–1891* (Dublin: Wolfhound Press, 1983), 20. See also Paul-Dubois, 504.

73. The phrase comes from Fr. Walter McDonald, who attended Maynooth in the 1870s and joined its faculty in 1881. He later directed its graduate Dunboyne Establishment. See Walter McDonald, *Reminiscences of a Maynooth Professor* (London: Jonathan Cape, 1926), 171.

74. Ibid.; O'Shea, 20.

75. Larkin, *Historical Dimensions*, 1255.

76. The centrality of religious practice among Irish Catholics left an indelible impression on the Italian observer Ernesto Buonaiuti. See his evocative *Impressions of Ireland*, trans. Bernard Maguire (Dublin: M. H. Gill and Son, 1913), 17.

77. Stations were masses and other official devotions held in private homes throughout a parish on a rotational basis. Stations had originated in penal times as unofficial

Church practice, but they continued into the new regime as recognized practice. On the institutionalization of stations, see Larkin, *Pastoral Role,* chap. 4. Donnelly has discussed how the public response to the apparitions of the blessed virgin at Knock, Co. Mayo, in 1879–80 represented a contested meeting place for the institutionalized Marianism of late nineteenth-century Catholicism and the customary rituals more associated with the pre-Cullenite regime. For a detailed case study of these incidents, see James S. Donnelly Jr., "The Marian Shrine of Knock: The First Decade" *Éire-Ireland,* 28 (Summer 1993): 54–97. On the incomplete nature of the Tridentine transformation of religious practices in the nineteenth century, see Timothy G. McMahon, "Religion and Popular Culture," 853–57; Connolly, *Priests and People,* 272–78. On the maintenance of other observances into the twentieth century, see Mary Kenny, *Goodbye to Catholic Ireland: A Social, Personal and Cultural History from the Fall of Parnell to the Realm of Mary Robinson* (London: Sinclair-Stevenson, 1997), 48–51.

78. Séamus Fenton, *It All Happened; Reminiscences* (Dublin: M. H. Gill, 1949), 208–10. Fenton recalled that the clothing of the statue was a practice carried to the Continent by Irish monks in the medieval period. Moreover, he claimed that German priests had told him that the practice continued in parts of Bavaria into the twentieth century.

79. For an account of women religious becoming submissive to episcopal authority, see Magray, 107–26.

80. Tom Inglis, *Moral Monopoly: The Catholic Church in Modern Irish Society* (Dublin: Gill and Macmillan, 1987), 187–214.

81. See Mary Kenny, 43–54. See also McDonald, chap. 1. Novels authored by priests are also particularly rich sources on the theme of the mother's encouragement of a vocation. See, for example, Gerald O'Donovan, chap. 1 and passim; Joseph Guinan, *The Curate of Kilcloon* (Dublin: M. H. Gill and Son, 1912), especially 8–9; and Joseph Guinan, *The Moores of Glynn* (New York: Benzinger Brothers, 1907).

82. Buonaiuti, 16; Joseph Guinan, *The Soggarth Aroon* (Dublin: Talbot Press, 1925), 109. Guinan refers to a similar sense that the priest was set apart in his *Curate of Kilcloon.* See Guinan, *Curate,* 97–101.

83. Paul-Dubois, 490.

84. Guinan, *Curate,* 57–61. Guinan called the belief in animal cures "but another manifestation of the people's child-like faith, and of their confident belief in the far-reaching, beneficent power of the priest."

85. John J. Horgan, *Parnell to Pearse: Some Recollections and Reflections* (Dublin: Browne and Nolan, 1948), 58–59.

86. Breandán Mac Suibhne, "Soggarth Aroon and Gombeen-Priest: Canon James Mac-Fadden (1842–1917)," in *Radical Irish Priests, 1660–1970,* ed. Gerard Moran (Dublin: Four Courts Press, 1998), 161–63.

87. Larkin, *Pastoral Role,* 260–61; Larkin, *Historical Dimensions,* 1253; O'Shea, 14.

88. Paul-Dubois, 494.

89. The theme of clerical help in secular affairs appeared continually in works of fiction. Especially relevant are novels written by clerics themselves, such as Guinan and the more famous Patrick Augustine Sheehan. For representative works, see Guinan's *The Soggarth Aroon* and *The Curate of Kilcloon*. See also Patrick Augustine Sheehan, *My New Curate, a Story: Gathered from the Stray Leaves of an Old Diary* (Boston: Marlier, Callanan, and Company, 1925); and Patrick Augustine Sheehan, *Luke Delmege* (New York: Longmans, Green and Co., 1928).

90. Larkin, *Historical Dimensions*, 1248.

91. Quoted in R. F. Foster, *Modern Ireland: 1600–1972* (New York: Viking Penguin, 1989), 341. For a full accounting of the hierarchy's campaign against the board, see Donald Akenson, *The Irish Education Experiment: The National System of Education in the Nineteenth Century* (London: Routledge and Kegan Paul, 1970), 294–315. See also O'Farrell, 93.

92. Miller, *Church, State, and Nation*, 29.

93. Ibid., 30. For information on clerical responsibility generally in education, see Akenson, *Irish Education Experiment*; T. J. McElligott, *Secondary Education in Ireland, 1870–1921* (Blackrock, Co. Dublin: Irish Academic Press, 1981); and E. Brian Titley, *Church, State, and the Control of Schooling in Ireland, 1900–1944* (New York: Gill and Macmillan, 1983).

94. McCarthy, 7–8; F. H. O'Donnell, *A History of the Irish Parliamentary Party, Vol. II: Parnell and the Lieutenants Complicity and Betrayal, with an Epilogue to the Present Day* (London: Longmans, Green and Company, 1910), 450–52.

95. O'Donnell, 454. The journalist P. D. Kenny gave a similar analysis of clerical dominance leading to Irish incapacity in the realm of economics. See P. D. Kenny, *Economics for Irishmen* (Dublin: Maunsel and Co., 1907).

96. Sir Horace Plunkett, *Ireland in the New Century* (Dublin: Irish Academic Press, 1983).

97. Ibid., 106–10.

98. Ibid., 110.

99. Ibid., 107–8, 119. It should be noted that Plunkett's comments on church building had been inspired by contemporary commentary. For a particularly effective pictorial representation of this criticism, see McCarthy, frontispiece. Also, for an example of similar comments in fiction see Gerald O'Donovan, 223.

100. Larkin broached the subject of investment in church plant in an article in the *AHR* in 1967 and reprinted it, with qualifications, in *Historical Dimensions* in 1976. In the intervening years, Lee and others had discussed the general growth of the Irish economy throughout the latter nineteenth century, calling into question one of the foundational assumptions of Larkin's argument. For a further analysis of the question, which outlines the overall debate, see Líam Kennedy, "The Roman Catholic Church and Economic Growth in Nineteenth Century Ireland," *Economic and Social Review*, 10 (Oct. 1978): 45–60. Cf. Emmet Larkin, "Economic Growth, Capital Investment, and the Roman Catholic Church in Nineteenth-Century Ireland, *AHR*, 72 (1967): 852–84; and J. J. Lee, "Capital in the Irish Economy,"

in *The Formation of the Irish Economy,* ed. L. M. Cullen (Cork: Mercier Press, 1969). See also Sidney Brooks, *The New Ireland* (Dublin: Maunsel and Co., 1907), chap. 5.

101. Michael O'Riordan, *Catholicity and Progress in Ireland* (London: K. Paul, Trench, Trübner and Co, 1905). For comments about O'Riordan and a reiteration of an earlier review of *Catholicity and Progress,* see Horgan, 133–36.

102. O'Riordan, 126, chaps. 5 and 7 through 10. His primary example of economic advance in a Catholic country was in Belgium.

103. Ibid., 210.

104. Paul-Dubois, 498.

105. Buonaiuti, 17.

106. Mac Suibhne, "Soggarth Aroon," 183–84.

107. James C. Scott, *Weapons of the Weak: Everyday Forms of Peasant Resistance* (New Haven, Conn.: Yale Univ. Press, 1985), 285–87.

108. One finds, for example, in Guinan's novels cases of parishioners seeking to pay dues to their priest while actually cheating him of the expected amount of oats and of parishioners grousing about what they perceive as preferential treatment given to a priest's family members. See Guinan, *Soggarth Aroon,* 59–65; and Guinan, *Curate,* 212–19.

109. See chapter 2.

110. Paul-Dubois, 490.

111. For a brief discussion of clerical opposition to Fenianism, see R. V. Comerford, *The Fenians in Context: Irish Politics and Society, 1848–82* (Dublin: Wolfhound Press, 1998), 113–14. For contemporary comments on priests restraining violence during the Land War, see Paul-Dubois, 486–89; George A. Birmingham [J. O. Hannay, pseud.], *Irishmen All* (New York: Frederick A. Stokes, 1913), 179; Brooks, 72.

112. *Leader,* 2 Jan. 1903. The correspondent was J. M. Hone, later a literary historian and the president of the Irish Academy of Letters. Hone, who was educated at Cambridge, would have been just twenty years old at the time. On Hone, see Henry Boylan, *A Dictionary of Irish Biography,* 2nd ed. (New York: St. Martin's Press, 1988), 162–63.

113. *Leader,* 2 Jan. 1903. Hone had responded to an article from the preceding issue, "The Work We Have Before Us," written by J. J. O'Toole under his pseudonym Imaal.

114. Ibid.

115. Ibid. Moran referred to Catholics as "idolators" and Protestants as "saved" in protest against the coronation oath, in which the British monarch declares the Catholic doctrine of transubstantiation to be "idolatrous and blasphemous."

116. Ibid.

117. Maume, *D. P. Moran,* 23. According to Maume, Fletcher first contributed in 1911 by giving his views on the *Ne temere* decree, and he continued publishing in the *Leader* into the 1920s.

118. Boyce, *Nationalism,* 228–46.

119. D. P. Moran, *Philosophy,* 37.

120. See W. B. Yeats, "The Irish National Theatre and the Three Sorts of Ignorance," *UI*, 24 Oct. 1903. Also, Yeats printed an account of his defense of *Playboy* in the occasional journal, the *Arrow*. See *Arrow* 1, 23 Feb. 1907. Lyons presents an account of the rising tension and eventual division between Irish-Ireland and Anglo-Irish Ireland that revolved around the work of the theatre. See Lyons, *Culture and Anarchy*, chap. 3. Also see R. F. Foster, *W. B. Yeats*, 359–432.

121. Timothy G. McMahon, "Cultural Nativism," 68–70. See also Lyons, *Culture and Anarchy*, 61; and Maume, *D. P. Moran*, 24.

122. D. P. Moran, "The Gaelic and the Other Movement," *ACS*, 8 July 1899. Boyce makes a similar charge against Hyde, that he was "seeking to destroy that English culture of which he was a product." See Boyce, *Nationalism*, 239. Like Moran, however, Hyde personally, and the League leadership collectively, restated continually that their aim was not to eradicate English from Irish public life, but rather to maintain Irish as a living language. See Timothy G. McMahon, "Gaelic League," 62–63. See also Douglas Hyde, "A Plea for the Irish Language," *Dublin University Review* 2 (Aug. 1886): 666–76; Hyde, "Necessity," 159; and Hyde, *Language, Lore, and Lyrics: Essays and Lectures*, ed. Breandán Ó Conaire (Dublin: Irish Academic Press, 1986), 194.

123. D. P. Moran, *Philosophy*, 81; Timothy G. McMahon, "Gaelic League," 72–74. Hutchinson errs egregiously in basing his claim that Moran hoped to "undermine the influence of Protestants" in the Gaelic movement on a quote from 1903 in which Moran stated that the League had originated from an Anglo-Irish conviction. Rather than implying a social stratum roughly equivalent to the Anglo-Irish landed elite, as Hutchinson seems to imply, Moran was referring to that part of Ireland in which English was the vernacular, just as all Irish writing in English—including the contents of the *Leader*—were "Anglo-Irish." See Hutchinson, *Dynamics*, 180, 193, fn. 55. See also *Leader*, 18 Apr. 1903.

124. Jeremiah O'Donovan, "The Celtic Revival of Today," *Irish Ecclesiastical Record*, 4th ser., 5 (Mar. 1899): 238–56. O'Donovan later left the priesthood and wrote novels as Gerald O'Donovan.

125. See John Kelly and Ronald Schuchard, eds., *The Collected Letters of W. B. Yeats. Vol. III, 1901–1904* (Oxford: Clarendon Press, 1994), 329, 348, 459, 461; and R. A. Anderson, *With Plunkett in Ireland: The Co-op Organiser's Story* (Dublin: Irish Academic Press, 1983), 136–47.

126. W. B. Yeats, *Memoirs, Autobiography—First Draft Journal*, transcribed and ed. Denis Donoghue (New York: Macmillan, 1973), 54. See also Gareth W. Dunleavy and Janet Egelson Dunleavy, *Douglas Hyde: A Maker of Modern Ireland* (Berkeley: Univ. of California Press, 1991), 132.

127. Allan Wade, ed., *The Letters of W. B. Yeats* (London: R. Hart-Davis, 1954), 226–27. See also John Kelly and Eric Domville, eds., *The Collected Letters of W. B. Yeats. Vol. I, 1865–1895* (Oxford: Clarendon Press, 1986), 342–53; Dunleavy and Dunleavy, 132–33, 181; Dominic Daly, 86–90.

128. R. F. Foster, *W. B. Yeats*, 206–8, 219–21, 226, 235–36, 246–48, 266–73, 279, 309–14, 417. See also *Beltaine* (May 1899), 4; *Beltaine* (Feb. 1900), 2, 4; *Samhain* (1901), 3–13, 20–38; *Samhain* (1902), 3, 6–8; *Samhain* (1903), 3–8; *Samhain* (1904), 8–10. For the discussion of donating the proceeds from the sale of *Samhain* to the Oireachtas, see Yeats to Gregory, 19–20 Jan. 1902, in Kelly and Schuchard, 147. For an overview of Hyde's work as a playwright in conjunction with Yeats and Lady Gregory, see Douglas Hyde, *Selected Plays of Douglas Hyde 'An Craoibhin Aoibhinn' with translations by Lady Gregory*, ed. Gareth W. Dunleavy and Janet Egelson Dunleavy (Gerrards Cross, Buckinghamshire: Colin Smythe; Washington, D.C.: Catholic Univ. of America Press, 1991), 13–23. On Yeats's visit to Galway, see *ACS*, 3 Oct. 1908.

129. Yeats to Lady Gregory, 30 Jan. 1904, in Kelly and Schuchard, 538.

130. Yeats to Quinn, 22 June 1904, in Kelly and Schuchard, 610–11.

131. The most important account of the Gaelic revival in the United States is the work of Ní Bhroiméil. She perhaps overstates the control exercised over the movement in Ireland by Irish Americans, but her lively treatment of their critical support is required reading for those interested in the revival era. See Una Ní Bhroiméil, *Building Irish Identity in America, 1870–1915: The Gaelic Revival* (Dublin: Four Courts Press, 2003).

132. Quoted in Dunleavy and Dunleavy, 244.

133. Lady Gregory to Quinn, 28 Sept. 1904, in Kelly and Schuchard, 652.

134. Quinn to Yeats, 13 July 1906, in Alan Himberd and George Mills Harper, eds. *The Letters of John Quinn to William Butler Yeats* (Ann Arbor, Mich.: UMI Research Press, 1983), 76–77.

135. Dunleavy and Dunleavy, 276–78.

2. PRIESTS AND PEOPLE IN THE GAELIC REVIVAL

1. *ACS*, 21 Dec. 1901.

2. Garvin, *Nationalist Revolutionaries*, especially chaps. 4 and 5; Gearóid Ó Tuathaigh, "The Irish-Ireland Idea: Rationale and Relevance," in *Culture in Ireland: Division or Diversity? Proceedings of the Cultures of Ireland Group Conference*, ed. Edna Longley (Belfast: Institute of Irish Studies, 1991), 58; and Miller, *Church, State, and Nation*, 42–43.

3. Leon Ó Broin, "The Gaelic League and the Chair of Irish at Maynooth," *Studies* 52 (Winter 1963), 348–62; Corish, *Maynooth*, 75.

4. Ó Broin, "The Gaelic League," 349; McDonald, 58–59.

5. Corish, *Maynooth*, 205, 213.

6. Ibid., 213.

7. O'Farrelly, *Leabhar*, 101.

8. Desmond Bowen, *The Protestant Crusade in Ireland, 1800–70: A Study of Protestant-Catholic Relations Between the Act of Union and Disestablishment* (Dublin: Gill and Macmillan, 1978), 226–28; Blaney, 75–77.

9. David Greene, "The Irish Language Movement," in *Irish Anglicanism, 1869–1969; Essays on the Role of Anglicanism in Irish Life, Presented to the Church of Ireland on the Occasion of*

the *Centenary of Its Disestablishment, by a Group of Methodist, Presbyterian, Quaker and Roman Catholic Scholars,* ed. Michael Hurley (Dublin: Allen Figgis, 1970), 111.

10. Edward M. Hogan, *The Irish Missionary Movement: A Historical Survey* (Dublin: Gill and Macmillan, 1990), especially parts 1 and 2.

11. Mary Kenny, 20.

12. Kevin Collins, *Catholic Churchmen and the Celtic Revival in Ireland, 1848–1916* (Dublin: Four Courts Press, 2002). As this chapter will argue, Collins overstates the impact of interested churchmen on the language revival.

13. Barry M. Coldrey, *Faith and Fatherland: The Christian Brothers and the Development of Irish Nationalism, 1838–1921* (Dublin: Gill and Macmillan, 1988), 157; and Tierney, *Eoin MacNeill,* 14–15. For an exhaustive catalog of the Ó Faoláin correspondence, see Pádraig Ó Macháin, ed., *A Catalogue of Irish Manuscripts in Mount Melleray Abbey, Co. Waterford* (Dublin: Dublin Institute for Advanced Studies, 1991).

14. Coldrey, 161.

15. On MacHale, see Fenton, 187–88; Peadar Ua Laoghaire, *Mo Sgéal Féin* (Dublin: Browne and Nolan, 1915), 104–5. On Bourke's contributions to *The Nation,* see Patrick F. Tally, "Catholic, Celtic, and Constitutional: A. M. Sullivan's *Nation* and Irish Nationalism, 1858–73," (master's thesis, Univ. of Wisconsin-Madison, 1993), 74–85. On Bourke and Glynn, see their correspondence in NLI, MS 3254, JGP, notebook No. 1 (1875–90). See also John A. Claffey, ed., *Glimpses of Tuam since the Famine* (Ferbane, Co. Offaly: Old Tuam Society, 1997), 122–27, 133–38, 154–61.

16. O'Farrelly, *Leabhar,* 98–99.

17. On Fleming, see Diarmuid Breathnach and Máire Ní Mhurchú, *1882–1982, Beathaisnéis, a hAon* (Dublin: An Clóchamhar Teoranta, 1986), 109–10.

18. John Fleming to Maurus Ó Faoláin, 9 Sept. 1886, MMA, MS 8(1)/137, LMOF.

19. Much of this correspondence is extant in manuscript or print. For example, see NLI, MS 3254, JGP, notebook No. 1 (1875–90), 2, 37–40, 64–174; and O'Farrelly, *Leabhar,* 104–26.

20. Eugene O'Growney, "The National Language," *Irish Ecclesiastical Record,* 3rd ser., 11 (Nov. 1890), 986–87. The article was signed E. Growney.

21. Ibid.

22. O'Growney estimated that interest in Gaelic was limited among priests to "eight or nine in the regular orders," only two or three among senior secular priests, and a "handful of the younger priests, willing, it may be, and earnest, but without influence or opportunities." Ibid., 985.

23. Ibid., 989.

24. Ibid., 991.

25. In several letters to Ó Fáolain, Fleming maintained that Atkinson bore no prejudice against Catholics. See especially the letter from Fleming to Ó Fáolain, 20 Mar. 1895, MMA, MS 8(1)/174, LMOF.

26. Donnelly, "The Marian Shrine of Knock," 67.

27. O'Growney to MacPhilpin, [Nov. 1890?], in NLI MS 3254, JGP, notebook No. 1 (1875–90).

28. "The National Language—A Remarkable Paper in the *Ecclesiastical Record*," *Tuam News*, 14 Nov. 1890.

29. O'Growney to MacNeill, n.d., quoted in O'Farrelly, *Leabhar*, 113. Browne had encouraged O'Growney and other interested students to found a short-lived Irish Society at Maynooth in 1886. See ibid., 101–2.

30. The decision of the trustees came on 15 October 1891, and MacNeill refers to O'Growney's opportunity at Maynooth in his supplementary article. See ibid., 111–12. Cf. Eoin MacNeill, "Why and How the Irish Language Is to Be Preserved," *Irish Ecclesiastical Record*, 3rd ser., 12 (Dec. 1891): 1099–1108. The article was signed J. McNeill. See also Hutchinson, *Dynamics*, 120–27; Ó Tuathaigh, "The Irish-Ireland Idea," 57–60.

31. The Gaelic Union faced recurring financial shortages, and the working membership was limited to a handful of individuals, including Fleming, Rev. Maxwell Close, and Richard J. O'Mulrenin, all of whom were intermittently ill or overextended with work. For background on these difficulties, see MMA, especially MSS 8(1)/140, 8(1)/145, 8(1)/162, and 8(1)/168, LMOF. On circulation figures, see O'Farrelly, *Leabhar*, 139.

32. Corish, *Maynooth*, 213.

33. O'Farrelly, *Leabhar*, 133. This background comes from a speech delivered by O'Hickey at Maynooth shortly after O'Growney's death. It appeared subsequently in the *Irish Ecclesiastical Record*. Cf. Michael P. O'Hickey, "Father O'Growney," *Irish Ecclesiastical Record*, 4th ser., 4 (Nov. 1899): 426–43.

34. Gerald O'Donovan, 177.

35. F. A., "Recollections of Father O'Growney," *Irish Record* (Mar. 1903), quoted in O'Farrelly, *Leabhar*, 180.

36. On Henebry, see Breathnach and Ní Mhurchú, *Beathaisneis, a Dó*, 35–36.

37. Quoted in O'Farrelly, *Leabhar*, 108.

38. F. A., "Recollections," 181.

39. Ibid., 182. See also Gerald O'Donovan, 179.

40. NLI MS 11, 537, Conradh na Gaeilge, *Leabhar-liosta ammneach i Sintiúsí Cinnbliadhna na Céad Ball, 1893–1897 (i Láimh-scríbhneoireacht na gCéad Chisteoirí i. Seághan Ó hÓgáin, Seosamh Laoide, i Stiophán Bairéad)*/First Membership Book and List of Annual Subscriptions, 1893–1897 (in the Handwriting of the First Treasurers, John Hogan, Joseph Lloyd, and Stephen Barrett). See also Gaelic League, *Report of the Gaelic League, 1894* (Dublin: Gaelic League, 1894), 26–41. The number of clergymen in Ireland in 1891, according to census figures, was 3,502. See "Statistics of Ireland: Roman Catholic Church," in *Thom's* (1905), 743.

41. NLI MSS 11, 537, Conradh na Gaeilge, *Leabhar-liosta*.

42. Ibid.

43. French, 44–46.

44. Miller, *Church, State, and Nation*, 135–36.

45. Dunleavy and Dunleavy, 132; R. F. Foster, *Paddy and Mr. Punch: Connections in Irish and English History* (London: A. Lane, 1993), 274; Sean O'Casey, *Drums Under the Windows* (London: Macmillan, 1945), 178. For an amusing first-hand account of one of Hyde's "illnesses," see Douglas Hyde, *Mise agus an Conradh (go dtí 1905)* (Dublin: Oifig an tSoláthair, 1937), 72–87.

46. Quoted in McCartney, "Hyde, D. P. Moran, and Irish Ireland," 51; O'Farrell, 229.

47. See for example, *ACS*, 15 Dec. 1900. See also William J. Walsh, *Bilingual Education. Gaelic League Pamphlet—no. 8* (Dublin: Gaelic League, 1900).

48. Letter from E[dmond] Morrissey to MacNeill, 20 Nov. 1895, in NLI, MS 10,900, EMP Belfast File. Similarly, Bishop John Clancy of Elphin and Bishop Richard Owens of Clogher joined the League's honorary council in March 1899. Seven weeks later, Clancy indicated that the bishop of Galway and the archbishop of Tuam adhered to the movement. See *ACS*, 18 Mar., 6 May 1899.

49. *ACS*, 19 Aug. 1899, 2 Mar. 1901.

50. S. J. Barrett, ed., *Imtheachta an Oireachtas, 1899. The Proceedings of the Third Oireachtas held in Dublin on Wednesday, 7th June, 1899, including the Cardinal's Speech, Oireachtas Ode, Oireachtas Address, Prize Essays, Stories and Poems* (Dublin: Gaelic League, 1900), 11.

51. *ACS*, 15 Apr., 12 Aug. 1899, 23 June 1900.

52. *ACS*, 30 June 1900.

53. Organisation Committee of the Gaelic League, *Instructions for Organisers* (Dublin: Gaelic League, 1903), 2; Donncha Ó Súilleabháin, *Na Timirí i ré tosaigh an Chonartha, 1893–1927* (Dublin: Conradh na Gaeilge, 1990), 4.

54. O'Hickey to Ó Faoláin, 8 Aug. 1896, MMA, 8(1)/47, LMOF.

55. Ibid., 14 Sept. 1896, MMA, 8(1)/51, LMOF. A summary of O'Hickey's campaign for the chair appears in Ó Broin, "The Gaelic League," 351–53. See also Pádraig Eric Mac Fhinn, *An tAthair Mícheál O hIceadha* (Dublin: Sáirséil and Dill, 1974), 33–40.

56. O'Hickey to Ó Faoláin, 11 Feb. 1898, MMA, 8(1)/62, LMOF. Several of O'Hickey's lectures from this period are included in the booklet *Language and Nationality*, published posthumously. See Michael P. O'Hickey, *Language and Nationality, with Preface by Douglas Hyde* (Waterford: Waterford News, 1918).

57. On subscriptions to *Fáinne an Lae*, see O'Hickey to Ó Faoláin, 11 Feb. 1898, MMA, 8(1)/62, LMOF. See also Corish, *Maynooth*, 284–85.

58. O'Farrell, 228; MacDonagh, *States of Mind*, 114; Garvin, *Nationalist Revolutionaries*, chap. 4.

59. Boyce, *Nationalism*, 242–43; MacDonagh, *States of Mind*, 115; Garvin, *Nationalist Revolutionaries*, 64–66.

60. O'Hegarty, 615.

61. *Leader*, 6 Dec. 1902, 7 Nov. 1908. O'Hickey privately wrote Ó Faoláin that he, too, saw the "hand of Providence" in the growth of the *Leader*. See O'Hickey to Ó Faoláin, 19 Oct. 1900, MMA, 8(1)/67, LMOF.

62. O'Hickey to Ó Faoláin, 24 Aug. 1896, MMA, 8(1)/48, LMOF.

63. *ACS*, 8 July 1899.

64. *UI*, 27 Dec. 1902.

65. Quoted in O'Farrelly, *Leabhar*, 104.

66. Quoted in ibid., 111. The books included John Mitchell's *Jail Journal*, Thomas Davis's *Essays*, "Gavan Duffy's Book" (possibly his recent history of Young Ireland movement), and works about Parnell.

67. For example, see his letter calling on Irish Americans to support the League financially, which appeared in the *Irish World* (New York), 21 Jan. 1899.

68. Patrick Buckley, *Faith and Fatherland: The Irish News, the Catholic Hierarchy, and the Management of Dissidents* (Belfast: Belfast Historical and Educational Society, 1991), 41.

69. O'Hickey, *Language and Nationality*, 52. The lecture in question was entitled "Nationality according to Thomas Davis," and it was delivered as one of O'Hickey's required lectures to the students at Maynooth. A later public lecture in Dublin, "The True National Idea," discussed many of the same ideas and served as the basis of the League's first penny pamphlet. Cf. M. P. O'Hickey, *The True National Idea. Gaelic League Pamphlet—No. 1* (Dublin: Gaelic League, 1900).

70. *ACS*, 10 Mar. 1900; Miller, *Church, State, and Nation*, 38; Mac Fhinn, *Ó hIceadha*, 33, 46–47. See also O'Hickey to Ó Faoláin, 21 Feb. 1900, MMA, 8(1)/65, LMOF.

71. Norma Borthwick, *Gaelic League, Annual Report for 1898* (Dublin: Gaelic League, 1898), 2.

72. The 178 branches listed for 1900 are those that appear in the ledger of League membership as having paid their first dues prior to 31 December 1900. Each subsequent entry includes only newly formed branches paying dues between 1 January and 31 December of the respective year. The numbers given are, however, necessarily inexact. Some branches had more than one president over the course of this period, and the length of one's presidency is not delineated in the ledger. When more than one president is listed, I have chosen the first name as my referent. It is, further, important to note that some individuals served as the president of more than one branch, sometimes concurrently. In some cases, branches were established in the various schools of a parish, and as manager, the priest appears to have been nominal president of all such branches. It also seems possible that a priest could have moved to another parish and started a new branch at that location. In all such cases, I have counted the priest more than once, electing to base totals on the number of branches and the number of first-time office-holders. Of the total of 537, 126 are listed as "C.C." and 45 are listed simply as "Rev." It is certainly possible that some or all of those listed as "Rev." were parish priests, but since the abbreviations "P.P.," "V. Rev.," or "Adm." appear regularly, I have considered all "Rev." entries to be junior clergy. Two others included as senior priests in my calculation were one dean and one prior.

73. On MacRedmond, see *ACS*, 17 Nov. 1900. For Hallinan, see *ACS* 14 Feb. 1903. On his career generally, see John Begley, *The Diocese of Limerick from 1641 to the Present Time* (Dublin: Brown and Nowlan, 1938), 590–92.

74. Gaelic League, *Annual Report of the Gaelic League, 1899–1900* (Dublin: Gaelic League, 1900), 15–22; Gaelic League, *Annual Report of the Gaelic League, 1901–02* (Dublin: Gaelic League, 1902), 104–13; Gaelic League, *Annual Report of the Gaelic League, 1902–03* (Dublin: Gaelic League, 1903), 146–60; NAI, BRS Gal. 1/1/1, Minutes of the St. Grellan's Branch of the Gaelic League, 1902–03, 28 Sept. 1902; and McCarthy, 326.

75. Paul-Dubois, 506.

76. See NAI, RIC CSB 1903/28,288/S, Report of the Crime Special Sergeants for February 1903.

77. NAI, RIC CSB 1902/26,268/S, Annual Return of Secret Societies and other Nationalist Associations, as of 31 December 1901. The total estimated membership was 15,086; members under Fenian control, 3,219 (21.3 percent); members under clerical control, 9,873 (65.4 percent). This leaves approximately 1990 members (13.2 percent) under undetermined leadership.

78. Connradh na Gaedhilge Coiste Thiobraid Árann Theas, *Bláith-Fhleasg ó Thiobraid Árann: A Garland from Tipperary, 1893–1943* (Clonmel: Irish Self-Determination League of Great Britain, 1943), 21–23.

79. See *ACS*, 15, 22 Aug. 1908; *Leader*, 3 July 1903, 3 Mar. 1906, 30 Mar. 1907, 25 July 1908.

80. Breathnach and Ní Mhurchú, *Beathaisnéis, a hAon*, 49.

81. *Clár: Feis Íbh-Ráthaigh, 1904, Dánta agus Seanchaidheacht* (Dublin: An Cló-Chumann Teoranta, 1904), 57, 60. Emphasis added.

82. Ó hAnnracháin to Fionán MacColuim, 20 Mar. 1903, in NLI, MS 24,393, FMP, Letters 1902–03. Active priests included Fr. Jeremiah O'Donovan, administrator of the Loughrea Cathedral; Fr. Francis Cassidy, parish priest at Kilchreest; Fr. Patrick Egan, parish priest at Duniry and Kilnelaghan; and Fr. Bernard Bowes, parish priest at Kilnadeema and Kilteskill. See the lists of clergy serving in the diocese of Clonfert and for the united dioceses of Galway and Kilmacduagh, in *Thom's* (1905), 1043, 1045. The listing for Clonfert includes 41 priests, excluding the bishop (22 parish priests and 19 curates); the listing for Galway and Kilmacduagh includes 40 priests, excluding the bishop (21 parish priests and 19 curates). These dioceses include parishes in counties Roscommon, Offaly, and Mayo, but they are concentrated in south Galway.

83. Ó hAnnrachain to MacColuim, 20 Mar. 1903, in NLI, MS 24,393, FMP, Letters 1902–03.

84. Blaney, 110–18.

85. *ACS*, 18 Apr. 1903.

86. *ACS*, 4 July 1903.

87. McGavock to MacNeill, 6 Nov. 1903, in NLI, MS 10,901, EMP, File 4: Ulster; McGavock to MacNeill, 22 Nov. 1903, in ibid.

88. McGavock to MacNeill, 23 Jan. 1904, in ibid.

89. McGavock to MacNeill, 8 Mar. 1904, in ibid.

90. Miller, *Church, State, and Nation*, 37–38.

91. Ibid., 97–98, 126–29.

92. Pearse to Séamas Ó Ceallaigh, 26 Dec. 1904, in *The Letters of P. H. Pearse*, ed. Seamas Ó Buachalla (Gerrards Cross, Buckinghamshire: Colin Smythe, 1980), 88.

93. Ibid.

94. *Leader*, 7 Dec. 1901.

95. *ACS*, 29 Sept. 1900.

96. *ACS*, 1 Sept. 1900.

97. *ACS*, 8 Sept. 1900. Moran sounded a similar note on the centenary of the Christian Brothers: "The Christian Brothers did no more against Irish-Ireland than the patriots of the various schools of the last century; but they did as much. They found Ireland largely Irish, and after a hundred years of endeavor they, with other agencies, left it Anglicized." See *Leader*, 21 June 1902.

98. *ACS*, 15 Sept. 1900. See also Mary E. L. Butler, *Irishwomen and the Home Language. Gaelic League Pamphlet—no. 6* (Dublin: Gaelic League, 1901); Mary E. L. Butler, *Two Schools: A Contrast, Leaflets, No. 2* (Dublin: Gaelic League, 1901).

99. *Leader*, 6 Oct. 1900.

100. *ACS*, 4 Oct. 1902.

101. On Farragher's many activities, see Peter Costello, ed., *Liam O'Flaherty's Ireland* (Dublin: Wolfhound Press, 1996), 14–15. See also Tierney, *Eoin MacNeill*, 87, 250; and W. L. Micks, *An Account of the Constitution, Administration, and Dissolution of the Congested Districts Board for Ireland, from 1891–1923* (Dublin: Eason and Son, 1925), 63–64.

102. *ACS*, 21 Sept. 1901.

103. *UI*, 9 Aug. 1901; *Leader*, 10 Aug. 1901.

104. *Leader*, 10 Aug. 1901.

105. Undated letter to MacNeill, quoted in Miller, *Church, State, and Nation*, 35.

106. *ACS*, 16 Nov. 1901.

107. Ibid.

108. Ibid.

109. *ACS*, 16 Nov., 21 Dec. 1901.

110. *ACS*, 30 Nov. 1901.

111. *UI*, 23 Nov. 1901.

112. *ACS*, 7 Dec. 1901.

113. *ACS*, 14 Dec. 1901.

114. Ibid.

115. *ACS*, 4 Jan. 1902.

116. Ibid.

117. Ibid.

118. *ACS*, 1 Nov. 1902. No reference is made to these questions in the official reports of the Ard-Fheis that appeared throughout May and early June 1902.

119. Ibid. See also the letter from Agnes O'Farrelly and Edith Drury in *ACS*, 1 Nov. 1902.

120. O'Hickey had received this privilege on previous visits to Aran, and according to *ACS*, he had filled in for Farragher and his curate on one occasion. See *ACS*, 1 Nov. 1902.

121. *FJ*, 12 Sept. 1902.

122. Deanery conferences were gatherings of the deans of a diocese, senior priests, whose collective statements are important guides to opinion among the priests in a diocese.

123. Miller, *Church, State, and Nation*, 80–83; *ACS*, 20 Sept., 4, 11 Oct. 1902.

124. *ACS*, 11 Oct. 1902.

125. *FJ*, 29 Sept. 1902; *ACS*, 4 Oct. 1902. See also Jeremiah O'Donovan, *An O'Growney Memorial Lecture* (Dublin: Gaelic League, 1902).

126. *FJ*, 11, 13, 18, 20, 22 Oct. 1902.

127. *ACS*, 18, 25 Oct., 1, 8, 15 Nov. 1902; *UI*, 25 Oct. 1902.

128. For references to proposed arbitration, see *FJ*, 11 Oct. 1902; *ACS*, 18 Oct., 8, 15 Nov. 1902; *UI*, 25 Oct. 1902; NLI, MS P. 7194, Coiste Gnótha Minutes, 6 Dec. 1902, 5 Jan. 1903.

129. Timothy G. McMahon, "'To Mould an Important Body of Shepherds': The Gaelic Summer Colleges and the Teaching of Irish History," in *Reading Irish Histories: Texts, Contexts, and Memory in Modern Ireland*, ed. Lawrence W. McBride (Dublin: Four Courts Press, 2003), 124.

130. *ACS*, 15 Nov. 1902.

131. NLI, MS P. 7194, Coiste Gnótha Minutes, 6 Dec. 1902.

132. The phrase was coined by the Irish-Ireland journalist W. P. Ryan.

133. See *Autobiography of the Ruairi O'More Branch of the Gaelic League, Portarlington* (Dublin: Gaelic League, 1906); W. P. Ryan, *The Pope's Green Island* (London: J. Nisbet, 1912), 103–15; Martin J. Waters, "Peasants and Emigrants: Considerations of the Gaelic League as a Social Movement," in *Views of the Irish Peasantry, 1800–1916*, ed. Daniel J. Casey and Robert E. Rhodes (Hamden, Conn.: Archon Books, 1977), 171–74; Miller, *Church, State, and Nation*, 133–34.

134. *ACS*, 4 Nov. 1905.

135. Ibid.; *UI*, 2 Dec. 1905.

136. *UI*, 30 Sept. 1905.

137. *UI*, 11 Nov. 1905.

138. *UI*, 21 Oct. 1905.

139. *ACS*, 4 Nov. 1905.

140. Ibid.

141. *ACS*, 11 Nov. 1905.

142. *UI*, 23, 30 Sept. 1905.

143. Quoted in *UI*, 11 Nov. 1905.

144. *ACS*, 18 Nov. 1905; W. P. Ryan, *Pope's Green Island*, 106.

145. Hyde's statement, paraphrased by O'Leary, and quoted in *UI*, 14 July 1906.

146. *FJ*, 9 July 1906.

147. Ibid.

148. O'Leary sent the letter, dated 14 June 1906, to priests throughout the country. According to both Griffith and Ryan, however, he did not send it to priests who were prominent in the Gaelic League. It was printed in full in the *UI* and the *IP*. See *UI*, 7 July 1906; *IP*, 7 July 1906.

149. Ibid.

150. Ibid.

151. W. P. Ryan, *Pope's Green Island*, 109.

152. Ibid., 109–10.

153. Ibid., 113.

154. Ibid.

155. Ibid., 114–15; *IP*, 18 Aug. 1906; *SF*, 18 Aug. 1906; *FJ*, 10 Aug. 1906.

156. W. P. Ryan, *Pope's Green Island*, 114.

157. See the report of the parish priest of Ring, Co. Waterford, opposing the Gaelic League because it espoused the "dangerous" doctrine of "free thought" in the *Leader*, 23 Feb. 1907.

158. For example, the Clontarf branch of Cumann na nGaedheal was occasionally confused with the same area's Gaelic League branch. See *Leader*, 30 May, 6, 20 June 1903; *ACS*, 6, 13 June 1903.

159. *Leader*, 30 May 1903.

160. *UI*, 2 Dec. 1905.

161. Ibid.

162. Cited in *SF*, 19 May 1906.

163. Jacques, *Irish Education as It Is and Should Be* (Dublin: Gill, 1906). "Jacques" was a pseudonymous contributor to several newspapers, including the *II*, the *IP* and *SF*.

164. *IP*, 17 Mar. 1906. Cf. Eireannach, "The Clerical Manager Question," *Leader*, 8 Dec. 1906.

165. O'Farrell, 221; McDonald, *Reminiscences*, 308.

166. *IP*, 30 June 1906.

167. Quoted in O'Farrell, 221.

168. *IP*, 29 Dec. 1906; Waters, "W. P. Ryan," 207–14. The McCann family, which owned the *Peasant*, began hearing about clerical concerns from the bishop of Meath in November 1906 and later received correspondence from Cardinal Logue. The newspaper closed down in December, until Ryan found other financing and moved the paper to Dublin in February 1907 as the *Peasant and Irish Ireland* (*PII*). From January 1909 until December 1910, the paper appeared under the title *Irish Nation and the Peasant* (*INP*). The quotation here comes from the final edition of the *IP* on 29 Dec. 1906, in which Ryan published his full correspondence with Cardinal Logue.

169. McDonald, *Reminiscences*, 299–311.

170. *INP*, 4 Sept. 1909. See also W. P. Ryan, *Pope's Green Island*, 180–81.

171. Paul-Dubois, 510.

172. Mary Kenny, 16–18.

173. Waters, "W. P. Ryan," 187–95. See also George L. Bernstein, *Liberalism and Liberal Politics in Edwardian England* (Boston: Allen and Unwin, 1986).

174. The bill was inspired by the Nonconformist core supporters of the Liberals who had been outraged by a 1902 act passed by the predecessor Tory government that extended tax aid to Anglican- and Catholic-controlled schools.

175. On French anticlerical legislation and the *Bloc des Gauches*, see James F. MacMillan, *Twentieth-Century France: Politics and Society, 1898–1991* (London: Edward Arnold, 1992), 15–18; and Gordon Wright, *France in Modern Times: From the Enlightenment to the Present* (New York: W. W. Norton and Co., 1981), 265–69. Pope Pius X issued *Vehementer* in February 1906 and *Gravissimo* in August 1906. In 1907 Logue also fretted about the growth of labor unions in Ireland under socialist inspiration. Although he believed in the right of working people to combine for just wages, he noted with fear that "when these people get together as they did a few days ago in England, and earlier in Stuttgart, and even at meetings in Dublin of our own people, one of the cries I find coming up from amongst them is THE CRY FOR SECULARISM IN THE SCHOOLS," which he considered "dangerous" because it "would lead finally to the destruction of religion amongst the people." Quoted in Miller, *Church, State, and Nation*, 270–71.

176. *ACS*, 11 Jan. 1908. Barry followed up this letter with another printed on 8 Feb. 1908. See also *ACS*, 21 Jan., 4 Feb. 1905 for earlier letters from Barry complaining about the League's nonsectarian and nonpolitical constitution.

177. *Leader*, 12 Nov. 1904.

178. Corish, *Maynooth*, 290.

179. *ACS*, 9 Nov. 1906.

180. Corish, *Maynooth*, 283.

181. *SF*, 12 May 1906. Intriguingly, archeology was one of the subjects on which O'Hickey was required to lecture annually to the students, suggesting that he may have scheduled the lecture to conflict with the lord lieutenant's visit.

182. Corish, *Maynooth*, 261–62. On the examination system, see the anonymous letter (probably written by O'Hickey) that appeared in the lead editorial in *ACS*, 23 Nov. 1907. *Irisleabhar Mauighe Nuadhad*, quoted in *ACS*, 2 May 1908. The *Irisleabhar* indicated that more than half of those claiming a knowledge of Irish (110 of 212) were either good or fair speakers, though more than 42 percent of the senior house remained "ignorant" of Irish.

183. Liam Mac an tSagairt, *Father Larry Murray* (Dún Laoghaire: Éigse Oirialla, 1983), 5.

184. Ibid., 6–9. See also Diarmuid Breathnach and Máire Ní Mhurchú, *1882–1982: Beathaisnéis, a Ceathair* (Dublin: An Clóchamhar Teoranta, 1994), 147–49.

185. *PII*, 2, 30 Nov., 14, 21 Dec. 1907, 4 Jan. 1908; *ACS*, 2, 9, 16, 23, 30 Nov. 1907, 28 Dec. 1907; *SF*, 9, 23, 30 Nov. 1907, 4 Jan. 1908.

186. *ACS*, 16 Nov. 1907. The dioceses were Armagh, Dublin, Clogher, Cork, Tuam, Cashel, Ferns, Derry, Dromore, Achonry, Ardagh, Killaloe, Kilmore, and Ossory.

187. *SF*, 23 Nov. 1907.

188. *SF*, 30 Nov. 1907. Corish describes this warning as having occurred in October 1906, after Mannix accused O'Hickey of leaking details to the press of earlier dispensations, though I have not found any record of these dispensations in the Irish-Ireland press in 1906. The specific language of the trustees was that anyone communicating "domestic secrets" to the press was guilty of "a grave violation of duty." See Corish, *Maynooth*, 290.

189. Mannix to Ó Dalaigh, 19 Dec. 1907, quoted in *ACS*, 28 Dec. 1907. The Mannix/Ó Dalaigh correspondence appeared in *ACS* and the following week in *SF* and the *PII*.

190. *ACS*, 28 Dec. 1907. Emphasis added.

191. *PII*, 13 June 1908. For a sampling of the ongoing exchanges about compulsory Irish within Maynooth, see *ACS*, 11 Jan., 15, 22 Feb. 1908; and *Leader*, 20 June, 4, 11, 18 July 1908.

192. O'Farrell, 90–91, 213, 219–20. See also Miller, *Church, State, and Nation*, 64.

193. Miller, *Church, State, and Nation*, 65.

194. Ibid., chap. 9.

195. Ibid., 203. The bill received the royal assent on 1 August 1908.

196. See P. H. Pearse, *A Significant Irish Educationalist: The Educational Writings of P. H. Pearse*, ed. Seamas Ó Buachalla (Dublin: Mercier Press, 1980).

197. *ACS*, 8 Feb.1908.

198. *ACS*, 1 Feb. 1908.

199. *ACS*, 2 May 1908.

200. Ibid.

201. *ACS*, 22 Aug. 1908.

202. *ACS*, 5 Dec. 1908.

203. Ibid.

204. W. P. Ryan, *Pope's Green Island*, 150–51.

205. Miller, *Church, State, and Nation*, 197.

206. *ACS*, 12 Dec. 1908.

207. Ibid.

208. *ACS*, 6, 20 Feb. 1909; Timothy G. McMahon, "'To Mould an Important Body of Shepherds,'" 134.

209. Comerford, "Nation, Nationalism," 34.

210. *ACS*, 30 Jan. 1909. See also Miller, *Church, State, and Nation*, 236.

211. Miller, *Church, State, and Nation*, 237. See *ACS*, 6 Mar. 1909.

212. *ACS*, 30 Jan. 1909.

213. Ibid.

214. *ACS*, 20 Feb. 1909.

215. *ACS*, 22 May 1909.

216. Timothy G. McMahon, "'To Mould an Important Body of Shepherds,'" 134–35.

217. *ACS*, 6 Mar. 1909.

218. Ibid.; *SF*, 6 Mar. 1909; *INP*, 6 Mar. 1909.

219. W. P. Ryan, *Pope's Green Island*, 182.

220. Ibid. Parish priests subscribed £5 and curates £2.

221. *INP*, 20 Mar. 1909. Emphasis added. This letter, signed "Layman," was answered the following week by a signatory "Exul.," later identified by Ryan as the Modernist priest Fr. John Tyrrell, S.J., who agreed wholeheartedly with the Layman's sentiments.

222. *ACS*, 6 Mar. 1909.

223. Ibid.

224. For example, see report of the meeting in favor of compulsory Irish in Wexford in *ACS*, 13 Feb. 1909; also, see report of the North Donegal United Irish League in *ACS*, 10 Apr. 1909.

225. *SF*, 3 July 1909.

226. W. P. Ryan, *Pope's Green Island*, 160–61; *ACS*, 3 July 1909.

227. Michael P. O'Hickey, *An Irish University or Else—* (Dublin: M. H. Gill and Son, 1909).

228. W. P. Ryan, *Pope's Green Island*, 161–63; *ACS*, 3, 10, 17, 24 July 1909.

229. O'Hickey, *An Irish University*, 20. The pronouncement appeared on 20 January 1909. O'Hickey's pamphlet contains three letters written after it appeared, including one dated 20 January that even comments on the pronouncement. See also *ACS*, 20 Feb. 1909.

230. *ACS*, 7 Aug. 1909.

231. Ibid. The statement was signed by Cardinal Logue, the Bishop of Waterford and Lismore, and the Bishop of Cloyne. Several accounts of the O'Hickey case have appeared in print, some more measured than others, which tend to be sympathetic to either the bishops or to O'Hickey. For an overview, see Miller, *Church, State, and Nation*, 239–41. For two contemporary accounts sympathetic to O'Hickey, see W. P. Ryan, *Pope's Green Island*, 160–64; and McDonald, *Reminiscences*, 235–75, 368–78. For a more recent account, highly sympathetic to O'Hickey, see Lucy McDiarmid, "The Man who Died for the Language: The Rev. Dr. Michael O'Hickey and the 'Essential Irish' Controversy of 1909," *Éire-Ireland* 35 (Spring-Summer, 2000): 188–218. For two accounts more sympathetic to the Maynooth authorities, see Ó Broin, "The Gaelic League and the Chair of Irish at Maynooth," 348–62; and Corish, *Maynooth*, 288–96.

232. *ACS*, 7 Aug. 1909.

233. Ibid.

234. *ACS*, 16 Apr. 1909.

235. Miller, *Church, State, and Nation*, 236. It was entirely in keeping with Walsh's sense of propriety that he remained silent publicly, particularly after the standing committee's pronouncement.

236. During May and June 1910, *ACS* carried extensive coverage of the senate's actions. The report of the final vote appears on 2 July 1910. See also W. P. Ryan, *Pope's Green Island*, 168–69. It is significant that Hyde's compromise proposal is similar to those discussed in

correspondence between Colonel Maurice Moore, Eoin MacNeill, Canon Arthur Ryan, Fr. O'Hickey, and Archbishop Walsh. See Miller, *Church, State, and Nation*, 236–39.

237. *IP*, 29 Dec. 1906. Emphasis added.

238. Many of the most active Gaelic Leaguers at the local level were schoolteachers, who were under enormous pressure to conform to the whims of their managers. For example, in 1898 and 1899, the largest teachers' union, Irish National Teachers Organization, had tried unsuccessfully to stand up to the power of the managers, and the priests (with the assistance of the bishops) reasserted their primacy over the schools. The timing of this controversy is potentially significant because it immediately predates the period of the League's fastest expansion. See Miller, *Church, State, and Nation*, 28–34.

239. Gerald O'Donovan, 83.

240. On Logue, see Barrett, 12. For an account of antimodernism among clergy more widely, see Garvin, *Nationalist Revolutionaries*, 58–60.

241. Guinan, *Curate*, 174–75: "It [the Gaelic League] is trying to make the laborer more intelligent, self-respecting and temperate; the farmer more up-to-date and progressive; the shop-keeper more business-like, and the manufacturer more pushing and self-advertising, after the manner of his foreign competitor. It tells us to copy the business methods and commercial code of the Englishman, his powers of initiative and constructiveness, but not to feel ashamed of our kindly Irish manners and customs."

242. For Ryan, see Connradh na Gaedhilge Coiste Thiobraid Árann Theas, 21–23. For references to Frs. Thomas Wall of Limerick and Lorcan O'Kieran of Monaghan, see NAI, RIC CSB 1915 "Other Papers, 1911–1920", Item 1. List of Clergymen who have come under Notice Owing to their Disloyal Language or Conduct During 1915, n.d.

243. Gerald O'Donovan, 83.

3. "ALL CREEDS AND ALL CLASSES"? JUST WHO MADE UP THE GAELIC LEAGUE?

1. Eoin MacNeill, "A Plea and A Plan for the Extension of the Movement to Preserve and Spread the Gaelic Language in Ireland," *GJ*, 4 (Mar. 1893), 179.

2. Garvin, *Nationalist Revolutionaries*, 79–80.

3. Hutchinson, *Dynamics*, 179.

4. The literature on the role of the lower-middle classes in revolutionary and later fascist movements is extensive and originated perhaps with Marx's own writings on reactionaries among the artisanate. See Arno Mayer, "The Lower Middle Class as Historical Problem," *Journal of Modern History* 47 (Sept. 1975): 409–36. For a case study that exemplifies the theme, see Robert Gellately, *The Politics of Economic Despair: Shopkeepers and German Politics, 1890–1914* (London: Sage Publications, 1974). For discussions of what has been variously called "integral nationalism," "eastern nationalism," and "ethnic nationalism," see Carlton J. H. Hayes, *The Historical Evolution of Modern Nationalism* (New York: Russell and Russell, 1968); Hans Kohn, *Nationalism: Its Meaning and History* (Princeton: Van Norstrand,

1965); Peter Alter, *Nationalism* (London: E. Arnold, 1994), especially chap. 2; Anthony D. Smith, *National Identity* (Reno: Univ. of Nevada Press, 1991), chap. 1.

5. Geoffrey Crossick and Heinz-Gerhard Haupt, eds., *Shopkeepers and Master Artisans in Nineteenth-Century Europe* (London: Metheuen, 1984); and Rudy J. Koshar, ed., *Splintered Classes: Politics and the Lower Middle Classes in Interwar Europe* (New York: Holmes and Meier, 1990).

6. NLI, MS 11, 537: Conradh na Gaeilge, *Leabhar-liosta ammneach i Sintiúsí Cinnbliadhna na Céad Ball, 1893–1897 (i Láimh-scríbhneoireacht na gCéad Chisteoirí i. Seághan Ó hÓgáin, Seosamh Laoide, i Stiophán Bairéad)*/First Membership Book and List of Annual Subscriptions, 1893–1897 (in the Handwriting of the First Treasurers, John Hogan, Joseph Lloyd, and Stephen Barrett); NLI, MS 11,538: Conradh na Gaeilge, *Leabhar-liosta na gCraobh i na n-Oifigeach a Bhíonnta I na Sintiúsí Cinnbliadhna, 1897–1898 go dtí 1905–1906 (i lámh-scríbhneoireacht an Chisdeora i Stiophán Bairéad)*/First List of Branches with Officers and Annual Subscriptions, 1897–1898 to 1905–1906 (in the Handwriting of the Treasurer Stephen Barrett). A third volume in this sequence was held at the Gaelic League Headquarters on Harcourt Street, Dublin, and graciously made available to the author in May 1996 by the then-League secretary Seán Mac Mathúna.

7. Gaelic League, Membership Book, Harcourt Street, Dublin.

8. In the annual report for 1906–7 the number of affiliated branches within Ireland is recorded as 480, while in a corresponding table in the annual report for 1907–8, the number given for 1906–7 is only 433. A similar disparity appears between the reports for 1907–8 and 1908–9. See *Imtheachta an Ard-Fheis, 1906–7* (Dublin: Gaelic League, 1907); *Imtheachta an Ard-Fheis, 1907–8* (Dublin: Gaelic League, 1908); *Imtheachta an Ard-Fheis, 1909* (Dublin: Gaelic League, 1909).

9. For example, Brooks counted 900 branches in 1906; Redmond-Howard, 1,000 in 1912; and the *Times* (London), 1,200 in 1913. Key and Garvin relied on Brooks and Redmond-Howard, respectively. See Brooks, 27; L. G. Redmond-Howard, *The New Birth of Ireland* (London: Collins' Clear Type Press, 1913), 217–18; *The Times, The Ireland of To-day* (Boston: Small, Maynard and Company, 1915 reprint edition), 38; Robert Kee, *The Green Flag: A History of Irish Nationalism* (London: Weidenfeld and Nicolson, 1972), 431; Garvin, *Nationalist Revolutionaries*, 79.

10. Ó Fearáil, 30; Shane O'Neill, "Politics of Culture," 43–44. For other estimates of League size, see Breandán Mac Aodha, "Was This a Social Revolution?" in *The Gaelic League Idea*, ed. Seán Ó Tuama (Cork: Mercier Press, 1972), 21; Brian Ó Cúiv, "The Gaelic Cultural Movements and the New Nationalism," in *The Making of 1916: Studies in the History of the Rising*, ed. Kevin B. Nowlan (Dublin: Stationary Office, 1969), 12.

11. *Imtheachta an Ard-Fheis, 1909*, 20.

12. *ACS* reported on 20 June 1908 that Bairéad had developed insomnia because of financial shortfalls; these would prompt austerity measures after 1910. See Timothy G. McMahon, "Gaelic League," 98–99.

13. See *GJ*, 9 (July 1899); Ó Fearáil, 17, 42, 44; Shane O'Neill, "Politics of Culture," 43–44.

14. Gaelic League, *Annual Report of the Gaelic League, 1902–03* (Dublin: Gaelic League, 1903), 146–60; Ó Cuív, "Gaelic Cultural Movements," 12.

15. Mac Aodha, 21–22.

16. *ACS*, 5 Nov. 1904.

17. *The Irish Language and Irish Intermediate Education: III: Dr. Hyde's Evidence. Gaelic League Pamphlet—no. 13* (Dublin, [1901?]), 1; *Leader*, 1 Dec. 1900.

18. NAI, RIC CSB 1902/26,268/S, Estimate of the Numerical Strength of Secret Societies and Other Nationalist Associations for the Year Ending 31st December 1901.

19. *ACS*, 11 Nov. 1899, 9 June 1900.

20. The total represents the average of the 36 metropolitan-area contingents for which data were available. The range of size went from a low of 24 for the Ballymullen branch to a high of 300 for the Drapers' branch. There were also 8 branches for which no data appeared. See *ACS*, 14 Mar. 1904.

21. Shane O'Neill, "Politics of Culture," 45–46.

22. *GJ*, 4 (Feb. 1894), 250; *GJ*, 7 (July 1896), 33; *GJ*, 7 (Dec. 1896), 126; *GJ*, 7 (Mar. 1897), 174–75.

23. *Leader*, 12 Nov. 1904.

24. Ibid.

25. See above, chap. 2. On Orange resistance to a League presence in County Down, see *ACS*, 16 Dec. 1911.

26. *Leader*, 2 Mar. 1907.

27. *Leader*, 7 Dec. 1907.

28. Birmingham, *An Irishman Looks*, 293.

29. Ibid., 294.

30. *ACS*, 9 June 1900.

31. *ACS*, 6 July 1901.

32. *ACS*, 21 Oct. 1911.

33. *Leader*, 30 Nov. 1907.

34. *ACS*, 26 Oct. 1912.

35. Eugene O'Growney, *Simple Lessons in Irish, Giving the Pronunciation of Each Word*, Part 1 (Dublin: Gaelic League, 1903); Eugene O'Growney, *Simple Lessons in Irish, Giving the Pronunciation of Each Word*, Part 5 (Dublin: Gaelic League, 1902); Ó Fearáil, 17.

36. *ACS*, 29 Nov. 1902.

37. Ibid.

38. *ACS*, 21 Jan. 1905.

39. *Dana*, 9 (Jan. 1905), 273.

40. Waters, "Peasants and Emigrants,"168–71.

41. Ibid., 171.

42. Shane O'Neill, "Politics of Culture," chap. 1.

43. See Breathnach and Ní Mhurchú, *Beathaisnéis, a hAon;* Breathnach and Ní Mhurchú, *Beathaisnéis, a Dó;* Breathnach and Ní Mhurchú, *1882–1982: Beathaisnéis, a Trí* (Dublin: An Clóchamhar Teoranta, 1992); Breathnach and Ní Mhurchú, *Beathaisnéis, a Ceathair;* Breathnach and Ní Mhurchú, *1882–1982: Beathaisnéis, a Cúig* (Dublin: An Clóchamhar Teoranta, 1997). Useful individual studies include Máirtín Mac Niocláis, *Seán Ó Ruadháin: Saol agus Saothar* (Dublin: An Clóchamhar Teoranta, 1991); Máiréad Ní Chinnéide, *Máire de Buitléir: Bean Athbheochana* (Dublin: Comhar Teoranta, 1993); Ó Cearúil; Diarmaid Ó Doibhlin, ed., *Duanaire Gaedhilge Róis Ní Ógáin: Cnuasach de na Sean-amhráin is Áille is Mó Clú* (Dublin: An Clóchamhar Teoranta, 1995); Riobard Bheldon, *Amhráin agus Dánta,* ed. Pádraig Ó Macháin (Dublin: Poddle Press, 1995); Ó Súilleabháin, *Na Timirí.* A general account of the League appears in Proinsias Mac Aonghusa, *Ar Son na Gaeilge: Conradh na Gaeilge, 1893–1993* (Dublin: Conradh na Gaeilge, 1993).

44. Rosters of the Coistí Gnótha have been taken from official lists submitted to the Ard-Fheiseanna. See Conradh na Gaeilge, *Cunntas ar Árd-Fheis, 1904* (Dublin: Gaelic League, 1904), 21–22; Conradh na Gaeilge, *Imtheachta an Ard-Fheis, 1914* (Dublin: Gaelic League, 1914), 31–32.

45. *ACS,* 9, 23 May 1903.

46. Ó Luing, 48–58; Timothy G. McMahon, "Social Bases," 22–24.

47. A fourth member of the 1913–14 committee had been raised a Protestant and converted to Catholicism as an adult. This was the Honourable William Gibson, later Lord Ashbourne. Gibson was a very liberal Catholic. See Breathnach and Ní Mhurchú, *Beathaisnéis, a Dó,* 58–59.

48. For the 1903–4 committee, information about ages was found for 32 of the 38 committee persons; for 1913–14, 28 of 34 are included. All the data about leaders are to be found in the volumes of Breathnach and Ní Mhurchú's *Beathaisnéis.* A comprehensive index of entries appears at the end of the fifth volume of the series.

49. Until 1904 the stipulated number of members serving on the committee was thirty, plus three officers, but the number varied somewhat from year to year because as members resigned or died, the committee would co-opt new members to fill the roster. Moreover, between 1904 and 1913 the stipulated number was increased to forty-five members.

50. There were seven women on the Coiste Gnótha in 1906–7; the committee then had forty-five members. Thus, the percentage of women serving (about 16 percent) did not markedly increase.

51. These figures are based on attendance tables published in the annual Gaelic League reports from 1903–4 through 1913–14. O'Farrelly attended 106 of 130 meetings, while Hyde attended 56 of 130. It should be noted that Hyde's attendance improved once he moved to Dublin from County Roscommon in 1908, but in no year during this period did he attend more meetings than O'Farrelly.

52. See Mary E. Daly, *Dublin, the Deposed Capital: A Social and Economic History, 1860–1914* (Cork: Cork Univ. Press, 1985), 64–66; W. A. Armstrong, "The Use of Information about

Occupation I as a Basis for Social Stratification," in *Nineteenth-Century Society: Essays in the Use of Quantitative Methods for the Study of Social Data*, ed. E. A. Wrigley (Cambridge: Cambridge Univ. Press, 1972), 191–214. Personal and familial data on occupations have been taken from entries in *Beathaisnéis*.

53. For the purposes of identifying a native speaker, I have included only those who grew up in an Irish-speaking household and/or those whose immediate or extended family made a point of speaking to them in Irish. The respective figures are 34 percent for 1903 and 32 percent for 1913.

54. Signs of upward mobility included such things as having Irish-speaking parents who raised the child as an English speaker; pursuing secondary or tertiary educational opportunities; or pursuing an occupation with more social cachet than that of one's parents (such as a civil-service position when one's parents had a small farm). Significant travel experiences included journeying outside of Ireland for career advancement or spending time abroad for study or employment. Here are the exact figures: 30 of 38 (79 percent) in 1903 and 22 of 34 (65 percent) in 1913. Seven of the latter 22 had served on the 1903 executive.

55. Recognizing this limitation, I discuss below anecdotal information (gleaned from correspondence and police and press reports) about other areas—all of which suggests that the urban data are largely representative for the rest of the country.

56. Gaelic League, *Report of the Gaelic League, 1894* (Dublin: Gaelic League, 1894), 26–34.

57. Mac Giolla Domhnaigh, 7–53.

58. The first such entry appeared in *ACS*, 16 Mar. 1899. The figure of 168 represents only those new members resident in Dublin.

59. Garvin, for instance, labeled one section of his discussion of the league "Many Young Men of Twenty Go to Language School." See Garvin, *Nationalist Revolutionaries*, 86.

60. Using biographical data gleaned from the census and the *Beathaisnéis* collection, I have found the ages of 95 of the members from Dublin, Cork, and Belfast. In each instance, I have related the age to the year in which the person joined the League. For 1894, I was able to identify 26 from Dublin and 8 from Cork. For 1895, I identified 11 from Belfast; and for 1899, 50 from the second Dublin cohort.

61. *ACS*, 12 Aug. 1899; Timothy G. McMahon, ed., *Pádraig Ó Fathaigh's War*, 4.

62. Ó Cobhthaigh, *Douglas Hyde*, 57.

63. The Catholic Young Men's Society had shown an interest in the language since the parliamentarian William O'Brien encouraged them to do so in 1892. See *GJ*, 6:2 (May 1895). See also William O'Brien, *Irish Ideas* (Port Washington, N.Y.: Kennikat Press, 1970), 47–77.

64. *ACS*, 9 Sept., 11 Nov. 1899; 16 June 1900; 28 Feb. 1903.

65. Mary Colum, *Life and the Dream* (Chester Springs, Penn.: Dufour Editions, 1966), 96.

66. W. P. Ryan, *Pope's Green Island*, 87.

67. On Esmonde, see *ACS*, 20 Apr. 1901. For Spring Rice, see *ACS*, 6, 20 Dec. 1902, 11 July 1903; Breathnach and Ní Mhurchú, *Beathaisnéis, a Ceathar*, 168; Colum, 164.

68. Senia Paseta, *Before the Revolution: Nationalism, Social Change, and Ireland's Catholic Elite, 1879–1922* (Cork: Cork Univ. Press, 1999), 140.

69. Breathnach and Ní Mhurchú, *Beathaisnéis, a Dó*, 142. For the industrial committee, see NLI, MS 9804, Conradh na Gaeilge, *Minutes of the Industrial Committee, 1902–11*. References to Power's attendance at Oireachtas committee meetings can be found up through 1914–15. For example, see Gaelic League, *Imtheachta an Ard-Fheis, 1915* (Dublin: Gaelic League, 1915), 34.

70. *ACS*, 1 Mar. 1902.

71. Ní Chinnéide, 7–18. See also Breathnach and Ní Mhurchú, *Beathaisnéis, a hAon*, 27. See also Joseph Sweeney, "Why 'Sinn Féin'?" *Éire-Ireland* 6 (Summer 1971), 33–40.

72. Butler, *Irishwomen*.

73. Ibid.

74. On education, see Butler, *Two Schools*, 4. For a fictional example of Butler's ideal of a woman sacrificing for her country and her husband, see her novel *The Ring of Day* (London: Hutchinson, 1906).

75. Butler, *Irishwomen*, 10.

76. On the role of Butler's thought in Irish-Ireland circles, see the fine overview in Frank Biletz, "Women and Irish-Ireland: The Domestic Nationalism of Mary Butler" *New Hibernia Review* 6 (Spring 2002): 59–72.

77. Breathnach and Ní Mhurchú, *Beathaisnéis, A Cúig*, 51–52. See also *SF*, 4 Dec. 1907; *ACS*, 15 Dec. 1900, 29 Jan. 1910.

78. Sean O'Casey to John Hutchinson, 10 Sept. 1953, in Sean O'Casey, *The Letters of Sean O'Casey, Vol. Two: 1942–1954*, ed. David Krause (New York: Macmillan, 1980), 990.

79. Ibid.

80. Tim Pat Coogan, *De Valera: Long Fellow, Long Shadow* (London: Hutchinson, 1993), 40.

81. Denis Gwynn, quoted in ibid., 41.

82. Breathnach and Ní Mhurchú, *Beathaisneis, a Cúig*, 53.

83. Sample sizes: Dublin I (1894), 71; Dublin II (1899), 58; Belfast (1895–97), 41; Cork (1894), 21. In the Belfast sample, I found several individuals whose surnames and addresses matched the householders listed in the *Belfast and Province of Ulster Directory*, but because they were apparently not the householder, I have not included them in my calculation. Among these, most of the householders for whom the directory included an occupation would have fallen into category III as skilled artisans. It is likely, though not certain, that the member living in such a household would also have been included in category III, and this would have altered the relative percentages for occupational categories significantly.

84. MacNeill, "A Plea and a Plan," 177–79.

85. *GJ*, 5: 12 (Mar. 1895), 177.

86. See NLI, MS 10,901, EMP, Munster Files and Connacht Files for Lists Pertaining to County Kerry and County Galway; UCD Archives, MS LA1/E/20, EMP, for County Cork.

87. UCD Archives, MS LA1/E/20, EMP. The Cork list includes four priests and one professional (Maurice Healy, the solicitor and member of parliament) who are a part of the sample.

88. The Londonderry data were collected from Gaelic League annual reports and compared to the census and directories, including the *Derry Almanac and Directory* (Londonderry: Londonderry Sentinel, 1894); *Derry Almanac, North-West Directory, and General Advertiser for 1901* (Londonderry: Londonderry Sentinel, 1901); and the *South Derry and District Almanac and Diary for 1902* (Cookstown, Co. Tyrone: Mid-Ulster Printing Works, 1902).

89. Miroslav Hroch, "Social and Territorial Characteristics in the Composition of the Leading Groups of National Movements," in *The Formation of National Elites: Comparative Studies on Governments and Non-Dominant Ethnic Groups in Europe, 1850–1940 Vol. VI*, ed. Andreas Kappeler, Fikret Adinir, and Alan O'Day (New York: New York Univ. Press, 1992), 268–69. See also Alan O'Day, "Ireland's Catholics in the British State, 1850–1922," in *The Formation of National Elites: Comparative Studies on Governments and Non-Dominant Ethnic Groups in Europe, 1850–1950, Vol. VI*, ed. Andreas Kappeler, Fikret Adanir, and Alan O'Day (New York: New York Univ. Press, 1992), 53. O'Day analyzes the leadership of several political nationalist organizations in Ireland but touches only briefly on the cultural revival.

90. See chapter 2.

91. See Sybil Gribbon, *Edwardian Belfast: A Social Profile* (Belfast: Appletree Press, 1982), 16. A sense of the varied interests of the club can be found in its publication, the *Belfast Naturalists' Field Club Report and Proceedings*, edited by the Gaelic enthusiast Francis Joseph Bigger.

92. Mac Giolla Domhnaigh, 7; NLI, MS 10,900, EMP, Belfast File. For a report about the classes of the Naturalists' Field Club, see *GJ*, 5 (May 1894).

93. Brett, 120; Gribbon, 47; Hepburn, *A Past Apart*, 69, 144–49; Fred Heatley, "Community Relations and the Religious Geography, 1800–86," in *Belfast: : The Making of the City, 1800–1914*, ed. J. C. Beckett (Belfast: Appletree Press, 1983), 129–42.

94. An example of earlier elite solidarity can be found in the subscriptions supporting construction of St. Patrick's Catholic church (completed in 1815). Of the £4,100 collected, Protestants subscribed £1,300. See Heatley, 133.

95. Edmond Morrissey to Eoin MacNeill, 20 Nov. 1895, NLI, MS 10,901, EMP, Belfast File.

96. See ibid. for the printed circular letter of April 1896 about a meeting of the Belfast Gaelic League.

97. These included Boyd himself, the attorney F. J. Bigger, two ministers, and the poet and scholar Rose Young, whose family owned more than 2,000 acres of land near Glengorm, Co. Antrim.

98. This was Dr. Walter Bernard.

99. According to *Thom's*, Boland had shops at No. 1 Grafton Street and on Johnson's Court, valued at £120 and £18 respectively. By comparison, others among the category II members included Michael Maher, whose two shops had rateable valuations of £24 and £33; the vintner Michael Flanagan, whose shop was valued at £35; and the butcher and parliamentarian William Field, whose shop had a valuation of £28. See *Thom's* (1894), 1400, 1430, 1444, 1503, 1511, 1537.

100. Breathnach and Ní Mhurchú, *Beathaisnéis, a Trí*, 68; *Thom's* (1894), 1389.

101. See the *Belfast and Province of Ulster Directory, for 1895*, entry for J. Moore, at 11 Shaftesbury Square. See also NAI 1901 Census for Belfast, A98/88, Returns for Shaftesbury Square, Odd Numbered Addresses. In 1901, Moore was listed as the head of the household, which included his wife, five children, and a maidservant.

102. In Dublin for 1894 black-coated workers made up forty of the forty-one category III members (98 percent); in Dublin, for 1899 thirty-two of thirty-seven (87 percent); in Belfast, thirteen of eighteen (72 percent); and in Cork, just five of ten (50 percent).

103. Mary E. Daly, *Dublin*, 4.

104. Benedict Anderson, *Imagined Communities: Reflections on the Origin and Spread of Nationalism* (London: Verso, 1991), 52–58.

105. Brian O'Higgins, "Unique Branch of the Gaelic League," *Wolfe Tone Annual* 13 (1944–45), 62.

106. Dermot Keogh, *The Rise of the Irish Working Class: The Dublin Trade Union Movement and Labour Leadership, 1890–1914* (Belfast: Appletree Press, 1982), 65, 74.

107. Using the counties of Clare, Cork, Donegal, Galway, Kerry, Mayo, and Waterford as representative of Irish-speaking counties, one finds twenty-three of the seventy identified migrants (33 percent) in this category. Breaking the data down further, the resulting totals include eleven of the twenty migrants in 1894 (55 percent) and twelve of the fifty migrants (24 percent) in 1899.

108. Eoin MacNeill's salary as a first-class clerk in the Accountant General's Office was £300 a year. See Tierney, *Eoin MacNeill*, 9, 43. In the late-nineteenth and early-twentieth centuries a person needed an income of about £250 to maintain what Farmar refers to as "full-blown middle-class family respectability." See Tony Farmar, *Ordinary Lives: The Private Lives of Three Generations of Ireland's Professional Classes* (Dublin: Gill and Macmillan, 1995), 25–33.

109. O'Higgins placed the shop assistant's salary at between £15 and £25 a year, but Keogh, whose focus is primarily on assistants in larger draperies, established an assistant's income at between £40 and £50 a year. See Brian O'Higgins, "My Songs and Myself," *Wolfe Tone Annual*, 17 (1949), 60; and Keogh, 68–76.

110. O'Casey, *Drums*, 8.

111. The wards corresponding to this description and those in which the 39 members resided were those of North Dock, Mountjoy, North City, South City, Rotunda, Inns Quay,

Wood Quay, Merchants' Quay, Usher's Quay, and Arran Quay. See Joseph V. O'Brien, *"Dear, Dirty Dublin": A City in Distress, 1899–1916* (Berkeley: Univ. of California Press, 1982), 12–24.

112. The average property valuation is based on a comparison of information from the table "Area, Valuation, Houses, and Population in Each Municipal Ward or District Electoral Division in the City or County Borough of Dublin," in *Thom's* (1905), 1379. The total for the valuation contains the valuation of both houses and land in 1901. The total for the number of houses includes both inhabited and uninhabited houses. Valuations of the habitations of Gaelic Leaguers include those found in *Thom's* (1894 and 1895). I have divided the total valuation by the total number of houses, without making a distinction between inhabited and uninhabited buildings; therefore, these are crude totals and should be considered only for purposes of comparison.

113. Maurice Goldring, *Pleasant the Scholar's Life: Irish Intellectuals and the Construction of the Nation State* (London: Serif, 1993), 47.

114. *ACS,* 18 Nov. 1899.

115. *ACS,* 3 Nov. 1900.

116. See *ACS,* 15 Apr. 1899; *FL,* 4, 11 Nov. 1899. Also, see O'Higgins, "My Songs," 60; Gaelic League, *Imtheachta an Ard-Fheis, 1902–03* (Dublin: Gaelic League, 1903), 150–51.

117. The twenty-six branches were in the wards of North Dock, Mountjoy, Rotunda, Inns Quay, North City, South City, Wood Quay, Merchants' Quay, Usher's Quay, and New Kilmainham.

118. See Mary E. Daly, *Dublin,* 22, 33–36, 277–78.

119. On the Catholic Commercial Club, see Paseta, 105. The cost of a new bicycle was roughly £5 for a modest model, making them the virtual preserve of middle-class riders in Ireland. See Farmar, 32.

120. For their participation in interdenominational billiards tournaments, see Martin Maguire, "The Organisation and Activism of Dublin's Protestant Working Class, 1883–1935," *Irish Historical Studies* 29 (May 1994): 65–87.

121. Ibid., 75–80. See also NAI, DMP CSB 1896/4072/S., "Report on Dublin Literary Societies from Which IRB and INA Are Recruited", 13 Nov. 1896. Attached to the file are newspaper clippings referring to meetings in Inchicore with the Lyngs, William Rooney, and Arthur Griffith.

122. *IT,* 4 Mar. 1892; and Mary E. Daly, *Dublin,* 164.

123. *ACS,* 5 Nov. 1904. See also *Programme for a Public Meeting to be Held in the Pembroke Industrial School, Ringsend, for the Purpose of Establishing a Branch of the Gaelic League, on Sunday, 16th October* (Dublin: Gaelic League, 1904).

124. *INP,* 24 Sept. 1910; *ACS,* 24 Sept 1910, 23 Sept. 1911.

125. *ACS,* 7 Oct. 1899, 22 June 1901.

126. NAI, RIC CSB 1902/27,855/S., Report for the County of Londonderry, "Gaelic League. New Branch Formed in Londonderry City," 11 Nov. 1902. See also the attached files dated 20, 27 Nov., 19 Dec. 1901.

127. *ACS*, 5 Dec. 1903.

128. *ACS*, 19 Apr. 1902.

129. John M. O'Reilly, *The Threatening Metempsychosis of a Nation. Gaelic League Pamphlet—no. 24* (Dublin: Gaelic League, 1901), 8.

130. Ibid.

131. *ACS*, 29 Dec. 1900.

132. *Thom's* (1905), 35, 41. The population figure is for 1901, and it is included in *Thom's* with information about market dates.

133. *Leader*, 26 Oct. 1906, 2, 9 Nov. 1907.

134. Patrick Macartan to Joseph McGarrity, 13 Jan. 1906, NLI MS 17,457 Joseph McGarrity Papers, Letters from Patrick Macartan 1904–1911, File 3 [1906]. For published reports about Maguire's activities in Dromore, see *ACS*, 7 May, 11 Nov. 1904.

135. *Leader*, 26 Oct. 1906, 9 Nov. 1907.

136. P. S. Dinneen, "The Gaelic League and Non-Sectarianism," *Irish Rosary* (Jan. 1907): 5–13. Dinneen signed this article with the Irish spelling of his name: Pádraig Ua Duinnín. For a fictional account that includes similar sentiments, see Birmingham, *Benedict Kavanagh*, 59.

137. *ACS*, 7 June, 1, 8 Nov. 1902, 12 Mar. 1904. See also Bew, *Ideology*, 88–89.

138. *ACS*, 7 June 1902.

139. *FJ*, 20 Mar. 1908. See also Murray, 62. Parental objections were reported in twenty-five of the fifty-seven schools under Protestant management.

140. *ACS*, 2 Dec. 1911.

141. Padraig Ó Snodaigh, *Hidden Ulster: The Other Hidden Ireland* (Dublin: Clodhanna, 1973), 89, 91.

142. Earnán de Blaghd, *Trasna na Bóinne: Imleabhar I de Chuimhní Cinn* (Dublin: Sáirséil and Dill, 1957), 128; Greene, 116.

143. *FJ*, 28 May 1907. The Venerable Archdeacon William Hutch, parish priest of Midleton, had made his remarks at a Gaelic League feis in Midleton at which a Protestant nationalist member of parliament, Captain A. J. C. Donelan, addressed the gathering. See *FJ*, 27 May 1907.

144. This was Rolleston's conclusion as well. See *FJ*, 28 May 1907.

145. *Leader*, 11, 25 May 1907.

146. O'Casey, *Drums*, 172.

147. de Blaghd, *Trasna na Boinne*, 127–28.

148. *ACS*, 11 Mar. 1905. See also O'Casey, *Drums*, 171–72; de Blaghd, *Trasna na Boinne*, 127–130.

149. Greene, 117.

150. For example, see Garvin, *Nationalist Revolutionaries*, 85; MacDonagh, *States of Mind*, 114–15. A full treatment of Hannay's involvement in the League and his troubles in 1906 appears in French, 26–52.

151. For example, see his letters to the *Church of Ireland Gazette*, 3, 17, 20 June, 8 July, 28 Oct., 4 Nov. 1904, 15 Dec. 1905. See also his three-part series in the *Irish Protestant*, 20, 27 May, 8 June 1905.

152. Hannay, *Is the Gaelic League Political?* 8.

153. French, 45, 50.

154. Ibid., 50.

155. Birmingham, *Benedict Kavanagh*, 7.

156. *Church of Ireland Gazette* quoted in *SF*, 13 Oct. 1906.

157. Ibid.

158. On the cultural renaissance in Belfast and what distinguished it from the Dublin literary revival, see Flann Campbell, *The Dissenting Voice: Protestant Democracy in Ulster from Plantation to Partition* (Belfast: Blackstaff Press, 1991), 361–75; John Hewitt, "The Northern Athens and After," in Beckett, 76–82; Jonathan Bardon, *Belfast: An Illustrated History* (Dundonald: Blackstaff Press, 1982), 167–68.

159. On the *SVV*, see Richard Harp, "The *Shan Van Vocht* (Belfast, 1896–1899) and Irish Nationalism," *Éire-Ireland* 24 (Autumn 1989): 42–52.

160. Hobson, 14–15.

161. Editorial from the *Irish Protestant*, quoted in *ACS*, 14 Oct. 1905.

162. Blaney, 181–86.

163. *ACS*, 16 July 1904. See also Eamon Phoenix, Pádraic Ó Cléireacháin, Eileen McAuley, and Nuala McSparran, eds., *Feis na nGleann: A Century of Gaelic Culture in the Antrim Glens* (Belfast: Stair Uladh, 2005).

164. Hyde, *Language, Lore and Lyrics*, 179. The speech took place at Carnegie Hall, 26 November 1905.

165. *ACS*, 24 June 1899, 24 Feb. 1900, 24 Nov. 1900, 12 Oct. 1901.

166. *FJ*, 20 Mar. 1908.

167. *ACS*, 23, 30 Dec. 1911; Timothy G. McMahon, "'To Mould an Important Body of Shepherds'," 133.

168. Dinneen, "Gaelic League and Non-Sectarianism," 9.

169. In the years before independence, large numbers of urban Leaguers followed this advice and made repeated visits to the Irish-speaking districts. For one of MacNeill's early appeals, see *GJ*, 6 (Oct. 1895).

170. Ó Cearúil, 9.

171. *FL*, 12 Nov. 1898.

172. *ACS*, 15 Feb. 1908. On Nugent, see the reports in *ACS* for the Newry District between 1899 and 1901. See also Ó Súilleabháin, *Na Timirí*, 11–12; Ó Cearúil, 29–31, 51.

173. For example, in 1908, *ACS* included a report that showed that more than £2,660 of the nearly £5,400 expended the preceding year had gone to "Organisers, Teachers, and Subsidies to Irish-speaking Districts." See *ACS*, 7 Mar. 1908.

174. The two best introductions to the work of League *timirí* and *muinteoirí táistil* have appeared in Irish. See Ó Súilleabháin, *Na Timirí*; and Ó Cearúil.

175. See CCCA, MS U203/135–138, Papers of Liam Ó Buachalla, Banteer, Co. Cork. These selections include letters between Ó Buachalla and various companies, including Philip Pierce and Co. of Wexford, J. B. Brooks and Co. of Birmingham, John O'Neill Cycle Co. of Dublin, and A. Tighe and Co. of Cork. Note: the CCCA incorporates materials formerly held in the Cork Archives Institute, at which the author first examined the Ó Buachalla papers.

176. Timothy G. McMahon, *Pádraig Ó Fathaigh's War*, 4.

177. O'Casey, *Drums*, 8. See also the poem by Alice Milligan, "The Man on the Wheel," which was inspired by Concannon's work in the Gaeltacht. Quoted in Ó Cearúil, 1–2.

178. Ó Cearúil, 12.

179. All biographical data and subsequent calculations are based on a comparison of information from appendix 1 in Ó Cearúil's volume with that contained in Breathnach and Ní Mhurchú collections, *Beathaisnéis*.

180. For example, Ó Buachalla began teaching in County Wexford outside of his home district, but he left that first position apparently because of homesickness to return to the Banteer and Millstreet areas in County Cork. Colm Ó Gaora worked in his home district as well, until he accepted an organizing position that covered a wider swath of Connacht. Tómas Ó Conba of Limerick city consistently taught in communities along the Shannon estuary. And Pádraig Ó Fathaigh continued to live on his mother's farm at Lurgan, Co. Galway, throughout his teaching career. See NLI, MS G. 672, FMP, Letters to Tómas Ó Conba, 1905–20; Ó Gaora, *Mise*, 64–90; C. Quinn, ed., *Descriptive List of the Papers of Liam Ó Buachalla, Banteer, County Cork (1882–1941)* (Cork: Cork Archives Institute, 1994), i–iii; Timothy G. McMahon, *Pádraig Ó Fathaigh's War*, 4.

181. Timothy G. McMahon, "'To Mould an Important Body of Shepherds'," 130, 136.

182. See Gaelic League, *Annual Report 1901–02*, 36–51.

183. The issue of how to accomplish their goals in the Gaeltacht was a long source of controversy among Gaelic Leaguers themselves. For the "anti-organizer" argument, see *An Muimhneach Óg*, 1 (June 1903), 4; and *FJ*, 18, 24 Sept. 1906. For the initial decision to conduct flying visits across the widest possible area, see *ACS*, 23 Sept. 1899.

184. *Gaelic League Reports, 1898*, 3–4; and *Annual Report, 1901–02*, 104–13.

185. J. M. Synge, *The Aran Islands and Other Writings*, ed. Robert Tracy (New York: Vintage Books, 1962), 316, 332.

186. *ACS*, 4 Mar. 1911.

187. Ibid.

188. Gaelic League, *Annual Report, 1901–02*, 48.

189. Paul-Dubois, 301–2.

190. Ibid., 304.

191. NLI, MS 24,393 FMP, 1902–03, Census of the Irish-Speaking Communities for Bolus Promontory.

192. Calculations based on tables of population and emigration in *Thom's* (1905), 727–28.

193. For example, see the reports on the returns for the counties of Kerry, Galway, Mayo, Cork, Donegal, appearing respectively in *ACS*, 13 Apr., 18, 25 May, 15 June, 20 July, 10 Aug. 1912.

194. This figure is based on a comparison of the branches from 1901 to the list of market and fair towns in *Thom's* (1905), 34–41.

195. For a discussion of the interconnections of towns with their surrounding townlands, see Lee, *Modernisation*, 97–99.

196. Garret Fitzgerald, "Estimates for Baronies of Minimum Level of Irish-speaking Amongst Successive Decenniel Cohorts: 1771–1781 to 1861–1871," *Proceedings of the Royal Irish Academy* 84c, (1984): 150.

197. The image of the "gombeen-man" is a well-established one in Ireland, and the tense lending relationship has been explored in much contemporary and later scholarly literature. For example, see Synge, *Aran Islands,* 320; Líam Kennedy, "Farmers," 365; and David S. Jones, "The Cleavage Between Graziers and Peasants in the Land Struggle, 1890–1910," in *Irish Peasants: Violence and Political Unrest, 1780–1914,* ed. Samuel Clark and James S. Donnelly Jr. (Madison: Univ. of Wisconsin Press, 1983), 374–413.

198. Ó hAnnracháin told the Ard-Fheis in 1902 that many priests who were Gaelic Leaguers and who presided at League meetings nonetheless hired only English-speaking teachers in the schools that they managed. Gaelic League, *Annual Report, 1901–02,* 48. A similar example of a priest revivalist attacking native culture was Canon James MacFadden, parish priest of Glenties, Co. Donegal. See Mac Suibhne, "Soggarth Aroon," 183–84.

199. *ACS,* 1 Nov. 1902, 3, 24 Jan. 1903.

200. *An Muimhneach Óg,* 1 (June 1903).

201. Ibid.

202. P. S. Dinneen, *Lectures on the Irish Language Movement Delivered under the Auspices of Various Branches of the Gaelic League* (Dublin: M. H. Gill, 1904), 21. On Dinneen's complaints that not enough attention was paid to the Gaeltacht, see ibid., 52–53.

203. *ACS,* 25 Nov. 1905.

204. For example, see *FJ,* 18, 24 Sept. 1906. See also the extended discussion in *ACS* during 1912 about saving the Gaeltacht that was inspired by the release of the 1911 county census returns. For a particularly pointed statement calling on the Ard-Fheis to focus its attention on the Gaeltacht, see the letter of Gobnait Ní Bhruadair in *ACS,* 22 June 1912.

205. For instance, in County Kerry, the general decline was less than 4 percent, but the fall in the number of Irish speakers was nearly 15 percent. See *ACS,* 13 Apr. 1912.

206. Ibid.

207. *ACS,* 15 June 1912.

208. *ACS,* 25 May 1912.

209. Timothy G. McMahon, "Gaelic League," 100–1.

210. *ACS,* 13 Apr., 1 June, 24 Aug. 1912.

211. *ACS,* 24 Aug. 1912.

4. COOPERATING WITH THE COOPERATORS:
BRANCH ACTIVITIES AND THE REGENERATION OF IRELAND

1. Conradh na Gaeilge, *Prospectus of the Fifth Oireachtas, or Literary Festival* (Dublin: Gaelic League, 1901), 1.

2. *ACS,* 21 Jan. 1905.

3. Michael P. O'Hickey, *Language and Nationality with Preface by Douglas Hyde* (Waterford: Waterford News, 1918), ii.

4. There is a very clear element of gendering in these appeals. Moran was particularly prone to refer to the Irish-Ireland movement as a "manly" movement, and in 1904, he published a cartoon representative of the "new" Ireland, embodied by a muscular male nude grappling with the serpent of Anglicization. See *Leader,* 16 July 1904. This gendered aspect of the "dependency" question merits significant future study.

5. See Mathews, 5–34; and Biletz, "Boundaries."

6. For instance, see *ACS,* 9 Sept. 1899.

7. W. P. Ryan, *Pope's Green Island,* 64.

8. Timothy G. McMahon, "'To Mould an Important Body of Shepherds'," 128–30; Elizabeth Devine, "The Connacht Irish College," *Catholic Bulletin* 2 (Jan. 1912): 9–14; and K. Magner, "Ballingeary," *Catholic Bulletin* 2 (Sept. 1912): 640–45.

9. Devine, 14.

10. After attending the Connacht College, for instance, Pádraig Ó Fathaigh included dancing, singing, and drama readings in his classes in south Galway. Timothy G. McMahon, *Pádraig Ó Fathaigh's War,* 4–5.

11. *ACS,* 9 Sept. 1899.

12. Horgan, 105.

13. For the Keating branch, see *FJ,* 8 Apr. 1903. For a similar report about the Central branch, see *FJ,* 11 May 1908.

14. Horgan, 109.

15. For a concise account of Dwyer's life, see Boylan, 103. The Michael Dwyer branch formed in June 1900, and its first vice president was Michael Mullen, a migrant from the Aran Islands, who later became an active socialist. For representative reports about the branch and about Mullen leading discussions about the Boer War, see *ACS,* 7 July, 11 Aug., 8 Sept. 1900.

16. Letter from Canon A. Morrissey to Liam Ó Buachalla, 15 [Jan.?] 1910, CCCA MS U203/59, Liam Ó Buachalla Papers. Emphasis as written.

17. *Leader,* 7 Apr. 1906.

18. Ibid., 14, 21 Apr. 1906.

19. Ibid., 14 Apr. 1906.

20. Ibid., 21 Apr. 1906.

21. NAI, BRS, Galway 1/1/1, Minute Book of the St. Grellan's Branch of the Gaelic League, [n.d., probably 27 Jan. 1903].

22. Ibid.

23. Ibid., 3, 28 Oct., 13, 20 Nov., 9, 20, 30 Dec. 1902, 6, 13, 20, 27 Jan. 1903. The branch subscribed to the *Leader*, the *New Ireland Review*, the *United Irishman*, *An Claidheamh Soluis*, the *Connaught Leader*, the *Evening Herald*, and the *Evening Telegraph*.

24. *FJ*, 12 Mar. 1908. MacFadden had attended a six-hour-long meeting of the Gaelic League Coiste Gnótha the evening prior to delivering this lecture on the Irish language and Irish industries.

25. Ibid. MacFadden's emphasis on tenants' rights in this speech is perhaps understandable given that his audience was made up of United Irish League members.

26. Horgan, 192.

27. Quoted in *Leader*, 21 Dec. 1901. Kennedy has shown that the absolute increase of publicans, innkeepers, and grocers in the years after the famine, in conjunction with the continued decrease in overall population, resulted in their increased visibility and power in local and national politics. See Kennedy, "Farmers," 342–44. 28. In 1845, Ireland had 15,000 licensed houses, whereas in 1905, the number was 30,000. See Paul-Dubois, 363.

29. Ibid.

30. Moran consistently referred to the figure of £13 million spent on alcoholic beverages, while Paul-Dubois claimed that the figure was as high as £15 million. The Frenchman also stated that the government collected more than £5 million in taxes on those sales. Cf. *Leader*, 15 Mar. 1902; Paul-Dubois, 363.

31. *ACS*, 21 Sept. 1901.

32. See *Leader*, 21 Mar. 1903; Joseph V. O'Brien, *Dear, Dirty Dublin*, 80.

33. Moran's references to "Bung" inspired one of the more memorable scenes in the "Circe" episode of James Joyce's *Ulysses*. See Timothy G. McMahon, "Cultural Nativism," 77–78.

34. *ACS*, 21 Sept. 1901.

35. *The Irish Language Movement and the Gaelic League* (Dublin: Gaelic League, 1912), 14.

36. Ibid.

37. Ibid.

38. O'Farrell, 223–24.

39. *ACS*, 21 Sept. 1901.

40. See Diarmaid Ferriter, *A Nation of Extremes: the Pioneers in Twentieth-Century Ireland* (Dublin: Irish Academic Press, 1999).

41. O'Farrell, 224.

42. *ACS*, 21 Sept. 1901.

43. *ACS*, 15, 22, 29 Apr. 1899, 7 July 1900.

44. *ACS*, 12 Oct. 1901, 12 July 1902.

45. Dunleavy and Dunleavy, 179.

46. Lady Augusta Gregory, *Lady Gregory's Diaries, 1892–1902*, ed. James Pethica (Gerrards Cross, Buckinghamshire: Colin Smythe, 1996), 293.

47. Murphy, *Patrick Pearse*, 37. For a lively account of MacGarvey's tobacco shop, see Seán Ó Cearnaigh, *An Stad: Críoláir na hAthbheochana* (Dublin: Comhar Teoranta, 1993).

48. O'Casey, *Drums*, 185.

49. W. P. Ryan, *Pope's Green Island*, 186.

50. NLI, MS 10,900, EMP, Dublin, Belfast, and Dublin County File for 1904–05.

51. *ACS*, 17 May 1902.

52. *ACS*, 22 Nov. 1902.

53. *ACS*, 17 May 1902.

54. Ibid.

55. *ACS*, 22, 29 Nov., 13 Dec. 1902.

56. *ACS*, 22, 29 Nov. 1902. A correspondent named Pádraig Ua Murchadha from Enniscorthy asserted that the Anti-Treating League had received a complete endorsement from the Ard-Fheis, which prompted Diarmuid Ó Cruadhlaoich to deny that the "sectarian" organization had received the imprimatur of the congress. In all likelihood the original writer was Fr. Patrick Murphy, who lived at the House of Missions in Enniscorthy. He was a leader of both the Gaelic League and the Anti-Treating League in County Wexford. Given the context of the debate, it is noteworthy he chose not to sign his name with its ecclesiastical prefix. On Murphy, see Breathnach and Ní Mhurchú, *Beathaisnéis, a Cuig*, 212–13. Murphy's active interest in the language movement is evident in his correspondence with one of his traveling teachers. See CCCA MS U203/46, Liam Ó Buachalla Papers, Letters pertaining to County Wexford.

57. *ACS*, 29 Nov. 1902.

58. Ibid.

59. Ibid.

60. *ACS*, 13 Dec. 1902.

61. Ibid.

62. On the DTAS and the IAPI, see Elizabeth Malcolm, *"Ireland Sober, Ireland Free": Drink and Temperance in Nineteenth-Century Ireland* (Syracuse: Syracuse Univ. Press, 1986), 176, 190, 251–70.

63. Kevin Danaher, *The Year in Ireland* (Cork: Mercier Press, 1972), 58. The most important study of St. Patrick's Day and its variety of meanings is Cronin and Adair's *The Wearing of the Green*. See also Peter Alter, "Symbols of Irish Nationalism," in *Reactions to Irish Nationalism*, ed. Alan O'Day (London: Hambledon Press, 1987); Timothy G. McMahon, "Gaelic League," 125–29; and Jacqueline R. Hill, "National Festivals, the State, and 'Protestant Ascendancy' in Ireland, 1790–1829," *Irish Historical Studies* 24 (May 1984): 30–51.

64. Timothy P. O'Neill, *Life and Tradition in Rural Ireland* (London: Dent, 1977), 64.

65. *Leader,* 15 Feb., 1, 22 Mar. 1902.

66. Ibid., 15 Feb. 1902.

67. Ibid., 1 Mar. 1902.

68. Ibid.

69. Ibid., 25 Jan. 1901.

70. Ibid., 22 Mar. 1902.

71. Ibid.

72. Ibid., 13 Sept. 1902.

73. Ibid., 28 Mar. 1903.

74. Ibid.

75. Ibid., 6 Feb. 1904. According to the IAPI, the police courts reported only thirty-two cases of public drunkenness on St. Patrick's Day in 1903, as opposed to sixty-nine in 1902.

76. *ACS,* 14 Mar. 1908.

77. *FJ,* 16 Mar. 1908.

78. Hutchinson, *Dynamics,* 168–80.

79. *Leader,* 5 Jan. 1901. See also, Maume, *D. P. Moran,* 13–14.

80. Maume, *Long Gestation,* 49, 63. See also Hutchinson, *Dynamics,* 168–78; and Biletz, "Boundaries," chaps. 3 and 5. Moran would advocate state protectionism after the creation of the Irish Free State. See Maume, *D. P. Moran,* 43–52.

81. Hutchinson, *Dynamics,* 120–27, 180–81. Joe Lee is equally hard on Hyde, referring to his "ideological isolation" and his "retreat from reality" because Hyde nostalgically invoked childhood memories of Irish men wearing knee breeches rather than factory-made trousers. Such a characterization misreads Hyde's evocation of what he saw as a more self-sufficient period in recent Irish history. See Lee, *Modernisation,* 137–41.

82. See MacFadden's comments about saving agriculture through reinvigorating cottage industries. *FJ,* 12 Mar. 1908. See also Pearse's Irish-language leading article on cottage industries, "Deuntuis Cois Teanadh" [Fireside Industries] in *ACS,* 4 Apr. 1903.

83. *FJ,* 12 Mar. 1908.

84. For a discussion of the effort to "modernize on Irish terms," see Mathews, *Revival,* 23–28. Hyde was more likely than MacNeill to use racialist phrases like "Celtic characteristics" and "our turn of thought." According to one authority, MacNeill specifically avoided such racialist terminology because he found it unsatisfactory. Also, Hyde's thinking on his approach to modernity, as represented by commerce and industry specifically, underwent changes during his adult years. As a Trinity College student, he claimed that preserving Irish "will neither make money nor help to make money." But as League president, he extolled the manner in which his organization was contributing to the industrial output of Ireland. On MacNeill, see Donal McCartney, "MacNeill and Irish-Ireland," in *The Scholar Revolutionary: Eoin MacNeill,* ed. F. X. Martin and F. J. Byrne (Shannon: Irish Univ. Press, 1973). For a comparison of Hyde's early ideas to his later thought, see Hyde, "A Plea," 666–76; and his speech to a Carnegie Hall audience in 1906, quoted in Hyde, *Language, Lore, and Lyrics,* 189.

85. *ACS*, 25 June 1904. The phrase occurs in a review of Thomas Concannon's *Focla Gnótha agus a gCora Cainte* (1904), a Gaelic dictionary of business terminology.

86. Ibid.

87. UCD Archives, MS LA 1/E/71, EMP. This passage comes from one of several undated items that were almost certainly the rough notes for a speech MacNeill made to the Dublin Central branch in February 1905. In both the notes and a press account of the speech he lays out a program of basic terminology that he considered necessary starting points to update the language: everyday household items; terms related to domestic economy; texts in basic logic; scientific and mechanical terms; and agricultural terms. See UCD Archives, MS LA1/E/67–71, EMP. See also *II*, 9 Feb. 1905.

88. *II*, 9 Feb. 1905.

89. For a compelling, if problematic, discussion of the role of print capitalism in linking persons of like experience to an imagined community, see Benedict Anderson, 9–46.

90. Maume, *Long Gestation*, 49, 63.

91. *ACS*, 8 July 1899. Emphasis added.

92. Ibid.

93. *ACS*, 6 Apr. 1901. Cf. Paul-Dubois, 434: "Those who remain here are the feeble and the dreamers, those who emigrate are the strong and the young."

94. *Leader*, 29 Sept., 6 Oct. 1900.

95. Ibid., 15, 22, 29 Sept. 1900.

96. W. P. O'Riain, *Lessons from Modern Language Movements: What Native Speech Has Achieved for Nationality. Gaelic League Pamphlet—no. 25* (Dublin: Gaelic League, 1901), 32.

97. *ACS*, 10 Aug. 1901.

98. Ibid.

99. *ACS*, 12 May 1900.

100. *ACS*, 30 June 1900.

101. *Leader*, 27 Oct. 1900.

102. *ACS*, 27 Oct. 1900.

103. *ACS*, 10 Dec. 1904.

104. Ibid.

105. *ACS*, 11 July 1902. See also NLI, MS 9804, Conradh na Gaeilge, *Minutes of the Industrial Committee, 1902–11*. The minutes are most complete for the period 1902–6, and then they run intermittently until 1911.

106. *ACS*, 20 Dec. 1902.

107. *ACS*, 23, 31 May, 13, 27 June 1903. The lone reply came from Messrs. Doyle and Co., Wexford town, a regular sponsor of the industrial exhibition at the annual County Wexford feis.

108. *ACS*, 1 Aug. 1903.

109. For a personal account of his parliamentary activities, see John P. Boland, *Irishman's Day: A Day in the Life of an Irish M. P.* (London: Macdonald, 1944).

110. Letter from "Eilís" to MacColuim, 21 Jan. 1903, in NLI, MS 24,393, FMP, Correspondence from Organizers and Others, 1902–03. See also *ACS*, 12, 19 Sept. 1903.

111. Bridget Boland, *At My Mother's Knee* (London: Bodley Head, 1978), 48.

112. Ibid. See also the episode in Guinan's *Curate of Kilcloon*, in which the energetic curate, Fr. Melville, attempts unsuccessfully to establish a peat business for his parishioners. See Guinan, *Curate*, 81–85.

113. *ACS*, 29 Aug. 1903.

114. Ibid.

115. Cronin was also a contributor to the *Leader*. See Maume, *D. P. Moran*, 14.

116. *ACS*, 23 Dec. 1905.

117. Ibid.

118. *IP*, 3 Feb. 1906.

119. *ACS*, 4 Mar. 1905.

120. *FJ*, 17 Apr. 1906.

121. Liam Ó Bolguidhir, "The Early Years of the Gaelic League in Kilkenny," *Old Kilkenny Review* (1992): 1014–26.

122. *FJ*, 17 Apr. 1906.

123. Ibid.

124. Ibid. O'Hanrahan was active in the branch from its foundation. See Ó Bolguidhir, 1018, 1023.

125. Ó Bolguidhir, 1021.

126. E. J. Riordan, *Modern Irish Trade and Industry* (London: Metheuen, 1920), 275; Horgan, 123–24.

127. One of the most important members of the original group was Liam de Roiste, a member of the Celtic Literary Society and the Gaelic League in Cork. See Horgan, 120.

128. Riordan, 266.

129. *II*, 13 Feb. 1905.

130. On the Dublin IDA, see *ACS*, 28 Jan. 1905. To obtain a sense of how closely associated the League was with the formation of the IIDA in Dublin, one can follow a series of letters in the *II* that specifically mention the role that the League ought to play in invigorating local industries. See *II*, 8, 9, 11, 13, 15 Feb. 1905. In Galway, Fr. A. J. Considine chaired the committee that formed the IDA. See *FJ*, 16, 17 May 1906.

131. Riordan, 275.

132. *ACS*, 2 Dec. 1905; *IP*, 10 Feb. 1906.

133. The Trade Marks Act of 1905 empowered the Board of Trade in London to register associations to issue trademarks to corporations whose products met specified requirements. The Irish trademark was officially registered to the Irish Industrial Development Association (Incorporated) on 8 December 1906, and the association began issuing trademarks on 1 January 1907. See Horgan, 123; Riordan, 276–77.

134. The specific requirement was that more than 50 percent of the cost of production had to go toward the cost of Irish labor. Also, preference was given to companies that could show that they had used only, or mainly Irish raw materials. See Riordan, 277.

135. Maume, *D. P. Moran*, 14.

136. *FJ*, 17, 18 Sept. 1908, 6, 7 Aug. 1909.

137. *FJ*, 17 Sept. 1908, 6, 7 Aug. 1909.

138. Quoted in Riordan, 272. The quotation is undated, but in another portion of the statement the *News-Letter* refers to trade statistics from 1907. It probably comes from 1909, when the IIDA conference met in Belfast.

139. *II*, 2 Jan. 1904. The speech took place on 30 Dec. 1903.

140. Ibid.

141. *FJ*, 4 Mar. 1903.

142. *SF*, 21 Feb. 1914. See also, *SF*, 28 Feb., 14 Mar., 13 June 1913. On Hughes, see Thomas Morrissey, "Saving the Language: 'The Impatient Revolutionary,'" *Studies* 77 (Autumn 1988): 352–57. Thomas Johnson had been a member of a Gaelic League branch in Belfast. Anthony J. Gaughan, *Thomas Johnson, 1872–1963: First Leader of the Labour Party in Dáil Éireann* (Mount Merrion, Co. Dublin: Kingdom Books, 1980), 18. O'Brien's involvement was tangential and based at least in part on his father's having been a student of the aged language enthusiast John Fleming. See William O'Brien, *Forth the Banners Go: Reminiscences of William O'Brien, as told to Edward MacLysaght* (Dublin: Three Candles, 1969), 18–26, 231–2. Larkin became so interested in the educational teachings of Pearse that he sent his sons to St. Enda's as students. On Larkin's nationalism, see Emmet Larkin, *James Larkin, Irish Labour Leader, 1876–1947* (London: Pluto Press, 1965), 182–84. For a reference to Larkin's sons at St. Enda's, see Hyde Memoir, 21. In a conversation with the author in October 1998, Emmet Larkin confirmed that both of James Larkin's sons had attended St. Enda's.

143. Among those with whom O'Casey felt kinship was Donal Ó Murchadha, one-time secretary of the Dublin Coiste Ceanntair, who disagreed with Hyde over supporting "Larkinism." Cf. O'Casey, *Drums*, 131–32; Hyde Memoir, 19–28.

144. See the speech of Lord Dunraven and the subsequent comments from other delegates at the Galway meeting in 1908. See *FJ*, 17 Sept. 1908.

145. *ACS*, 17 June 1899, 13 Dec. 1902.

146. *ACS*, 22 June 1899.

147. *ACS*, 23 Dec. 1905. The second part of the article appeared in the following week. MacGinley had originally expressed his opinions in a speech at the Rory O'More branch in Portarlington on 8 October 1905.

148. *ACS*, 24 Nov. 1900. For examples of *timirí* reports that give a comparative sense of the use of Irish at the fair in Dungarvan, see *ACS*, 1 Dec. 1900, 11 July 1903.

149. *ACS*, 23 Dec. 1905.

150. *ACS*, 13 May 1905.

151. NAI, CSORP 1903/17,607 "Gaelic League Meeting at Cloghane on 20 Aug. 1903." See also *ACS,* 19 Sept. 1903.

152. On the cooperative movement, see R. A. Anderson; Trevor West, *Horace Plunkett, Cooperation and Politics: An Irish Biography* (Gerrards Cross, Buckinghamshire: Colin Smythe, 1986); and Paul-Dubois, 443–51.

153. Lyons, *Culture and Anarchy,* 74–75. Although Moran supported Plunkett's early career, he abandoned him after *Ireland in the New Century* appeared in 1904. See Maume, *D. P. Moran,* 15–17.

154. For instance, Finlay spoke in Derry and Dromore in 1904 and in Kilskeery in 1906. See *ACS,* 20 Feb., 6 Aug. 1904; *IH,* 22 Oct. 1904; *Leader,* 13 Oct. 1906.

155. The articles, entitled *"Airgead Saor"* ["Free Money"], appeared intermittently in *ACS* from 24 Mar. 1900 to 12 May 1900.

156. Douglas Hyde, *Duilleóigín 2A, Bancanna Tíre/IAOS Pamphlet 2A, Rural Banks* (Dublin: Irish Agricultural Organisation Society, 1900).

157. See *ACS,* 7 Mar. 1903; 21 Nov. 1908; 10 Dec. 1910.

158. *ACS,* 21 Nov. 1908.

159. Irish Agricultural Organisation Society, *Seventh Report of the Irish Agricultural Organisation Society Ltd., for the Year Ending December 31st 1901* (Dublin: Irish Agricultural Organisation Society, 1902), 7–8.

160. *IH,* 6 Aug. 1904.

161. Paul-Dubois, 449.

162. Synge, *Aran Islands,* 316–17.

163. *IH,* 25 Apr., 9 May 1903.

164. See *IH,* 30 July 1904. On O'Conor-Eccles's career, see *Times,* 15 June 1911.

165. *Leader,* 9 Nov. 1907.

166. Ibid., 2 Nov. 1907.

167. Ibid.

168. Ibid. Moran's series about Kilskeery was entitled "Irishisation and How 'Tis Done."

169. Thomas MacDonagh O'Mahony, quoted in "Report of the Workings of the Cahirciveen Branch of the Gaelic League," in *Clár: Feis Íbh-Ráthaigh, 1904,* 60.

5. The Grand Opportunity: Festivals and the Gaelic Revival

1. "Brian na Banban" (Brian O'Higgins, pseud.) in the *Leinster Leader,* quoted in *ACS,* 27 May 1911.

2. Manning, 4–7; Turner, 16.

3. O'Leary, *Prose Literature,* 375.

4. "An t-Oireachtas: An Irish Language Prize Meeting," *GJ,* 7 (Jan. 1897), 129. See also Donncha Ó Súilleabháin, *Scéal an Oireachtais, 1897–1924* (Dublin: An Clóchamhar Teoranta, 1984).

5. "An t-Oireachtas," 129.

6. Ibid. One of the founders of the Feis Ceoil was the bombastic and somewhat contro-versial Thomas O'Neill Russell. For an overview of his life, see Breathnach and Ní Mhurchú, *Beathaisnéis, a Trí,* 148–50. Eoin MacNeill once said of Russell that "he is the gentlest of ex-tremists, the blandest of revolutionaries. In Dublin, in whose social life he is a picturesque figure, he wages war day in day out, having as little consideration for common or received opinions as an earthquake for a hamlet." Quoted in *IP,* 23 June 1906.

7. "An t-Oireachtas," 130.

8. Ó Suilleabháin, *Scéal,* 157; *GJ,* 8 (June 1897), 20. The figure of 103 *entries* does not, however, reflect precisely the number of *competitors* because some individuals entered more than one competition. All calculations, therefore, should be viewed as approximations.

9. *GJ,* 8 (June 1897), 20. Competition Number 7 asked for "an essay in Irish or English on the subject 'How to popularize the Irish language.'" It was sponsored by the land activist William O'Brien, who was not then serving in parliament, and it offered the largest prize of the first Oireachtas, £10. The winner of the competition was the poet and journalist Alice Milligan, who wrote in English.

10. Tierney, *Eoin MacNeill,* 28.

11. *GJ,* 8 (June 1897), 20. These included Cork (12), Galway (7), Kerry (6), Donegal (4), Waterford (4), Clare (2), and Mayo (1).

12. Ibid. Both Ó Foghludha and Ó Séaghda became well-known Irish writers and translators under their respective pseudonyms, Feargus Finnbhéil and Conan Maol. Ó Foghludha, who later translated French plays into Irish, won the competition to compose "A Song of the Gaelic Movement, with Chorus, suitable for singing at Gaelic League meet-ings." His "Go Mairidh ár nGaedhilg Slán" became the rallying song of the Gaelic League, and as we will see below, it would play a prominent part in the Dublin processions. For information on Ó Foghludha, see Breathnach and Ní Mhurchú, *Beathaisnéis, a Dó,* 107. On Ó Séaghda, see Breathnach and Ní Mhurchú, *Beathaisnéis, a hAon,* 103–4.

13. There were actually twenty-five names listed among the prizewinners and com-mended, but four of them were listed in multiple competitions: John J. Hynes (2 times), Tadhg O'Donoghue (3), Diarmuid Ó Foghludha (3), and J. H. Lloyd (2).

14. Ó Suilleabháin, *Scéal,* 13.

15. All press opinions quoted in *GJ,* 8 (June 1897), 20–24.

16. Ibid., 17.

17. W. P. Ryan, *Pope's Green Island,* 68.

18. Tadhg Ó Donnchadha, ed., *Imtheachta an Oireachtas, 1901, Leabhar a hAon* (Dublin: Gaelic League, 1903), 10. The number of entries from within Ireland was, however, only 318.

19. *FL,* 26 Mar. 1898.

20. *FL,* 2 Apr. 1898.

21. *Annual Report of the Gaelic League for 1898,* dated 30 September 1898, quoted in Ó Suilleabháin, *Scéal,* 194. For general comments on the feis Ceoil in Belfast, see the report by

O'Neill Russell in the *SVV*, 6 June 1898. For an account of the tableaux directed by Alice Milligan, see the report "Gaelic Tableaux in Belfast" in the same issue of the *SVV*.

22. Ó Suilleabháin, *Scéal*, 195.

23. For example, see NLI, MS 10,900, EMP, Leinster File, which contains invitations to dozens of feiseanna in a single province.

24. *ACS*, 19 Aug., 2 Sept. 1899, 13 Jan. 1900. See also *Programme of Feis na n-Deisi, to be held in the Town Hall, Dungarvan, on Sunday, August 11th, 1901* (Dungarvan: Brenan and Company, 1901).

25. See the report of Ua Laoghaire's speech at the Munster feis in 1900 in *Leader*, 29 Sept. 1900. He served as the president of the *Feis na Mumhan* General Committee in 1907. See *Feis na Mumhan, 1907, City Hall Cork, September 16th to 21st. An Clár: Programme* (Cork: Guy and Co., 1907). On the Fermoy feis, see *Leader* 2 Aug. 1902; *ACS*, 12 July 1902, 19 Sept. 1903.

26. Hyde delivered the Oireachtas ode from 1897 to 1903. Among those who gave the ode on later occasions were the Deise poet Roibeard Bheldon (1905) and Conchur Ó Deasúna (1906) of Ballyvourney, Co. Cork, who won prizes for prose and poetry at the Oireachtas throughout his adult life. Among those giving the oration were Fr. J. M. O'Reilly of Achill Island in 1898; Pádraig Ó Seaghdha of Co. Kerry via Belfast in 1900; Canon James MacFadden of The Glenties, Co. Donegal, in 1902; and Pádraig Mac Suibhne of Fermoy in 1906. See Ó Suilleabháin, *Scéal*, 200–1.

27. In its discussion of the Oireachtas committee report in 1903, the Ard-Fheis resolved that "in order to have the competitions at the Oireachtas of a thoroughly representative character, the committee recommend that arrangements should be made to bring first and second prize winners in the Irish style of singing, story-telling, dialogue, and recitation at the provincial and county feiseanna to Dublin to compete at the Oireachtas." See *ACS*, 23 May 1903. Cf. Ó Suilleabháin, *Scéal*, 194–95; *ACS*, 9 Jan., 27 Feb. 1904.

28. Ó Suilleabháin, *Scéal*, 194. In the first year of operation, fourteen festivals received approval to join in the travel arrangements. In 1905, the number grew to twenty-four festivals. The financial aspects of this scheme raised concerns for at least one revivalist who wrote into *ACS* to complain that such incentives might lead branches to "teach to the test," a biting complaint often leveled by Irish-Irelanders against the intermediate schools of Ireland. See *ACS*, 27 Feb. 1904.

29. For example, see the report of the Oireachtas committee in *ACS*, 26 Apr. 1902.

30. For examples of feiseanna limiting competitors to the local populace, see *Feis Dhroichid na Banndan. Bandon Convent Grounds, Sunday, July 22nd, 1906 Programme* (Cork: Eagle Printing Co., 1906), 5; and *Clár. Feis na Gaillimhe/Galway Feis, County Hall, Galway, August 16 & 17* (Dublin: An Cló-Chumann Teoranta, 1906), 4.

31. *ACS*, 23 May 1903. In practice, however, the Organization committee (Coiste an Timthireachta) did not deal with scheduling festivals. That duty devolved to the Oireachtas committee. See Ó Suilleabháin, *Scéal*, 194.

32. For example, see the postcard from national secretary Pádraig Ó Dalaigh to Cornelius O'Leary at Rathcoole, Co. Cork, about a proposed feis that might conflict with a previously scheduled festival at Dromogh. Ó Dalaigh to O'Leary, 18 Apr. 1906, CCCA, MS U. 163/15, C. T. O'Leary Papers. The Dromagh syllabus had been licensed at the meeting of the Oireachtas committee on 31 March. See ACS, 7 Apr. 1906. Also see the postcard from Fionán MacColuim to the local secretary and traveling teacher Liam Ó Buachalla, asking him to reschedule an outing by members of his branch, so that they could attend the Cullen feis. MacColuim to Ó Buachalla, 24 June 1910, CCCA, MS U. 203/10, Liam Ó Buachalla Papers.

33. Seán T. Ó Ceallaigh, Seán T., 88: "Ní raibh ionam féin ach tosnaitheoir dáiríre, ach mar sin féin bhí an Ghaeilge go líofa agam. B'fhéidir nach raibh sí i gconaí cruinn ó thaobh an ghraiméir de, ach is cosúil nár chuir sé sin lá buairimh ar éinne. Bhí moltóirí an-ghann agus níor ghá dóibh aon scrúdú a sheasamh iad féin." ["Truthfully I was only a beginner, but even so I had a lot of Irish. Perhaps it was not always gramatically precise, but apparently that did not bother anyone. Judges were very scarce, and there would not have been any examinations without them."]

34. Ibid.

35. ACS, 29 Apr. 1905.

36. Ibid.

37. ACS, 16 Dec. 1905.

38. FJ, 10 Aug. 1906. The actual resolution, as reported in the proceedings of the Ard-Fheis, read: "That a feis, or event in the nature of a feis, held in a district where there is a branch of the Gaelic League, without the approval of the branch, or of the coiste ceanntair (if any), or the Coiste Gnótha, should be deemed a bogus feis; and any person competing thereat shall be disqualified for a period of three years from competing at the Oireachtas or at any feis held under the auspices of any Gaelic League body." Quoted in Ó Suilleabháin, Scéal, 195.

39. FJ, 10 Aug. 1905.

40. Ibid.

41. Ibid.

42. Ibid. This was the same congress that reelected MacGinley and the Protestant rector of Westport, Canon J. O. Hannay, to the executive committee in spite of concerns among some conservative priests that the League encouraged nonsectarian cooperation.

43. Four of the "Irish Language" competitions at the Wexford feis in 1905 required students, ranging in age from under 11 up to 16 years, to display knowledge of various conversation primers and to recite prayers. Similarly, three of the "Literary" competitions at the Bandon feis in 1906 required students to display familiarity with materials from the approved national schools program in Irish and to recite specified prayers. See Feis agus Aonach Loch g-Carmain/County Wexford Feis and Aonach Ros Mhic Treóin, on Whit Sunday and

Whit Monday and the following day, June 11th, 12th, and 13th, 1905 (Enniscorthy, n.p., 1905); and *Feis Dhroichid na Banndan,* 6.

44. See Competitions 16, 20 and 23, in *Feis na Mumhan, 1907,* 35, 41–3, 49–51.

45. *ACS,* 18 July 1903.

46. Ibid.

47. *ACS,* 3 Dec. 1903.

48. Ibid.

49. Ibid. There were also fourteen dancing competitions and five musical competitions.

50. *Imtheachta an Ard-Fheis, 1907,* quoted in Ó Suilleabháin, *Scéal,* 195.

51. Although he does not give a precise count, Ó Suilleabháin points out that a proportion of the syllabi failed ["Theip ar na comortais chomhréir"] when submitted for review.
See Ó Suilleabháin, *Scéal,* 195.

52. *Feis agus Aonach Loch g-Carmain; Clár Feis Íbh-Ráthaigh, 1904, Dánta augs Seanchaid-
heacht* (Dublin: An Cló-Chumann Teoranta, 1904); *Feis Uíbh Ráthaigh, 1910, Clár na Feise*
(Tralee: *"Star"* and *"People,"* 1910); *Feis na Mumhan, 1903* (Cork: Cork Sun Co., 1903); *Feis na
Mumhan, 1907; Feis na Mumhan, Clár na Chuirme Ceóil, Dia Luain, 16adh Meádhon Fóghmhair*
(Cork: Guy and Co., [1907?]); *Feis na Mumhan, 1910, to be held in Cork, September 9th, 10th,
and 11th. An Clár/Programme* (Cork: Guy and Co., 1910); *Feis Tuadh-Mumhan, 1907, Syllabus,
List of Competitions, Prizes, Conditions* (Limerick: O'Connor and Co., 1907); *Clár Feis Tuadh-
Mhumhan, 1908* (Limerick: O'Connor and Co., 1908); *Clár Feis Tuadh-Mhumhan, 1910* (Limer-
ick: O'Connor and Co., 1910); *Feis Tuadh-Mumhan, 1910, Syllabus, List of Competitions, Prizes,
Conditions* (Limerick: O'Connor and Co., 1910); *Feis Dhaingin Uí Chúise, 1905, Tionólfar sa
Daingean i Sgoileannaibh na mBrathair Dia Sathairn an 22adh Lá a's Dia Domhnaigh and 23adh
Lá d'Iúl, 1905* (Tralee: Kerry Sentinel, 1905); *Feis Dhaingin Uí Chúise, 1906* (Tralee: Kerryman
Printing Co., 1906); *Feis Cholmáin, 1906, Clár na hOibre* (Dublin: An Cló-Chumann Teoranta,
1906); *Seventh Annual Feis i Aonach Loch gCarmáin, 1908, Whit Sunday & Whit Monday, June 7th
and 8th in New Ross* (Enniscorthy: Echo Printing and Publishing Co., 1908); *Clár. Feis na Gail-
limhe/Galway Feis, County Hall, Galway, August 16 & 17* (Dublin: An Cló-Chumann Teoranta,,
1906); *Feis Dhroichid na Banndan; Feis Mór Lios-Tuathail, 10adh Iul 1910. Clar na Féise* (Tralee:
Kerryman, 1910); *Feis Laoighise i Osraidhe, do Tionólfar Fé Chúram Choiste Ceanntair Laoighise
agus Osraidhe, i bPort Laoighise, ar 15adh Lá de'n bhFóghmhar, 1907, An Clár* (Dublin: An Cló-
Chumann Teoranta,, 1907); *Programme of Feis na n-Deisi; Feis Laighean i Midhe, Rotunda, Baile
Átha Cliath, Dia Sathairn, 15adh Márta, 1902. Leabhar na Feise (Book of the Feis)* (Dublin: n.p.,
1902); *Feis na Mumhan, Cillairne, 1904* (Cork: n.p., 1904); *Imtheachta Feise na Mumhan, 1904. List
of Subscribers and Prize-Winners Together with Remarks of Judges, Detailed Balance Sheet, and Auditor's Report* (Tralee: Ryle and Quirke Printers, 1905); *Feis na Mumhan, Cilláirne, 1905* (Tralee:
"Star" and *"People"* Offices, 1905); *Syllabus of Uisneach Feis to be held in Athlone, on Saturday &
Sunday, June 8th & 9th, 1912* (Athlone: Athlone Printing Works Co., 1912); *Clár Feis Fhearmanach, 1916. I nInisceithleann, ar an 29adh Lá de Mheitheamh* (Enniskillen: Fermanagh Herald Office, 1916); *Feis Lair na n-Eireann, to be held in Mullingar, on Sunday, the 2nd of July, 1916, Clár na*

Feise (Mullingar: Westmeath Examiner Printing Works, 1916); *Clár Feise Charman i Ros-Mic-Treóin, Whit Sunday & Monday, May 19th & 20th, 1918* (Wexford: Hanrahan Printer, 1918); *Feis Mór Uisnigh, 1912, Bower Convent Grounds, and Midlands Industrial Exhibition, Father Mathew Hall, 7th, 8th and 9th June. Clár* (Athlone: Athlone Printing Works Co. 1912).

53. *Aeríocht* (pl., *aeríochtaí*) is Gaelic for an open-air function, while *scoruigheacht* (pl., *scoruigheachtaí*) is Gaelic for an indoor event.

54. See Douglas Hyde, *Selected Plays.* Noel McGonagle has written more generally about the emergence of literature in Irish as a result of League work, including plays by P. T. Mac-Ginley which became well known through feis performances. See Noel McGonagle, "Writing in Gaelic since 1880," in *Irish Studies: A General Introduction,* ed. Thomas Bartlett, Chris Curtin, Riana O'Dwyer, and Gearóid Ó Tuathaigh (Dublin: Gill and Macmillan, 1988).

55. *ACS,* 25 Mar. 1899.

56. Ibid.

57. UCD Archives, MS P11/A/3, WPRP, "Quests and Companions," 39. "Seanchas" translates as story-telling or chatting. One such gathering spot was Cathal MacGarvey's tobacco shop *An Stad.* See Ó Cearnaigh.

58. MacNeill to Mrs. [Taddie] MacNeill, 25 Aug. 1900, UCD Archives, MS LA1/G/44, EMP. Hyde, O'Hickey, Lady Gregory, W. B. Yeats, Bishop MacCormack of Galway, John Dillon M. P., and William O'Malley M. P., attended the feis.

59. Seán T. Ó Ceallaigh, *Seán T.,* 89.

60. *ACS,* 23 June 1900.

61. *ACS,* 22 May 1909.

62. Ibid.

63. Moran made a similar point at the Munster feis in 1907. He published his address as a two-part series in the *Leader.* His comments can be seen as part of a discussion opened up in early 1907 by contributors to the *Leader,* who suggested that Irish-Irelanders should create their own music halls, pantomimes, and children's literature based on English models. "I am not sure that I would go so far as that," Moran said, "but I would like to see Irish going in almost everywhere it could get a footing." See *Leader,* 23, 30 Nov. 1907.

64. *Clár Feis na Gaillimhe,* 32–33.

65. Ibid., 4. The initial use of a clothing requirement took place at the Feis Uladh in 1900. See *ACS,* 22 Sept. 1900.

66. *Thom's* (1905), 34.

67. For example, League secretary Pádraig Ó Dalaigh was a resident of Dungarvan prior to moving to Dublin; Patrick Mac Suibhne was also from the Dungarvan area and lived in Fermoy in 1906; Eoghan Ó Neachtáin, one-time editor of *ACS* and a Gaelic columnist in the *II,* was from Galway city; Kerry activist Thomas MacDonagh O'Mahony lived at Cahirciveen, and Fionán MacColuim, the head *timire* for Munster, often visited the area surrounding Cahirciveen; and the Gaelic enthusiast and member of parliament for West Kerry Thomas O'Donnell was a frequent visitor to Dingle.

68. As at the Oireachtas of 1897, some individuals entered more than one competition; indeed, at Feis Íbh-Ráthaigh the organizers encouraged people to test themselves in more than one discipline by creating a special prize—the Iveragh Cup—which recognized the strongest overall contestant in a total of three competitions. The preponderance of certain names in specific geographic regions makes determining the precise number of repeat entries an impossibility. (In these specific programs, four of which originated in counties Cork and Kerry, one finds the Christian names of Patrick, Michael, and Seán, and the surnames of Murphy, McCarthy, and O'Sullivan appearing repeatedly.) Therefore, I have based all calculations on the number of entries rather than the number of individuals involved.

69. The precise numbers are 958 entries from men and boys and 474 from women and girls.

70. The percentage of female entries in increasing order was 18 percent at Dungarvan (1901); 29 percent at Galway (1906); 30 percent at Cahirciveen (1904); 36 percent at Dingle (1906); 37 percent at Bandon (1906); and 38 percent at Fermoy (1906).

71. For example, at Feis Dhroichid na Banndan, competition 4a. was restricted to "children attending any school in the *coiste ceanntair* area, and for juniors (under 20) attending Gaelic League classes in the district," but competition 5 was limited to "juniors (under 17)." See *Feis Droichid na Banndan*, 6–7. One does, however, find some competitions specifying that they are only for "boys" or "girls," but others are open to "juniors," suggesting that the latter category may have been intended for young adults rather than school-aged children.

72. For the purposes of the age calculations, I have excluded those competitions for which there was no indication of the intended competitors and those which were open to juniors *and* adults. This gives a net aggregate of 1,477 competitors.

73. At the Feis na n-Deisi, 70 percent of those entering were in "senior" competitions, but this incredibly high percentage appears to have been the result of two factors: first, as the smallest of the feiseanna under consideration, any variation in the real number of competitors is magnified as a percentage of the whole; and second, the feis syllabus contained far fewer events aimed specifically at juniors than the later festivals. The percentage of adult competitors at other festivals was: 47 percent at Galway; 35 percent at Fermoy; and 33 percent at Bandon.

74. The Galway feis in 1906 had 19 individual events, 10 for adults and 9 for juniors. Feis Cholmain at Fermoy had 14 individual events, 8 for juniors and 6 for adults.

75. Concannon first visited Dingle in 1900, and the *Kerry Sentinel* of 3 Mar. 1900 reported that people from all walks of life attended his public presentation. The following year, however, Ó hAnnracháin noted that few signs of the excitement generated by his predecessor's presence remained. Local revivalists in Dingle continued to encourage the movement, as evidenced by their support of Irish industries, their creation of an annual feis in 1903, and their involvement in the Dingle summer college. In 1910, however, MacColuim recorded scathing comments about the lack of interest in the revival shown by persons in

Dingle and the Corkaguiney district in what appears to have been the draft of a letter he intended to publish in the local press. He laid part of the blame on the League executive for not pursuing the region more actively, but he also indicted the local population for not taking up the cause: "Corkaguiney—except for a few bilingual schools—is a 'dead limb' of the great Irish-Ireland tree, because for some cause which calls for full explanation, the 'limb' has not kept pace with the growth of the tree itself. Let those who can ensure its growth see to it. Ireland demands it." Quoted in Pádraig Mac Fhearghusa, *Conradh na Gaeilge i gCiarraí: A History of the Gaelic League in Kerry* (Tralee: Kenno, 1995), 23–24. On the foundation of the summer college, see ibid., 30. On the drop in interest shortly after Concannon's visit, see *ACS*, 19 Jan. 1901. Evidence of the Dingle branch's activity can be found in many brief reports in *ACS*. For example, see *ACS*, 10 Dec. 1904. For MacColuim's observations, see NLI, MS 24,434, FMP, Draft Letter Re: the Position of the Gaelic League in Corkaguiney, Co. Kerry, 1910.

76. Mac Fhearghusa, 25; *ACS*, 28 Feb. 1903. See also MacDonagh O'Mahony's annual report in *Clár: Feis Íbh-Ráthaigh*, 57–61.

77. *Feis Dhaingin Uí Chúise*, 15–19. Competitions 37 through 39 were directed at children under 15, under 13, and under 11 respectively.

78. In Competitions 1 through 9, contestants were asked either to write essays, to transcribe songs or poems from a native speaker, or to discuss Irish history and literature. See ibid., 3–4.

79. Ó Donnchadha, 10. Competitions 35 and 37 (instrumental) brought in 35 and 31 entries respectively, and competition 27 (vocal) brought in 28.

80. *ACS*, 23 May 1903.

81. O'Leary, *Prose Literature*, 93–96, 173–75.

82. *ACS*, 23 May 1903. There were a total of six competitors in this competition. See also Ó Suilleabháin, *Scéal*, 182.

83. Competition No. 1 asked for an essay on Gaelic literature in the nineteenth century, and two competitors sent in entries. Competition 13 called for an original composition of a piece meant for declamation and received two entries. Competition No. 8, sponsored by the Gaelic Society of New York, called for submissions to be judged and recognized on a county by county basis. Although judges awarded prizes to entrants from counties Donegal, Mayo, Galway, Kerry, Cork, and Waterford, no prize went to the lone submission from Clare. According to the judges' comments, the Clare competitor was "evidently a learner, and does not show sufficient excellence to deserve the prize." See Ó Donnchadha, 146, 153, 155.

84. Ibid., 159.

85. Ibid., 158. Similar splits between successful and unsuccessful contestants are found elsewhere in adjudicators' comments. For example, see the comments for Competition No. 22 at the Oireachtas in 1903, Collection of previously unpublished folk poems taken down from a native speaker: "All the competitors, save the two prize winners, show gross carelessness in both writing and compiling their papers, and none of their collections are of

sufficient merit to gain the third prize." *ACS*, 23 May 1903. According to Ó Suilleabháin, ten people had submitted collections to Competition No. 22. See Ó Suilleabháin, *Scéal*, 169.

86. Ó Suilleabháin, *Scéal*, 157–60.

87. Most historical essay competitions at provincial feiseanna dealt with topics of local interest. See O'Leary, *Prose Literature*, 173.

88. *Clár: Feis Íbh-Ráthaigh 1904*, 11.

89. *Féis Dhaingin Uí Chúise*, 1906, 3. Competition No. 2: "Aiste sgriobhtha ar thoradh saothair Dhomhnaill Uí Chonnail ar Thréitibh agus ar Náisuntacht [*sic*] na nGaodhal."

90. *Feis Mór Lios-Tuathail*, 10.

91. For perceptive discussions of the Ranch War, see Paul Bew, *Conflict and Conciliation in Ireland, 1890–1910: Parnellites and Radical Agrarians* (Oxford: Clarendon Press, 1987), especially chaps. 5 and 6; and Fergus Campbell, *Land and Revolution*, chap.3.

92. *Eighth Report of the Irish Agricultural Organization Society Ltd., Year Ending December 31st 1902* (Dublin: Irish Agricultural Organization Society, 1903), 56.

93. A copy of the leaflet appears in the tenth report of the society, for the year 1904.

94. These subjects appeared in Oireachtas competitions in 1898, 1899, 1902, 1903, and 1904 respectively. See Ó Suilleabháin, *Scéal*, 157–79.

95. *ACS*, 16 July 1904. On Gleeson's association with Lily and Elizabeth Yeats and the Dun Emer Guild, see Nicola Gordon Bowe, "Two Early Twentieth Century Irish Arts and Crafts Workshops in Context: An Túr Gloine and the Dun Emer Guild and Industries," *Journal of Design History* 2 (1989): 193–206.

96. *Feis agus Aonach Loch gCarmáin, 1905*, 47–60; *Feis i Aonach Loch Garmáin, 1908*, 71–92.

97. For example, see *Feis i Aonach Loch Garmáin, 1908*, 75.

98. Ibid.

99. On Lloyd, see Breathnach and Ní Mhurchú, *Beathaisnéis, a Cúig*, 69–70. For his appearance at Glasgow, see *ACS*, 9 Nov. 1901.

100. Among the plays staged at festivals cited above were Dinneen's *An Tobar Draoicheachta* and Ua Laoghaire's *Medbh* and *Tadg Saor*.

101. See *Samhain* (1901), 6; and *Samhain* (1903), 3.

102. Douglas Hyde, *Selected Plays*, 15–16.

103. For an account of the difficulties faced by enthusiasts for Gaelic drama, see O'Leary, *Prose Literature*, 296–304.

104. See *Samhain* (1903), 3; *ACS*, 7 July 1906.

105. *Feis i Aonach Loch Garmáin, 1908*, 65.

106. Ibid.

107. *Feis na Mumhan, 1910*, 15.

108. See the report from Cathaoir (probably Fr. Cathaoir Ó Braonáin) in *ACS*, 27 Feb. 1904.

109. Kenmare spent lavishly on improvements to his mansion and demense in the 1870s and 1880s, and his tenants extended him the mixed complement of being a "considerate

landlord," while holding that "the best landlord is good for nothing." See Donnelly, *Land and the People*, 382.

110. *Feis na Mumhan, 1907*, 5.

111. The Earl of Kenmare is listed first among subscribers to the 1904 Munster feis. He and two others subscribed £5 apiece to the festival, the largest sums by individuals. See *Imtheachta Feise na Mumhan, 1904*, 11.

112. *ACS*, 5 Aug. 1905. See also Dunleavy and Dunleavy, 248.

113. On Bellingham's politics, see F. S. L. Lyons, *Charles Stewart Parnell* (New York: Oxford Univ. Press, 1977), 254. In 1916, his son, Sir Edward Bellingham considered a run for parliament in North Louth, but, according to Maume, he accepted the Irish parliamentary party nominee as the rightful candidate and withdrew. See Maume, *Long Gestation*, 170.

114. *ACS*, 9 Aug. 1902, 5 Sept. 1903, 29 July 1905. See also *FJ*, 15 June 1908.

115. Subscribers' lists were not consistent in the information they included. Most lists included only the name of a donor and the amount given.

116. Two individuals gave £10 to League festivals: the parliamentarian and land agitator William O'Brien gave £10 to the first Oireachtas to fund a prize; and the Dublin-based architect J. F. Fuller gave the same amount to the Munster feis in 1904 to provide prizes for special competitions between schoolchildren from County Kerry. Eight individuals were listed as giving 6d. to the Munster feis that same year. See *GJ*, 8 (June 1897), 20; and *Imtheachta Feise na Mumhan, 1904*, 15. An anonymous donor also gave £10 to the Wexford feis in 1908. This may have been Sir Thomas Grattan Esmonde, M.P., who was listed as a patron of the feis but whose name does not otherwise appear as a contributor. See *Feis i Aonach Loch Garmáin, 1908*, 93.

117. *Imtheachta Feise na Mumhan, 1904*, 11–15. Cork branches of the League did contribute to the Kerry-based festival, and a comparison of the 1904 list to the subscriptions received in 1907—when the festival had returned to Cork city—indicates that these branch contributions were consistent regardless of the location of the festival. Cf. *Feis na Mumhan, 1907*, 83.

118. *Imtheachta Feise na Mumhan, 1904*, 11–15.

119. W. P. Ryan, *Pope's Green Island*, 186.

120. *PII*, 25 July 1908.

121. Ibid.

122. *PII*, 12 Dec. 1908; *INP*, 10 July 1909.

123. W. P. Ryan, *Pope's Green Island*, 189–90.

124. See *SVV*, 4 July, 12 Dec. 1898; 2 Jan. 1899. See also *FL*, 19, 26 Nov., 3 Dec. 1898.

125. Hyde presents an evocative account of the feis in his memoir in which he lauds Bishop (later Cardinal) O'Donnell for his courtesy and intellect. See Hyde Memoir, 10.

126. *SF*, 30 Jan. 1909. In the event, John P. Boland, M.P., entered the resolution, which was seconded by Fr. Malachy Brennan. Brennan, as seen in chapter 2, was later forced to resign from the Gaelic League executive by his bishop in response to this action. The UIL convention passed Boland's resolution by a 3-to-1 majority.

127. W. P. Ryan, *Pope's Green Island*, 190–91; Waters, "W. P. Ryan," 291–92.

128. The date of the event was 10 August 1908. The title "Killarney Fete and Fancy Fair" appears on a draft poster for the event which can be found in NLI, MS 24,413, FMP, *Conradh na Gaeilge*, Posters and Notices of Feiseanna, 1908–09.

129. For example, in 1905, Bishop Mangan told Irish-speaking families in Dingle and Ballyferriter that while he supported the League, he felt that it was imperative for the children of the Irish-speaking districts to learn English. According to *ACS*, he was especially concerned that they learn their Christian doctrine in English because they would "in due course emigrate, and that they must be taught the English catechism in order that they may understand the religious instruction which they will receive abroad." See *ACS*, 19 Aug. 1905.

130. Ryan lauded Fr. Ó Braonáin's zeal for the movement. See *PII*, 9, 16 Mar. 1907.

131. *PII*, 9 Mar. 1907.

132. Letter from Ó Braonáin to MacColuim, 21 Feb. 1903, in NLI, MS 24,393, FMP, Correspondence 1902–03.

133. Hyde Memoir, 41. O'Kelly (who wrote under the pseudonym "Sceilg") had been fired from the *FJ* in the spring of 1905. O'Kelly's supporters, including Ó Braonáin, believed that Hyde and other members of the executive had set out to injure their friend because he edited the Irish-Ireland journal *Banba*, which was often critical of the executive. Hyde was innocent of the charges flung at him and "listened aghast as the attack developed, but soon sat back in my chair and did not move a muscle or wink an eye-lid after that." For an account sympathetic to O'Kelly, see Murphy, *Patrick Pearse*, 32–33.

134. In the report of the Oireachtas committee meeting at which they discussed the circumstances of the feis, it is described as "unlicensed." See *ACS*, 12 Sept. 1908. Also in the report of the same meeting carried by Ryan in the *PII*, he notes that the feis program itself states that it was not organized for League purposes.

135. *ACS*, 22 Aug. 1908. Ua Laoghaire had only recently been made a canon. Bishop Mangan alluded to the elevation in a self-deprecating reference to his own inability to think of the Castlelyons priest as anything but "An tAthair Peadar," the affectionate nickname by which most Irish-Irelanders identified him.

136. *PII*, 22 Aug. 1908.

137. *PII*, 12 Sept. 1908. The "Fixtures" list included the dates and locations of upcoming festivals and concerts. Through 13 June 1908, *Feis na n-Airne* does not appear in the Fixtures list.

138. W. P. Ryan, *Pope's Green Island*, 190.

139. NLI, MS 24,413, FMP, Posters and Notices of Feiseanna, 1908–09.

140. See above, chap. 2.

141. Letter from John Clark to MacNeill, 30 May 1905, in NLI, MS 10,901, EMP, Ulster File.

142. Letter from Annie McGavock to MacNeill, 8 Mar. 1904, in NLI, MS 10,901, EMP, Ulster File.

143. Breathnach and Ní Mhurchú, *Beathaisnéis, a hAon*, 30–31.

144. Ibid.

145. *ACS*, 16 July 1904. For a general outline of the careers of Smiley and Dixon, see *Who Was Who, Vol. I, 1897–1915* (London: St. Martin's Press, 1988, 6th ed.), 146, 482. On the 1905 by-election, see Bardon, 159–60; and Boyle, 138–39.

146. *ACS*, 16 July 1904.

147. UCD, Archives, MS LA1/E/11, EMP, "Feis na nGleann."

148. *Irish Weekly*, quoted in *ACS*, 16 July 1904.

149. MacNeill, "Feis na nGleann."

150. *Irish Weekly*, quoted in *ACS*, 16 July 1904. 151. NAI, RIC CSB Preces, 1902/27,484/S., Precis for 16–31 July; NAI, RIC CSB 1902/27,624/S., Precis for August; and NAI, RIC CSB 1902/27,742/S., Precis for 16–30 September.

152. *ACS*, 19 Sept. 1903.

153. *Leader*, 26 Oct. 1907.

154. Ibid., 30 Mar. 1907. *"An Fear Mór"* [Séamas Ó hEochaidh, pseud.], "Tiobruid Árann, 1908–10," in Connradh na Gaedhilge Coiste Thiobraid Árann Theas, *Bláith-Fhleasg*, 48.

155. *Am Bàrd* (Aug. 1901), 53.

156. Ibid.

157. Ibid., 54.

158. *FJ*, 11 May 1908.

159. For example, the *FJ* referred to the crowd at the opening concert of the 1908 festival as only "fairly large," and it lukewarmly described the closing concert as "one of the most successful events of its kind held in connection with this fixture. See *FJ*, 11, 14 May 1908.

160. For instance, in June 1904, the Blackrock branch held a concert on 12 June; the Celbride, Co. Kildare, branch sponsored one on 19 June; and the Swords branch held a concert on 26 June. Also on the weekend of 26 June, the Columcille branch sponsored an excursion to Limerick, so that its members and guests could visit the Thomond feis. See *ACS*, 11 June 1904.

161. Seán T. Ó Ceallaigh, *Seán T.*, 86. The *FJ* reached the same conclusion, suggesting that the feis suffered by comparison to the Oireachtas. See *FJ*, 26 May 1906.

162. *FJ*, 26 May 1906.

163. W. P. Ryan, *Pope's Green Island*, 69.

164. MacNeill, "Feis na nGleann."

165. Quoted in *ACS*, 8 June 1912.

6. THE MARCH OF A NATION: DUBLIN'S LANGUAGE PROCESSIONS

1. William Dawson, "My Dublin Year," *Studies* 1 (Dec. 1912): 706.

2. The Coiste Gnótha instituted Irish Language Week in 1902 as a way to bolster slow returns to the Language Fund. See *Leader* 8, 22 Feb., 15, 22 Mar. 1902; *ACS* 8, 15, 22 Mar.

1902; *II*, 13 Mar. 1906. See also NLI, MS 19,318, Coiste Ceanntair Atha Cliath, Circulars from 1905–06, 29–30. For a representative report of a meeting of the Coiste an Bhailighthe (collection committee), see *INP*, 28 Aug. 1909.

3. Three studies of processions and accompanying demonstrations have particularly shaped the following interpretation. See Mary Ryan, "The American Parade: Representations of the Nineteenth-Century Social Order," in *The New Cultural History*, ed. Lynn Hunt (Berkeley: Univ. of California Press, 1989); and Owens, "Constructing the Repeal Spectacle"; Owens, "Nationalism without Words."

4. *Leader*, 22 Feb. 1902.

5. NLI, MS 9790, Minutes of the Coiste an Timthireachta, Coiste Ceanntair Atha Cliath, 25 Nov. 1905.

6. Ibid., 19 Jan. 1906.

7. NLI, MS 19,318, Circulars from 1905–06, Letter dated 13 February 1906 and signed by Padraig Mac Giolla Iosa, secretary of the planning committee.

8. Owens, "Constructing the Repeal Spectacle," 83.

9. *ACS*, 21 Mar. 1903; *Leader*, 21 Mar. 1903.

10. *IT* quoted in *Leader*, 19 Mar. 1904, and in *ACS*, 17 Mar. 1906.

11. *ACS*, 25 Sept. 1909; *II*, 19 Sept. 1910, 18 Sept. 1911.

12. *ACS*, 18 Mar. 1905. See also the report in the *II* from "Jacques" about the crowd watching the procession, dated 20 Sept. 1909.

13. NAI, DMP CSB 1902/26591/S., Precis for Mar. 1902; NAI, DMP CSB 1903/28320/S. Precis for Mar. 1903; NAI, DMP CSB 1904/29494/S., Precis for Mar. 1904; NLI, DMP CSB 1911/3235/S., Precis for September 1911.

14. This is based on 10,000 marchers taking approximately fifty minutes to pass a point. If the earlier processions took somewhere between ninety minutes and two hours (i.e., approximately twice as long) to pass that point, a figure of 20,000 would seem a reasonable minimum estimate. Further, since the DMP suggest that the early processions grew in comparison to the 18,000 marchers of 1902, I have extended my estimate to an upper level of 25,000.

15. Metropolitan Dublin had a population of about 404,000 in 1911. See Mary E. Daly, "Social Structure of the Dublin Working Class, 1871–1911," *Irish Historical Studies* 23 (Nov. 1982): 121.

16. The first public reference to Ingoldsby appeared in 1905: "All Ireland will join in *An Craoibhín's* tribute to the organizers of the demonstration . . . above all to Padraic Mac Giolla Iosa, the 'organiser of victory.'" See *ACS*, 18 Mar. 1905.

17. Ibid. See also A. J. Nowlan, "Phoenix Park Public Meetings," *Dublin Historical Record* 14 (May 1958): 111.

18. *ACS*, 12 Sept. 1908. On Ó hAnnrachain, see Boylan, 295.

19. NLI, MS 11,536, Leabhar Seachtmhain na Gaedhilge, 1903: Minutes of the 1909 Demonstration Committee, 10 Sept. 1909. The presence of minutes related to the 1909

demonstration in an address book related to the distribution of Language Week collection materials testifies to the lingering lack of professionalism within League committees.

20. *ACS,* 14 Mar. 1903.

21. Ibid.

22. O'Casey, *Drums,* 129.

23. *II,* 10 June 1907.

24. *II,* 20 Sept. 1909.

25. See the advance reports from *ACS,* 10 Mar. 1906, 19 Sept. 1908, 18 Sept. 1909.

26. *ACS,* 10 Mar. 1906.

27. "Go Máiridh ár nGaedhilge Slán," Rallying Song of the Gaelic League (Dublin: Gaelic League, 1905).

28. NLI MS 9790, Coiste an Timthireachta, 4 May 1907.

29. *II,* 10 June 1907.

30. For example, see NLI, MS 19,318, Circulars from 1905–06, Letter dated 13 Feb. 1906.

31. In 1906, the subcommittee deputed Ingoldsby and Ó Ceallaigh to call upon the Dublin Trades Council and the Dublin County Committee of the GAA. See NLI, MS 9790, Coiste an Timthireachta, 11 Feb. 1906.

32. The Wolfe Tone Memorial Committee emerged from efforts to commemorate the centennial of the 1798 Rising led by Theobald Wolfe Tone. Originally conceived as a front by members of the IRB, the commemoration committee eventually included numerous constitutional nationalists. As part of the commemoration, the foundation stone for the Wolfe Tone Memorial was laid in August 1898 amid much fanfare, but there was not enough money to pay for the rest of the monument. Republicans established the Memorial Committee to complete the project and to siphon off money for arms; however, most members of the Memorial Committee were not IRB members. See Timothy J. O'Keefe, "'Who Fears to Speak of '98?' The Rhetoric and Rituals of the United Irishmen Centennial, 1898," *Eire-Ireland* 27 (Fall 1992): 67–91; and Ó Broin, *Revolutionary Underground,* chaps. 5 and 6.

33. *ACS,* 12 Sept. 1908.

34. Ibid.

35. Ibid.

36. Ibid.

37. Ibid.

38. Ibid.

39. Ibid. A similar meeting took place on 6 September 1909. For a report, see *ACS,* 11 Sept. 1909.

40. The subcommittee received a letter from the honorary secretary of the INF complaining about their placement and stating that similar complaints had been ignored by procession organizers in 1904. Subcommittee members stated that this correspondence offered them the first insights into the INF's threatened withdrawal. See NLI, MS 9790, Coiste an Timthireachta, 15 Mar. 1906.

41. Ibid., 7, 9, 15 Mar. 1906, 9 Feb., 9 Mar. 1907.

42. Ibid., 15 Mar. 1906.

43. O'Brien, *Dear, Dirty Dublin*, 65–66.

44. *INP*, 24 Sept. 1910.

45. *Leader*, 24 Sept. 1910.

46. Ibid.

47. *ACS*, 24 Sept. 1910.

48. *II*, 18 Mar. 1913.

49. *Leader*, 19 Mar. 1904.

50. NLI, MS 9790, Coiste an Timthireachta, 25 Feb. 1906.

51. *PII*, 26 Sept. 1908.

52. Ibid.

53. *II*, 20 Sept. 1909.

54. Ibid.

55. Anton J. J. Großmann, *Irische Nationalbewegungen, 1884–1915* (Munich: Minerva Publikation, 1978), 44.

56. *ACS*, 10 Mar. 1906.

57. Ibid.

58. Sir Jonah Barrington, *Personnal Sketches of His Own Times,* 3rd ed. (London: George Routledge and Sons, 1869), 140–44.

59. Alter, "Symbols of Irish Nationalism," 18–19.

60. *II*, 14 Mar. 1904, 21 Sept. 1908; *ACS*, 19 Mar. 1904, 19 Sept. 1908. See also Timothy G. McMahon, "'To Mould an Important Body of Shepherds,'" 122–24.

61. *II*, 10 June 1907. The *Independent* included a pencil drawing of the tableau. On Keating, see Bernadette Cunningham, *The World of Geoffrey Keating: History, Myth and Religion in Seventeenth-Century Ireland* (Dublin: Four Courts Press, 2000); and Boylan, 55. On the place of the *Foras Feasa ar Éirinn*, see R. F. Foster, *Modern Ireland*, 38–43.

62. Brian Boru appeared in the processions of 1907 and in 1911, while Malachy II appeared in 1908. See *ACS*, 19 Sept. 1908; 18 Sept. 1911; and *II*, 10 June 1907; 18 Sept. 1911.

63. On the MacHale branch, see chap. 1, fn. 51.

64. *II*, 18 Sept. 1911.

65. Into the twenty-first century, the Sinn Féin party motto remains Tiocaigh ár Lá/ Our day will come.

66. The connection between the parliamentary party and the *FJ* was so pronounced that Moran dubbed all political bombast "sunburstry." See Timothy G. McMahon, "Cultural Nativism," 75–76.

67. The Parliament Act passed in August 1911. The procession took place on 20 Sept. 1911. The act, which reduced the House of Lords' veto to a suspensary veto, virtually assured passage of Home Rule by the Liberal government under H. H. Asquith.

68. In 1910, four branches set up tableaux depicting the Gaelic summer colleges in the four provinces of Ireland. See *ACS*, 24 Sept. 1910.

69. *II*, 12 Mar. 1906. Compare this emigrant scene to ones described by Canon Guinan in his novels. For example, in *The Moores of Glynn*, one of the Moore children, Frank, emigrates after dropping out of the seminary. While in America, he contracts tuberculosis. He returns home to die in a chapter entitled "The Prodigal's Return." See Guinan, *Moores of Glynn*, 256–69.

70. *Programme or Clár Móir-Shiubhail na nGaedheal/Irish Language Procession, Sunday 18th September 1910* (Dublin: Demonstration Committee, 1910), 24. See also, *II*, 19 Sept. 1910.

71. *Programme or Clár Móir-Shiubhail na nGaedheal*, 24.

72. In 1911, for example, the tableau of the Drumcondra branch focused on "Anglicizing via the System of Education." According to the *II*, the theme stressed the "effect in alienating young minds from their natural tendencies" inherent in Irish schools. See *II*, 19 Sept. 1911. References to the various battles over educational policy run throughout the Irish-Ireland press of the period. A good summary of the arguments and the part played by the League in getting Irish recognized as a school subject appears in Donncha Ó Súilleabháin, *Cath na Gaeilge sa Choras Oideachais, 1893–1911* (Dublin: Conradh na Gaeilge, 1988).

73. *II*, 12 Mar. 1906.

74. *II*, 12 Mar. 1906 includes a sketch of the tableau. The phrase "usual insignia" appears in the description of his cloak.

75. *II*, 10 June 1907.

76. The unsigned memorandum on which this policy was based was promulgated in March 1901. See Gareth W. Dunleavy, "Hyde's Crusade for the Language and the Case of the Embarrassing Packets," *Studies* 73 (Spring 1984): 12–25.

77. Timothy G. McMahon, "Gaelic League," 120–25.

78. Dunleavy, "Hyde's Crusade," 17.

79. *II*, 2 Mar. 1905. See also *FJ*, 2, 4, 6 Mar. 1905. The *FJ* for 6 March includes a letter from Ó Dalaigh expressing his frustration at mixed signals he had received from postal officials and from the published guide for use of the postal service that had been issued in January 1905.

80. Dunleavy, "Hyde's Crusade," 16; *II*, 7 Mar. 1905. The story in the *II* also drew a contrast between the reluctance of the post office to handle correspondence addressed in Irish and its readiness to handle Gaelic correspondence in Scotland.

81. *II*, 13 Mar. 1905.

82. *FJ*, 13 Mar. 1905.

83. Dunleavy, "Hyde's Crusade," 24. In Northern Ireland, the postal policy remained unchanged until 1959.

84. *II*, 20 Sept. 1909; *FJ*, 20 Sept. 1909.

85. The phrase comes from Eugene O'Curry, the nineteenth-century scholar whose lectures on medieval life and literature were essential reading for the men and women of the language revival. Quoted in Seumas MacManus, *The Story of the Irish Race* (Old Greenwich,

Conn.: Devin-Adair, 1966), 168, fn. 9. MacManus also discusses the assembly at Druim-ceat, which he spells Drimceatt. He bases his account largely on that given by Bishop John Healy in his popular book on *Ireland's Ancient Schools and Scholars*. See John Healy, *Ireland's Ancient Schools and Scholars* (Dublin: Sealy, Bryers and Walker, 1902), 320–24; also cf. Mac-Manus, 165–68.

86. *FJ*, 20 Sept. 1909.

87. *II*, 20 Sept. 1909.

88. Ibid.

89. See above, chapter 2.

90. *II*, 20 Sept. 1909.

91. For example, see *ACS*, 14 Mar. 1903.

92. NLI, MS 9790, Coiste an Timthireachta, 9 Mar. 1906.

93. On the expansion of the AOH into southern Ireland, see Hepburn, *A Past Apart*, 157–72, which reprints his article "The Ancient Order of Hibernians in Irish Politics, 1905–14," from *Cithara* 10 (May 1971): 5–18.

94. NLI, MS 9790, Coiste an Timthireachta, 20 Feb. 1906; 7 Mar. 1906. Also, see the report of the public procession planning meeting in *II*, 3 Mar. 1905.

95. All calculations are based on published reports of the contingents in the language section, which were provided by Ingoldsby's corps of press stewards. See *II*, 12 Mar. 1906.

96. NLI, MS 9790, Coiste an Timthireachta, 16 Feb. 1906. For reports on 1905, see *II*, 24 Feb.; 10, 13 Mar. 1905.

97. *II*, 3 Mar. 1905.

98. *Leader*, 17 Mar. 1906; *ACS*, 17 Mar. 1906.

99. *IP*, 17 Mar. 1906.

100. O'Brien, *Dear, Dirty Dublin*, 66–67.

101. *Leader*, 17 Mar. 1906.

102. See NLI, MS 19,318, Circulars from 1905–06, Letter dated 9 Apr. 1906. The letter invites delegates to discuss the proposed change of date at a meeting on 27 April. For the reasoning behind the further change to September, see *Leader*, 19 Sept. 1908.

103. *INP*, 19 June 1909.

104. *INP*, 27 Aug. 1910.

105. *Evening Mail*, 17 Mar. 1902, quoted in Tymoczko, 239. "God Save Ireland" was the title of a song inspired by the last words uttered by three revolutionary nationalists in 1867. The song was one of the unofficial anthems of the Irish parliamentary party between 1880 and 1916. See Alter, "Symbols of Irish Nationalism," 6–8.

106. *Leader*, 22 Mar. 1902. See also Tymoczko, 240.

107. *Leader*, 19 Mar. 1904.

108. Quoted in *ACS*, 17 Mar. 1906.

109. *ACS*, 24 Sept. 1910.

110. Dawson, 706.

111. Ibid.

112. *INP*, 27 Aug. 1910. See also *PII*, 26 Sept. 1908; *INP*, 25 Sept. 1909, 17, 24 Sept. 1910.

113. *ACS*, 23 Sept. 1911.

114. *II*, 18 Mar. 1913. The records for the organization subcommittee are extremely thin for this period. Based on press references to the procession, however, it is unlikely that the decision to hold the procession was taken before the very late autumn of 1912.

CONCLUSION

1. Hyde Memoir, 19.

2. Ibid., 18.

3. Ó Fearáil, 44; Timothy G. McMahon, *Pádraig Ó Fathaigh's War*, 9.

4. Timothy Corcoran, "The Native Speaker as Teacher," *Irish Monthly* 51 (Apr. 1923): 187–90.

5. For instance, see MacDonagh, *States of Mind*, 116–25; Terence Brown, 37–53, 113. For a more tempered account of their stridency, see Gearóid Ó Tuathaigh, "Cultural Visions in the New State: Embedding and Embalming," in *De Valera's Irelands*, ed. Gabriel Doherty and Dermot Keogh (Cork: Cork Univ. Press, 2003).

6. Donald H. Akenson, *A Mirror to Kathleen's Face: Education in Independent Ireland, 1922–1960* (Montreal: McGill-Queen's Univ. Press, 1975), 52; Timothy G. McMahon, "'To Mould an Important Body of Shepherds,'" 136, 139.

7. For instance, see Michael Wheatley, *Nationalism and the Irish Party: Provincial Ireland, 1910–1916* (Oxford: Oxford Univ. Press, 2005), 63.

8. David Hogan [Frank Gallagher, pseud.], *The Four Glorious Years* (Dublin: Irish Press, 1953).

9. On provincial political transformations, see Wheatley, 250–66; Fergus Campbell, *Land and Revolution*, 166–285; Charles Townshend, *The British Campaign in Ireland, 1919–1921: The Development of Political and Military Policies* (Oxford: Oxford Univ. Press, 1975), 1; Charles Townshend, *Easter 1916: The Irish Rebellion* (London: Allen Lane, 2006), 300–43; Timothy G. McMahon, *Pdraig Ó Fathaigh's War*, 8–12.

10. For the best academic account of the civil war in Ireland, see Michael Hopkinson, *Green against Green: The Irish Civil War* (Dublin: Gill and Macmillan, 1988). For a fascinating account of the multiple understandings of democracy and their impact on the civil war and the foundation of the Irish Free State, see Tom Garvin, *1922: The Birth of Irish Democracy* (Dublin: Gill and Macmillan, 2005).

11. For an important work that addresses economic programs and national identity in the Free State era, see Mary E. Daly, *Industrial Development and Irish National Identity, 1922–1939* (Dublin: Gill and Macmillan, 1992).

12. Timothy G. McMahon, "Religion and Popular Culture," 856–57.

Glossary

aeríocht (pl., *aeríochtaí*): an open-air concert

Ard Chraobh: Central branch (Dublin)

Ard-Fheis: national congress

coiste ceanntair (pl., *coistí ceanntair*): a district council

Coiste Gnótha: the national executive committee

Conradh na Gaeilge: Gaelic League

craobh (pl., *craobhacha*): a branch

feis (pl., feiseanna): a festival

muinteoir táistil (pl., *muinteoirí táistil*): a traveling teacher

Oireachtas (pl., Oireachtais): the national festival

scoruigheacht (pl., *scoruigheachtaí*): an indoor concert

timire (pl., *timirí*): a traveling organizer

Bibliography

I. PRIMARY SOURCES

A. Archives Visited and Papers Consulted

1. National Library of Ireland, Manuscript Collections

Eoin MacNeill Papers
Fionán MacColuim Papers
Gaelic League Papers (Various)
John Glynn Papers
Joseph McGarrity Papers
Pádraig Ó Fathaigh Papers
Stiofán Báiread Papers

2. National Archives of Ireland

Census of Ireland, Returns, 1901 and 1911
Chief Secretary's Office, Registered Papers
Dublin Metropolitan Police, Monthly Preces
Royal Irish Constabulary, Crime Special Branch Reports
Royal Irish Constabulary, Inspector General's Monthly Confidential Reports
Royal Irish Constabulary, Monthly Preces
St. Grellan's Branch of the Gaelic League, Ballinasloe, Co. Galway, Minutes

3. Trinity College, Dublin, Archives

J. O. Hannay Papers
Nelly O'Brien Papers

4. University College Dublin, Archives Department

Documents Related to the Firing of Fr. Michael P. O'Hickey
Eoin MacNeill Papers
Richard Mulcahy Papers
Very Rev. Peadar Canon Ua Laoghaire Papers
W. P. Ryan Papers

5. University College Dublin, Department of Irish Folklore

Memoir of Douglas Hyde

6. Mount Melleray Abbey Archive

Correspondence of Abbot Maurus Ó Faoláin

7. Cork City and County Archives

C. T. O'Leary Papers
Liam de Roiste Papers
Liam Ó Buachalla Papers

B. Newspapers and Periodicals

An Claidheamh Soluis
An Macaomh
An Muimneach Óg
Arrow
Belfast Naturalists' Field Club Report on the Celtic Language and Literature
Beltaine
Catholic Bulletin
Dana
Freeman's Journal
Irish Book Lover
Irish Ecclesiastical Record
Irish Homestead
Irish Independent
Irish Monthly
Irish Nation and the Peasant

Irish Peasant

Irish Review

Irish Times

Irisleabhar na Gaedhilge/The Gaelic Journal

Journal of the Ivernian Society

Leader

New Ireland Review

Nineteenth Century and After

Northern Patriot

Peasant and Irish Ireland

Samhain

Shan Van Vocht

Sinn Féin

Studies

United Irishman

C. *Other Contemporary Publications*

1. *Gaelic League Numbered Pamphlets*

O'Hickey, Michael P. *The True National Idea. Gaelic League Pamphlet—no. 1.* Dublin:
Gaelic League, 1900, 2nd ed.

*The Case for Bilingual Education in the Irish-Speaking Districts. Gaelic League, Pamphlet
No. 2.* Dublin: Gaelic League, 1900.

Martyn, Edward. *Ireland's Battle for Her Language. Gaelic League Pamphlet—no. 4.*
Dublin: Gaelic League, 1900.

Parliament and the Teaching of Irish. Gaelic League Pamphlet—no. 5. Dublin: Gaelic
League, 1901.

Butler, Mary E. L. *Irishwomen and the Home Language. Gaelic League Pamphlet—no. 6.*
Dublin: Gaelic League, 1901.

Hyde, Douglas. *A University Scandal. Gaelic League Pamphlet—no. 7.* Dublin: Gaelic
League, 1901.

Walsh, William J. *Bilingual Education. Gaelic League Pamphlet—no. 8.* Dublin: Gaelic
League, 1901.

The Irish Language and Irish Intermediate Education. Gaelic League Pamphlet—no. 11.
Dublin: Gaelic League, 1901.

*The Irish Language and Irish Intermediate Education: Dr. Hyde's Evidence. Gaelic League
Pamphlet—no. 13: 3.* Dublin: Gaelic League, [1901?].

O'Farrelly, Agnes. *The Reign of Humbug. Gaelic League Pamphlet—no. 19.* Dublin: Gaelic League, 1901.

Kavanagh, P. F. *Ireland's Defence: Her Language. Pamphlet No. 23.* Dublin: Gaelic League, 1902.

O'Reilly, John M. *The Threatening Metempsychosis of the Nation. Gaelic League Pamphlet—no. 24.* Dublin: Gaelic League, 1901.

O Riain, W. P. [W. P. Ryan, pseud.] *Lessons from Modern Language Movements: What Native Speech Has Achieved for Nationality. Gaelic League Pamphlet—no. 25.* Dublin: Gaelic League, [1901?].

O'Hickey, Michael P. *The Nationalisation of Irish Education, Pamphlet No. 27.* Dublin: Gaelic League, 1902.

———. *The Irish Language Movement: Its Genesis, Growth, and Progress, Pamphlet No. 28.* Dublin: Gaelic League, 1902.

Farquharson, Louisa E. *Ireland's Ideal, Pamphlet No. 31.* Dublin: Gaelic League, 1905.

Lane-Poole, Stanley. *The Irish Battle of the Books, Originally Contributed to the Fortnightly Review, Pamphlet No. 32.* Dublin: Cahill and Co., 1907.

Moonan, George A. *The Spirit of the Gaelic League, Pamphlet No. 33.* Dublin: Gaelic League, 1905.

2. Gaelic League Numbered Leaflets

Connradh na Gaedhilge. *Dhá Adhbhar Déag/Twelve Reasons, Leaflets No. 1.* Dublin: Gaelic League, 1901.

Butler, Mary E. L. *Two Schools: A Contrast, Leaflets, No. 2.* Dublin: Gaelic League, 1901.

3. Other Pamphlets

An Ard-Chraobh de Chonnradh na Gaedhilge, *Cunntas Bliadhantamhail, 1902–1903.* Dublin: An Cló-Chumann, 1903.

Borthwick, Norma. *Gaelic League, Annual Report for 1898.* Dublin: Gaelic League, 1898.

Catalogue of Irish Books Published by Connradh na Gaedhilge. Dublin: An Clódhanna, 1908.

Connradh na Gaedhilge. *Objects of the Gaelic League.* Dublin: Gaelic League, [1901?].

———. *Prospectus of the Fifth Oireachtas or Literary Festival.* Dublin: Gaelic League, 1901.

————. *Rules of Craobh na n-Áirne.* Tralee: The Kerryman Printing Co., [1909?].

Corkery, Daniel. *What's This about the Gaelic League?* Dublin: Gaelic League, 1943.

Douglas Hyde and the Revival of the Irish Language. New York: Press of Una, 1905.

Gaelic League. *Report of the Gaelic League, 1894.* Dublin: Gaelic League, 1894, and subsequent annual reports, 1895–1915. Titles vary.

Hannay, J. O. *Is the Gaelic League Political? A Lecture Delivered under the Auspices of the Branch of the Five Provinces on January 23rd, 1906.* Dublin: Gaelic League, 1906.

Hyde, Douglas. *The Gaelic League and Politics.* Dublin: Cahill, 1915.

The Irish Language Movement and the Gaelic League. Dublin: Gaelic League, 1912.

Meehan, J. W. *The Gaelic League and Organisation. Inaugural Address to the First Meeting of the Coiste Conndae Mhuigheo.* Westport: *Mayo News* Office, 1912.

Nutt, Alfred. *The Critical Study of Gaelic Literature: Indispensable for the History of the Gaelic Race.* 1904. Reprint, New York: Lenox Hill, 1971.

[O'Conor-Eccles, Charlotte]. *'For as We Are, Shall Banba Be': Simple Advice to be Followed by All Who Desire the Good of Ireland, and Especially by Gaelic Leaguers.* Dublin: An Cló-Chumann, 1905, 2nd ed.

O'Hickey, Michael P. *Irish Education and the Irish Language.* Dublin: n.p., 1899.

O'Leary, Peadar. *Irish or Infidelity, Which?* Dublin: Leader, 1909.

Organisation Committee of the Gaelic League. *Instructions for Organisers.* Dublin: Gaelic League, 1903.

Programme for a Public Meeting to be Held in the Pembroke Industrial School, Ringsend, for the Purpose of Establishing a Branch of the Gaelic League, on Sunday, 16th October. Dublin: Gaelic League, 1904.

Programme or Clár Móir-Shiubhail na nGaedheal/Irish Language Procession, Sunday 18th September 1910. Dublin: Demonstration Committee, 1910.

Prospectuses. Dublin: Gaelic League, 1901.

A Statement of the Position of Modern Irish in the National University. Dublin: Irish Book Company, 1911.

4. *Feis and Processions Programs*

Clár Feise Charman i Ros-Mic-Treóin, Whit Sunday & Monday, May 19th & 20th, 1918. Wexford: Hanrahan Printer, 1918.

Clár Feis Fhearmanach, 1916. I nInisceithleann, ar an 29adh Lá de Mheitheamh. Enniskillen: Fermanagh Herald Office, 1916.

Clár Feis Íbh-Ráthaigh, 1904, Dánta agus Seanchaidheacht. Dublin: An Cló-Chumann Teoranta, 1904.

Clár Feis na Gaillimhe/Galway Feis, County Hall, Galway, August 16 & 17. Dublin: An Cló-Chumann Teoranta, 1906.

Clár Feis Tuadh-Mhumhan, 1908. Limerick: O'Connor and Co., 1908.

Clár Feis Tuadh-Mhumhan, 1910. Limerick: O'Connor and Co., 1910.

Clár Oirachtais, 1912. Dublin: Gaelic League, 1912.

Feis agus Aonach Loch g-Carmain/County Wexford Feis and Aonach Ros Mhic Treóin, on Whit Sunday and Whit Monday and the following day, June 11th, 12th, and 13th, 1905. Enniscorthy, n.p., 1905.

Feis Cholmáin, 1906, Clár na hOibre. Dublin: An Cló-Chumann Teoranta, 1906.

Feis Dhaingin Uí Chúise, 1905, Tionólfar sa Daingean i Sgoileannaibh na mBrathair Dia Sathairn an 22adh Lá a's Dia Domhnaigh and 23adh Lá d'Iúl, 1905. Tralee: Kerry Sentinel, 1905.

Feis Dhaingin Uí Chúise, 1906. Tralee: Kerryman Printing Co., 1906.

Feis Dhroichid na Banndan. Bandon Convent Grounds, Sunday, July 22nd, 1906. Cork: Eagle Printing Works, 1906.

Feis Laighean i Midhe, Rotunda, Baile Átha Cliath, Dia Sathairn, 15adh Márta, 1902. Leabhar na Feise (Book of the Feis). Dublin: n.p., 1902.

Feis Lair na n-Eireann, to be held in Mullingar, on Sunday, the 2nd of July, 1916, Clár na Feise. Mullingar: Westmeath Examiner Printing Works, 1916.

Feis Laoighise i Osraidhe, do Tionólfar Fé Chúram Choiste Ceanntair Laoighise agus Osraidhe, i bPort Laoighise, ar 15adh Lá de'n bhFóghmhar, 1907, An Clár. Dublin: An Cló-Chumann Teoranta, 1907.

Feis Mór Lios-Tuathail, 10adh Iul 1910. Clar na Féise. Tralee: Kerryman, 1910.

Feis Mór Uisnigh, 1912, Bower Convent Grounds, and Midlands Industrial Exhibition, Father Mathew Hall, 7th, 8th and 9th June. Clár. Athlone: Athlone Printing Works Co., 1912.

Feis na Mumhan, 1903. Cork: Cork Sun Co., 1903.

Feis na Mumhan, 1907, City Hall Cork, September 16th to 21st. An Clár: Programme. Cork: Guy and Co., 1907.

Feis na Mumhan, 1910, to be held in Cork, September 9th, 10th, and 11th. An Clár/Programme. Cork: Guy and Co., 1910.

Feis na Mumhan, Cillairne, 1904. Cork, n.p., 1904.

Feis na Mumhan, Cilláirne, 1905. Tralee: "Star" and "People" Offices, 1905.

Feis na Mumhan, Clár na Chuirme Ceóil, Dia Luain, 16adh Meádhon Fóghmhair. Cork: Guy and Co., [1907?].

Feis Tuadh-Mumhan, 1907, Syllabus, List of Competitions, Prizes, Conditions. Limerick: O'Connor and Co., 1907.

Feis Tuadh-Mumhan, 1910, Syllabus, List of Competitions, Prizes, Conditions. Limerick: O'Connor and Co., 1910.

Feis Uíbh Ráthaigh, 1910, Clár na Feise. Tralee: "Star" and "People," 1910.

Imtheachta Feise na Mumhan, 1904. List of Subscribers and Prize-Winners Together with Remarks of Judges, Detailed Balance Sheet, and Auditor's Report. Tralee: Ryle and Quirke Printers, 1905.

Mor Shiubhail na n-Gaedheal, Clar. Irish Language Procession, Sunday, September 20th, 1908. Dublin: Tower Press, 1908.

Programme of Feis na n-Deisi, to be held in the Town Hall, Dungarvan, on Sunday, August 11th, 1901. Dungarvan: Brenan and Company, 1901.

Seventh Annual Feis i Aonach Loch Gcarmáin, 1908, Whit Sunday & Whit Monday, June 7th and 8th in New Ross. Enniscorthy: Echo Printing and Publishing Co., 1908.

Syllabus of Uisneach Feis to be held in Athlone, on Saturday & Sunday, June 8th & 9th, 1912. Athlone: Athlone Printing Works Co., 1912.

5. Local Directories

Belfast and Province of Ulster Directory for 1895. Belfast: Belfast News-Letter, 1895.

The Derry Almanac and Directory, for 1894. Derry: Londonderry Sentinel, 1894.

The Derry Almanac, North-West Directory, and General Advertiser, for 1901. Derry: Londonderry Sentinel, 1901.

Guy's County and City of Cork Directory for 1894. Cork: Francis Guy, 1894.

The South Derry and District Almanac and Diary for 1902. Cookstown, Co. Tyrone: Mid-Ulster Printing Works, 1902.

Thom's Official Directory of the United Kingdom of Great Britain and Ireland, for the Year 1894. Dublin: Alexander Thom, 1894, and subsequent annual directories, 1895–1905.

6. Books and Articles

Anderson, R. A. *With Plunkett in Ireland: The Co-op Organiser's Story.* Dublin: Irish Academic Press, 1983.

Autobiography of the Ruari O'More Branch of the Gaelic League, Portarlington. Dublin: Gaelic League, 1906.

Barrett, S. J., ed. *Imtheachta an Oireachtas, 1899. The Proceedings of the Third Oireachtas held in Dublin on Wednesday, 7th June, 1899, including the Cardinal's Speech,*

Oireachtas Ode, Oireachtas Address, Prize Essays, Stories and Poems. Dublin: Gaelic League, 1900.

Barrington, Sir Jonah. *Personal Sketches of His Own Times,* 3rd ed. London: George Routledge and Sons, 1869.

Bheldon, Riobard. *Amhráin agus Dánta,* ed. Pádraig Ó Macháin. Dublin: Poddle Press, 1995.

Birmingham, George A. (J. O. Hannay, pseud.). *Benedict Kavanagh.* London: Hodder and Stoughton, 1913.

———. *Irishmen All.* New York: Frederick A. Stokes, 1913.

———. *An Irishman Looks at His World.* London: Hodder and Stoughton, 1919.

Boland, Bridget. *At My Mother's Knee.* London: Bodley Head, 1978.

Boland, John P. *Irishman's Day: A Day in the Life of an Irish M. P.* London: Macdonald, 1944.

Brooks, Sidney. *The New Ireland.* Dublin: Maunsel and Co., 1907.

Buonaiuti, Ernesto. *Impressions of Ireland,* trans. Bernard Maguire. Dublin: M. H. Gill and Son, 1913.

Butler, Mary E. L. *The Ring of Day.* London: Hutchinson, 1906.

Clery, Arthur E. "The Gaelic League, 1893–1919." *Studies* 8 (1919): 398–408.

Colum, Mary. *Life and the Dream.* Chester Springs, Penn.: Dufour Editions, 1966.

Congested Districts Board for Ireland. *First Annual Report of the Congested Districts Board for Ireland.* Dublin: Alexander Thom, 1893, and subsequent annual reports, 1894–1910.

Corcoran, Timothy. "The Native Speaker as Teacher." *Irish Monthly* 51 (Apr. 1923): 187–90.

Crosbie, Thomas. "A Plea for the Study of Gaelic." *New Ireland Review* 6 (Oct. 1896): 109–12.

Davis, Thomas. *Prose Writings: Essays on Ireland,* ed. T.W. Rolleston. London: W. Scott, 1889.

Dawson, William. "My Dublin Year." *Studies* 1 (Dec. 1912): 694–708.

de Blaghd, Earnán. *Trasna na Bóinne: Imleabhar I de Chuimhní Cinn.* Dublin: Sáirséil and Dill, 1957.

Department of Agriculture and Technical Instruction. *Ireland, Industrial and Agricultural.* Dublin: Browne and Nolan, 1902.

Desart, Lady Ellen. "The Gaelic League," *Nineteenth Century and After* 345 (Nov. 1905): 755–62.

Devine, Elizabeth. "The Connacht Irish College." *Catholic Bulletin* 2 (Jan. 1912): 9–14.

Dinneen, P. S. *Lectures on the Irish Language Movement.* Dublin: M. H. Gill, 1904.

———. "The Gaelic League and Non-Sectarianism." *Irish Rosary* (Jan. 1907): 5–13.

Duffy, Sir Charles Gavan. *The Revival of Irish Literature.* London: T. Fisher Unwin, 1894.

———. *Short Life of Thomas Davis.* London: T. Fisher Unwin, 1895.

Fenton, Séamus. *It All Happened; Reminiscences.* Dublin: M. H. Gill, 1949.

Gregory, Lady Augusta, ed. *Ideals in Ireland.* London: At the Unicorn, 1901.

———. *Lady Gregory's Diaries, 1892–1902,* ed. James Pethica. Gerrards Cross, Buckinghamshire: Colin Smythe, 1996.

Guinan, Joseph. *The Moores of Glynn.* New York: Benzinger Brothers, 1907.

———. *The Curate of Kilcloon.* Dublin: M. H. Gill and Son, 1912.

———. *The Soggarth Aroon.* Dublin: Talbot Press, 1925.

Hannay, J. O. "The Gaelic League." *Independent Review* 8 (Nov. 1905): 302–14.

Healy, John. *Ireland's Ancient Schools and Scholars.* Dublin: Sealy, Bryers and Walker, 1902.

Henry, Robert Mitchell. *The Evolution of Sinn Féin.* 1920. Reprint, Freeport, N.Y.: Books for Libraries Press, 1971.

Hobson, Bulmer. *Ireland: Yesterday and Tomorrow.* Tralee: Anvil Books, 1968.

Hogan, David [Frank Gallagher, pseud.]. *The Four Glorious Years.* Dublin: Irish Press, 1953.

Horgan, John J. *Parnell to Pearse: Some Reflections and Recollections.* Dublin: Browne and Nolan, 1948.

Hyde, Douglas. "A Plea for the Irish Language." *Dublin University Review* 2 (Aug. 1886): 666–76.

———. "The Necessity for De-Anglicising Ireland." In *The Revival of Irish Literature,* ed. Sir Charles Gavan Duffy. London: T. Fisher Unwin, 1894.

———. "Abstract of a Lecture on Celtic Language and Literature." *Belfast Naturalists' Field Club Report and Proceedings,* 2nd ser., 4 (1895): 204–05.

———. *Duilleóigín 2A, Bancanna Tíre/IAOS Pamphlet 2A, Rural Banks.* Dublin: Irish Agricultural Organisation Society, 1900.

———, ed. *Imtheachta an Oireachtas, 1900, Leabhar II: Trí Sgéalta (do fuair an Chéad Duais), Conchubhar Ó Deasúmhna do Chuir Síos.* Dublin: Gaelic League, 1902.

———. "Half-Holiday Lecturers at St. Enda's: Dr. Douglas Hyde on the Language Movement." *An Macaomh* 1 (Christmas 1909): 50–51.

———. "Opening Lecture of the Professor of Modern Irish at Dublin University College." *New Ireland Review* 32 (May 1910): 139–49.

———. "Canon Peadar O'Leary and Dr. Kuno Meyer." *Studies* 9 (June 1920): 297–301.

———. "The Irish Language Movement: Some Reminiscences." *Manchester Guardian Commercial* (10 May 1923): 38–40.

———. *Mise agus an Connradh (go dtí 1905)*. Dublin: Oifig an tSoláthair, 1937.

———. *A Literary History of Ireland*. London: Benn, 1967.

———. *Language, Lore, and Lyrics: Essays and Lectures*, ed. Breandán Ó Conaire. Dublin: Irish Academic Press, 1986.

———. *Selected Plays of Douglas Hyde, 'An Craoibhin Aoibhinn' with Translations by Lady Gregory*, edited with an introduction by Gareth W. Dunleavy and Janet Egelson Dunleavy. Gerrards Cross, Buckinghamshire: Colin Smythe; Washington, D.C.: Catholic Univ. of America Press, 1991.

Imtheachta an Oireachtas, 1900: Leabhar I: do Cruinniughadh i mBaile Átha Cliath, i mBealtaine, 1900. Dublin: Gaelic League, 1902.

Irish Agricultural Organisation Society. *Seventh Report of the Irish Agricultural Organisation Society Ltd., for the Year Ending December 31st 1901*. Dublin: Irish Agricultural Organisation Society, 1902.

———. *Eighth Report of the Irish Agricultural Organisation Society Ltd., for the Year Ending December 31st 1902*. Dublin: Irish Agricultural Organisation Society, 1903.

Jacques. *Irish Education as It Is and as It Should Be*. Dublin: Gill, 1906.

Joynt, Maud. "The Future of the Irish Language." *New Ireland Review* 8 (June 1900): 193–99.

Judge, J. M. "The Irish Movement: A Talk with the Man in the Street." *New Ireland Review* 29 (May 1908): 169–78.

Kenny, P. D. *Economics for Irishmen*. Dublin: Maunsel and Co., 1907.

MacNeill, Eoin. "Why and How the Irish Language Is to Be Preserved." *Irish Ecclesiastical Record*, 3rd ser., 12 (Dec. 1891): 1099–1108. [The article was signed J. McNeill.]

———. "A Plea and a Plan for the Extension of the Movement to Preserve and Spread the Gaelic Language in Ireland." *Gaelic Journal* 4 (Mar. 1893): 179.

———. "The Gaelic League." *Gaelic Journal* 4 (Nov. 1893): 226.

———. "Some Notes of Our National Literature." *New Ireland Review* 1 (May 1894): 138–49.

Mac Suibhne, Conchubhar. "How to Gaelicise the Pale." *Catholic Bulletin* 1 (Apr. 1911): 205–06.

Magner, K. "Ballingeary." *Catholic Bulletin* 2 (Sept. 1912): 640–45.

Mahony, Thomas MacDonagh. "The Present State of Ireland." *New Ireland Review* 11 (Aug. 1899): 341–47.

McCarthy, Michael J. F. *Priests and People in Ireland.* Dublin: Hodges and Figgis, 1903.

McDonald, Walter. *Reminiscences of a Maynooth Professor.* London: Jonathan Cape, 1926.

Micks, W. L. *An Account of the Constitution, Administration, and Dissolution of the Congested Districts Board for Ireland, from 1891–1923.* Dublin: Eason and Son, 1925.

Moore, George. "The Irish Literary Renaissance and the Irish Language." *New Ireland Review* 8 (Apr. 1900): 65–72.

Moran, D. P. "Is the Irish Nation Dying?" *New Ireland Review* 10 (Dec. 1898): 208–14.

———. "The Future of the Irish Nation." *New Ireland Review* 10 (Feb. 1899): 345–59.

———. "The Pale and the Gael." *New Ireland Review* 11 (June 1899): 230–44.

———. "Politics, Nationality, and Snobs." *New Ireland Review* 12 (Nov. 1899): 129–43.

———. "The Gaelic Revival." *New Ireland Review* 12 (Jan. 1900): 257–72.

———. "The Battle of Two Civilizations." *New Ireland Review* 13 (Aug. 1900): 323–36.

———. *The Philosophy of Irish Ireland.* Dublin: James Duffy, 1905.

O'Brien, William. *Irish Ideas.* Port Washington, N.Y.: Kennikat Press, 1970.

O'Casey, Sean. *Drums under the Windows.* London: Macmillan, 1945.

———. *The Letters of Sean O'Casey, Vol. Two: 1942–54,* ed. David Krause. New York: Macmillan, 1980.

———. *The Letters of Sean O'Casey, Vol. Three: 1955–58,* ed. David Krause. Washington, D.C.: Catholic Univ. of America Press, 1989.

———. *The Letters of Sean O'Casey, Vol. Four: 1959–64,* ed. David Krause. Washington, D. C.: Catholic Univ. of America Press, 1992.

Ó Ceallaigh, Seán T., and Proinsias Ó Conluain. *Seán T.: Scéal a Bheatha á Insint ag Seán T. Ó Ceallaigh.* Dublin: Foilseacháin Náisiúnta Teoranta, 1963.

Ó Ceallaigh, Tomás. "Can We Save the Language?" *Catholic Bulletin* 1 (Apr. 1911): 186–90.

Ó Cobhthaigh, Diarmid. *Douglas Hyde.* Dublin: Maunsel, 1917.

Ó Crohan, Tomás. *The Islandman.* Oxford: Oxford Univ. Press, 1978.

Ó Dalaigh, Patrick. *Annual Report of the Gaelic League, 1901–2, and Proceedings of the Ard-Fheis, 1902, with Summary of Accounts, List of Branches, &c.* Dublin: Gaelic League, 1902.

Ó Donnchadha, Tadhg, ed. *Imtheachta an Oireachtais, 1901, Leabhar a hAon.* Dublin: Gaelic League, 1903.

O'Donnell, F. H. *A History of the Irish Parliamentary Party, Vol. II: Parnell and the Lieutenants Complicity and Betrayal, with an Epilogue to the Present Day.* London: Longmans, Green and Company, 1910.

O'Donoghue, Eamon. "A Plea for the Old Tongue." *Journal of the Ivernian Society* 3 (Apr.–June 1911): 183–90.

O'Donovan, Gerald. *Father Ralph.* Dingle: Brandon, 1993.

O'Donovan, Jeremiah. "The Celtic Revival of Today." *Irish Ecclesiastical Record*, 4th ser., 5 (Mar. 1899): 238–56.

———. "Is Ireland Doomed? Part I" *New Ireland Review* 11, no. 2 (Apr. 1899): 67–75.

———. "Is Ireland Doomed? Part II" *New Ireland Review* 11, no. 3 (May 1899): 131–38.

———. *An O'Growney Memorial Lecture.* Dublin: Gaelic League, 1902.

O'Farrelly, Agnes, ed. *Leabhar an Athar Eoghan/The O'Growney Memorial Volume.* Dublin: M. H. Gill and Son, 1904.

Ó Gaora, Colm. *Mise.* Dublin: Oifig an tSolátair, 1943.

O'Growney, Eugene. "The National Language," *Irish Ecclesiastical Record*, 3rd ser., 11 (Nov. 1890): 982–92. The article was signed E. Growney.

———. *Simple Lessons in Irish; Giving the Pronunciation of Each Word*, Part 1. Dublin: Gaelic League, 1903.

———. *Simple Lessons in Irish; Giving the Pronunciation of Each Word*, Part 2. Dublin: Gaelic League, 1904.

———. *Simple Lessons in Irish; Giving the Pronunciation of Each Word*, Part 3. Dublin: Gaelic League, 1904.

———. *Simple Lessons in Irish; Giving the Pronunciation of Each Word*, Part 4. Dublin: Gaelic League, 1902.

———. *Simple Lessons in Irish; Giving the Pronunciation of Each Word*, Part 5. Dublin: Gaelic League, 1902.

Ó hAnnracháin, Peadar. *Mar Chonnac-sa Éire.* Dublin: Oifig Díolta Foillseacháin Rialtais, 1937.

———. *Fé Bhrat an Chonnnartha.* Dublin: Oifig an tSolátair, 1944.

O'Hegarty, P. S. *A History of Ireland under the Union, 1801–1922: With an Epilogue Carrying the Story down to the Acceptance in 1927 by de Valera of the Anglo-Irish Treaty of 1921.* New York: Kraus, 1969.

O'Hickey, Michael P. "Nationality According to Thomas Davis." *New Ireland Review* 9 (May 1898): 129–215.

———. "Father O'Growney." *Irish Ecclesiastical Record*, 4th ser., 4 (Nov. 1899): 426–43.

———. *An Irish University or Else—.* Dublin: M. H. Gill and Son, 1909.

————. *Language and Nationality, with Preface by Douglas Hyde.* Waterford: *Waterford News,* 1918.

O'Higgins, Brian. "Unique Branch of the Gaelic League." *Wolfe Tone Annual* 13 (1944–45).

————. "My Songs and Myself." *Wolfe Tone Annual* 17 (1949).

O'Riordan, Michael. *Catholicity and Progress in Ireland.* London: K. Paul, Trench, Trübner and Co., 1905.

Paul-Dubois, Louis A. *Contemporary Ireland,* with an introduction by Tom Kettle. Dublin: Maunsel and Co., 1911.

Pearse, P. H.. *The Letters of P. H. Pearse,* with a foreword by F. S. L. Lyons, ed. Seamas Ó Buachalla. Gerrards Cross, Buckinghamshire: Colin Smythe, 1980.

————. *A Significant Educationalist: The Educational Writings of P. H. Pearse,* ed. Seamas Ó Buachalla. Dublin: Mercier Press, 1980.

Phillips, W. Alison. *The Revolution in Ireland, 1906–1923.* London: Longmans, Green and Co., 1923.

Plunkett, Sir Horace. *Ireland in the New Century.* Dublin: Irish Academic Press, 1983.

Redmond-Howard, L. G. *The New Birth of Ireland.* London: Collins' Clear Type Press, 1913.

Riordan, E. J. *Modern Irish Trade and Industry.* London: Metheuen, 1920.

Russell, G. W. *Co-operation and Nationality.* Dublin: Irish Academic Press, 1982.

Ryan, W. P. *The Pope's Green Island.* London: J. Nisbet, 1912.

Sheehan, Patrick Augustine. *My New Curate, a Story: Gathered from the Stray Leaves of an Old Diary.* Boston: Marlier, Callanan, and Company, 1925.

————. *Luke Delmege.* New York: Longmans, Green and Co., 1928.

Sigerson, Dr. George. "Irish Literature: Its Origin, Environment, and Influence." In *The Revival of Irish Literature,* ed. Sir Charles Gavan Duffy. London: T. Fisher Unwin, 1894.

Synge, J. M. *In Wicklow, West Kerry, and Connemara.* Dublin: Maunsel, 1911.

————. *The Aran Islands and Other Writings,* ed. Robert Tracy. New York: Vintage Books, 1962.

[*Times.*] *The Ireland of To-Day.* Reprint, Boston: Small, Maynard and Company, 1915. Originally published as a special section of the *Times* in 1913.

Ua Laoghaire [O'Leary], Peadar. "The Ivernian Society: Inaugural Address." *Journal of the Ivernian Society* 1 (Oct. 1908): 65–68.

————. *Mo Sgéal Féin.* Dublin: Browne and Nolan, 1915.

Yeats, W. B. *Memoirs: Autobiography—First Draft Journal,* transcribed and ed. Denis Donoghue. New York: Macmillan, 1973.

————. *Where There Is Nothing, and The Unicorn from the Stars*, ed. Katherine Worth. Washington, D. C.: Catholic Univ. of America Press, 1987.

II. SECONDARY SOURCES

Akenson, Donald H. *The Irish Education Experiment: The National System of Education in the Nineteenth Century.* London: Routledge and Kegan Paul, 1970.

————. *A Mirror to Kathleen's Face: Education in Independent Ireland, 1922–1960.* Montreal: McGill-Queen's Univ. Press, 1975.

Alter, Peter. "Symbols of Irish Nationalism." In *Reactions to Irish Nationalism,* ed. Alan O'Day. London: Hambledon Press, 1987.

————. *Nationalism.* London: E. Arnold, 1994.

Anderson, Benedict. *Imagined Communities: Reflections on the Origins and Spread of Nationalism.* London: Verso, 1991.

Andrews, Líam. "The Very Dogs in Belfast Will Bark in Irish: The Unionist Government and the Irish Language, 1921–43." In *The Irish Language in Northern Ireland,* ed. Aodán MacPóilin. Belfast: Ultach Trust, 1997.

Armstrong, W. A. "The Use of Information about Occupation I as a Basis for Social Stratification." In *Nineteenth-Century Society: Essays in the Use of Quantitative Methods for the Study of Social Data,* edited by E. A. Wrigley. Cambridge: Cambridge Univ. Press, 1972.

Augusteijn, Joost. *From Public Defiance to Guerrilla Warfare: The Experience of Ordinary Volunteers in the Irish War of Independence, 1916–1921.* Dublin: Irish Academic Press, 1994.

Bardon, Jonathan. *Belfast: An Illustrated History.* Dundonald: Blackstaff Press, 1982.

Bartlett, Thomas, Chris Curtin, Riana O'Dwyer, and Gearóid Ó Tuathaigh, eds. *Irish Studies: A General Introduction.* Dublin: Gill and Macmillan, 1988.

Beckett, J. C., ed. *Belfast: The Making of the City, 1800–1914.* Belfast: Appletree Press, 1983.

Beckett, J. C., and R. E. Glasscock, eds. *Belfast: The Origin and Growth of an Industrial City.* London: British Broadcasting Corportation, 1967.

Begley, John. *The Diocese of Limerick from 1641 to the Present Time.* Dublin: Brown and Nowlan, 1938.

Bernstein, George L. *Liberalism and Liberal Politics in Edwardian England.* Boston: Allen and Unwin, 1986.

Bew, Paul. *Conflict and Conciliation in Ireland, 1890–1910: Parnellites and Radical Agrarians.* Oxford: Clarendon Press, 1987.

——. *Ideology and the Irish Question: Ulster Unionism and Irish Nationalism, 1912–1916.* Oxford: Clarendon Press, 1994.

Biletz, Frank. "The Boundaries of Irish National Identity, 1890–1912." Ph.D. diss., Univ. of Chicago, 1994.

——. "Women and Irish-Ireland: The Domestic Nationalism of Mary Butler." *New Hibernia Review* 6 (Spring 2002): 59–72.

Blaney, Roger. *Presbyterians and the Irish Language.* Belfast: Ultach Trust, 1996.

Bourke, Marcus. *The O'Rahilly.* Tralee: Anvil Books, 1967.

Bowe, Nicola Gordon. "Two Early Twentieth Century Irish Arts and Crafts Workshops in Context: An Túr Gloine and the Dun Emer Guild and Industries." *Journal of Design History* 2 (1989): 193–206.

Bowen, Desmond. *The Protestant Crusade in Ireland, 1800–70: A Study of Protestant-Catholic Relations Between the Act of Union and Disestablishment.* Dublin: Gill and Macmillan, 1978.

Boyce, D. George. *Nationalism in Ireland.* London: Routledge, 1991.

Boyce, D. George, and Alan O'Day, eds. *The Making of Modern Irish History: Revisionism and the Revisionist Controversy.* London: Routledge, 1996.

Boylan, Henry. *A Dictionary of Irish Biography,* 2nd ed. New York: St. Martin's Press, 1988.

Boyle, J. W. "The Belfast Protestant Association and the Independent Orange Order, 1901–1910." *Irish Historical Studies* 13 (Sept. 1962): 117–52.

Brady, Ciaran, ed. *Interpreting Irish History: The Debate on Historical Revisionism, 1938–1994.* Dublin: Irish Academic Press, 1994.

Breathnach, Diarmuid, and Máire Ní Mhurchú. *1882–1982: Beathaisnéis, a hAon.* Dublin: An Clóchamhar Teoranta, 1986.

——. *1882–1982: Beathaisnéis, a Dó.* Dublin: An Clóchamhar Teoranta, 1990.

——. *1882–1982: Beathaisnéis, a Trí.* Dublin: An Clóchamhar Teoranta, 1992.

——. *1882–1982: Beathaisnéis, a Ceathair.* Dublin: An Clóchamhar Teoranta, 1994.

——. *1882–1982: Beathaisnéis, a Cúig.* Dublin: An Clóchamhar Teoranta, 1997.

Brett, C. E. B. "The Edwardian City: Belfast about 1900." In *Belfast: The Origin and Growth of an Industrial City,* ed. J. C. Beckett and R. E. Glasscock. London: British Broadcasting Corporation, 1967.

Brown, Malcolm. *The Politics of Irish Literature: From Thomas Davis to W. B. Yeats.* Seattle: Univ. of Washington Press, 1973.

Brown, Terence. *Ireland: A Social and Cultural History, 1922 to the Present.* Ithaca, N.Y.: Cornell Univ. Press, 1985.

Browne, Ray B., and Michael T. Marsden, eds. *The Cultures of Celebration*. Bowling Green, Ohio: Bowling Green State Univ. Popular Press, 1994.

Buckley, Patrick. *Faith and Fatherland: The Irish News, the Catholic Hierarchy, and the Management of Dissidents*. Belfast: Belfast Historical and Educational Society, 1991.

Butlin, R. A., ed. *The Development of the Irish Town*. London: Croom Helm, 1977.

Cahalan, James M. *Modern Irish Literature and Culture: A Chronology*. New York: G. K. Hall, 1993.

Callanan, Frank. *The Parnell Split, 1890–91*. Cork: Cork Univ. Press, 1992.

———. *T. M. Healy*. Cork: Cork Univ. Press, 1996.

Campbell, Fergus. *Land and Revolution: Nationalist Politics in the West of Ireland, 1891–1921*. Oxford: Oxford Univ. Press, 2005.

Campbell, Flann. *The Dissenting Voice: Protestant Democracy in Ulster from Plantation to Partition*. Belfast: Blackstaff Press, 1991.

Candy, Catherine. *Priestly Fictions: Popular Irish Novelists of the Early 20th Century*. Dublin: Wolfhound Press, 1995.

Cannadine, David. "The Context, Performance and Meaning of Ritual: The British Monarchy and the 'Invention of Tradition.'" In *The Invention of Tradition*, ed. Eric Hobsbawm and Terence Ranger. Cambridge: Cambridge Univ. Press, 1983.

Canny, Nicholas. *Kingdom and Colony: Ireland and the Atlantic World, 1560–1800*. Baltimore: Johns Hopkins Univ. Press, 1988.

Casey, Daniel J., and Robert E. Rhodes, eds. *Views of the Irish Peasantry, 1800–1916*. Hamden, Conn.: Archon Books, 1977.

Casteleyn, Mary. *A History of Literacy and Libraries in Ireland: The Long-Traced Pedigree*. Brookfield, Mass.: Gower, 1984.

Cealtra, Inis. "The President on the League: Our Idea of a University." *Catholic Bulletin* 28 (June 1938): 483–91.

Chancellor, Valerie E. *History for Their Masters: Opinion in the English History Textbook, 1800–1914*. New York: A. M. Kelley, 1970.

Claffey, John A., ed. *Glimpses of Tuam since the Famine*. Ferbane, Co. Offaly: Old Tuam Society, 1997.

Clark, Samuel. "The Importance of Agrarian Classes: Agrarian Class Structure and Collective Action in Nineteenth-Century Ireland." In *Ireland: Land, Politics, and People*, ed. P. J. Drudy. Cambridge: Cambridge Univ. Press, 1982.

Clark, Samuel, and James S. Donnelly Jr., eds. *Irish Peasants: Violence and Political Unrest, 1780–1914*. Madison: Univ. of Wisconsin Press, 1983.

Coldrey, Barry M. *Faith and Fatherland: The Christian Brothers and the Development of Irish Nationalism, 1838–1921.* Dublin: Gill and Macmillan, 1988.

Collins, Kevin. *Catholic Churchmen and the Celtic Revival in Ireland, 1848–1916.* Dublin: Four Courts Press, 2002.

Colls, Robert, and Philip Dodd, eds. *Englishness: Politics and Culture, 1880–1920.* London: Croom Helm, 1986.

Comerford, R. V. "Nation, Nationalism, and the Irish Language." In *Perspectives on Irish Nationalism,* ed. Thomas E. Hachey and Lawrence J. McCaffrey. Lexington: Univ. Press of Kentucky, 1989.

———. *The Fenians in Context: Irish Politics and Society, 1848–82.* Dublin: Wolfhound Press, 1998.

———. *Ireland: Inventing the Nation.* London: Hodder Arnold, 2003.

Connolly, S. J. *Priests and People in Pre-Famine Ireland, 1780–1845.* Dublin: Gill and Macmillan, 1982.

———. *Religion and Society in Nineteenth-Century Ireland: Studies in Irish Economic and Social History, 3.* Dundalk: Dundalgan Press, 1985.

Connradh na Gaedhilge Coiste Thiobrad Árann Theas. *Bláith-Fhleasg ó Thiobraid Árann: A Garland from Tipperary, 1893–1943.* Clonmel: Irish Self-Determination League of Great Britain, 1943.

Coogan, Tim Pat. *De Valera: Long Fellow, Long Shadow.* London: Hutchinson, 1993.

Coolahan, John. "Imperialism and the Irish National School System." In *"Benefits Bestowed?": Education and British Imperialism,* ed. J. A. Mangan. Manchester: Manchester Univ. Press, 1988.

Corish, Patrick J. *The Irish Catholic Experience: A Historical Survey.* Dublin: Gill and Macmillan, 1985.

———. *Maynooth: 1795–1995.* Dublin: Gill and Macmillan, 1995.

Costello, Peter, ed. *Liam O'Flaherty's Ireland.* Dublin: Wolfhound Press, 1996.

Cronin, Mike, and Daryl Adair. *The Wearing of the Green: A History of St. Patrick's Day.* London: Routledge, 2002.

Cronin, Seán. "Nation Building and the Irish Language Revival Movement." *Éire-Ireland* 13 (Spring 1978): 7–14.

Crossick, Geoffrey, and Heinz-Gerhard Haupt, eds. *Shopkeepers and Master Artisans in Nineteenth-Century Europe.* London: Metheuen, 1984.

Cullen, L. M. *An Economic History of Ireland since 1660.* New York: Barnes and Noble Books, 1972.

———. "The Cultural Basis of Modern Irish Nationalism." In *The Roots of Nationalism: Studies in Northern Europe*, ed. Rosalind Mitchison. Edinburgh: Donald, 1980.

Cunningham, Bernadette. *The World of Geoffrey Keating: History, Myth and Religion in Seventeenth-Century Ireland*. Dublin: Four Courts Press, 2000.

Daly, Dominic. *The Young Douglas Hyde: The Dawn of the Irish Revolution and Renaissance, 1874–1893*. Dublin: Irish Univ. Press, 1974.

Daly, G. "On Formulating National Goals." In *Ireland in the Year 2000: Towards a National Strategy: Issues and Perspectives; Proceedings of a Colloquy, Kilkea Castle, February 1983*. Dublin: An Foras Forbatha, 1983.

Daly, Mary E. "Social Structure of the Dublin Working Class, 1871–1911." *Irish Historical Studies* 23 (Nov. 1982): 121–33.

———. *Dublin, the Deposed Capital: A Social and Economic History, 1860–1914*. Cork: Cork Univ. Press, 1984.

———. *Industrial Development and Irish National Identity, 1922–1939*. Dublin: Gill and Macmillan, 1992.

———. "Forty Shades of Grey? Irish Historiography and the Challenges of Multidisciplinarity." In *Ireland Beyond Boundaries: Mapping Irish Studies in the Twenty-First Century*, ed. Liam Harte and Yvonne Whelan. London: Pluto Press, 2007.

Danaher, Kevin. *The Year in Ireland*. Cork: Mercier Press, 1972.

D'Arcy, Fergus A. "Wages of Labourers in the Dublin Building Industry, 1667–1918." *Saothar: Journal of the Irish Labour History Society*, 14 (1989): 17–32.

de Blaghd, Earnán. "Hyde in Conflict." In *The Gaelic League Idea*, ed. Seán Ó Tuama. Cork and Dublin: Mercier Press, 1972.

Deutsch, Karl. *Nationalism and Social Communication*. Cambridge, Mass.: Technology Press of the Massachusetts Institute of Technology, 1953.

Dixon, F. E. "Dublin Exhibitions, Part I." *Dublin Historical Record*, 26 (June 1973): 93–100.

———. "Dublin Exhibitions, Part II." *Dublin Historical Record*, 26 (Sept. 1973): 137–46.

Donnelly, James S., Jr. *The Land and the People of Nineteenth-Century Cork: The Rural Economy and the Land Question*. London: Routledge and Kegan Paul, 1975.

———. "The Marian Shrine of Knock: The First Decade." *Éire-Ireland*, 28 (Summer 1993): 54–99.

Drotner, Kirsten. *English Children and Their Magazines, 1751–1945*. New Haven: Yale Univ. Press, 1988.

Drudy, P. J., ed. *Ireland: Land, Politics, and People.* Cambridge: Cambridge Univ. Press, 1982.

Dudley Edwards, Ruth. *Patrick Pearse: The Triumph of Failure.* London: Gollancz, 1977.

Dunleavy, Gareth W. "Hyde's Crusade for the Language and the Case of the Embarrassing Packets." *Studies* 73 (Spring 1984): 12–25.

Dunleavy, Gareth W., and Janet Egelson Dunleavy. *Douglas Hyde: A Maker of Modern Ireland.* Berkeley: Univ. of California Press, 1991.

Ellmann, Richard. *James Joyce.* Oxford: Oxford Univ. Press, 1982.

Eyler, Audrey S., and Robert F. Garratt, eds. *The Uses of the Past: Essays on Irish Culture.* Newark: Univ. of Delaware Press, 1988.

Farmar, Tony. *Ordinary Lives: The Private Lives of Three Generations of Ireland's Professional Classes.* Dublin: Gill and Macmillan, 1995.

Ferriter, Diarmaid. *A Nation of Extremes: the Pioneers in Twentieth-Century Ireland.* Dublin: Irish Academic Press, 1999.

Fitzgerald, Garret. "Estimates for Baronies of Minimum Level of Irish-speaking Amongst Successive Decenniel Cohorts: 1771–1781 to 1861–1871." *Proceedings of the Royal Irish Academy* 84c (1984): 117–55.

Fitzpatrick, David. *Politics and Irish Life, 1913–1921: Provincial Experience of War and Revolution.* Cork: Cork Univ. Press, 1998.

Foster, John Wilson. "Yeats and the Folklore of the Irish Revival." *Éire-Ireland,* 17 (Summer 1982): 6–18.

———. *Fictions of the Irish Literary Revival: A Changeling Art.* Syracuse: Syracuse Univ. Press, 1987.

———. "Who Are the Irish?" *Studies,* 77 (Winter 1988): 403–21.

Foster, R. F. *Modern Ireland, 1600–1972.* New York: Viking Penguin, 1989.

———. "Anglo-Irish Literature, Gaelic Nationalism, and Irish Politics in the 1890s." In *Ireland after the Union: Proceedings of the Second Joint Meeting of the Royal Irish Academy and the British Academy, London, 1986.* Oxford: Oxford Univ. Press, 1989.

———. *Paddy and Mr. Punch: Connections in Irish and English History.* London: A. Lane, 1993.

———. *W. B. Yeats, A Life: Vol. I, The Apprentice Mage.* Oxford: Oxford Univ. Press, 1997.

Frayne, John P., ed. *Uncollected Prose by W. B. Yeats, Vol. I: First Reviews and Articles, 1886–1896.* New York: Columbia Univ. Press, 1970.

Freeman, T. W. "Irish Towns in the Eighteenth and Nineteenth Centuries." In *The Development of the Irish Town*, ed. R. A. Butlin. London: Croom Helm, 1977.

French, R. B. D. "J. O. Hannay and the Gaelic League." *Hermathena: A Dublin University Review* 52 (Spring 1966): 26–52.

Gailey, Andrew. *Ireland and the Death of Kindness: the Experience of Constructive Unionism, 1890–1905*. Cork: Cork Univ. Press, 1987.

Garvin, Tom. *The Evolution of Irish National Politics*. New York: Holmes and Meier, 1981.

———. "Priests and Patriots: Irish Separatism and Fear of the Modern, 1890–1914." *Irish Historical Studies* 25 (May 1986): 67–81.

———. *Nationalist Revolutionaries in Ireland, 1858–1928*. Oxford: Clarendon Press, 1987.

———. *1922: The Birth of Irish Democracy*. Dublin: Gill and Macmillan, 2005.

Gaughan, J. Anthony. *Thomas Johnson, 1872–1963: First Leader of the Labour Party in Dáil Éireann*. Mount Merrion, Co. Dublin: Kingdom Books, 1980.

———. *A Political Odyssey: Thomas O'Donnell, M. P. for West Kerry, 1900–1918*. Mount Merrion, Co. Dublin: Kingdom Books, 1983.

Geertz, Clifford. *The Interpretation of Culture*. New York: Basic Books, 1973.

Gellately, Robert. *The Politics of Economic Despair: Shopkeepers and German Politics, 1890–1914*. London: Sage Publications, 1974.

Gellner, Ernest. *Nations and Nationalism*. Ithaca, N. Y., 1983.

Glandon, Virginia E. *Arthur Griffith and the Advanced Nationalist Press: Ireland, 1900–1922*. New York: P. Lang, 1985.

Goldring, Maurice. *Pleasant the Scholar's Life: Irish Intellectuals and the Construction of the Nation State*. London: Serif, 1993.

Gramsci, Antonio. *An Antonio Gramsci Reader: Selected Writings, 1916–1935*, ed. David Forgacs. New York: Schocken Books, 1988.

Greene, David. "The Irish Language Movement." In *Irish Anglicanism, 1869–1969; Essays on the Role of Anglicanism in Irish Life, Presented to the Church of Ireland on the Occasion of the Centenary of Its Disestablishment, by a Group of Methodist, Presbyterian, Quaker and Roman Catholic Scholars*, ed. Michael Hurley. Dublin: Allen Figgis, 1970.

Gribbon, Sybil. *Edwardian Belfast: A Social Profile*. Belfast: Appletree Press, 1982.

Großmann, Anton J. J. *Irische Nationalbewegungen, 1884–1915*. Munich: Minerva Publikation, 1978.

Grote, Georg. *Torn Between Politics and Culture: The Gaelic League, 1893–1993*. New York: Waxmann, 1994.

Hachey, Thomas E. and Lawrence J. McCaffrey, eds. *Perspectives on Irish National-ism*. Lexington: Univ. Press of Kentucky, 1989.

Harp, Richard. "The *Shan Van Vocht* (Belfast, 1896–1899) and Irish Nationalism." *Éire-Ireland* 24 (Autumn 1989): 42–52.

Hayes, Carlton J. H. *The Historical Evolution of Modern Nationalism*. New York: Russell and Russell, 1968.

Heatley, Fred. "Community Relations and the Religious Geography, 1800–86." In *Belfast: The Making of the City, 1800–1914*, ed. J. C. Beckett. Belfast: Appletree Press, 1983.

Hepburn, A. C. "The Ancient Order of Hibernians in Irish Politics, 1905–14." *Cithara* 10 (May 1971): 5–18.

———. "Work, Class, and Religion in Belfast, 1871–1911." *Irish Economic and Social History*, 10 (1983): 33–50.

———. *A Past Apart: Studies in the History of Catholic Belfast, 1850–1950*. Belfast: Ulster Historical Foundation, 1996.

Herr, Cheryl. *Joyce's Anatomy of Culture*. Urbana: Univ. of Illinois Press, 1986.

Hewitt, John. "The Northern Athens and After." In *Belfast: The Origin and Growth of an Industrial City*, ed. J. C. Beckett. Belfast: Appletree Press, 1983.

Hill, Jacqueline. "National Festivals, the State, and 'Protestant Ascendancy'in Ire-land, 1790–1829." *Irish Historical Studies* 24 (May 1984): 30–51.

Himberd, Alan, and George Mills Harper, eds. *The Letters of John Quinn to William Butler Yeats*. Ann Arbor: UMI Research Press, 1983.

Hobsbawm, Eric. *Nations and Nationalism since 1780: Programme, Myth, Reality*. Cambridge: Cambridge Univ. Press, 1990.

Hobsbawm, Eric, and Terence Ranger, eds. *The Invention of Tradition*. Cambridge: Cambridge Univ. Press, 1983.

Hogan, Edward M. *The Irish Missionary Movement: A Historical Survey*. Dublin: Gill and Macmillan, 1990.

Hogan, Robert, Richard Burnham, and Daniel P. Poteet, eds. *The Modern Irish Drama: A Documentary History, IV: The Rise of the Realists, 1910–1915*. Dublin: Dolmen Press, 1979.

Hopkinson, Michael. *Green against Green: The Irish Civil War*. Dublin: Gill and Macmillan, 1988.

Hoppen, K. T. *Elections, Politics, and Society in Ireland, 1832–1885*. Oxford: Clarendon Press, 1984.

Hroch, Miroslav. "Social and Territorial Characteristics in the Composition of the Leading Groups of National Movements." In *The Formation of National Elites:*

Comparative Studies on Governments and Non-Dominant Ethnic Groups in Europe, 1850–1950, vol. 6, ed. Andreas Kappeler, Fikret Adanir, and Alan O'Day. New York: New York Univ. Press, 1992.

———. *Social Preconditions of National Revival in Europe: A Comparative Analysis of the Social Composition of Patriotic Groups among the Smaller European Nations.* New York: Columbia Univ. Press, 2000.

Hunt, Lynn, ed. *The New Cultural History*. Berkeley: Univ. of California Press, 1989.

Hutchinson, John. *The Dynamics of Cultural Nationalism: The Gaelic Revival and the Creation of the Irish Nation State.* London: Allen and Unwin, 1987.

———. "Cultural Nationalism, Elite Mobility, and Nation-Building: Communitarian Politics in Modern Ireland." *British Journal of Sociology*, 38 (Dec. 1987): 482–501.

———. "Irish Nationalism." In *The Making of Modern Irish History: Revisionism and the Revisionist Controversy*, ed. D. George Boyce and Alan O'Day. London: Routledge, 1996.

Inglis, Brian. "Moran of *The Leader* and Ryan of *The Irish Peasant.*" In *The Shaping of Modern Ireland*, ed. Conor Cruise O'Brien. Toronto: Univ. of Toronto Press, 1960.

Inglis, Tom. *Moral Monopoly: The Catholic Church in Modern Irish Society.* Dublin: Gill and Macmillan, 1987.

Jackson, Alvin. *The Ulster Party: Irish Unionists in the House of Commons, 1884–1911.* Oxford: Clarendon Press, 1989.

———. "The Failure of Unionism in Dublin." *Irish Historical Studies* 26 (Nov. 1989): 377–95.

———. "Irish Unionism." In *The Making of Modern Irish History: Revisionism and the Revisionist Controversy*, ed. D. George Boyce and Alan O'Day. London: Routledge, 1996.

Jones, David S. "The Cleavage Between Graziers and Peasants in the Land Struggle, 1890–1910." In *Irish Peasants: Violence and Political Unrest, 1780–1914*, edited by Samuel Clark and J. S. Donnelly, Jr. Madison: Univ. of Wisconsin Press, 1983.

Kappeler, Andreas, Fikret Adanir, and Alan O'Day, eds. *The Formation of National Elites: Comparative Studies on Governments and Non-Dominant Ethnic Groups in Europe, 1850–1950*, vol. 6. New York: New York Univ. Press, 1992.

Kee, Robert. *The Green Flag: A History of Irish Nationalism.* London: Weidenfeld and Nicolson, 1972.

Keenan, Desmond. *The Catholic Church in Nineteenth-Century Ireland: A Sociological Study.* Dublin: Gill and Macmillan, 1983.

Kelly, John, and Eric Domville, eds. *The Collected Letters of W. B. Yeats. Vol. I, 1865–1895.* Oxford: Clarendon Press, 1986.

Kelly, John, Warwick Gould, and Deirdre Toomey, eds. *The Collected Letters of W. B. Yeats, Vol. II, 1896–1900.* Oxford: Clarendon Press, 1997.

Kelly, John, and Ronald Schuchard, eds. *The Collected Letters of W. B. Yeats. Vol. III, 1901–1904.* Oxford: Clarendon Press, 1994.

Kennedy, Líam. "The Roman Catholic Church and Economic Growth in Nineteenth-Century Ireland" *Economic and Social Review* 10 (Oct. 1978): 45–60.

———. "Farmers, Traders, and Agricultural Politics in Pre-Independence Ireland." In *Irish Peasants: Violence and Political Unrest, 1780–1914,* ed. Samuel Clark and James S. Donnelly Jr. Madison: Univ. of Wisconsin Press, 1983.

Kenny, Mary. *Goodbye to Catholic Ireland: A Social, Personal and Cultural History from the Fall of Parnell to the Realm of Mary Robinson.* London: Sinclair-Stevenson, 1997.

Keogh, Dermot. *The Rise of the Irish Working Class: The Dublin Trade Union Movement and Labour Leadership, 1890–1914.* Belfast: Appletree Press, 1982.

Kohn, Hans. *Nationalism, Its Meaning and History.* Princeton: Van Norstrand, 1965.

Koshar, Rudy J., ed. *Splintered Classes: Politics and the Lower Middle Classes in Interwar Europe.* New York: Holmes and Meier, 1990.

Larkin, Emmet. *James Larkin: Irish Labour Leader, 1876–1947.* London: Pluto Press, 1965.

———. "The Devotional Revolution in Ireland, 1850–1875," *American Historical Review* 77 (Fall 1972): 625–52.

———. *The Historical Dimensions of Irish Catholicism.* New York: Arno Press, 1976.

———. *The Pastoral Role of the Roman Catholic Church in Pre-Famine Ireland, 1750–1850.* Dublin: Four Courts Press, 2005.

Lee, J. J. "Capital in the Irish Economy." In *The Formation of the Irish Economy,* ed. L. M. Cullen. Cork: Mercier Press, 1969.

———. *The Modernisation of Ireland.* Dublin: Gill and Macmillan, 1973.

———. *Ireland, 1912–1985: Politics and Society.* Cambridge: Cambridge Univ. Press, 1989.

Longley, Edna, ed. *Culture in Ireland: Division or Diversity: Proceedings of the Cultures of Ireland Group Conference.* Belfast: Institute of Irish Studies, 1991.

Lyons, F. S. L. *John Dillon.* London: Routledge and Kegan Paul, 1968.

———. *Ireland since the Famine.* London: Fontana Paperbacks, 1973.

———. *The Irish Parliamentary Party, 1890–1910.* Westport, Conn.: Greenwood Press, 1975.

———. *Charles Stewart Parnell.* New York: Oxford Univ. Press, 1977.

———. *Culture and Anarchy in Ireland, 1890–1939.* Oxford: Clarendon Press, 1979.

Mac an tSagairt, Liam. *Father Larry Murray.* Dún Laoghaire: Éigse Oirialla, 1983.

Mac Aodha, Brendán S. "Was This a Social Revolution?" In *The Gaelic League Idea,* ed. Seán Ó Tuama. Cork: Mercier Press, 1972.

Mac Aonghusa, Proinsias. *Ar Son na Gaeilge: Conradh na Gaeilge, 1893–1993.* Dublin: Conradh na Gaeilge, 1993.

MacDonagh, Oliver. *Ireland: The Union and Its Aftermath.* London: Allen and Unwin, 1977.

———. *States of Mind: A Study of the Anglo-Irish Conflict, 1780–1980.* London: Allen and Unwin, 1983.

MacDonagh, Oliver, W. F. Mandle, and Pauric Travers, eds. *Irish Culture and Nationalism, 1750–1950.* London: St. Martin's Press, 1983.

Mac Fhearghusa, Pádraig. *Conradh na Gaeilge i gCiarraí: A History of the Gaelic League in Kerry.* Tralee: Kenno, 1995.

Mac Fhinn, Pádraig Eric. *An tAthair Mícheál Ó hIceadha.* Dublin: Sáirséil and Dill, 1974.

Mac Giolla Domhnaigh, Gearóid. *Conradh Gaeilge Chúige Uladh ag tús an 20ú chéid.* Monaghan: Comhaltas Uladh de Conradh na Gaeilge, 1995.

MacKenzie, John M. *Propaganda and Empire: The Manipulation of British Public Opinion, 1880–1960.* Manchester: Manchester Univ. Press, 1984.

MacManus, Seumas. *The Story of the Irish Race.* Old Greenwich, Conn.: Devin-Adair, 1966.

MacMillan, James F. *Twentieth-Century France: Politics and Society, 1898–1991.* London: Edward Arnold, 1992.

Mac Niocláis, Máirtín. *Seán Ó Ruadháin: Saol agus Saothar.* Dublin: An Clóchomhar Teoranta, 1991.

Mac Póilin, Aodán, ed. *The Irish Language in Northern Ireland.* Belfast: Ultach Trust, 1997.

Mac Suibhne, Breandán. "Soggarth Aroon and Gombeen-Priest: Canon James MacFadden (1842–1917)." In *Radical Irish Priests, 1660–1970,* ed. Gerard Moran. Dublin: Four Courts Press, 1998.

Magray, Mary Peckham. *The Transforming Power of the Nuns: Women, Religion, and Cultural Change in Ireland, 1750–1900.* New York: Oxford Univ. Press, 1998.

Maguire, Martin. "The Organisation and Activism of Dublin's Protestant Working Class, 1883–1935." *Irish Historical Studies* 29 (May 1994): 65–87.

Malcolm, Elizabeth. "Popular Recreation in Nineteenth-Century Ireland." In *Irish Culture and Nationalism, 1750–1950*, ed. Oliver MacDonagh, W. F. Mandle, and Pauric Travers. London: St. Martin's Press, 1983.

———. *"Ireland Sober, Ireland Free": Drink and Temperance in Nineteenth-Century Ireland*. Syracuse: Syracuse Univ. Press, 1986.

Mangan, J. A. *"Benefits Bestowed"? Education and British Imperialism*. Manchester: Manchester Univ. Press, 1988.

Manning, Frank, ed. *The Celebration of Society: Perspectives on Contemporary Cultural Performance*. Bowling Green, Ohio: Bowling Green Univ. Popular Press, 1983.

Martin, F. X. *Leaders and Men of the Easter Rising: Dublin 1916*. Ithaca, N.Y.: Cornell Univ. Press, 1967.

Martin, F. X., and F. J. Byrne, eds. *The Scholar Revolutionary: Eoin MacNeill*. Shannon: Irish Univ. Press, 1973.

Mathews, P. J. *Revival: The Abbey Theatre, Sinn Féin, the Gaelic League, and the Co-operative Movement*. Notre Dame, Ind.: Univ. of Notre Dame Press, 2003.

Maume, Patrick. *"Life That Is Exile": Daniel Corkery and the Search for Irish Ireland*. Belfast: Institute of Irish Studies, 1993.

———. *D. P. Moran*. Dundalk: Dundalgan Press, 1995.

———. "In the Fenians' Wake: Ireland Nineteenth-Century Crises, and Their Representation in the Sentimental Rhetoric of William O'Brien, MP, and Canon Sheehan." *Bullán* 4 (Autumn 1998): 59–80.

———. *The Long Gestation: Irish Nationalist Life, 1890–1918*. New York: St. Martin's Press, 1999.

Mayer, Arno. "The Lower Middle Class as Historical Problem." *Journal of Modern History* 47 (Sept. 1975): 409–36.

McBride, Lawrence. "A Literary Life of a Socially and Politically Engaged Priest: Canon Patrick Augustine Sheehan (1852–1913)." In *Radical Irish Priests, 1660–1970*, ed. Gerard Moran. Dublin: Four Courts Press, 1998.

———, ed. *Reading Irish Histories: Texts, Contexts, and Memory in Modern Ireland*. Dublin: Four Courts Press, 2003.

McCartney, Donal. "Hyde, D. P. Moran, and Irish-Ireland." In *Leaders and Men of the Easter Rising: Dublin 1916*, ed. F. X. Martin. Ithaca, N.Y.: Cornell Univ. Press, 1967.

———. "MacNeill and Irish-Ireland." In *The Scholar Revolutionary: Eoin MacNeill*, ed. F. X. Martin and F. J. Byrne. Shannon: Irish Univ. Press, 1973.

McCracken, Donal P. *The Irish Pro-Boers, 1877–1902*. Johannesburg: Perskor, 1989.

McDiarmid, Lucy. "The Man Who Died for the Language: The Rev. Dr. O'Hickey and the 'Essential Irish' Controversy of 1909." *Éire-Ireland* 35 (Spring–Summer 2000): 188–218.

McElligott, T. J. *Secondary Education in Ireland, 1870–1921.* Blackrock, Co. Dublin: Irish Academic Press, 1981.

McGonagle, Noel. "Writing in Gaelic since 1880." In *Irish Studies: A General Introduction,* ed. Thomas Bartlett, Chris Curtin, Riana O'Dwyer, and Gearóid Ó Tuathaigh. Dublin: Gill and Macmillan, 1988.

McMahon, Sean. "Art and Life Blended: Douglas Hyde and the Literary Revival." *Éire-Ireland* 14 (1979): 112–25.

McMahon, Timothy G. "The Gaelic League and the Irish-Ireland Movement." Master's thesis, Univ. of Wisconsin-Madison, 1994.

———. "Cultural Nativism and Irish-Ireland: *The Leader* as a Source for Joyce's *Ulysses.*" *Joyce Studies Annual.* Austin: Univ. of Texas Press, 1996.

———, ed. *Pádraig Ó Fathaigh's War of Independence: Recollections of a Galway Gaelic Leaguer.* Cork: Cork Univ. Press, 2000.

———. "The Social Bases of the Gaelic Revival, 1893–1910." Ph.D., Univ. of Wisconsin-Madison, 2001.

———. "'All Creeds and All Classes?' Just Who Made up the Gaelic League?" *Éire-Ireland* 37 (Fall–Winter 2002): 118–68.

———. "'To Mould an Important Body of Shepherds': The Gaelic Summer Colleges and the Teaching of Irish History." In *Reading Irish Histories: Texts, Contexts, and Memory in Modern Ireland,* ed. Lawrence W. McBride. Dublin: Four Courts Press, 2003.

———. "Religion and Popular Culture in Nineteenth-Century Ireland." *History Compass* 5 (2007): 845–64.

Miller, David W. *Church, State, and Nation in Ireland, 1898–1921.* Dublin: Gill and Macmillan, 1973.

———. "Irish Catholicism and the Great Famine." *Journal of Social History* 9 (1975): 81–98.

———. "Mass Attendance in Ireland in 1834." In *Piety and Power: Essays in Honour of Emmet Larkin,* ed. S. J. Brown and David W. Miller. Belfast: Institute of Irish Studies, 2000.

———. "Landscape and Religious Practice: A Study in Mass Attendance in Pre-Famine Ireland." *Éire-Ireland* 40 (Spring/Summer 2005): 90–106.

Mitchison, Rosalind, ed. *The Roots of Nationalism: Studies in Northern Europe.* Edinburgh: Donald, 1980.

Moran, Gerard, ed. *Radical Irish Priests, 1660–1970*. Dublin: Four Courts Press, 1998.

Morrissey, Thomas. "Saving the Language: 'The Impatient Revolutionary.'" *Studies* 77 (Autumn 1988): 352–57.

Murphy, Brian Patrick. "Father Peter Yorke's 'Turning of the Tide' (1899): The Strictly Cultural Nationalism of the Early Gaelic League." *Éire-Ireland* 23 (Spring 1988): 35–44.

———. *Patrick Pearse and the Lost Republican Ideal*. Dublin: James Duffy, 1991.

Murray, Peter. "Irish Cultural Nationalism in the United Kingdom State: Politics and the Gaelic League, 1900–1918." *Irish Political Studies* 8 (1993): 55–72.

Newsinger, John. "The Catholic Church in Nineteenth-Century Ireland." *European History Quarterly* 25 (Apr. 1995): 247–67.

Ní Bhroiméil, Una. *Building Irish Identity in America, 1870–1915: The Gaelic Revival*. Dublin: Four Courts Press, 2003.

Ní Chinnéide, Máiréad. *Máire de Buitléir, Bean Athbheochana*. Dublin: Comhar Teoranta, 1993.

Nolan, William, and Thomas G. McGrath, eds. *Tipperary: History and Society*. Templeogue, Co. Dublin: Geography Publications, 1985.

Nowlan, A. J. "Phoenix Park Public Meetings." *Dublin Historical Record* 14 (May 1958): 102–13.

Nowlan, Kevin B. *The Making of 1916: Studies in the History of the Rising*. Dublin: Stationery Office, 1969.

Ó Bolguidhir, Liam. "The Early Years of the Gaelic League in Kilkenny." *Old Kilkenny Review* 4 (1992): 1014–26.

O'Brien, Conor Cruise, ed. *The Shaping of Modern Ireland*. Toronto: Univ. of Toronto Press, 1960.

O'Brien, Joseph V. *William O'Brien and the Course of Irish Politics, 1881–1918*. Berkeley: Univ. of California Press, 1976.

———. *"Dear, Dirty Dublin": A City in Distress, 1899–1916*. Berkeley: Univ. of California Press, 1982.

O'Brien, William. *Forth the Banners Go: Reminiscences of William O'Brien, as Told to Edward MacLysaght*. Dublin: Three Candles, 1969.

O'Brien, William, and Desmond Ryan, eds. *Devoy's Post Bag, Vol. II, 1880–1928*. Dublin: C. J. Fallon, 1953.

Ó Broin, Leon. "The President and the Irish Revival." *Irish Monthly* 66 (Sept. 1938): 587–95.

———. "The Gaelic League and the Chair of Irish at Maynooth." *Studies* 52 (Winter 1963): 348–62.

————. *Revolutionary Underground: The Irish Republican Brotherhood, 1858–1924.* Dublin: Gill and Macmillan, 1976.

Ó Cearnaigh, Seán. *An Stad: Croílár na hAthbheochana.* Dublin: Comhar Teoranta, 1993.

Ó Cearúil, Colm. *Aspail ar Son na Gaeilge: Timirí Chonradh na Gaeilge, 1899–1923.* Dublin: Conradh na Gaeilge, 1995.

Ó Conluain, Proinsias, and Donncha Ó Céileachair. *An Duinníneach: An tAthair Pádraig Ó Duinnín, a Shaol, a Shaothar agus an Ré inar Mhair Sé.* Dublin: Sáirséil and Dill, 1976.

O'Connell, Maurice, ed. *People Power: Proceedings of the Third Annual Daniel O'Connell Workshop.* Dublin: Institute of Public Administration, 1993.

Ó Cuív, Brian, ed. *A View of the Irish Language.* Dublin: Stationery Office, 1969.

————. "The Gaelic Cultural Movements and the New Nationalism." In *The Making of 1916: Studies in the History of the Rising,* ed. Kevin B. Nowlan. Dublin: Stationery Office, 1969.

O'Day, Alan, ed. *Reactions to Irish Nationalism.* London: Hambledon Press, 1987.

————. "Ireland's Catholics in the British State, 1850–1922." In *The Formation of National Elites: Comparative Studies on Governments and Non-Dominant Ethnic Groups in Europe, 1850–1950,* vol. 6, ed. Andreas Kappeler, Fikret Adanir, and Alan O'Day. New York: New York Univ. Press, 1992.

Ó Doibhlin, Diarmaid. *Duanaire Gaedhilge Róis Ní Ógáin: Cnuasach de na Seanamhráin is Áille is Mó Clú.* Dublin: An Clóchomhar Teoranta, 1995.

Ó Domhnall, Micheal. *Iolscoil na Mumhan, Coláiste na Rinne: Geárr-Stair.* Cork: Cló na Laoi Teoranta, 1987.

O'Farrell, Patrick. *Ireland's English Question: Anglo-Irish Relations, 1534–1970.* New York: Schocken Books, 1971.

Ó Fearáil, Pádraig. *The Story of Conradh na Gaeilge.* Dublin: An Clódhanna Teoranta, 1975.

Ó Fiaich, Tomás. "The Great Controversy." In *The Gaelic League Idea,* ed. Seán Ó Tuama. Cork: Mercier Press, 1972.

Ó hAilín, Tomas. "Irish Revival Movements." In *A View of the Irish Language,* ed. Brian Ó Cuív. Dublin: Stationery Office, 1969.

O'Keefe, Timothy J. "'Who Fears to Speak of '98?': The Rhetoric and Rituals of the United Irishmen Centennial, 1898." *Éire-Ireland* 27 (Fall 1992): 67–91.

O'Leary, Philip. "Uneasy Alliance: The Gaelic League Looks at the 'Irish' Renaissance." In *The Uses of the Past: Essays on Irish Culture,* ed. Audrey S. Eyler and Robert F. Garratt. Newark: Univ. of Delaware Press, 1988.

———. *The Prose Literature of the Gaelic Revival, 1881–1921: Ideology and Innovation.* University Park: Pennsylvania State Univ. Press, 1994.

———. *Gaelic Prose in the Irish Free State, 1922–1939.* Dublin: University College Dublin Press, 2004.

Ó Luing, Sean. *I Die in a Good Cause: A Study of Thomas Ashe, Idealist and Revolutionary.* Tralee: Anvil Books, 1970.

Ó Macháin, Pádraig. *A Catalogue of Irish Manuscripts in Mount Melleray Abbey, Co. Waterford.* Dublin: Dublin Institute for Advanced Studies, 1991.

Ó Monacháin, Seosamh. *Timire Aniar: Tomás Ó Mannacháin.* Dublin: Coiscéim, 1995.

O'Neil, Daniel J. "Irish Cultural Revitalization." *Plural Societies* 13 (Spring/Summer 1983): 3–16.

O'Neill, Shane. "The Politics of Culture in Ireland, 1899–1910." D.Phil., Oxford Univ., 1982.

O'Neill, Timothy P. *Life and Tradition in Rural Ireland.* London: Dent, 1977.

O'Shea, James. *Priest, Politics, and Society in Post-Famine Ireland: A Study of County Tipperary, 1850–1891.* Dublin: Wolfhound Press, 1983.

Ó Snodaigh, Padraig. *Hidden Ulster: The Other Hidden Ireland.* Dublin: Clodhanna, 1973.

Ó Súilleabháin, Donncha. *Scéal an Oireachtais, 1897–1924.* Dublin: An Clóchamhar Teoranta, 1984.

———. *Cath na Gaeilge sa Chóras Oideachais, 1893–1911.* Dublin: Conradh na Gaeilge, 1988.

———. *Conradh na Gaeilge i Londain, 1894–1917.* Dublin: Conradh na Gaeilge, 1989.

———. *Na Timirí i ré tosaigh an Chonartha, 1893–1927.* Dublin: Conradh na Gaeilge, 1990.

Ó Tuama, Seán, ed. *The Gaelic League Idea.* Cork: Mercier Press, 1972.

Ó Tuathaigh, Gearóid. "The Irish-Ireland Idea: Rationale and Relevance." In *Culture in Ireland: Division or Diversity? Proceedings of the Cultures of Ireland Group Conference,* ed. Edna Longley. Belfast: Institute of Irish Studies, 1991.

———. "Cultural Visions in the New State: Embedding and Embalming." In *De Valera's Irelands,* edited by Gabriel Doherty and Dermot Keogh. Cork: Cork Univ. Press, 2003.

Owens, Gary. "Constructing the Repeal Spectacle: Monster Meetings and People Power in Pre-Famine Ireland." In *People Power: Proceedings of the Third Annual Daniel O'Connell Workshop,* ed. Maurice O'Connell. Dublin: Institute of Public Administration, 1993.

————. "Nationalism without Words: Symbolism and Ritual Behavior in the Repeal 'Monster Meetings' of 1843–5." In *Irish Popular Culture, 1650–1850,* ed. James S. Donnelly Jr. and Kerby A. Miller. Dublin: Irish Academic Press, 1999.

Ozouf, Mona. *Festivals and the French Revolution,* trans. Alan Sheridan. Cambridge, Mass.: Harvard Univ. Press, 1988.

Paseta, Senia. *Before the Revolution: Nationalism, Social Change, and Ireland's Catholic Elite, 1879–1922.* Cork: Cork Univ. Press, 1999.

Phoenix, Eamon, Pádraic Ó Cléireacháin, Eileen McAuley, and Nuala McSparran, eds. *Feis na nGleann: A Century of Gaelic Culture in the Antrim Glens.* Belfast: Stair Uladh, 2005.

Quinn, C., ed. *Descriptive List of the Papers of Liam Ó Buachalla, Banteer, County Cork (1882–1941).* Cork: Cork Archives Institute, 1994.

Ryan, Mary. "The American Parade: Representations of the Nineteenth-Century Social Order." In *The New Cultural History,* ed. Lynn Hunt. Berkeley: Univ. of California Press, 1989.

Saddlemyer, Ann, ed. *Theatre Business: The Correspondence of the First Abbey Theatre Directors: William Butler Yeats, Lady Gregory, and J. M. Synge.* University Park: Pennsylvania State Univ. Press, 1982.

Saddlemyer, Ann, and Colin Smythe, eds. *Lady Gregory, Fifty Years After.* Gerrards Cross, Buckinghamshire: Colin Smythe, 1987.

Scholes, Robert, and Richard Kain, eds. *The Workshop of Daedalus: James Joyce and the Raw Materials for* A Portrait of the Artist as a Young Man. Evanston, Ill.: Northwestern Univ. Press, 1965.

Scott, James C. *Weapons of the Weak: Everyday Forms of Peasant Resistance.* New Haven, Conn.: Yale Univ. Press, 1985.

Smith, Anthony D. *Nationalism in the Twentieth Century.* New York: New York Univ. Press, 1979.

————. *The Ethnic Revival.* Cambridge: Cambridge Univ. Press, 1981.

————. *The Ethnic Origins of Nations.* New York: Basil Blackwell, 1986.

————. *National Identity.* Reno: Univ. of Nevada Press, 1991.

Smyth, W. J., and Kevin Whelan, eds. *Common Ground: Essays on the Historical Geography of Ireland. Presented to T. Jones Hughes.* Cork: Cork Univ. Press, 1988.

Sullivan, Eileen. *Thomas Davis.* Lewisburg, Penn.: Bucknell Univ. Press, 1978.

Sweeney, Joseph. "Why 'Sinn Féin'?" *Éire-Ireland* 6 (Summer 1971): 33–40.

Tally, Patrick F. "Catholic, Celtic, and Constitutional: A. M. Sullivan's *Nation* and Irish Nationalism, 1858–73." Master's thesis, Univ. of Wisconsin-Madison, 1993.

Tierney, Michael. "What Did the Gaelic League Accomplish? 1893–1963." *Studies* 54 (Winter 1963): 337–47.

———. *Eoin MacNeill: Scholar and Man of Action, 1867–1945*. ed. F. X. Martin. Oxford: Clarendon Press, 1980.

Titley, E. Brian. *Church, State, and the Control of Education in Ireland, 1900–1944*. New York: Gill and Macmillan, 1983.

Townshend, Charles. *The British Campaign in Ireland, 1919–1921: The Development of Political and Military Policies*. Oxford: Oxford Univ. Press, 1975.

———. *Easter 1916: The Irish Rebellion*. London: Allen Lane, 2006.

Turner, Victor. *Celebration: Studies in Festival and Ritual*. Washington, D.C.: Smithsonian Institution Press, 1982.

Tymoczko, Maria. *The Irish Ulysses*. Berkeley: Univ. of California Press, 1994.

Uí Mhorónaigh, Eibhlín, ed. *Ó Ghlúin go Glúin: Scéal Chonradh na Gaeilge i n-Aonach Urmhumhan, 1901–1993*. Dublin: Coiscéim, 1993.

United Kingdom. *Parliamentary Debates*. Commons, 5th ser., vol. 42 (1912).

Vaughan, W. E. *Landlords and Tenants in Ireland, 1848–1904*. Dublin: Economic and Social History Society of Ireland, 1984.

Wade, Allan, ed. *The Letters of W. B. Yeats*. London: R. Hart-Davis, 1954.

Walker, Brian. *Ulster Politics: The Formative Years, 1868–86*. Belfast: Institute of Irish Studies, 1989.

———. *Dancing to History's Tune: History, Myth and Politics in Ireland*. Belfast: Institute of Irish Studies, 1996.

———. "Public Holidays, Commemoration and Identity in Ireland, North and South, 1920–1960." In *De Valera's Irelands*, ed. Gabriel Doherty and Dermot Keogh. Cork: Mercier Press, 2003.

Warwick-Haller, Sally. *William O'Brien and the Irish Land War*. Dublin: Irish Academic Press, 1990.

Waters, Martin J. "W. P. Ryan and the Irish-Ireland Movement." Ph.D. diss., Univ. of Connecticut, 1970.

———. "Peasants and Emigrants: Considerations of the Gaelic League as a Social Movement." In *Views of the Irish Peasantry, 1800–1916*, ed. Daniel J. Casey and Robert E. Rhodes. Hamden, Conn.: Archon Books, 1977.

Weber, Eugen. *Peasants into Frenchmen: The Modernization of Rural France, 1870–1914*. Palo Alto: Stanford Univ. Press, 1976.

West, Trevor. *Horace Plunkett: Cooperation and Politics: An Irish Biography*. Gerrards Cross, Buckinghamshire: Colin Smythe, 1986.

Wheatcroft, Geoffrey. "The Disenchantment of Ireland." *Atlantic Monthly* 272 (July 1993): 65–84.

Wheatley, Michael. *Nationalism and the Irish Party: Provincial Ireland, 1910–1916.* Oxford: Oxford Univ. Press, 2005.

Whelan, Kevin. "The Catholic Church in County Tipperary, 1700–1900." In *Tipperary: History and Society,* ed. William Nolan and Thomas G. McGrath. Templeogue, Co. Dublin: Geography Publications, 1985.

———. "The Regional Impact of Catholicism, 1700–1850." In *Common Ground: Essays on the Historical Geography of Ireland: Presented to T. Jones Hughes,* ed. W. J. Smyth and Kevin Whelan. Cork: Cork Univ. Press, 1988.

White, Anna MacBride, and A. Norman Jeffares, eds. *The Gonne-Yeats Letters, 1893–1938: Always Your Friend.* London: Hutchinson, 1992.

Wright, Gordon. *France in Modern Times: From the Enlightenment to the Present.* New York: W. W. Norton and Co., 1981.

Wrigley, E. A., ed. *Nineteenth-Century Society: Essays in the Use of Quantitative Methods for the Study of Social Data.* Cambridge: Cambridge Univ. Press, 1972.

Wyatt, Anne. "Froude, Lecky, and 'the Humblest Irishman.'" *Irish Historical Studies* 19 (Mar. 1975): 261–85.

Index

Italic page numbers denote tables.